THE FINANCIAL CONSTITUTION OF EUROPEAN INTEGRATION

This open access book delivers a much-needed analysis of the interplay between the EU's financial constitution and European integration.

The economic rescue package NextGenerationEU has multiplied the EU's financial volume and thereby raised the question of the state of European integration anew. This open access book 'follows the money' and surveys the financial constitution of European integration from the perspective of law, political economy, and history.

Structured into three thematic parts, the book focuses on past and present developments of the fiscal structure of the EU as well as potential future outcomes. It raises an array of questions that are answered from different disciplinary perspectives and through the eyes of academia and practice: Can underlying design flaws of the European Monetary Union be identified? What about the legality and the economic implications of the innovative policy-making at the EU level in response to the COVID-19 pandemic? What do these reflections on the EU financial constitution reveal about the development of European integration as a whole?

The Financial Constitution of European Integration

Follow the Money?

Edited by
Ruth Weber

•HART•
OXFORD • LONDON • NEW YORK • NEW DELHI • SYDNEY

HART PUBLISHING
Bloomsbury Publishing Plc
Kemp House, Chawley Park, Cumnor Hill, Oxford, OX2 9PH, UK
1385 Broadway, New York, NY 10018, USA
29 Earlsfort Terrace, Dublin 2, Ireland

HART PUBLISHING, the Hart/Stag logo, BLOOMSBURY and the Diana logo are trademarks of Bloomsbury Publishing Plc

First published in Great Britain 2023

The publication of this work was supported by the Open Access Publication Fund of Humboldt-Universität zu Berlin, funded by the Deutsche Forschungsgemeinschaft (DFG, German Research Foundation) – 491192747. The publication of this work was further supported by the Research Training Group 'Dynamic Integration – Law in-between Harmonisation and Plurality in Europe' (DynamInt, GRK 2483), funded by the Deutsche Forschungsgemeinschaft (DFG, German Research Foundation) – 397044234.

Funded by DFG Deutsche Forschungsgemeinschaft German Research Foundation

HUMBOLDT-UNIVERSITÄT ZU BERLIN

A catalogue record for this book is available from the British Library.

A catalogue record for this book is available from the Library of Congress.

Library of Congress Control Number: 2023942364

ISBN: HB: 978-1-50996-992-0
ePDF: 978-1-50996-991-3
ePub: 978-1-50996-993-7
Book DOI: 10.5040/9781509969944

Typeset by Compuscript Ltd, Shannon

PREFACE AND ACKNOWLEDGEMENTS

This volume is the result of a conference hosted on 9 and 10 June 2022 at Humboldt University Berlin and organised by the DFG (Deutsche Forschungsgemeinschaft) Research Training Group DynamInt. I am grateful for the support I received while organising it: I would like to thank the DynamInt members who were involved – the student assistants Dorothea Brumby, Sarah Cichon, Antonia Craven and Akwasi Osei-Dwomoh as well as the programme coordinators Kerstin Schuster and Rüdiger Schwarz and the PhD students Lennart Gau, Caterina Bresci and Alba Hernandez Weiss. My thanks also go to the DFG as well as to the European Law School Foundation for their financial support. Last but not least, I would like to express my gratitude to Matthias Ruffert who provided me with advice and support throughout the process of organising the conference and publishing the volume.

The conference was special simply because for many it was the first opportunity to travel to a conference after the restrictions imposed by the COVID-19 pandemic. Therefore, I would also like to thank all presenters who could not be part of this volume (Paul De Grauwe, Thu Nguyen and Charles Wyplosz) and the moderators of the panels (Marcin Baranski, Michael C Burda and Matthias Ruffert). I am grateful that the pandemic situation at the time allowed a conference to be held in presence largely without restrictions. The discussions at the conference were not only finally live again, but – more than that – also very lively. This helped me significantly when conceptualising this volume.

Above all, I am particularly grateful to all the authors of this volume. This is the first time I have edited a book and it fills me with profound gratitude to bring these authors together. Two authors did not attend the conference but fortunately later agreed to contribute to this volume: Bruno De Witte and Francesco Martucci. Further thanks go to the three blind reviewers as well as to Christoph Möllers who helped to sharpen the underlying question of the book.

Lastly, I would also like to thank some people in the editing process. First, Roberta Bassi from Hart Publishing who gave me plenty of good advice on my first editing project. I am also grateful to Verity Stuart who very kindly supported me in choosing the cover, and, together with Linda Goss and Ceri Warner, offered support during many other production phases. The University Library of Humboldt University and the DFG Research Training Group DynamInt provided financial support to realise this work as an open access publication. Finally, I would like to thank Antonia Craven and Maximilian Berger for their assistance in editing the contributions in accordance with the style guidelines. Antonia Craven merits special thanks because she supported the project from the beginning and enriched it with many ideas and inspirations.

Ruth Weber
Berlin, July 2023

CONTENTS

PART 3
INTEGRATION THROUGH FINANCIAL CONSTITUTION?

CONTRIBUTORS

Thomas Biebricher is a Heisenberg-Professor for Political Theory, History of Ideas and Theories of the Economy at the Goethe-Universität in Frankfurt am Main. His research focuses on neoliberalism and conservatism in theory and practice. His latest publications include *The Political Theory of Neoliberalism* (Stanford University Press, 2019) and *Geistig-moralische Wende: Die Erschöpfung des deutschen Konservatismus* 2nd edition (Matthes & Seitz, 2022).

Alberto de Gregorio Merino is Director at the Legal Service of the Council of the EU, in the directorate dealing with economic, financial and EU budget affairs. He is the Legal Adviser to Ecofin and to the Euro Group, to the Economic and Financial Committee, and to the Eurogroup Working Group. He is also legal adviser to Coreper and to the cabinet of the president of the European Council.

Bruno De Witte is Emeritus Professor of European Union Law at Maastricht University (Netherlands) and a visiting fellow of the Schuman Centre at the European University Institute in Florence.

Päivi Leino-Sandberg is Professor of Transnational European Law at the University of Helsinki and Deputy Director of the Erik Castrén Institute of International Law and Human Rights where she currently leads several international research projects. She specialises in EU constitutional and institutional law including Economic and Monetary Union (EMU), various questions of democratic governance, and the impact of legal expertise on EU policy-making.

N Piers Ludlow is Professor of International History at the London School of Economics. His research focuses on the history of the European Community/Union and on Britain's troubled relations with it. He is the author of *Roy Jenkins and the European Commission Presidency, 1976–1980: At the Heart of Europe* (Palgrave, 2016); his next book will be a detailed look at Britain's four decades as an EC/EU member state.

Francesco Martucci is Professor of European Law at the University Paris Panthéon-Assas. He is member of the Legal High Committee for Financial Markets of Paris (HCJP). His research focuses on European law and economic, financial and monetary law.

Claire Mongouachon is a senior lecturer in public law at the University of Aix-Marseille where she teaches European law as a member of the Centre d'Études et de Recherches Internationales et Communautaires (CERIC). Her main publications are related to economic European law and public economic law, with a focus on the interaction with German Law and the Philosophy of Economics (particularly ordoliberalism).

Christian Neumeier is a postdoctoral researcher at Humboldt-Universität zu Berlin. He holds a PhD in law from Humboldt-Universität and an LL.M. from Yale Law School. He studied law in Heidelberg, Bonn, and Oxford and clerked for the German Federal Constitutional Court.

Matthias Ruffert is Professor of Public Law and European Law at the Law Faculty of the Humboldt-Universität zu Berlin and Spokesperson of the Research Training Group 'Dynamic Integration (DynamInt)' at Humboldt-Universität zu Berlin (funded by the German Research Foundation – Deutsche Forschungsgemeinschaft, DFG). His previous engagements include being Professor of Public Law, European Law and Public International Law at the Friedrich-Schiller-University Jena, a judge at the Administrative Court of Appeal of Thuringia, and a member of the Thuringian Constitutional Court.

Frank Schorkopf is Chair for Public Law and European Law at the Georg-August-University Goettingen, Institute of International and European Law. He was a research assistant at the University of Hamburg, a senior research fellow at the Max Planck Institute for Comparative Public Law and International Law, and a law clerk at the German Federal Constitutional Court, inter alia. He is a full Member of the Goettingen Academy of Science and Humanities. His research interests are German and European public law and the legal history of European integration.

Paul Tucker is a research fellow at the Mossavar-Rahmani Center for Business and Government (Harvard Kennedy School), and author of *Global Discord* (Princeton University Press, 2022) and *Unelected Power* (PUP, 2018). He is a senior fellow at the Center for European Studies (Harvard University), president of the UK's National Institute for Economic and Social Research, and a Governor of the Ditchley Foundation. He was a central banker at the Bank of England and Basel and chaired the Systemic Risk Council.

Luuk van Middelaar is a political theorist and historian. He is a professor of EU law at Leiden University and a political commentator for NRC Handelsblad. He is the author of *The Passage to Europe* (Yale University Press, 2009/2013), *Alarums & Excursions* (Agenda Publishing, 2019), *Pandemonium* (Agenda Publishing, 2021) and *Le Réveil géopolitique de l'Europe* (Collège de France, 2022). Van Middelaar was the chief speechwriter and a close adviser to European Council President Herman Van Rompuy (2010–2014). In 2022, he founded the Brussels Institute for Geopolitics.

Ruth Weber is a postdoctoral researcher in the Research Training Group 'Dynamic Integration (DynamInt)' at Humboldt-Universität zu Berlin. She is currently working on her habilitation thesis on budgetary powers and democracy in the

European multi-level system. Her award-winning dissertation (PhD in Paris and Freiburg) was published by Mohr Siebeck in 2019. She clerked at the German Federal Constitutional Court and the French Constitution Council, inter alia.

Claudia Wutscher is Associate Professor at the Institute for Austrian and European Public Law at the University of Economics and Business Vienna (WU Vienna), Austria. Her main areas of research include law of EMU, banking and financial markets law, Common Markets law, energy law, budgetary law and legal theory.

Introduction

'Follow the Money!'

RUTH WEBER

1. 'Too Small, Too Big – Follow the Money!'

The 'first really significant push for integration since Maastricht'[1] – this is how the German philosopher Jürgen Habermas commented on the decision to issue common European debts in 2020. The recovery fund NextGenerationEU (NGEU) was set to cope with the economic consequences of the Covid-19 pandemic. With it, the European Union's financial volume has multiplied. Ten years ago, when Habermas discussed European integration with the politician Joschka Fischer (Greens), the legal scholar Christian Calliess and the economist Henrik Enderlein, the latter replied to the question of whether Europe is far too big in the details and far too small in the bigger picture: 'Too small and too big: an economist would always say "Follow the money!"'[2] In effect, the budgetary power would always be decisive.

From the perspectives of financial, fiscal and also budgetary law, NGEU adds an entirely new dimension to the question of European integration. Which legal problems does this development cause? How should it be contextualised politically, economically and historically? Will it lead to new 'constitutional controversies'[3] making a reassessment of the basics of EU law necessary? These questions give reason to examine and discuss the state of European integration in view of its

[1] Jürgen Habermas, '30 Jahre danach: Die zweite Chance. Merkels europapolitische Kehrtwende und der innerdeutsche Vereinigungsprozess' (2020) 9 *Blätter für deutsche und internationale Politik* 41, 42; original wording: 'Der Entschluss zur gemeinsamen europäischen Schuldenaufnahme, der erst durch das Ausscheiden Großbritanniens möglich geworden ist, könnte den seit Maastricht ersten wirklich bedeutenden Integrationsschub einleiten.'

[2] Jürgen Habermas et al, 'Europa und die neue Deutsche Frage: Ein Gespräch mit Jürgen Habermas, Joschka Fischer, Henrik Enderlein und Christian Calliess' (2011) 5 *Blätter für deutsche und internationale Politik* 45, 62; original wording: 'Zu klein und zu groß: Der Ökonom würde immer sagen "Follow the money!"' in response to the question 'Ist Europa nicht im Kleinen viel zu groß und im Großen viel zu klein?'.

[3] See Maximilian Steinbeis, 'Follow the Money' (*Verfassungsblog*, 10 June 2022) https://verfassungsblog.de/follow-the-money, who speaks of 'much-needed constitutional controversies' to overcome 'Euroscepticism'.

financial constitution. The approach of this book is 'financial' as it deals with various aspects of EU financing, and finances within the EU. The term 'constitution' is employed in a broad sense. Its point of reference is 'European integration' and thus an ongoing process. Hence, the interplay between the EU's financial constitution and European integration is the focal point of this book.

What does it mean when the financial volume distributed at the EU level becomes increasingly bigger? Does more money also mean more power – and what implications does this have on democratic control? Modern statehood is characterised by the fact that budgetary powers are subject to democratic decision-making. The fact that 'money is the nerve of all things' has been reflected since antiquity in the proverbial phrase *pecunia nervus rerum*. As Michael Stolleis illustrates in a book of the same name, the phrase gained enormous popularity from the sixteenth and seventeenth centuries onwards. He suspects it to be 'an essential point of the self-understanding of the time'.[4] *Rerum* was also replaced by *belli* ('of war') during this period. The increased financial needs caused by wars constituted a basic problem that conditioned the emergence of modern state finances in the early modern period.[5] The question of who has budgetary power is essential for the emergence of nation states and modern democracies. Thus, the slogan 'no taxation without representation' epitomises the discontent over the lack of representation in the British Parliament of settlers on the American continent, despite the levying of taxes, which eventually led to American independence and its democratic constitution. In the English-speaking world, the phrase 'power of the purse' has also emerged, suggesting budgetary power is a crucial expression of power of Parliament. In the German discourse, one often encounters the phrase that budgetary power is the 'royal right' (*Königsrecht*) of Parliament. All of these expressions reflect the importance of the question of budgetary power for democracy.[6] Moreover, it is a recurring argumentative figure in court decisions, especially in constitutional courts. For the Bundesverfassungsgericht (German Federal Constitutional Court), it is the 'overall responsibility, with sufficient political discretion regarding revenue and expenditure'[7] that is one of the most

[4] Michael Stolleis, *Pecunia nervus rerum: Zur Staatsfinanzierung in der frühen Neuzeit* (Frankfurt am Main, Klostermann, 1983) 65: 'Im 16. und 17. Jahrhundert gewannen die Sätze "pecunia nervus rerum" und "pecunia nervus belli" eine solche Beliebtheit, daß man vermuten darf, hier einen wesentlichen Punkt des Selbstverständnisses der Zeit gefunden zu haben.'

[5] ibid 70; also see Michael Stolleis, '"Pecunia nervus rerum" – Die Finanzfrage in der deutschen Staatsräsonliteratur des 17. Jahrhunderts' in Aldo De Maddalena and Hermann Kellenbenz (eds), *Finanzen und Staatsräson in Italien und Deutschland in der frühen Neuzeit* (Berlin, Duncker & Humblot, 1992) 21–36; Charles Tilly, *Coercion, Capital and European States, AD 990–1992* (Oxford, Wiley-Blackwell, 1993) 87–91; Linda Colley, *The Gun, the Ship and the Pen. Warfare, Constitution and the Making of the Modern World* (London, Liveright Publishing Corporation, 2021) 25–34.

[6] References to these expressions can also be found several times in this volume, see the chapters by Päivi Leino-Sandberg (ch 8), Frank Schorkopf (ch 10), Bruno De Witte (ch 11) and Luuk van Middelaar (ch 12).

[7] See BVerfGE 123, 267, para 256: 'What is decisive, however, is that the overall responsibility, with sufficient political discretion regarding revenue and expenditure, can still rest with the German *Bundestag*.'

important reservations of the national legal order.[8] After all, many essential political disputes are an expression of either public expenditure or revenue, or the link between these.

2. An Ever-Transforming Financial Constitution of European Integration

NGEU reveals key questions regarding the state of the budgetary powers in the multi-level system of the European Union and of the 'financial constitution of European integration'. The economic crisis triggered by the Covid-19 pandemic outbreak provided the impetus for the creation of NGEU. Based on a Franco-German proposal by the German chancellor Angela Merkel and the French president Emmanuel Macron, the European Commission led by Ursula von der Leyen launched the proposal to establish NGEU. On 21 July 2020, the 27 EU heads of state and government in the European Council agreed on a fund that differed from the Commission's proposal only in its details. The fund comprised €750 billion, of which €390 billion were to be grants and €360 billion loans.[9] Above all, the main novelty is the fact that the EU itself is issuing bonds on a large scale which are to be paid for by the EU through additional revenues in the period from 2028–58. Where this revenue will come from – whether from own EU taxes or by increasing the member states' contributions – has not yet been clarified.

The EU Recovery and Resilience Instrument (EURI) sets up the general distribution regime.[10] Most of the reconstruction fund is disbursed through a new Reconstruction and Resilience Facility (RRF), and the remainder through existing programmes (ReactEU, Horizon Europe, InvestEU, Rural Development, Just Transition Fund, RescEU).[11] Whereas Article 175 of the Treaty on the Functioning of the European Union (TFEU) is pronounced as the legal basis for the RRF, Article 122 TFEU serves as the legal basis for EURI. Article 122 TFEU enables the Council to act without a parliamentary veto.[12]

The allocation key for the money was based on unemployment rates for the distribution in 2021–22, and the total loss in GDP between 2020 and 2022

[8] See also BVerfGE 129, 124; 132, 195; 135, 317; 142, 123; 146, 216; 151, 202; 154, 17.

[9] The prices indicated in this text are the initial 2018 prices. They have increased due to inflation since then.

[10] Council Regulation (EU) 2020/2094 establishing a European Union Recovery Instrument to support the recovery in the aftermath of the COVID-19 crisis [2020] OJ LI433/23.

[11] For an overview see European Commission, 'Recovery and Resilience Facility' (*European Commission Website*) https://commission.europa.eu/business-economy-euro/economic-recovery/recovery-and-resilience-facility_en; for further details see the chapters by Alberto de Gregorio Merino (ch 5), Claudia Wutscher (ch 6) and Francesco Martucci (ch 7) in this volume.

[12] This point is highlighted and treated by several contributions to this volume, see Matthias Ruffert (epilogue), Alberto de Gregorio Merino (ch 5), Päivi Leino-Sandberg (ch 8), Frank Schorkopf (ch 10) and Bruno De Witte (ch 11).

for the distribution in 2023. Furthermore, the allocation of money is linked to reforms. In order for the Commission to review these, member states must submit their national plans to it. The review criteria correspond to Country-Specific Recommendations (CSRs) from the European Semester, referring to growth potential, job creation, economic and social resilience, and the green and digital transitions. The payment requests are then decided on by the Council by a qualified majority. Additionally, there is an emergency brake mechanism for the effective use of the funds in the Council, which implies that the control does not lie solely with the Commission.[13]

The Russian war of aggression against Ukraine has shifted the focus to defence policy, inflation and the energy crisis. Consequently, the Commission developed the REPowerEU strategy, according to which the EU aims to be more independent of fossil fuels, especially from Russia, by 2030. In February 2023, the Council and the European Parliament approved that money from NGEU can be used to finance the REPowerEU programme.[14] Although the NGEU funds were originally earmarked for a strictly limited one-off situation, they are now being channelled into more recent crisis-related programmes. As a reaction to these unexpected events, the use of NGEU funds has been diversified, leading to an even broader impact of NGEU. However, this modification remains controversial. In crises, decisions with major implications for public budgets are often taken in a limited amount of time. This poses numerous challenges to democratic decision-making, which are compounded by the multi-level system. The recent developments – marked by the Covid-19 pandemic and subsequently the war in Ukraine – show that the financial constitution of European integration is transforming significantly.

The new legal instrument NGEU in particular has already given rise to discussion in legal literature. Through its combination of great topicality and novelty, NGEU triggers legal questions that have not yet been resolved. Some commentators emphasise the legal creativity[15] and the transformative character of the reconstruction fund.[16] However, there is no consensus on whether the instrument is compatible with EU law. While some find that the limits of legal

[13] See the chapters by Claire Mongouachon (ch 3), Thomas Biebricher (ch 4), Alberto de Gregorio Merino (ch 5), Päivi Leino-Sandberg (ch 8) and Frank Schorkopf (ch 10) in this volume for further details.

[14] Regulation (EU) 2023/435 of the European Parliament and of the Council amending Regulation (EU) 2021/241 as regards REPowerEU chapters in recovery and resilience plans and amending Regulations (EU) No 1303/2013, (EU) 2021/1060 and (EU) 2021/1755, and Directive 2003/87/EC [2023] OJ L63/1.

[15] Frank Schorkopf, 'Die Europäische Union auf dem Weg zur Fiskalunion: Integrationsfortschritt durch den Rechtsrahmen des Sonderhaushalts "Next Generation EU"' (2020) 73 *Neue Juristische Wochenschrift* 3085, 3087.

[16] Martin Nettesheim, '"Next Generation EU": Die Transformation der EU-Finanzverfassung' (2020) 145 *Archiv des öffentlichen Recht* 381; Hanno Kube and Frank Schorkopf, 'Strukturveränderungen der Wirtschafts- und Währungsunion: Normativer Grund der Legitimation und Akzeptanz' (2021) 21 *Neue Juristische Wochenschrift* 1650.

interpretation were adhered to,[17] others express concerns.[18] In particular, the interpretation of various provisions of EU primary law is being questioned, especially with regard to NGEU's legal basis (Article 122 TFEU), the possibility for the EU to take on debt (Article 125 TFEU), and Articles 310 and 311 TFEU on the question of revenue categories and the balance of the EU budget. Moreover, the compatibility with national constitutional law is also being discussed.[19]

3. Writing an Interdisciplinary 'Follow up' to a 'Budgetary Saga'

These legal issues play an essential role in various contributions to this book.[20] However, this volume intends to go beyond a purely legal focus as the legal questions addressed touch upon political science, history and political economy. The analyses of these disciplines provide broader evaluations of the developments[21] as well as specific studies on the role of the European Parliament,[22] for example. Previous and forthcoming collective works on issues related to the EU budget and EU fiscal federalism show that bringing together various disciplines is a promising approach.[23] It is precisely for this reason that the title of the volume – *The Financial*

[17] Bruno De Witte, 'The European Union's COVID-19 Recovery Plan: The Legal Engineering of an Economic Policy Shift' (2021) 58 *CML Rev* 635; Paul Dermine, 'The EU's Response to the COVID-19 Crisis and the Trajectory of Fiscal Integration in Europe: Between Continuity and Rupture' (2021) 47 *Legal Issues of Economic Integration* 337; Frédéric Allemand, 'Le financement du plan de relance européen' (2021) 2 *Revue des Affaires Européennes* 797; Armin Steinbach, 'The Greening of the Economic and Monetary Union' (2022) 59 *CML Rev* 329.

[18] Matthias Ruffert, 'Europarecht für die nächste Generation: Zum Projekt Next Generation EU' (2020) 39 *Neue Zeitschrift für Verwaltungsrecht* 1777; Enzo Cannizzaro, 'Neither Representation nor Taxation? Or, "Europe's Moment" – Part I' (2020) 2 *Editorial European Papers* 703; Enzo Cannizzaro, 'Neither Representation nor Values? Or, "Europe's Moment" – Part II' (2020) 3 *Editorial European Papers* 1101; Caroline Heber, 'Europarechtliche Grenzen für den Wiederaufbaufonds' (2021) 56 *Europarecht* 416; Anastasia Iliopoulou-Penot, 'L'instrument pour la relance Next Generation EU: "Where there is a political will, there is a legal way"?' (2021) 57 *Revue Trimestrielle de Droit Europeen* 527; Päivi Leino-Sandberg and Matthias Ruffert, 'Next Generation EU and Its Constitutional Ramifications : A critical assessment' (2022) 59 *CML Rev* 433.

[19] See for example the proceedings before the Bundesverfassungsgericht resulting in BVerfG, Judgment of the Second Senate of 6 December 2022–2 BvR 547/21 –, see discussion of the decision in Matthias Ruffert's epilogue.

[20] See chapters in Part II of this volume.

[21] Martin Höpner, 'Vollendung der Währungsunion? Der europäische Aufbaufonds' (2021) 49 *Leviathan* 488; J Adam Tooze, *Welt im Lockdown: Die globale Krise und ihre Folgen* (München, CH Beck, 2021); Luuk van Middelaar, *Das europäische Pandämonium: Was die Pandemie über den Zustand der EU enthüllt* (Berlin, Suhrkamp, 2021).

[22] Carlos Closa Montero, Felipe González de León and Gisela Hernández González, 'Pragmatism and the Limits to the European Parliament's Strategies for Self-Empowerment' (2021) 9 *Politics and Governance* 163.

[23] Stefan Becker, Michael W Bauer and Alfredo De Feo (eds), *The New Politics of the European Union Budget* (Baden-Baden, Nomos, 2017) gathers contributions on the topic from practitioners and political scientists in particular; Thiess Büttner and Michael Thöne, *The Future of EU-Finances*

Constitution of European Integration – combines not only a constitutional legal analysis but also the very attempt to approach the constitution of European integration through the perspective of different disciplines.

With NGEU and its first large-scale issuing of debts on an EU level, debating the future of the European Union's fiscal architecture has gained fundamental importance. When 'following the money', the perspective of only one discipline does not suffice. While the budgetary and monetary perspective includes the disciplines of law and political economy, insights from the fields of history and political philosophy are essential in order to better understand the overarching processes of European integration and disintegration. The interdisciplinary approach is intended to provide a broad picture, including, on the one hand, legal-technical details as well as, on the other hand, findings of historical analyses, political theory and economy. The link between these different approaches is their common perspective: they all 'follow the money'.

The authors' individual focus depends on the epistemological interest of their disciplinary horizon as well as the focal point of their own research or practice. The aim of this book is not to provide a comprehensive overview of the current state of affairs of questions arising from EU finances. It is not intended to be a 'handbook of the EU financial constitution'. Rather, the current situation is to be scrutinised from various perspectives – implying not only descriptive but also normative elements.

Given the great topicality of NGEU – the funds from the RRF are currently being disbursed – previous publications mostly deal with individual aspects of its legality or economic impact. A recent publication by the European University Institute is one of the first collaborative works on the matter.[24] However, as the volume was edited at a time when the negotiations and decision-making processes of NGEU were still underway – the member states' parliaments had not yet given their approval – Alfredo De Feo formulates in his closing words: 'The follow up of this budgetary saga will be the object of further studies by scholars in the coming years.'[25] This volume presents one component for the rewriting of this 'saga'.

(Tübingen, Mohr Siebeck, 2016) brings together policy papers by lawyers and economists on the future of EU finances; Luca Zamparini and Ubaldo Villani-Lubelli, *Features and Challenges of the EU Budget: A Multidisciplinary Analysis* (Cheltenham, Edward Elgar Publishing, 2019); Guillaume Grégoire and Xavier Miny, *The Idea of Economic Constitution in Europe: Genealogy and Overview* (Leiden, Brill Nijhoff, 2022); Alicia Hinarejos and Robert Schütze (eds), *EU Fiscal Federalism: Past, Present, Future* (Oxford, Oxford University Press, forthcoming 2023).

[24] Brigid Laffan and Alfredo De Feo, *EU Financing for Next Decade, Beyond the MFF 2021–2027 and the Next Generation EU* (online open access, Florence, European University Institute, 2020) https://cadmus.eui.eu/handle/1814/69015.

[25] ibid 342. The importance of these questions is also underlined in Diane Fromage and Anna Herranz-Surrallés, *Executive-Legislative (Im)balance in the European Union* (Oxford, Hart, 2020) 15 and 16, see also 303 ff (epilogue by Peter L Lindseth).

4. The Structure of the Book

The interplay of European integration and its financial constitution is dealt with in three thematic parts, each containing four chapters. The first part covers potential underlying design flaws of the European Monetary Union (EMU). It contains four chapters written by an economist (Sir Paul Tucker), two lawyers (Christian Neumeier and Claire Mongouachon) and a political theorist (Thomas Biebricher). The second part of the volume focuses on addressing the legality of the innovative law-making at the EU level in response to the Covid-19 pandemic. Here, four chapters combine the views of legal practitioners and researchers (Alberto de Gregorio Merino, Claudia Wutscher, Francesco Martucci and Päivi Leino-Sandberg). The third part looks at developments of the EU financial constitution tying together a more comprehensive narrative of European integration. In this part, two chapters are written by legal scholars (Frank Schorkopf and Bruno De Witte) and two by historians and/or political philosophers (N Piers Ludlow and Luuk van Middelaar). The volume concludes with an epilogue by Matthias Ruffert (Humboldt-Universität zu Berlin).

The first part of the book deals with possible underlying design flaws of the EMU. First, Sir Paul Tucker (Harvard Kennedy School) asks a question that is both pertinent and pressing: does the European Central Bank (ECB) care about inflation? Tucker examines the unusual role of the ECB in EU fiscal policy and argues that the ECB is prioritising eurozone stability over inflation. Tucker delineates general developments in central banking and offers an explanation as to why central bankers' incentives may no longer be harnessed to their core mandate. Going into more detail about the ECB, he highlights its exceptional position compared to other central banks as in his eyes 'the ECB became the existential guarantor of the European Project itself'. Compared to other central banks, the ECB is confronted with an unprecedented 'grand dilemma': In the absence of a conventional fiscal authority in the eurozone, 'it finds itself synthesising one, under the rubric of monetary policy, whenever the economic–financial pillars of the Union are crumbling'. This is a 'job immeasurably more difficult than that of its supposed peers' that leads to 'the ECB's greatest challenge', ie 'to navigate itself back toward the proper role of technocratic trustee for monetary-system stability'. Understanding this linkage of monetary, economic and fiscal union is crucial for the leading question of this volume, ie the financial constitution of European integration. Finally, at the end of his chapter, Tucker points out that 'the designers of Europe's monetary union faced conflicting incentives they could not reconcile: to push the European project forward by introducing a single currency, but not to push it so far forward that, via establishing some kind of fiscal union, a political union loomed around the next corner before the peoples of Europe clearly wanted or could support it'.

While Tucker extrapolates from this the observation for the current development of the ECB that the 'upshot is a fragility that the ECB's leaders have to remember, and navigate, every second of every day', Christian Neumeier (Humboldt-Universität zu Berlin) follows up on one of the underlying questions. He writes about the origins of the EMU and what its designers thought about the consequences that Tucker clearly points out are evident to this day. Neumeier provides an explanation for one of the 'primary puzzles' of European monetary integration: 'the asymmetry between the monetary and the economic side of the EMU'. After presenting historical and economic literature on the history of the EMU, he focuses on a memorandum by German foreign minister Hans Dietrich Genscher published in the spring of 1988. For Neumeier, this memorandum was central to the shape that the EMU would later take. According to him, the importance of the memorandum 'was to advocate for a monetary union on the one hard condition that it would have an independent central bank, but without at the same time making any specific proposals as to how economic and fiscal integration should proceed'. 'Who … invented the asymmetrical monetary union?' he asks and suggests it was 'Genscher and a close group of German officials'. To back up this argument, Neumeier draws on archival sources of the political archive of the German Foreign Office and interviews with two civil servants involved in the process of drafting the memorandum, Wilhelm Schönfelder and Peter Wilhelm Schlüter. For Neumeier, the files show 'that Genscher himself was responsible for the final version of the memorandum'. But, Schönfelder drafted it and Schlüter was the 'intellectual mastermind behind' it. Neumeier stresses that '[a]symmetry was not invented by the ordoliberal Eurosceptics who usually defend it in contemporary German politics. It was a structure invented by a group of strongly pro-European German officials, some with ordoliberal leanings, and fought through by pro-European politicians who believed in European integration to a degree that has become rare these days.' Moreover, he underlines that '[a]symmetry … had a strong tactical component. To make the institutional structure of the central bank front and centre sidelined the main internal opponent of monetary integration and was designed to assuage a public which trusted independent experts more than elected politicians.'

The question of who decides and should decide on essential fiscal decisions is central to Claire Mongouachon's chapter (Aix-Marseille Université). Her main focus lies on reforms of the EU fiscal framework, especially the review of the EU's economic governance launched by the European Commission in 2020 and following reform proposals by member states such as France. She approaches this topic by questioning the degree of its 'politicisation'. Her starting point is that fiscal rules have traditionally been considered a 'technical field', but have become increasingly 'politicised'. Law, especially European budgetary rules, demonstrates 'a major tool for depoliticising budgetary matters'. As 'fully-fledged element[s] of the financial constitution of the Union (and of the member states)' these rules took 'fiscal policy flexibility from the hands of elected politicians'. According to Mongouachon, budgetary rules emerge as a result of the asymmetry addressed in the chapters by Tucker and Neumeier: '[T]hey are at the heart of the asymmetry between monetary union and economic union – caught in tension as they stand between the two.' Mongouachon stresses that the reforms introduced by the Stability and Growth Pact (SGP) and the Treaty on Stability, Coordination and Governance in the EMU (TSCG) were seen as a kind of automation of rules aimed at financial stability and safe assets, depriving member states of broader policy choices. The pandemic and its 'new political and societal challenges' have 'led to heightened awareness [of] … new challenges and the need for massive public investment by states'. Recent proposals formulated by French institutions and academics demand a 'greening' of the rules as well as the 'parliamentarisation' of the eurozone. Mongouachon concludes by underlining the need to create a new institutional framework to arbitrate between the different objectives that could guide the implementation of EU fiscal rules in the future.

Thomas Biebricher (Goethe-Universität Frankfurt am Main) questions the end of neoliberalism as a possible consequence of NGEU. Biebricher's starting point is the observation that the global trade frictions in the wake of the Covid-19 pandemic, and in particular the NGEU funds adopted in response to it, have led to an increased perception of the end of neoliberalism. With the outbreak of the Ukraine war, he notes, this claim has been further exacerbated. Biebricher begins his chapter by providing the history of neoliberalism focusing on the ideas formulated in the Walter Lippmann Colloquium in 1938. According to Biebricher, some of the preconditions of neoliberalism can be found in the economic governance of the EMU: 'From the beginning, the Europe of Maastricht was to be one where rules were supposed to reign supreme.' His main concern is then to question two strongly diverging assessments, as NGEU was 'hailed as a departure from the long-standing neoliberal script in Europe that had been reiterated and affirmed in the eurozone crisis' on the one side, and was 'condemned as the final nail in the coffin of Europe as a space of competition and fiscal responsibility under the banner of what was sometimes called "corona socialism"' on the other. He comes to the interim conclusion that 'NGEU is not a departure from austerity neoliberalism but, arguably, its perfection', pointing in particular to the conditionality of the NGEU funds. But Biebricher does not just confine himself to this statement. Rather, he then broadens the view to future developments and addresses the importance of observing how the distribution and use of funds are handled in practice. Beyond this, he raises fundamental questions about the construction of the EU's financial constitution, asking about permanent debt at the European level and EU taxes: 'Issuing debt on a permanent basis would undoubtedly trigger a debate over whether the EU should have … the right to levy taxes and, if this were the case, this would undoubtedly prompt renewed questions regarding an institutional restructuring of the EU in order to remedy its various democratic deficits. The end result could possibly be a supranational executive that has the right to tax and is democratically accountable to parliament – not the most desirable prospect from a neoliberal perspective.'

The second part of the volume focuses on the legal assessment of recent developments in EU financial constitutional law, especially with regard to NGEU. Firstly, Alberto de Gregorio Merino (Director at the Legal Service of the Council of the European Union) presents an inside perspective on NGEU and the rule of law mechanism. He seeks to explain 'the permeability between the Community of money and the Community of values on which the Union is founded'. For his legal analysis, he stresses that the EU treaties are 'a living document': this, together with a 'finalistic interpretation', guides his interpretation of key financial provisions of the TFEU. His view regarding the central question of the volume is straightforward – NGEU and the rule of law mechanism demonstrate 'the fundamental integration value of the budget of the Union': For him, EU budgetary law 'carries … principles of paramount constitutional value, the interpretation and application of which are key in shaping the paths for integration'. In interpreting the provisions of the treaties, he also addresses concerns: while he refers to Article 122 TFEU as 'a kind of "sleeping beauty"', he also urges that 'an excessive use of exceptionality clauses' must be avoided. Yet, he is convinced, the 'ghost of the Weimar Constitution does not risk haunting the Union legal order'. At the end of his chapter, he returns to his starting point – the link between money and values. He underlines the increasing importance of the values laid down in Article 2 of the Treaty on European Union (TEU) and also in the jurisprudence of the Court of Justice of the European Union (CJEU), and explicitly welcomes this. They are, he claims, part of the 'European constitutional identity' and 'substratum of a "European Constitutional patriotism"'.

Claudia Wutscher (Vienna University of Economics and Business) provides a legal assessment of NGEU and raises doubts about its compatibility with European and national constitutional law, especially in light of its unprecedented high volume. The starting point of her reflections is that the size of the measure does not play a central role in most legal assessments of EU law but is indispensable in assessing NGEU. She highlights the 'manifold legal issues' that arise in the context of NGEU. According to Wutscher 'arguing for NGEU's legality already requires contortions when interpreting primary law rules' but also with regards to national constitutional law and member states' budgetary autonomy. Wutscher refers not only to previous legal scholarly analyses but also deals with the Council Legal Service Opinion of 2020,[26] which adds a critical perspective to the view expressed in de Gregorio Merino's chapter. Finally, she underlines the importance of budgetary autonomy of the member states referring to their overall importance: 'Without budgetary autonomy, it would seem, no effective and independent state power can come into being, because the exercise of *any state power* requires the authority to decide on the procurement and allocation of the resources required for this purpose.' Despite various doubts, she concludes that 'member states' budgetary autonomy is not yet at risk from NGEU in its current form'.

[26] Council Legal Service, Opinion, Council Doc. 9062/20 (Brussels, 24 June 2020).

Francesco Martucci (Université Paris Panthéon-Assas) takes a closer look at a principle of EU law that is increasingly receiving wide attention: the principle of solidarity. Martucci argues that within the EMU 'the framework of discipline has been complemented by that of solidarity', with the measures taken in reaction to the Covid-19 pandemic bringing about a 'real change'. For Martucci, this can be seen in the words of the Advocate General Campos Sánchez-Bordona who referred to 'the biggest step forward in terms of solidarity which the European Union has taken in its history' in this context. To show this 'progress of solidarity', Martucci outlines an evolution of the EMU that can be understood as a development towards increasing solidarity. His starting point is fiscal discipline and the 'discipline framework organised by the Treaties' since Maastricht. Having outlined the normative framework and its development, he clarifies why 'the Covid-19 crisis marks a paradigm shift in the implementation of deficit excessive procedures' and 'brought about a substantial change in the conditionality'. Regarding NGEU, Martucci explores its 'remarkable' features. It is the enormous amount of money needed to pay it back that is decisive for him. This ultimately raises 'the recurring question of a European tax', ie 'a fundamental reform of the Union's own resources system'. For Martucci, not only NGEU but also the even more recent reactions to the energy crisis indicate a paradigm shift in terms of solidarity. He discusses emerging issues of EU law concerning newly adopted regulations, in particular regarding the question of the legal basis of the Regulation (EU) 2022/1854[27] and whether the EU had the competence to adopt it. According to Martucci, the answer to this is 'hardly apodictic'. He also relates this to 'a time when the threat of ultra vires is taken seriously in a renewed dialogue of judges'. Martucci concludes that the various crises have resulted in the EMU having 'a solidarity framework that interacts with the disciplinary framework'. For him, this shows that the EU 'is indeed moving forward thanks to crises that allow for deeper integration'.

While Martucci contours how the principle of solidarity has achieved enormous importance in current debates of EU law, Päivi Leino-Sandberg (University of Helsinki) opens up the perspective of fiscal integration beyond crisis management. She is critical of the use of the solidarity principle which she describes as follows: 'Today, we are witnessing how "the principle of solidarity" is being framed as a new general principle of law that can be used to justify derogating from the EU Treaties and thus expanding EU competence.' Overall, she criticises the way the EU has reacted to crises in the past 10 years: As a result, she says, democratic decision-making is at risk. According to her, the 'crisis-driven method of integration' is dominated by executive decision-making, paired with 'opportunistic exercise guided by institutional ambition', whereas legislative power is diminished. This, she says, also concerns budgetary powers: 'Budgetary democracy has been replaced by technocratic executive action, which, however noble in its intentions,

[27] Council Regulation (EU) 2022/1854 on an emergency intervention to address high energy prices [2022] OJ LI 261/1.

necessarily ends up limiting the effect of democratic politics.' Leino-Sandberg does not agree with the interpretation method of a 'living constitution' advocated by de Gregorio Merino. For her, it is characterised by a 're-framing of existing key Treaty provisions'. This leads her to the assessment that the 'only constraint on EU action is a political one: what the institutions can agree on'. With regard to NGEU, this would result in problems not only for the principle of conferral but also the separation of powers and thus ultimately democracy. As a consequence, not only the European Parliament loses power but also 'national parliaments tend to find themselves squeezed towards the dystopian nightmare painted earlier by the Bundesverfassungsgericht'. Her following diagnosis is not very comforting: 'In today's EU economic and fiscal policies, there is no question of "more democracy" – it is a model of "less democracy" at all levels.' At the end of her chapter, however, Leino-Sandberg emphasises that 'the ties' between the member states 'have grown over years' and asks whether they are 'now strong enough' for a 'federal evolution', which for her would have to be organised democratically above all.

In the third part, the developments of the EU financial constitution are further embedded in the broader evolution of European integration, starting with a focus on historical and current phenomena of the EU's financial and fiscal structure and ending with possible future developments. First, N Piers Ludlow (London School of Economics and Political Science) classifies historic budgetary breakthroughs as an important driving factor for integration in the latter half of the 1980s. According to Ludlow, there is 'a really important budgetary dimension to the 1980s *relance*' that the standard analyses of the decade do not include. His focus is less on the adoption of the Single Market programme in 1985 or the 1986 Single European Act but rather on the budgetary breakthroughs of 1984 and especially of 1988, when the Delors I package was adopted. The Delors I package represents a milestone in the history of integration that is often neglected. Ludlow's analysis focuses on a period of time that was marked by a serious crisis of the European Communities, which was, however, overcome. With the new decade, the Maastricht Treaty of 1992 finally marked a deepening of integration. Ludlow's thesis – that in the historical research of the 1980s the resolution of the budgetary conflicts has not been assessed sufficiently – is valuable for the evaluation of the central question of this volume: it seeks to understand the history of integration in relation to its financial constitution. Thus, after reading Ludlow's chapter, one may ask whether the thesis of 'budgeting for success' can be applied to other decades or even to current developments.

The following chapter by Frank Schorkopf (Georg-August-University Göttingen) refers to a different historical period as well as to the current political and legal situation. He first focuses on the demand for greater participation made by the European Parliament in the 1960s and 1970s. He argues that it was the transition to the own resources system at the beginning of the 1970s that made the introduction of universal suffrage of the European Parliament in 1979 possible. Subsequent changes in organisational law, such as the introduction of the conciliation procedure, were then suitable for increasing the competences of the parliament. According to Schorkopf, this demonstrates the 'normative surplus' of the EU's budgetary law. He then proceeds to draw a comparison to the current situation. He puts forward the argument that by allowing NGEU to raise debt at the EU level, member states have undertaken a systemic change to the budgetary and financial constitution. For Schorkopf, this is a significant deepening of integration. For this very reason, he stresses the question of representation and parliamentary legitimacy that should not be neglected in the current context. To sum up, Schorkopf sees budgetary and financial issues as 'a resource of an indirect integration surplus of the EU' which leads him to speak of 'integration through money' alluding 'to the formative school of thought "integration through law"'.

Bruno De Witte's (Maastricht University/European University Institute Florence) chapter ties in with this question focusing on 'integration through funding'. In his opinion, the EU's traditional way of achieving integration 'through law' is increasingly complemented by the pursuit of integration 'through funding'. De Witte does not focus on a single historical period but provides an analysis of constitutional law and thus evaluates the general development of budgetary and public finance law in the EU. According to De Witte, for much of its history, the EU budget has served as an instrument for redistribution among member states but also for achieving European policy goals. The latter function has become increasingly important in the context of the common European response to the Covid-19 crisis and the EU's environmental and climate policies. In this context, De Witte stresses the importance of structural funds by designating them as 'half-empty shells that can be filled with new policy goals every seven years, when the revised fund regulations are being adopted, and occasionally even within the seven-year period, in order to address new needs'. For him, NGEU is 'a tool for integration through funding', 'a multipurpose plan, aiming to foster structural transformation of the national economies', and 'a true instrument of strategic spending for the European Union'.

In referring to 'strategic spending', De Witte alludes to the subsequent chapter by Luuk van Middelaar (Leiden University), who addresses investment politics as 'a new capacity to project Union action into the future'. Van Middelaar takes the budgetary evolution of the Union as a starting point to outline a story of the European Union's executive and strategic emancipation. In contrast to Schorkopf's and Leino-Sandberg's chapters, he focuses on the executive rather than the parliament. Van Middelaar observes an evolution of European integration from 'rules-politics' to 'events-politics'; the latter also represented by the Covid-19 pandemic and the measures taken in response. This distinction leads van Middelaar to examine the evolution of the EU's spending capacity. According to him, it was initially characterised by 'programme spending', followed by 'emergency spending' and finally 'strategic spending'. 'Strategic spending' is crucial for van Middelaar as part of a larger capacity emerging at the European level which might represent a new form of executive political action: 'The test is, therefore, whether the EU is able to … acquire a projection capability, to spend now *and* to invest in the future. … Strategic spending … can be seen as the emergence of a European capacity to act in accordance with political aims.' Van Middelaar combines his observations on 'strategic spending' with an assessment of the geopolitical situation of the EU. In this way, he provides an outlook on future developments not only, but especially, for the EU's financial constitution.

5. 'Only Time Will Tell'

'Time will tell how this will play out. Officially, NGEU is supposed to be non-permanent, with the funds paid back by 2058 at the latest. However, it is safe to say that many in Brussels, Paris and beyond consider that an important precedent has been set'. This statement comes from Luuk van Middelaar's chapter. However, he is not alone with this assessment – almost all other chapters emphasise two things. First, with NGEU and the developments after the Covid-19 pandemic, a new era of the EU financial constitution has begun. Second, it remains to be seen what the consequences will be and what they will mean for the future of European integration.

What will the changes triggered by NGEU mean for democracy in the EU? What is the interplay between the power that more money confers and budgetary powers that ought to be decided on democratically? Will – as Frank Schorkopf supposes – the 'financial burdens postponed to the future … push the member states to introduce genuine EU taxes'? Will – as Thomas Biebricher suggests – this be the 'worst-case scenario for neoliberals'? One might ask with Claudia Wutscher, what role 'budgetary autonomy as the financial manifestation of democratic self-determination' will play in the future, or with Alberto de Gregorio Merino if future money will also be '"coloured" by the values of Article 2 TEU'. Francesco Martucci raises the question whether '[a]fter decades of discipline, the time of solidarity finally came'. Will 'cheque book diplomacy' play an equally important role in the future as it did in the late 1980s, as N Piers Ludlow illustrates, referring to 'an important sequence of Community breakthroughs linked to Kohl's readiness to get out his chequebook at crucial moments'. One could reiterate Christian Neumeier's concern about the concept of the Genscher Memorandum never asking 'the obvious question: whether the consensus on the German economic model would or even could work for all member states at the same time'. One might ask, alluding to Sir Paul Tucker, what choice will be made 'between living with an overmighty central bank … or … returning technocracy to its proper place but within a deeper economic union built on incentive-compatible foundations'. What paradoxes and simultaneities, yet unknown, will we be able to observe in the future in 'processes of depoliticisation and repoliticisation' one could ask with Claire Mongouachon. And what role will 'meaningful scholarly debate' play in this one could add with Matthias Ruffert. Also, Päivi Leino-Sandberg invites to a broader discussion by asking if 'the Union could finally allow a good crisis to go to waste, and be ready to graduate into a more deliberative and organised method of federal evolution'.

Finally, Bruno De Witte stresses that NGEU's 'policy steering effect still needs to be demonstrated'. This effect, its 'integration effect', according to him depends on three factors: Will the states 'be able to absorb the vast amounts of money allocated to them in the form of grants and loans'? Will this money 'actually be used for the purposes described in the national plans'? And will the money 'effectively produce the policy goals … which are set out in the programme'?[28] If one takes these questions to heart, one thing is certain for the future exploration of the financial constitution of European integration: we will not be able to stop but will be obliged to continue 'following the money'.

[28] Other authors in this volume also raise these questions. Thomas Biebricher (ch 4) points out that 'there will in all likelihood be a considerable potential for controversy when it comes to taking stock in 2026, as by then the NGEU funds will have to be fully spent'. Päivi Leino-Sandberg (ch 8) states: '[S]o far, these constitutional issues have not been debated in the EU, nor has the efficiency of such policies for ensuring EU objectives been thoroughly studied.'

PART 1

Design Flaws of the European Monetary Union?

1

Does the ECB Care about Inflation?

PAUL TUCKER*

My title might seem like an extraordinary question: what can I possibly mean by 'does the ECB care about inflation?' If I disclose my answer is 'no', the question and answer might, indeed, seem completely crazy – and so uninteresting. In this chapter, I will try to persuade the reader otherwise, or at least create a sense that the European Central Bank (ECB) has a problem it must somehow seek to reduce, if not solve.

I am going to unpack the question, point towards some evidence in a rather loose way, and offer an explanation for my answer. Partly, something really has gone wrong in advanced-economy central banking. Partly, the ECB's extraordinarily pivotal role in the European project pulls it in conflicting directions. The first is curable both in principle and in practice, although I do not mean to imply it would be easy given where the advanced-economy central banks as a whole find themselves. The second might be curable in theory but it is hard to see how – absent severe social dislocation, which could lead anywhere – Europe will find a way through the massive challenges presented by the serious constitutional deepening that is necessary to release the ECB into the community of regular central banks.

1. Unpacking the Question of whether the ECB Cares about Inflation

Very obviously the ECB cares somewhat about inflation. Almost everyone does, so I do not mean to ask whether the ECB cares about inflation at all. The

* Paul Tucker is a research fellow at the Mossavar-Rahmani Center for Business and Governor at the Harvard Kennedy School. He is the author of *Unelected Power: The Quest for Legitimacy in Central Banking and the Regulatory State* (Princeton, NJ, Princeton University Press, 2018), and of *Global Discord: Values and Power in a Fractured World Order* (Princeton, NJ, Princeton University Press, 2022). He was a central banker for 33 years (from autumn 1980 until late-2013). During that time, he was a secretary of the Bank of England's Monetary Policy Committee during its first (nearly) five years, and then spent nearly a dozen years as one of its members.

question makes sense only in the context of the ECB's treaty-based objective, which (paraphrasing) is first and foremost to maintain price stability, and subject to that, to support wider EU economic policies.[1]

The question, then, is not whether the ECB cares about inflation a bit; nor whether it gives inflation a much higher weight in trade-offs with other goods. Rather, it is whether the ECB is consistently directed to achieving price stability as a *necessary precondition* for turning to other things at all. That means expectations of medium to long-term inflation being anchored to the 2 per cent target, and, furthermore, that anchor being secure.

Does the ECB care about inflation in that sense? No, it does not – or, perhaps more accurately, for an extended period over recent years the ECB talked and set policy as though it did not. In this, the ECB was not alone among the major central banks, so part of what I have to say – about the contingent perils of gradualist policy, and about policy-makers' incentives – will concern advanced-economy central banks in general. But there is also a very important constitutional point about the ECB in particular, which I will discuss in the final part of this chapter.

2. Circumstantial Evidence that the ECB and Some Other Major Central Banks have not been Prioritising Inflation

During the 1990s there was something approaching a revolution in the practice of monetary policy. At its centre was a massive increase in transparency: transparency about objectives, policy settings, and, perhaps above all, in explanations of policy settings. Transparency fostered both economic efficiency and accountability. Policy-makers were supposedly tied to the mast by exposing themselves to scrutiny.[2]

But the notion that pellucid explanations of policy-makers' reasoning are supposedly the norm might be questioned if the explanations end up being elusive or even misleading. I fear we were close to that during much of 2021–22, and

[1] Under Art 127 of the Treaty on the Functioning of the European Union (TFEU), 'Without prejudice to the objective of price stability, the ESCB shall support the general economic policies in the Union with a view to contributing to the achievement of the objectives of the Union as laid down in Article 3 of the Treaty on European Union'. Contrary to commentary among economists, this is not a straightforward lexicographic objective (of the kind the Bank of England has). A plausible reading of the treaties is that anything done by the ECB, including in pursuit of the second objective, needs to be permissible under the first objective; and that anything done under the second objective involves supporting EU policy, and so cannot involve the ECB making discretionary choices on EU policy. For such a reading, see the following article by the current ECB General Counsel: Chiara Zilioli and Michael Ioannidis, 'Climate Change and the Mandate of the ECB: Potential and Limits of Monetary Contribution to European Green Policies' (2022) 59 *CML Rev* 363. As such, the word 'objective' (used in the French as well as the English version of the treaty) is somewhat misleading.

[2] Tucker, *Unelected Power* 420–24.

perhaps even in 2020. Before getting to those points about presentation, here are some broad-brush background facts, together with some observations on them.

In 2020, in response to the economic shock brought by the Covid-19 virus, the main central banks massively increased quantitative easing (QE) at the same time as governments provided badly needed fiscal support to families and businesses. In effect, we had money-financed fiscal stimulus. But, even at the time, it was not clear why additional monetary accommodation was warranted. After all, a good deal of the economy's productive capacity (aggregate supply) was shutting down. Of course, it was sensible to stabilise government bond markets when the seriousness of the pandemic dawned on people in the spring of 2020. But that warranted a market-maker of last operation that could be unwound when markets stabilised, not long-lasting additions to QE. It was almost as though central banks had forgotten that they can purchase government bonds for different purposes, and not all of them are QE, which should be thought of as monetary policy stimulus to aggregate demand.[3] Meanwhile, the financing costs available to credit-worthy governments via the bond markets were, due to forward rates being below any plausible long-term equilibrium for nominal rates, much better than those they instead took on via the fixed-to-floating rate swap delivered by ever-expanding QE.[4]

In 2021, when the US government enacted a new massive fiscal stimulus package, the Federal Reserve continued to add to its own monetary stimulus – as did the other major central banks. Putting it mildly, it was not easy to understand why the pace of QE – ie, the pace of incremental additions to monetary stimulus – should be maintained notwithstanding the scale of injection of demand from the federal government. And for other central banks, the enormous size of the US meant that the prospect of the US economy overheating was obviously relevant to their own deliberations.

In 2022, there was a very sharp rise in energy prices due to Russia's war on Ukraine (and OPEC's choice not to increase supply to stabilise prices). The main central banks initially maintained low policy rates and continued to add to QE. They said the rise in headline inflation from the cost shock would be temporary. That is, of course, correct for shocks to the price level, just so long as there are no second-round effects on inflation expectations, affecting wage- and price-setting.

[3] The distinct purposes include to stimulate aggregate demand (monetary policy); to provide emergency financing to government; to stabilise bond markets; to provide liquidity to those selling the bonds; and to relieve pressure (inventory risk) on intermediaries. The second to the fifth each entails moral hazard. Each of the five also needs its own regime and governance. See Stephen Cecchetti and Paul Tucker, 'Understanding how central banks use their balance sheets: A critical categorisation' (*VoxEU*, 1 June 2021) https://cepr.org/voxeu/columns/understanding-how-central-banks-use-their-balance-sheets-critical-categorisation.

[4] The debt swap is effected when QE is combined with central banks paying their policy rate of interest on the totality of reserves, not merely the marginal euro (dollar, pound) of reserves, which is all that is necessary to implement standard monetary policy. See Paul Tucker, 'Quantitative Easing, Monetary Policy Implementation, and the Public Finances' *Institute for Fiscal Studies Green Budget 2002* ch 7.

Of course, Covid-19 and the war on Ukraine presented extraordinarily difficult circumstances for macroeconomic policy-makers. But it is – and, at the time, was – striking that only from the middle of 2022 did the major central banks cease adding to QE and start raising their policy rates in earnest.[5] Since, at least in some countries, the aftermath of the pandemic seems to have brought a contraction in labour-market participation, entailing a lower path for aggregate supply (AS), that gradualism raises puzzling questions about the central banks' conjunctural judgements and policy strategies.

2.1. Presentation: Elisions, Obscurities and Risks

The main point of recalling that history is to examine monetary-policy explanations and transparency. The first surprising thing was that, when the change in policy stance eventually began, we were encouraged by the main central banks to think that they were *tightening* policy in the face of inflationary pressures. Indeed they were. But it seems likely that policy was still stimulating aggregate demand for a good part of 2022. For example, in a January 2023 interview, ECB policy-maker Philip Lane said: 'We're not yet at the level of interest rates needed to bring inflation back to 2 per cent in a timely manner.'[6] One might reasonably ask why not; why would the ECB choose to set its policy rate at a level it thought inadequate to achieve its target? An answer might be framed in terms of uncertainty and the balance of risks, looking ahead.

Elsewhere in this rich and instructive interview, Lane says: 'The debate about the exact timing [of starting to tighten policy] is misplaced.' As a general proposition, that makes sense. But it applies in particular situations only if inflation expectations are *securely* anchored to the target, so that there is zero need for pre-emptive action in order to avoid seeming complacent. By stipulating that the debate was misplaced, a senior policy-maker perhaps seemed to assume victory was assured.

Anyway, for months and months policy was tightened by central banks in the sense of being less loose, but not in the sense of restraining aggregate demand. That involved an elision of *changes* versus *levels*.

But there is one more thing. Lane underlined that in February 2022, the ECB 'signalled a faster pace of reduction of asset purchases'. Read or heard quickly, that

[5] As I understand it, the Bank of England stopped making QE purchases in late 2021 and commenced selling QE gilts roughly a year later; the Fed stopped QE purchases in March 2022, and started sales a quarter later; and the ECB stopped expanding their QE portfolio in July 2022, but reinvested redemptions until spring 2023, since when they have partly reinvested redemptions.

[6] Interview with Philip R Lane, Member of the Executive Board of the ECB, conducted by Martin Wolf, *Financial Times* (London, 17 January 2023) www.ecb.europa.eu/press/inter/date/2023/html/ecb.in230117~1ab0df6f3d.en.html. I must underline, given that I draw a lot from this interview, that Lane is unquestionably expert in these matters. I choose his remarks precisely because, in this interview and elsewhere, he is articulate and there is little risk that he does not understand what he is saying.

too might sound like tightening, but it isn't even that. Its meaning becomes clear if the sentence is translated into an equivalent proposition on interest rates: 'interest rates have been cut by X basis points per meeting, but now we are going to cut rates by smaller amounts at each meeting'. In other words, still cutting; and, back in the world of QE, still adding to the stimulus. So, I suppose, that is a second elision. Or, at least it looks that way unless further stimulus was warranted by new adverse shocks to aggregate demand (AD), or by news that older adverse AD shocks still working their way through the economy were bigger than previously grasped and outweighed any contraction in AS. But in that case, why not say so?

All that is noteworthy because one of the two big things about monetary policy is *getting the sign right*: to be restraining demand when one judges one needs to slow spending growth to maintain inflation in line with the target; and to be stimulating demand when necessary to achieve the target. To continue stimulating demand was substantively odd in my view. That is because it risked adding domestically generated inflationary pressures to the effects on headline inflation from the external cost shocks, and so raised the probability of unwelcome second-round effects in inflation expectations. Writing in spring 2023, it seems likely that this is becoming visible in the US, and perhaps elsewhere.

That takes us back to the demands of a norm of transparency, seen as a route to both efficiency and legitimacy, via accountability and discipline (including internally within central banks as concrete organisations). Given the complex combination of shocks affecting inflation, they have needed to publish their best-guess decompositions of excess inflation (relative to target) in terms of the effects of external terms-of-trade shocks (notably the energy price increases) and drivers of any domestically generated inflation, including adverse internal AS shocks (eg, to labour supply) and monetary conditions. Even if, for illustrative purposes, 80 per cent of the roughly peak 8 percentage point (pp) overshoot was attributable to the external cost shocks, the residue attributable to domestically generated inflation (20 per cent of 8pp: 1.6pp) would probably rank as the biggest overshoot since the regime of flexible inflation-targeting was introduced a quarter of a century ago.[7] (At least in the US, 80 per cent seems unrealistically high, underlining the point.)

While, as one policy-maker rightly pointed out to me, any such (staff) decompositions would be model-based, that is irrelevant to the unavoidability of policy-makers making such judgements themselves (ideally drawing on multiple models) in order to set policy, and their duty (given the transparency norm) to publish them. Also, while the opinions of different policy-makers within

[7] I have chosen 80% for my illustration mainly because (for mysterious reasons) people are fond of 80/20 splits, and also because Bank of England governor Andrew Bailey attributed 80% of the target overshoot in Britain to external cost shocks when testifying to the Westminster parliament during 2022. See Larry Elliot, '"Apocalyptic" food prices will be disastrous for world's poor, says Bank governor' *The Guardian* (London, 17 May 2022) www.theguardian.com/business/2022/may/16/apocalyptic-food-prices-will-be-disastrous-for-worlds-poor-says-bank-governor.

any jurisdiction's monetary committee might reasonably differ, that is not an argument against transparency, because it is hard for any of them to explain their votes without resort to at least implicit judgements on what has been driving the high inflation outturns.

2.2. What Might Explain the Elisions?

Of course, my own various substantive judgements, implied above, might easily be mistaken. But if, contrary to my view, the ECB's judgement was that policy needed to stay accommodative – and, even more important, that its policymakers were correct to want to carry on adding to the stimulus until mid-2022 – then the transparency norm, supposedly central to the 1990s' revolution, demanded that central bank policy-makers say so in terms, and defend that important judgement. That did not happen. There are various candidate explanations for this, but with some obscurity about which would be favoured by the policy-makers themselves.

One possibility is that, at least during the first part of 2022, the main central banks carried on believing their 'transitory inflation' story well after they stopped pressing it in public. That would have had to be based on a judgement that the energy price rises had delivered a cost shock but there had not been any change in nominal trends (and so in underlying inflationary pressures). It would also mean that when they said they were 'tightening', they did not have any plan for policy to be tight (in levels terms). The immediate point here is not that such a diagnosis and decision would definitely have been a mistake – a separate question – but, rather, that the apparent lack of candour about the (conditionally) intended stance of policy would have been a mistake.

A second possible explanation is that central bankers understood they were still stimulating aggregate demand but thought any excess demand would have a negligible effect on inflation. That might have reflected a view that the so-called Phillips Curve had not merely been mislaid (a serious practical problem) but, much more important, no longer captured any kind of reliable economic relationship; in other words, that there was no longer any meaningful constraint on the path of demand relative to the path of the economy's productive capacity. If so, that view needed declaring in terms, and defending.

A third, and perhaps more realistic, possibility is that the main elision – between *changes* in short-term interest rates and their *level* – arose because policy-makers have come to think they can rely on expectations of *future* policy settings to do the work of bringing the economy back into balance. This draws on the true belief that it is the entire yield curve that matters. As Lane rightly said in his Financial Times interview: 'After all, the yield curve jumps in anticipation of what we are expected to do and we've also proven an ability to move quickly.'

But on dissecting that main elision, we are reminded that it is the expected and realised path of *real* rates not of *nominal* rates that matters to the stance of monetary policy (and much more). Thus, policy-makers might have judged that, even in conditions of excess demand, it was ok for the prevailing (instantaneous) *nominal* policy rate to deliver a negative *short-term real* rate provided that market expectations (embodied in the yield curve) of *future* policy-rate settings would bear down on aggregate demand because the implied *path* for *real* interest rates – ie, after taking account of expectations of the path of inflation itself – would be high enough to do so. This kind of gradualism can be thought of as choosing to maintain negative real rates today, while signalling the prospect of positive short real rates tomorrow, and eventually real rates high enough to restrain AD. It is a strategy or plan that might appear to suit everyone, since it might reduce volatility in the economy and also in financial markets.

But, to work, that kind of policy strategy depends heavily on the expected profile for inflation and, more specifically, on the central bank being trusted to deliver on the inflation target. In other words, to repeat a central point, it relies on the anchor both holding and being secure. While dynamic stochastic general equilibrium (DSGE) models – and their outputs served up by technically proficient staff – might be used in ways that effectively encode credibility through a presumption of securely anchored inflation expectations, policy-makers themselves should not habitually inhale that addictive assumption.[8] These are points about people or, more accurately, about people and processes, and so about organisational fitness.

The root point is that *central bankers are themselves the nominal anchor.* Routinely relying on market expectations to do the heavy lifting is a risky strategy, entailing much more volatility down the road if economic agents have come to harbour scepticism about policy-makers' willingness to be unpopular in order to deliver inflation back to target, and hence to maintain medium-term inflation expectations in line with the target. Sometimes (not always) policy needs a down payment, to show you mean it; ie, to show more than that you will get round to restraining demand eventually. When that is so is a matter for policy-makers' judgement. It is a judgement they need to be open about and cogently defend, but most importantly one they need to remember they must make.[9]

It matters enormously for this reason. If ever the anchor does slip, it will be damn hard to know how far it has moved. That means it will be hard to know the rate of inflation expected in the future, which in turn means it will be hard to know the level of real rates currently and prospectively. Bluntly, it will be hard to

[8] Technically, this involves running the model with a reaction function for the policy rate that delivers inflation in line with the target, and minimises the costs of economic volatility, and so on. But if, in the real world, inflation expectations have slipped or are not securely anchored – meaning the expectations-formation process has changed in some way – then the necessary reaction function will be different, and probably not known ex ante.

[9] For similar sentiments, expressed differently, see former Bank of England governor Mervyn King, 'The King Canute Theory of Inflation' (*Bloomberg*, 24 November 2021) www.bloomberg.com/opinion/articles/2021-11-24/central-banks-should-abandon-the-king-canute-theory-of-inflation, based on Mervyn King, 'Monetary Policy in a World of Radical Uncertainty' (Institute of International Monetary Research, Annual Public Lecture, London, 23 November 2021).

judge whether monetary conditions are stimulating or restraining demand, and by how much.[10] Once in that situation, the policy-maker would have to make a best guess, and then wait and see. If they were unlucky and medium-term inflation expectations had risen by more than they guessed, then further tightening would become necessary to restore the anchor. But precisely because in that situation there would be growing uncertainty about medium-term expectations and increasing nervousness about credibility, the policy-makers would still not be confident about quite how high nominal interest rates would need to go.

This means that when monetary policy-makers occasionally go out of their way to say, speaking in general terms, that bringing inflation back down from above target is easier than getting inflation up from below target when the policy rate is stuck at the Zero Lower Bound (ZLB), they are not wrong as a general matter, but something is being obscured (a third elision). Namely, that if the anchor slips, they would not know how big and painful a recession would be needed to restore it.

Those were the implied stakes when, in late February 2023, the president of the New York Fed, who is vice chair of the Federal Open Markets Committee, said 'our job is to make sure we *restore* price stability' (emphasis added).[11] That was not the same as saying that inflation is too high and must be brought down but that underlying nominal trends remain consistent with price stability; and, given the speaker's experience and credentials, I discount the possibility that the vice chair misspoke. Instead, the word 'restore' plainly implied that price stability needed to be restored; ie, that, along the way of operating a gradualist rate strategy, the anchor had slipped. By contrast, in Lane's slightly earlier *Financial Times* interview, he carefully stressed that euro area inflation expectations were still anchored. That matters enormously, because any plausible justification of the ECB's own gradualist strategy has depended on exactly that.

2.3. The Hazards in 'Forward Guidance'

Much of that discussion is related to the phenomenon known as 'forward guidance', on which there is more to be said (not all of it good) than can be managed here.

[10] Of course, that judgement includes assessing where the actual and yield-curve implied risk-free real rate (r) is relative to the neutral real rate (the notorious r*) that prevails when the economy is, broadly speaking, in balanced equilibrium. But while r* is never directly observable, for a quarter of a century central bankers and others have been able to measure r with confidence. When the anchor is slipping, that becomes a lot more difficult. The sheer scale and persistence of QE has, meanwhile, probably distorted signals from bond yields, which in more normal times act as an independent (albeit erratic) conscience for monetary policy-makers by pricing expected inflation and inflation risk premia (compensating for uncertainty about future inflation) into nominal bond yields. I do not discuss here the effects of so-called quantitative tightening (QT) on this or on the other issues I explore.

[11] *Reuters*, 'Fed is "absolutely" committed to 2% target, Williams says' (22 February 2023) www.reuters.com/markets/us/fed-is-absolutely-committed-2-inflation-target-williams-says-2023-02-22.

First, it is vital to distinguish between, on the one hand, what has come to be known as Odyssean forward guidance when policy rates are stuck at the ZLB and, on the other hand, statements about future policy when nominal rates are no longer stuck at the ZLB, casually known as Delphic. That vital distinction has been blurred, elided or for a while just junked.

In Odyssean mode, the policy-maker is trying to commit to keep policy rates low for too long; ie, beyond the point of economic recovery and a return of underlying inflation to (or above) target. But the same sounds and scribbles – 'forward guidance' – have come to be employed habitually when, freed from the ZLB constraint, policy-makers are merely talking about what they are going to do. The first is a commitment, the second a prediction, and so they obviously do not have anything like the same analytical grounding. This fourth elision, moreover, is costly because policy-makers' unqualified predictions about their future choices are unreliable, not for any nefarious reason but because they do not know what is going to happen in the world. They do not know which known risks will crystallise, and which shocks will take them completely by surprise (unknown unknowns).

That being so, I would urge policy-makers to talk less about themselves, and more about the economy: about the economic outlook, with its many uncertainties, and about whether they judge the risks to the outlook for growth and for inflation to be symmetric or skewed, and why.

I urge that partly because Delphic guidance can impair the quality of decision making. Guidance of either variety cannot work unless there is a stable super-majority in a policy committee. If Guidance issued today is vulnerable to being dropped or changed at a future meeting because, say, just one member has changed his or her mind, and that possibility is widely understood, the initial guidance (now lower case) will be given little weight. Indeed, Odyssean Guidance is, in practice, absolutely pointless without a stable super-majority.

But after years of Odyssean Guidance, it was hard for financial market participants and others to grasp that Delphic Guidance is different. They found that hard because central bankers and their closest commentators continued to use the words 'forward guidance'. Same words, same meaning, yes? No.

As they bumped into those contradictions, leading central banks, very much including the ECB, tried to escape from their predicament by emphasising that policy would be 'data dependent'. And so, by God, it should be, because it is only by analysing an eclectic set of data – official statistics on the real economy, the monetary aggregates and other indications of nominal trends, surveys, anecdote – that one has any hope of making tolerably sound judgements about the economic outlook. It is a practice where policy-makers need to spend a lot of their own time scrutinising the conjunctural data, and thinking about how they fit together given various possible understandings (models) of how the economy works.

But policy-makers are finding it hard to stick to a (second-order) promise of being data dependent, which, under any ordinary understanding, would mean not making decisions until they have received all the data due out before the next formal policy meeting. That precludes revealing *before* a meeting what will be decided at that meeting, which, to pick only one example, is what the ECB seemed to do when, in mid-February 2023, it said that the policy rate would be raised by 50 basis points at the meeting to be held roughly a fortnight later.[12] In other words, policy seemed to be decided before all the data were in, so it was not easy to be convinced that policy choices depended wholly on the data, as not a few commentators pointed out at the time.

What, I think, may be going on here is partly the corrosive habit-persistence after years of forward guidance to which I have already alluded, but also partly a mode of making policy decisions via *negotiations* among members rather than collective *deliberation*. If anything akin to negotiation is the main mode of operation, a policy committee's leader(s) would rationally want to announce a deal once they have clinched one they can live with. This, I should say, is how the Fed seems to have operated at times over the past decade, and I hardly think it has more to recommend it there than in Europe. The underlying problem might be that both committees are too big, and that regional Fed presidents in the US and national governors in Europe have learned that, if the leader(s) wants consensus or at least a big majority, regular members can advance their own preferred policy by, in effect, negotiating via public speeches and interviews.

Anyway, it seems to me that continuing to use 'forward guidance' to imply that policy will only gradually reach the point of restraining demand can sometimes amount to deferring necessary action. That would be an exercise in hope: the technical hopes of staff seduced by DSGE models in the service of the political hopes of policy-makers interested in promising, say, inclusive growth (a worthy objective for elected politicians using their fiscal instruments).

While that predicament was perhaps most obvious at the Federal Reserve, there seemed to be an element of it at the ECB too. On both sides of the Atlantic, a previous generation would have quickly raised the policy rate to be restrictive in order to maintain the anchor, and might by the time of my writing (spring 2023) even have reached the point of beginning to ease the degree of restraint on demand. Instead, we might only now be entering the phase of restrictive policy.

The interesting question about this apparent shift in sentiment towards taking risks with inflation is, why? What can have induced independent policy-makers to loosen the binds that lie at the heart of their existence?

[12] Andrew Langley, 'ECB's Lagarde Reaffirms Intention for Half-Point March Hike' (*Bloomberg*, 15 February 2023) www.bloomberg.com/news/articles/2023-02-15/ecb-s-lagarde-reaffirms-intention-to-hike-by-half-point-in-march.

3. Incentives: Making Central Bank Independence Work

That vital question brings us to incentives, and hence the conditions for independence to work at all. The standard argument is rooted in the time-inconsistency problem made famous, analytically, by Finn E Kydland and Edward C Prescott.[13] The argument is plausible enough intuitively: even assuming that elected politicians consistently prioritise the electorate's aggregate welfare, they will sometimes exploit any short-term trade-off between economic activity (or jobs) and inflation, leading to higher medium-term inflation expectations without improving long-run output. When features of the real world are introduced – notably, the tendency of politicians to flip flop in their policy preferences – the arguments for not leaving monetary policy in elected hands are fortified.

There is also a different kind of argument for independence – a constitutional one. Since the monetary levers are always latently instruments of taxation (through surprise inflation or deflation), the last people who should hold them are the members of the elected executive (prime ministers, finance ministers, and so on) as that would violate one element of the separation of powers that lies at the heart of constitutional democracy: that taxation should be approved by a representative assembly of some kind.[14]

But those are both arguments – welfarist or constitutionalist – for not leaving executive government free to run monetary policy. They say nothing about why delegation to an independent body will work. Take, for example, a Rogoffian conservative central banker: why wouldn't the politicians appoint someone who looked 'conservative' but, when it came to it, wasn't, because in fact they were an ally of the politician. Or take a Walshian contract: why would the politician choose to enforce the contract against the erring central banker if the politician benefitted from the economic and credit boom; and since the politician might not enforce the contract, why wouldn't inflation expectations reflect that?[15] Both prescriptions are vulnerable to the time-inconsistency problem merely being relocated, as pointed out many years ago by the late Ben McCallum.[16] This poses a challenge to Larry Summers' important statement at the beginning of the 1990s that 'institutions [can] do the work of rules, and monetary rules should be avoided; instead, institutions should be drafted to solve time-inconsistency problems.'[17]

[13] Finn E Kydland and Edward C Prescott, 'Rules Rather than Discretion: The Inconsistency of Optimal Plans' (1977) 85 *The Journal of Political Economy* 473.

[14] Tucker, *Unelected Power* 287–92. When I first discussed this with the late Alberto Alesina, he was kind enough to say that he had not come across this argument before, and agreed with it.

[15] Kenneth Rogoff, 'The Optimal Degree of Commitment to an Intermediate Monetary Target' (1985) 100 *Quarterly Journal of Economics* 1169. Carl E Walsh, 'Optimal Contracts for Central Bankers' (1995) 85 *American Economic Review* 150.

[16] Bennett T McCallum, 'Two Fallacies Concerning Central Bank Independence' (1995) 85 *American Economic Review* 207.

[17] Lawrence Summers, 'Panel Discussion: Price Stability: How Should Long-term Monetary Policy Be Determined?' (1991) 23 *Journal of Money, Credit and Banking* 625.

How, exactly, can institutions do the work of rules? What does that depend on? After all, the relocated commitment problem afflicts even the Kydland-Prescott paper's advocacy of rules: why would anyone stick to the rule? Identifying a well-crafted rule that would be best (even optimal) if people stuck to it is not much use if, once humans are allowed in, it will be set aside.

3.1. Prestige and Esteem, but for What?

Here we can turn to insights on incentive-compatible institutions. If delegation to unelected central bankers is to do its work (and so be worth any legitimation convolutions), it needs somehow to harness the incentives of the regime's stewards, and their political overseers, who are all flesh and blood men and women.

Illumination comes, I think, from some papers by the late Alberto Alesina and Guido Tabellini.[18] They posit a choice between a politician (who targets aggregate welfare) and a technocrat (who is motivated by the esteem accruing to them if they are seen successfully to deliver a delegated mandate). Armed with that distinction, it becomes rational to delegate some kinds of task to the technocrat. The authors say something about the particular conditions that must hold for that to make sense in certain fields (eg, a time-inconsistency problem), but do not step back to address the wider necessary preconditions for the economy of esteem to do its work. I attempted to do that in *Unelected Power*.[19]

One precondition is that the political society must be capable of bestowing esteem; an apparently innocuous point that has some punch. If the only measure of prestige in a particular society is, say, wealth or perceived closeness to the ruler, delegation is not going to work. This precondition amounts, therefore, to a society needing to have multiple sources of prestige if monetary independence is to work (a point that I suspect does not find its way into International Monetary Fund (IMF) recommendations to a good chunk of the world).

A second precondition, which gets close to the bone today and opens up an illuminating perspective on central banks taking on more and more functions, is that appointed central bank leaders need to care (a lot) about the prestige accrued from delivering the mandate, or foregone if they do not. Milton Friedman was half onto something, but not what he thought, when in the early 1960s he claimed that 'the two most important variables in [central bankers'] loss function are avoiding accountability on the one hand and achieving prestige on the other'.[20] What he

[18] Alberto Alesina and Guido Tabellini, 'Bureaucrats or Politicians? Part I: A Single Policy Task' (2007) 97 *American Economic Review* 169.

[19] Tucker, *Unelected Power* chs 5 and 6.

[20] Letter from Milton Friedman to Stan Fischer, quoted in Stanley Fischer, 'Rules versus Discretion in Monetary Policy' in Benjamin M Friedman and Frank H Hahn (eds), *Handbook of Monetary Economics*, vol 2 (Amsterdam, Elsevier Science Publishers, 1990) 1155–84, 1181.

missed is that, in some circumstances, exposing oneself to accountability can help sharpen incentives, and so offers a route to prestige.

At this point, it is useful to unpack where those personal returns might come from. There are two main sources: professional esteem from a dispersed community of current and former central bankers, monetary economists and other specialist commentators; and, separately, wider public prestige from the political community itself (households as voters, but also the business and financial communities). Delegation works to harness central bankers only if they do care about such esteem and prestige.

Now imagine a central banker who has a public reputation for combatting, say, climate change and inequality, and other social-justice causes. Maybe if (steady state) inflation rises under their watch, they will not care much about ignominy among those who do care about price stability (the *Bild* newspaper in Germany, say) because their standing in the world is buttressed by their social-justice credentials. And maybe, in our thought experiment, they do not much care about the opinion of former central bankers and monetary economists since they have never really been part of that professional-cum-epistemic community. Alternatively, imagine a central banker whose key constituency of political supporters cares most about lax regulation that permits their donors to thrive: a kind of libertarian conservatism. In either case, and plenty of others, the harness is not going to be tight enough to underpin the warrant for delegating responsibility for price stability.

Put more broadly, delegation is unlikely to work as well as expected (or at least hoped) if office holders have access to alternative sources of esteem and prestige. Since the public interest depends on incentivising them to stick to and deliver the central bank's mandate, they have to desire prestige for and from *that*.

That poses a challenge if someone arrives in office already enjoying prestige (for something else), or gains it while in office for something other than sticking to and delivering the mandate (eg, for intervening in political issues or a devotion – genuine or apparent – to good causes). Somehow, the political community needs to put that prestige on hold, so as to orient the prestige-seeking office holder to the mandate. Whether that is realistic might turn, I suggest, on the attitudes of the relevant professional community, and on public attitudes toward that professional community. If the office holder craves professional esteem, the harness might bite notwithstanding pre-existing stardom. If not, and if the public do not think much of the professional community ('economists', with the word spat out in a certain way), then the harness will be loose. In those circumstances, the best that can be hoped for is that office holders care whether their prestige will be in jeopardy in the longer run if they screw up.

Ironically, and maybe tragically, here we are back to short-termism. Delegation to an insulated agency in order to sidestep the costs of political short-termism will struggle to work if the office holders are motivated by short-term prestige (sometimes casually termed celebrity).

3.2. Independence's Achilles Heel: Esteem and Prestige for Too Much

That economy-of-esteem account of the preconditions for effective monetary delegation opens a window onto how independence can be undermined. Here is how I put it in a piece for the IMF a few years ago (before headline inflation took off):

> It is important to remember that there have always been enemies of independence. Within a rich repertoire for undoing an economy's monetary constitution, they can deploy two broad strategies, each with obvious and opaque variants.
>
> One way to bring central banks to heel is through appointments. As seen recently in the United States, that is not easy when favored candidates fall well short of the normal credentials. More troubling are appointees who seem reasonable, excellent even, but turn out to be discreetly committed allies of leading politicians. The most famous case, also during turbulent times, is the former Fed chairman Arthur Burns, a leading economist who put Richard Nixon's 1972 reelection prospects ahead of the Fed's statutory mandate. No one should think that was the last example of a political outrider occupying the monetary corridors.
>
> The other way to undermine independence is through a change in mandate. The crude variant involves simply voting to compromise or repeal the central bank law. That isn't easy, because it is highly visible. The subtle, almost paradoxical, strategy gives the central bank *more* responsibility – so much so that any decent official would feel duty bound to consult political leaders on how to use their extensive powers. The more central banks acquiesce (even revel) in the 'only game in town' label, the easier it becomes for politicians to give them more to do, and so undo them.[21]

My analysis in *Unelected Power* suggested (but, given subsequent developments, I now feel did not bring out sufficiently) that those two strategies are intertwined. Independence is undermined by widening the mandate and appointing someone who cares more about those other causes (or, more accurately, other sources of prestige) than about the respect and standing that would come from delivering monetary-system stability.

3.3. Application to the ECB

When applied to the ECB, this leads to some reasonably clear conclusions. First, ECB policy-makers should not seek any credit for supporting any EU policies (under the ECB's second objective). Moreover, whenever supporting EU policies, it would be important to explain publicly why particular actions fit under the secondary treaty objective, and why the ECB was not making important

[21] Paul Tucker, 'On Central Bank Independence', *Finance & Development* (IMF, June 2020) www.imf.org/en/Publications/fandd/issues/2020/06/paul-tucker-unelected-power-on-central-bank-independence.

discretionary choices about the substance of EU policy or on how it bears on the ECB's operations. Second, and conversely, ECB policy-makers need willingly to impale themselves on medium-term inflation expectations being securely anchored to the 2 per cent inflation target.

And yet, it is more complicated than that, and here my tone will shift.

4. Why the ECB has the Hardest Job Among Advanced-Economy Central Banks

There is something distinctive about the ECB, uncomfortably so. It is both more and less than a normal central bank.[22]

4.1. Not a Regular Central Bank

The most obvious difference between the ECB and most of its notional peers is that it is not established by ordinary legislation (passed by the EU Council and Parliament, and revisable by them) but, rather, through a treaty among the EU's many member states (each with their own local ratification process, some involving national referenda). In practice, therefore, the ECB's independence is as deeply entrenched as it is possible to get. As I have argued elsewhere, this implies that the ECB's functions ought to be even more narrowly constrained; ie, more constrained than the regimes for central banks granted independence by ordinary legislation.[23] While legislators in the US, UK and Japan can alter the terms of their local monetary regime if the Fed, Bank of England or Bank of Japan stretch themselves too far in some perceived way, that is not feasible in Europe and so the binds need to be stricter from the start.

In its enthusiasm to pursue wider functions – sometimes, but not always, carefully wrapped in the language of providing 'support' for the EU's other policies and goals – the ECB cuts against this important condition for sustained legitimacy: not only its own, but that of the EU institutions more generally.

4.2. Deep Entrenchment Combined with Incomplete Economic Government

But the differences between the ECB and its ostensible peers run deeper than the degree of its constitutional entrenchment, with profound implications. Unlike

[22] This section draws on Tucker, *Unelected Power* 393–94.

[23] Paul Tucker, 'How the European Central Bank and Other Independent Agencies Reveal a Gap in Constitutionalism: A Spectrum of Institutions for Commitment' (2021) 22 *German Law Journal* 999.

those central banks serving national or federal democracies, the euro area's central bank does not work alongside a counterpart fiscal authority, let alone one elected by the people.

Appearing to recognise this, the EU's treaty-makers sought to substitute discipline for discretion by enshrining a legal principle of 'no bail outs' for member states participating in the monetary union. When it came to pass, however, that proved to be mere parchment. While member state governments had short-term incentives to sign up to 'discipline', they did not have more enduring incentives to abide by or enforce their agreement. So when the euro area faced an existential crisis, the lack of confederal fiscal capabilities in elected hands left the ECB as the only institution that could keep the currency union from shattering.

It is important to be clear about what this means: the ECB became the existential guarantor of the European project itself. Not merely a mighty citizen, but *the* essential citizen, the economic sovereign – a lot more than a normal central bank.[24]

4.3. Central Banking's Grand Dilemma Writ Large

Here we confront an especially problematic version of central banking's grand dilemma. In its standard form, this is the problem of the Stackelberg (sequential-move) game inscribed into the relations between a monetary authority and an elected fiscal authority. Even where policy-makers share the view that an adverse economic shock is best met with a combination of fiscal and monetary stimulus, the fiscal policy-maker has strong political incentives to do nothing – thereby avoiding the short-term political costs of carrying with them cabinet, donors, party base etc– safe in the knowledge the central bank will strive to do more within the limits of its mandate.

But the ECB faces this problem on a giant scale almost unknown to regular central banks.[25] Since there is no conventional fiscal authority for the euro area, it finds itself synthesising one, under the rubric of monetary policy, whenever the economic–financial pillars of the Union are crumbling.

Thus, the 'grand dilemma' becomes gruelling, leaving the ECB with a job immeasurably more difficult than that of its supposed peers. Because the ECB's independence is so deeply entrenched, its functions should (normatively, ie, given Europeans' deep political values) be tightly constrained. Because it lacks a fiscal counterpart, the opposite is inevitable in practice. The deep value of constitutional propriety and the imperative of preserving the people's welfare meet in headlong

[24] The language 'economic sovereign' echoes the notorious and morally repugnant Carl Schmitt, who argued that the actor who declares a state of exception is the true sovereign, and that that is always the executive branch of government (as the only 24/7 branch).

[25] I include the qualification 'almost' because the Federal Reserve faces a diluted version of the predicament given Congressional sclerosis.

collision. Both in terms of constitutional politics and quotidian politics, therefore, the ECB's greatest challenge is to navigate itself back toward the proper role of technocratic trustee for monetary-system stability.

It is hard to see how that can be accomplished without a deepening of the economic union – to some degree of fiscal union – in ways that are unpalatable for some member states. For constitutionalists, the choice lies between living with an overmighty central bank (underpinning a fragile currency union through its quasi-fiscal powers) or, alternatively, returning technocracy to its proper place but within a deeper economic union built on incentive-compatible foundations.

Meanwhile, the ECB's leaders, knowing they are the emergency cavalry, are not incentivised to be pre-emptive against inflation in a single-minded 'no risks with the anchor' way, because they must always consider whether an abrupt tightening of monetary and credit conditions could bring about a crisis among euro area members with cyclical or structural financing vulnerabilities.[26] It puts the ECB beyond any normal conception of a central bank, landing its leaders with a quite extraordinarily difficult job.

5. Summing up

The central background thought behind this chapter is the following: *inflation, meaning persistent inflation, is always and everywhere a political economy phenomenon.*

Friedman's famous statement about inflation being always a monetary phenomenon is true, but lies one step forward from the underlying problem. At the time of writing in spring 2023, we do not yet know whether the high inflation of recent years will persist or, if inflation does fall back, whether it will settle in line with or above target. If it does remain above target, the roots of the predicament will lie in flawed incentives: in the incentives of the monetary regime's designers, or of the regime's central banker stewards, or of those who appoint those stewards, or of those who oversee the stewards, or even of commentators, or some complex combination of some or all of those. We wait and see (and of course hope).

Given that basic proposition, the chapter's morphology of central bankers' incentives and interests underlines the importance of some welfare-oriented principles for the design of independent central banks. First, their functions and responsibilities must be as narrow as possible, as otherwise their leaders have too many routes to esteem and prestige. I believe the mandate should be

[26] Perhaps the new instrument for handling fragmentation crises, the Transmission Protection Instrument, will alter this dynamic, which would be a major achievement since, among other things, it would remove the shackles on monetary policy. But one could imagine that policy-makers might still be cautious about imposing monetary-policy shocks via sharper tightenings because until there is a crisis, they cannot be sure the new tool will work as intended. These are, to be clear, weighty judgements.

monetary-system stability, which includes the stability of the private part of the monetary system, but not more.[27]

Second, they need objectives that can be understood and tracked by interested members of the public, so that their personal ambitions cannot be achieved by self-declaratory success. Precisely because the price-stability objective is framed as a quantified target for inflation (typically 2 per cent), observers can see that outcomes have been miles away from target, and the central bankers have accordingly been taking a lot of public heat, personally. Although one takes zero pleasure in observing this, that shows that that part of the regime is working as intended.

In a way, it has been a reminder to central banks in general, and the ECB in particular, to attend to the core of the mandate: achieving price stability via a secure anchor for medium-to-long-term inflation expectations. The single-mindedness which that demands will, however, continue to be tested by the need for vigilance regarding the stability-cum-integrity of the euro area itself.

That is because, as was understood by many from its founding, the designers of Europe's monetary union faced conflicting incentives they could not reconcile: to push the European project forward by introducing a single currency, but not to push it so far forward that, via establishing some kind of fiscal union, a political union loomed around the next corner before the peoples of Europe clearly wanted or could support it. The upshot is a fragility that the ECB's leaders have to remember, and navigate, every second of every day.

So, the answer to my headline question is: 'No, the ECB is not focused above all else on maintaining price stability, and that is a bad thing, but how could things be otherwise after everyone realised that the ECB is the de facto emergency fiscal authority the European project's architects understandably hesitated to create elsewhere.'

That mitigation is not a licence to branch out beyond central banking, or to be casual about shocks to underlying inflationary trends. But it does introduce a constraint that is not faced by other central banks. Given the geopolitical situation, the last thing the West needs is another euro area crisis.[28]

Finally, it should be stressed that it is easier to make these various judgements as an observer than as an actor. But perhaps that is why, at least in aspiration, they might be of some slight use to those carrying such great responsibilities in such extraordinary times.

[27] Tucker, *Unelected Power* ch 20.
[28] See Tucker, *Global Discord* part V.

2

Inventing the Asymmetrical Monetary Union

CHRISTIAN NEUMEIER*

From the perspective of monetary economics, little seemed to suggest the foundation of the European Economic and Monetary Union (EMU) by the Maastricht Treaty in 1993. Establishing a monetary union without a relevant fiscal capacity, without automatic stabilisers,[1] and without a common economic policy was not something many economists would have recommended. Labour mobility was comparatively low and national economies still diverged significantly. Scholars of optimum currency areas (OCA), then and now the prevalent theoretical framework to assess potential monetary unions, publicly warned against monetary integration without further fiscal and economic integration.[2] Even those who otherwise disagreed with the broadly Keynesian foundation of OCA were wary. Contemporary critics ranged from Paul Krugman to Milton Friedman, from Barry Eichengreen to Ronald Reagan's chief economic adviser Martin Feldstein and German ordoliberal economist (and later chief economist of the ECB) Otmar Issing, who called the EMU a 'phantom'.[3]

* I would like to express my sincere gratitude to Wilhelm Schönfelder and Peter Wilhelm Schlüter for their kind openness to revisit the past. I am also grateful to the staff at the Political Archive of the Federal Foreign Office for their assistance. The text has benefitted from critical comments by Antonia Craven, Piers Ludlow, Florian Meinel, Luuk van Middelaar, Frank Schorkopf, Paul Tucker and Ruth Weber.

[1] Automatic stabilisers are fiscal mechanisms such as an unemployment insurance or a progressive income tax which automictically adjust to recessions, see Paul De Grauwe, *Economics of Monetary Union*, 13th edn (Oxford, Oxford University Press, 2020) 13.

[2] De Grauwe, *Economics of Monetary Union* 24; Francesco Paolo Mongelli, 'The OCA theory and the path to EMU' in Marco Buti et al (eds), *The Euro: The First Decade* (Cambridge, Cambridge University Press, 2010) 115–42. For a critique, see Waltraud Schelkle, *The Political Economy of Monetary Solidarity* (Oxford, Oxford University Press, 2017) 19–27.

[3] Paul Krugman, 'Policy problems of a monetary union' in Paul De Grauwe and Lucas Papademos (eds), *The European Monetary System in the 1990s* (London, Longman, 1990) 48–64, less critical about asymmetry, however, than in his later appraisal in 'Revenge of the Optimum Currency Area' (2013) 27 *NBER Macroeconomics Annual* 439; Milton Friedman, 'The Euro: Monetary Unity to Political Disunity' (*Project Syndicate*, 28 August 1997); *cf* Antonio Martino, 'Milton Friedman and the Euro' (2008) 28 *Cato Journal* 263; Barry Eichengreen, 'Is Europe an Optimum Currency Area?' in Silvio Borner and Herbert Grubel (eds), *The European Community after 1992* (Basingstoke, Macmillan, 1992) 138–64,

For historians (or anyone) thinking about European monetary integration, the asymmetry between the monetary and the economic side of the EMU presents one of its primary puzzles. Why would member states adopt a structure which many prominent economists opposed so adamantly? When, how and why did the asymmetrical monetary union (AMU) emerge as a concept? Who invented this unlikely and daring form of monetary union? Despite their general richness, existing historical accounts of the EMU have not focused on the conceptual history of asymmetry (section 1). This chapter will attempt to close this gap. It identifies a memorandum published by Germany's foreign minister Hans-Dietrich Genscher in the spring of 1988 as the conceptual origin of asymmetry (section 2). The chapter will explore the making of the memorandum (section 3) and its theoretical foundation (section 4), before briefly tracing how it began to shape government policy and the contours of monetary integration (section 5).

1. A Question Still Unanswered

The asymmetry between monetary integration on the one hand and economic and fiscal integration on the other hand is the defining characteristic of the Maastricht Treaty.[4] According to its original design, the European economy was to be governed mainly by the four market freedoms and whichever national economic and fiscal policies member states would adopt within the bounds of the fiscal rules established by Art 126 of the Treaty on the Functioning of the European Union (TFEU). While the Maastricht Treaty established some fora for policy coordination between member states and endowed the European Commission with monitoring powers, a set of fiscal rules for member state budgets was considered the most important piece of common economic government. Many observers have argued that this arrangement proved to be beset with fundamental problems. It is identified by many as the underlying cause for the structural imbalances between member states that fuelled the European debt crisis.[5] It is

reprinted in Barry Eichengreen, *European Monetary Unification* (Cambridge, MA, MIT Press, 1997) 51–71; Martin Feldstein, 'The Political Economy of the European Economic and Monetary Union: Political Sources of an Economic Liability' (1997) 11 *Journal of Economic Perspectives* 23; Otmar Issing, 'Europäische Notenbank – ein Phantom' *Frankfurter Allgemeine Zeitung* (Frankfurt am Main, 12 March 1988) 13. For a nuanced discussion see De Grauwe and Papademos, *The European Monetary System*.

[4] *cf* Barry Eichengreen, 'Sui Generis EMU' in Buti et al, *The Euro* 72–101.

[5] Adam Tooze, *Crashed: How a Decade of Financial Crises Changed the World* (London, Allen Lane, 2018) 91; Mark Copelovitch, Jeffry Frieden and Stefanie Walter, 'The Political Economy of the Euro Crisis' (2016) 49 *Comparative Political Studies* 811; Erik Jones, 'Getting the Story Right: How You Should Choose between Different Interpretations of the European Crisis (And Why You Should Care)' (2015) 37 *Journal of European Integration* 817; Krugman, 'Revenge'; Peter A Hall, 'The Economics and Politics of the Euro Crisis' (2012) 21 *German Politics* 355. *cf* Christos Hadjiemmanuil, 'The Euro Area in Crisis 2008–18' in Fabian Amtenbrink, Christoph Herrmann and René Repasi (eds), *The EU Law of Economic and Monetary Union* (Oxford, Oxford University Press, 2020) 1252–362.

blamed for the slow response to the financial crisis in 2008–2010 which brought the eurozone close to the point of collapse. When the crisis was finally averted, asymmetry, its critics argue, hampered economic growth and led to a recovery that was considerably slower than in the United States.[6]

1.1. Explaining Economic and Monetary Union

If 'why asymmetry?' is the obvious historical question to ask, one would assume that historians must already have explored its conceptual origins in more than sufficient detail. Surprisingly, this is not the case. There is a rich historical literature on why the EMU came about and how it took shape in the run-up to the Maastricht Treaty. Basically, scholars have offered three different historical explanations for the EMU.[7] They all offer rich insights and explain important aspects of the EMU. None of them, however, answers the more specific question of how and why asymmetry emerged as a concept. Existing accounts explain very convincingly why there would be *some kind* of monetary union at the end of the 1980s but less so why member states opted for the very specific and, as it soon turned out, fragile monetary union of the Maastricht Treaty.[8]

First, there is the still popular idea that the EMU was a political price to be paid by Germany for its reunification.[9] This account faces two objections. For one, it is not supported by the timeline of events. Reunification certainly facilitated the conclusion of the Maastricht Treaty. In particular, it played a role in the early agreement at the European Council meeting in Strasbourg in December 1989 on

[6] De Grauwe, *Economics of Monetary Union* 233.

[7] Of course, these explanations are not mutually exclusive. Any satisfactory historical account of the EMU will have to consider a number of factors ranging from the structural economic forces which pulled member states towards monetary union, the various national interests which made it politically plausible to enter into a monetary union, the specific actors at the helm of national governments, to the intellectual groundwork for monetary union which had been laid over 30 years of nearly constant discussion about monetary integration in the European Community. For a collection of views, see Michael Gehler and Wilfried Loth (eds), *Reshaping Europe: Towards a political, economic and monetary union 1984–1989* (Baden-Baden, Nomos, 2020); Amy Verdun (ed), *The Euro: European Integration Theory and Economic and Monetary Union* (London, Rowman & Littlefield, 2002). Harold James, *Making the European Monetary Union* (Cambridge, MA, Harvard University Press, 2012) 211 identifies four main explanations: European 'identity politics'; 'political entrepeneurship on part of the EC Commission'; 'a power struggle between nation-states'; and 'financial globalization'.

[8] Paul De Grauwe, 'The Fragility of the Eurozone's Institutions' (2010) 21 *Open Economies Review* 167; Orkun Saka, Ana-Maria Fuertes and Elena Kalotychou, 'ECB Policy and Eurozone Fragility: Was De Grauwe Right?' (2015) 54 *Journal of International Money and Finance* 168.

[9] David Marsh, *The Euro: The Politics of the New Global Currency* (New Haven, CT, Yale University Press, 2009) 133; Karl Kaltenthaler, *Germany and the Politics of Europe's Money* (Durham, NC, Duke University Press, 1998) 69; Loukas Tsoukalis, *The New European Economy Revisited*, 3rd edn (Oxford, Oxford University Press, 1997) 170. The main historical source for the claim appears to be the diary of one of Mitterrand's advisers, see Jacques Attali, *Verbatim: Chronique des années 1988–1991*, vol 3 (Paris, Fayard, 1995). The accuracy of these notes is disputed. For a balanced critique of the claim, see Andreas Rödder, *Deutschland einig Vaterland: Die Geschichte der Wiedervereinigung* (München, Beck, 2009) 264.

a fixed rather than a flexible date to begin negotiations for the common currency in earnest.[10] There is also ample evidence that Chancellor Helmut Kohl as well as foreign minister Hans-Dietrich Genscher, like most of their predecessors, held a deep and genuine conviction that German reunification would only be possible within a larger process of European integration.[11] Both truisms, however, hardly explain the specific contours of the EMU, which began to take form as early as 1988, when German reunification, albeit being a political aim of the Kohl government, was hardly seen as more than a mere possibility in the mid-term future. In 1987, the German government had for some time tried to hold out monetary integration in return for greater military cooperation with the French, without much success. That was obviously a very different bargain and a failed one, too.[12] In addition, this first explanation is also misleading, as it seems to suggest that the EMU was not in Germany's interest per se and was therefore opposed by the German public – after all, it was a price to be paid.[13] Largely based on some opinion polls after the Maastricht Treaty was long concluded, this assumption ignores the strength of public sentiment and economic interests which favoured monetary integration. The EMU enjoyed widespread contemporary support in parts of the German business and banking community, which lobbied quite vigorously for a monetary union.[14] Even labour unions were traditionally pro-European.[15] More importantly, as I will argue, this first explanation neglects that it was in fact the German government who put forward the conceptually decisive initiative for the asymmetrical version of a monetary union long before reunification was on the agenda.

The second prominent explanation for the EMU emphasises the long-term structural forces which pulled member states of the European Community into a

[10] For an analysis of the negotiation process, see Kenneth Dyson and Kevin Featherstone, *The Road to Maastricht: Negotiating Economic and Monetary Union* (Oxford, Oxford University Press, 1999); Colette Mazzucelli, *France and Germany at Maastricht: Politics and Negotiations to create the European Union* (New York, NY, Garland, 1997); Wilhelm Schönfelder and Elke Thiel, *Ein Markt – Eine Währung: Die Verhandlungen zur Europäischen Wirtschafts- und Währungsunion* (Baden-Baden, Nomos, 1994); David J Howarth, *The French Road to European Monetary Union* (Houndmills, Palgrave, 2001). For an extensive critique of the premise that France was opposed to reunification, see Tilo Schabert, *Wie Weltgeschichte gemacht wird: Frankreich und die deutsche Einheit* (Stuttgart, Klett-Cotta, 2002).

[11] Helmut Kohl, 'Europa und die deutsche Frage' (1981) 20 *Lutherische Monatshefte* 261, reprinted in Peter Hintze and Gerd Langguth (eds), *Helmut Kohl: Der Kurs der CDU* (Stuttgart, Deutsche Verlagsanstalt, 1993) 199–204. For Genscher's position on Europe, see n 59 below.

[12] *cf* Frédéric Bozo, 'In search of the Holy Grail: France and European Monetary Unification 1984–1989' in Gehler and Loth, *Reshaping Europe* 283–330, 300; Ulrich Lappenküper, *Mitterrand und Deutschland: Die enträtselte Sphinx* (München, Oldenbourg, 2011) 236.

[13] The claim is therefore often taken up by anti-euro propagandists, see Roland Vaubel, *Das Ende der Euromantik* (Wiesbaden, Springer, 2018) 1–18.

[14] For a nuanced overview, see Kaltenthaler, *Germany* 75; Henrik Meyer, *Deutsche Europapolitik unter Helmut Kohl: Die Auswirkungen des politischen Umfeldes auf die Integrationsbereitschaft der Bundesregierung* (Berlin, Köster, 2004) 191; Stefan Fröhlich, *Helmut Kohl und die deutsche Außenpolitik* (Paderborn, Schöningh, 2001) 246.

[15] Wolfgang Streeck, *More Uncertainties: West German Unions Facing 1992* (Berlin, WZB, 1990).

monetary union.[16] According to this view, the EMU is best explained as a spill-over effect of the European Single Act. In 1986, when member states agreed to abolish all capital controls by 1992, they effectively had little choice other than establishing a monetary union soon after. The unimpaired free movement of capital agreed in the Act, so the argument goes, would have likely unleashed disparities between national currencies which the European Monetary System (EMS) could not have coped with. This explanation mirrors neo-functionalist accounts of European integration as well as a contemporary narrative of the Commission which was eager to portray monetary integration as inevitable.[17] It is ultimately underpinned by an economic argument: Marcus Fleming and Robert Mundell's famous 'impossible trinity', first formulated in the early 1960s.[18] It shows that it is impossible for a country to have (a) fixed exchange rates, (b) no capital controls, and (c) an independent monetary policy at the same time. In 1987, this theorem came to the fore again, when it was prominently applied to the European Community by an expert commission established by the European Commission and chaired by the integrationist Italian economist Tomasso Padoa-Schioppa.[19] Based on this analysis, member states of the European Community faced a simple choice. If they went along with abolishing nearly all forms of capital controls, they could either (a) live with (possibly wildly) floating exchange rates or (b) forego an independent monetary policy and form some kind of monetary union. As fluctuating exchange rates seemed more undesirable than the alternative, this naturally led to the conclusion that they should enter into a monetary union. But a monetary union could come in a variety of forms. However convincing this second explanation might be in principle, it does not readily explain the conceptual origins of the asymmetric shape of the EMU.

The same is true for the third prominent explanation, which is based on the political economy of a monetary union. It argues that at the end of the 1980s, national economic interests converged so as to make the EMU a plausible step

[16] Richard E Baldwin and Charles Wyplosz, *The Economics of European Integration*, 6th edn (London, McGraw-Hill, 2020) 20; N Piers Ludlow, 'European Integration in the 1980s: On the Way to Maastricht?' (2013) 19 *Journal of European Integration History* 18; Andreas Wirsching, 'Stationen auf dem Weg nach Maastricht' (2003) 10 *Historisch-Politische Mitteilungen* 261; Tsoukalis, *The new European economy revisited* 164.

[17] For a critique, see Barry Eichengreen, 'A More Perfect Union? On the Logic of Economic Integration' in Barry Eichengreen, *European Monetary Unification* (Cambridge, Mass, MIT Press, 1997) 247–69.

[18] Robert A Mundell, 'The Monetary Dynamics of International Adjustment under Fixed and Flexible Exchange Rates' (1960) 74 *The Quarterly Journal of Economics* 227; J Marcus Fleming, 'Domestic Financial Policies under Fixed and under Floating Exchange Rates' (1962) 9 *IMF Staff Papers* 369. *cf* James M Boughton, 'On the Origins of the Fleming-Mundell Model' (2003) 50 *IMF Staff Papers* 1.

[19] Tommaso Padoa-Schioppa, *Efficiency, Stability, and Equity: A strategy for the evolution of the economic system of the European community – a report* (Oxford, Oxford University Press, 1987) 18; *cf* Fabio Masini, 'Tommaso Padoa-Schioppa: EMU as the Anchor Stone for Building a Federal Europe' in Kenneth Dyson and Ivo Maes (eds), *Architects of the Euro* (Oxford, Oxford University Press, 2016) 193–211; Ludlow, 'European Integration' 18; Tsoukalis, *The New European Economy Revisited* 164.

to take.[20] Germany, with its economy heavily dependent on exports, had a vital economic interest in locking in its European competitors into a system of fixed exchange rates, so that they could no longer devalue their currencies to become more competitive.[21] France, on the other hand, had a vital economic interest in breaking the monetary dominance of the Deutsche Mark and gaining a seat at the table of monetary policy making again, after seeing the Banque de France being forced to more or less follow the decisions of the Deutsche Bundesbank for almost a decade.[22] Countries with traditionally higher rates of inflation could possibly break inflationary cycles and benefit from lower interest rates for government bonds by entering into a monetary union.[23] One could go through the list of member states and stake out their respective interests and motivations. Doing so again provides good reason why there could be *a* monetary union at that historical juncture – without explaining asymmetry. To provide this more specific explanation, one would need to demonstrate that not only did interests converge on a monetary union but how they converged on asymmetry specifically.

A fourth influential account claims that the EMU is best understood as a neoliberal arrangement, another instance of the great triumph of neoliberal thought in the 1980s and 1990s.[24] There is indeed a strand in neoliberal thought on 'competitive federalism' that advocates for elements that, taken together, would not be too dissimilar to some of the arrangements of the Maastricht Treaty.[25] The theory of competitive federalism is, however, not germane to monetary unions. More importantly, the discretionary powers of the ECB at the heart of the EMU run directly contrary to neoliberal ideals of monetary policy. Noting a similarity in parts is therefore different from demonstrating that 'neoliberalism' is conceptually responsible for the EMU.

[20] Andrew Moravcsik, *The Choice for Europe: Social Purpose and State Power from Messina to Maastricht* (Ithaca, NY, Cornell University Press, 1998) 379; Philip Manow, *Social Protection, Capitalist Production: The Bismarckian Welfare State in the German Political Economy 1880–2015* (Oxford, Oxford University Press, 2020) 114; Malcolm Levitt and Christopher Lord, *The Political Economy of Monetary Union* (New York, NY, St. Martin's Press, 2000). *cf* Femke van Esch, 'Why States Want EMU: Developing a Theory on National Preferences' in Verdun, *The Euro* 51–68.

[21] Orfeo Fioretos, 'The Domestic Sources of Multilateral Preferences: Varieties of Capitalism in the European Community' in Peter A Hall and David Soskice (eds), *Varieties of Capitalism* (Oxford, Oxford University Press, 2001) 213–46, 235.

[22] Howarth, *The French Road* 118.

[23] James, *Making the European Monetary Union* 220; Manow, *Social Protection* 130.

[24] Kathleen R McNamara, *The Currency of Ideas: Monetary Politics in the European Union* (Ithaca, NY, Cornell University Press, 1998); Lloy Wylie, 'EMU: A Neoliberal Construction' in Verdun, *The Euro* 69–90; *cf* Thomas Biebricher, *The Political Theory of Neoliberalism* (Stanford, CA, Stanford University Press, 2018) 191.

[25] James M Buchanan, 'Competitive Federalism by Default' in Charles B Blankart and Dennis C Mueller (eds), *A Constitution for the European Union* (Cambridge, MA, MIT Press, 2004) 25–35; James M Buchanan and Dwight R Lee, 'On a Fiscal Constitution for the European Union' (1994) 5 *Journal des Économistes et des Études Humaines* 219; *cf* Biebricher, *The Political Theory of Neoliberalism* 55.

1.2. The Puzzle of Asymmetry

However sophisticated and nuanced current historical explanations of the EMU are (and they are more nuanced than I could portray them in my slightly stylised account), they do not fully explain the conceptual origins of asymmetry. This is not to suggest that they are not helpful or even wrong. While the narrative of a grand bargain between France and Germany that exchanged the EMU for reunification is unable to contribute much to the explanation of the AMU, the spill-over argument and the political economy account each provide an important foundation for understanding the dynamics at the end of the 1980s. Still, there is an explanatory gap in our understanding of how and why asymmetry came about – and it is a very puzzling one, too, for a number of reasons:

(1) As it has already been noted at the outset, there was no fully-fledged economic theory for asymmetry before the Maastricht Treaty was concluded. Nor has one been developed since (as far as I can see).[26] There was an argument that asymmetry might just work.[27] But most economists across the ideological spectrum were deeply critical and voiced their assessment in no uncertain terms. They talked about 'Alice in Euroland', 'voodoo economics', and 'a danger for Europe'.[28] To be clear, this is not to claim that there were no contemporary economic arguments for the Euro as such. Of course, some economists argued for a common currency at the time and most still do.[29] But to agree with the idea of a common currency in general is very different from offering a comprehensive theoretical justification for the asymmetrical features of the EMU. Just as simply defending certain elements of the status quo is not equivalent to a comprehensive justification of the AMU. To better understand this difference, it might be helpful to spell out what a comprehensive justification would require. To defend

[26] But *cf* Roel MWJ Beetsma and A Lans Bovenberg, 'The Optimality of a Monetary Union without a Fiscal Union' (2001) 33 *Journal of Money, Credit and Banking* 179.

[27] Tommaso Padoa-Schioppa, 'The EMS is not Enough: The Need for Monetary Union' (October 1987) in *The Road to Monetary Union in Europe* (Oxford, Oxford University Press, 2000) 93–110, 103–06. *cf* Daniel Cohen, 'The costs and benefits of a European currency' in Marcello de Cecco and Alberto Giovannini (eds), *A European Central Bank?* (Cambridge, Cambridge University Press, 1989) 195–208 and the scathing critique by Alberto Alesina in the same volume, 209–11.

[28] Willem H Buiter, 'Alice in Euroland' (1999) 37 *Journal of Common Market Studies* 181; Willem H Buiter et al, 'Excessive Deficits: Sense and Nonsense in the Treaty of Maastricht' (1993) 8 *Economic Policy* 57; Willem H Buiter, 'De budgettaire voodoo van Maastricht' (1992) *18 Economisch Statistische Berichten* 268; Barry Eichengreen, 'The political economy of fiscal policy after EMU' (1992) Center for International and Development Economics Research Working Paper No. C92-00. In 1992, 60 then prominent German economists signed a public letter calling the Euro 'A Danger for Europe', published under the hardly less dramatic title 'Die EG-Währungsunion führt zur Zerreißprobe' *Frankfurter Allgemeine Zeitung* (Frankfurt am Main, 11 June 1992) 15.

[29] For a collection of contemporary arguments by the Commission, see Michael Emerson, Daniel Gros and Alexander Italianer, *One market, one money: an evaluation of the potential benefits and costs of forming an economic and monetary union* (Oxford, Oxford University Press, 1992); European Commission (ed), *The economics of EMU: Background studies for 'One market, one money'* (Luxembourg, Office for Official Publications of the European Communities, 1991); Daniel Gros and Niels Thygesen, *European Monetary Integration* (London, Longman, 1992).

the AMU, one would need to argue that separating monetary from fiscal and economic policy is not only feasible but rather more advisable on economic and/or political grounds. While historically, one could make a secondary argument that (1) asymmetry was the only structure available politically at the time and (2) that an asymmetrical monetary union with all its problems was still preferable to no monetary union at all, that does not justify the status quo. It is therefore not an argument for asymmetry that the Euro has facilitated trade or might have otherwise yielded beneficial economic consequences. The same is true for those who defend the fiscal rules of the AMU with arguments about moral hazard and would prefer them to be even stricter. Regardless of whether this is a good argument, it is an argument only for one element of the asymmetric architecture of the EMU, not for the whole structure per se.

(2) The asymmetrical structure was not foreshadowed by any of the numerous plans and memoranda in the 30 years before the EMU – except for one, which is the subject of this chapter. Asymmetry was a genuine novelty. The previous plans, from the Marjolin Report in 1962 or the ambitious Werner Plan in 1970 to the more technical analysis of the MacDougall Report in 1977, had, in different forms but quite consistently, argued for a strong economic and fiscal equivalent to monetary integration. In 1987, the report of the Padoa-Schioppa commission had warned again that much greater economic coordination was needed for a monetary union to work.[30]

(3) There is a third and final reason why the asymmetry of the EMU is puzzling. It is difficult to explain it as simply a political compromise between the two competing views about European integration which dominated at the time. Depending on which side one took in the long-standing controversy about how economic integration should proceed, monetary policy was to fulfil very different objectives and was to be administered by very different kinds of institutions. Those who argued for further monetary integration before full economic integration (sometimes misleadingly dubbed 'monetarists') foresaw a much more political role for monetary policy. They were usually wary to hand monetary policy over to a completely independent central bank without some form of political control. Others such as the Netherlands, Germany and most notably the Bundesbank (which may count as a country of its own) took the view that monetary integration could only follow as the last step if it had been preceded by economic convergence (the (in)famous 'coronation theory').[31] The coronation camp was adamant about the independence of the

[30] Padoa-Schioppa, *Efficiency, Stability, and Equity* 84. The report hinted at different forms of wage bargaining in member states and went on to caution that 'fixed exchange rates would pose difficult problems for those countries whose international competitiveness in the past had depended upon periodic devaluations of their currencies'. It also noted that the independence of a central bank could not simply be reconstituted at the supranational level 'by mechanically adopting … the statutes of a central bank that has the required autonomy in a national context' (84). Paul Krugman in an annex to the report identified a potential disinflationary bias as one the main risks of monetary union (134–36).

[31] Marsh, *The Euro* 39; Kaltenthaler, *Germany* 71.

central bank but only in conjunction with a sufficiently integrated economic policy, ultimately run by a European government.

Neither theory envisaged what would become the structure of the EMU: an ostensibly depoliticised form of monetary policy ahead of full economic convergence, run by a strongly independent central bank with a mandate primarily focused on price stability, not on economic integration – without a corresponding economic government, sufficient labour mobility, and a relevant fiscal capacity at the community level. Integrationists succeeded in introducing a monetary union for the political purpose of fostering further integration but without the necessary institutional setting. The coronation camp, on the other hand, pushed through the complex institution of an independent central bank, but without the economic context necessary for it to function. Was this not the natural compromise between the two camps? If so, it meant that both sides gave up on the crucial functional premise of their theory without suggesting one to replace it.

2. Inventing Asymmetry: The Genscher Memorandum

Who then invented the asymmetrical monetary union? My suggestion is that it was Germany's foreign minister Hans-Dietrich Genscher and a close group of German officials. The first document at the European level to outline the contours of the AMU is the Delors Report of 1989. The invention of the AMU is therefore often ascribed to the Delors Committee and explained as a combination of the professional preferences and ideological dispositions of its members: central bankers who applied the newly found neoliberal consensus.[32] This genealogy is true as far as it goes. But the Delors Report, in this regard, only followed an earlier proposal in a memorandum by Genscher, which led to the appointment of the Delors Committee in the first place. It was the Genscher memorandum which led to a conceptual breakthrough after the 'very limited reform discussion of the mid 80s'.[33]

Genscher's leading role has been acknowledged, not least by his own memoir but also by his contemporaries and some historians. Jacques Delors, for instance, recognised that 'Genscher was the first to light the match'.[34] Many historical accounts mention the Genscher memorandum, albeit more in passing, as just one in the sequence of the many proposals and memoranda since the Marjolin

[32] McNamara, *The Currency of Ideas*; Tsoukalis, *The New European Economy Revisited* 165.

[33] James, *Making the European Monetary Union* 207.

[34] Hans-Dieter Heumann, *Hans-Dietrich Genscher: Die Biographie* (Paderborn, Schöningh, 2012) 220; Hans Tietmeyer, *Herausforderung Euro: Wie es zum Euro kam und was er für Deutschlands Zukunft bedeutet* (München, Hanser, 2005) 114; Karl Otto Pöhl, 'Der Delors-Bericht und das Statut einer Europäischen Zentralbank' in Theo Waigel (ed), *Unsere Zukunft heißt Europa* (Düsseldorf, Econ, 1996) 193–209.

Memorandum.[35] While the significance of the memorandum has not always been appreciated by historians of the EMU, some have sensed its importance without further exploring its origin and background.[36] Those who have seen its importance, like Kenneth Dyson and Kevin Featherstone in their masterful account of the Maastricht Treaty, could not make use of the archived files.[37] Even those who emphasise its importance for the overall process sometimes do so for the wrong reasons. The Genscher memorandum was consequential less in establishing an expert committee or its support for a European central bank than in inventing asymmetry.[38]

2.1. A Call for Monetary Integration

In February 1988, Genscher published a 'Memorandum for creating a European currency area and a European central bank'.[39] More precisely, he did not publish it but only brought copies of it with him to a prescheduled meeting with journalists.[40] It was the beginning of the German presidency in the European Council and Genscher decided to test the waters for a further step in monetary integration. He could have published an op-ed in a newspaper but handing out a memorandum to journalists was considered to have a potentially greater impact. To prepare a 'memorandum' which nobody could read beforehand signalled more thorough elaboration and had an air of diplomatic secrecy and grand political strategy. Yet, it was a very unusual step. Only at the beginning of the month, the government had adopted a resolution that a European currency union with a central bank

[35] Horst Ungerer, *A Concise History of European Monetary Integration: From EPU to EMU* (Westport, CT, Quorum Books, 1997) 197; *cf* the semi-official account by Éric Bussière and Ivo Maes, 'Die Entstehung der Wirtschafts- und Währungsunion' in Vincent Dujardin et al (eds), *Die Europäische Kommission 1986–2000: Geschichte und Erinnerungen einer Institution* (Luxemburg, Amt für Veröffentlichungen der Europäischen Union, 2019) 245–76, 249.

[36] James, *Making the European Monetary Union* 229; Bozo, 'In search of the Holy Grail' 302: 'a divine surprise for the French' and 'a major turning point' (306); Wilfried Loth, 'Between France and the Bundesbank: Hans-Dietrich Genscher, Helmut Kohl and the Breakthrough of the Monetary Union' in Gehler and Loth, *Reshaping Europe* 331–46; Malcolm Townsend, *The Euro and Economic and Monetary Union* (London, Harper, 2007) 58: 'bridged various positions and foresaw the outlines of the eventual agreement'.

[37] Matt Marshall, *The Bank: The Birth of Europe's Central Bank and the Rebirth of Europe's Power* (London, Random House, 1999) 78; Dyson and Featherstone, *The Road to Maastricht* 306, 326–32: Genscher as 'policy entrepeneur'.

[38] Fröhlich, *Helmut Kohl* 243: the expert committee was the 'decisive new element'; Dyson and Featherstone, *The Road to Maastricht* 330: 'more radical in content than any French initiatives on EMU in unequivocally supporting an ECB'.

[39] Reprinted in Henry Krägenau and Wolfgang Wetter (eds), *Europäische Wirtschafts- und Währungsunion: Vom Werner- Plan zum Vertrag von Maastricht: Analysen und Dokumentation* (Baden-Baden, Nomos, 1993) 309–310. It was labelled a 'basis for discussion' (*Diskussionsgrundlage*). Genscher later called it a *Denkschrift*, see Hans-Dietrich Genscher, *Erinnerungen* (Berlin, Siedler, 1995) 388.

[40] It was only later published in Europäische Zeitung, April 1988.

was merely a 'long-term objective'.[41] Monetary policy did not fall into Genscher's official portfolio and firmly belonged to the Treasury's remit. Genscher therefore published the memorandum, which was prepared for him by the Foreign Office, in a private capacity – whatever that meant.[42] It was not run through the normal government process.[43] There was no formal vote in Cabinet, nor was it even discussed. Other departments, especially the Treasury and the Bundesbank, were not consulted in advance. It is unclear whether Genscher personally informed Chancellor Kohl before he made the memorandum public.[44]

Considering its conceptual significance, the memorandum is surprisingly brief. It is densely argued and short on details – which might have helped its eventual success. It starts by offering three fundamental reasons for establishing a common currency area: two internal, one external. First, it argued that a common currency was the 'economically necessary complement' to the internal market. With this line of argument, the memorandum echoed the findings of the Padoa-Schioppa Report without mentioning it. Second, it argued that a common currency would serve as a 'catalyst' for the necessary convergence of economic policy. This sounded like a nod to the integrationist position and the Werner Report of 1970, which after intense debate had termed monetary union a 'leaven' for further integration.[45] Third, it argued that a European currency area would help 'reduce the dependence of member states of the EMS on the Dollar' and help to 'strengthen their capacity to act' on the global stage.

The memorandum then went on to list a set of 'prerequisites' for a common currency area. Genscher argued that monetary union primarily required a consensus on economic policy. More specifically, the consensus would need to be *ordnungspolitisch*. The memorandum employed the shibboleth of German ordoliberalism to lay out a vision for monetary integration dismissed by most German ordoliberals. First and foremost, the consensus would need to include the 'autonomy' of the central bank and a clear separation between monetary and fiscal policy. The central bank would need to be safeguarded against any obligation to fund government debt. Second, monetary union was only conceivable, Genscher held, if member states agreed on a clear priority for price stability.

[41] BT-Drs 11/1780, 8. The resolution was adopted in Cabinet as an answer to a parliamentary inquiry, see Kabinettsbeschluss, 3 February 1988.

[42] If you take an unnecessarily strict view, it was probably illegal, as ministers are not allowed to use government funds for party political purposes.

[43] Hans Tietmeyer, *Währungsstabilität für Europa: Beiträge, Reden und Dokumente zur europäischen Währungsintegration aus vier Jahrzehnten* (Baden-Baden, Nomos, 1996) 483.

[44] Marshall, *The Bank* 82 reports that Genscher later indicated he did not discuss it with Kohl because he had unsuccessfully tried to press his view in Cabinet before. Kohl's press secretary later denied the rumour that the Chancellor was not aware of the Genscher memorandum (see n 120). Kohl's office, the Chancellery (*Bundeskanzleramt*), was probably informed in advance. It had close ties to the Foreign Office since Kohl's point man for European policy, Joachim Bitterlich, was a former staffer of Genscher who had come over to the Chancellery.

[45] 'Report to the Council and the Commission on the realization by stages of Economic and Monetary Union in the Community' (1970) 26.

Member state governments would therefore need to accept what has been termed 'monetary dominance':[46] their fiscal and economic policies would need to follow the economic assessment and subsequent monetary decisions of the central bank. In a couple of terse sentences which did not reveal their true implication at first glance the memorandum hinted at the far-reaching ramifications of such a priority. In a broad field ranging from wage policy to taxing and spending, member states would need to 'pursue a policy that stabilises internal prices and costs and leads to a balanced trade account'.

2.2. Shifting Position

Despite its repeated reference to key concepts of ordoliberal doctrine, the Memorandum in substance represented a dramatic change of position compared to the long held German stance on monetary integration in Europe. In 1970, the Werner Report, which was published under the name of the then Prime Minister of Luxembourg Pierre Werner but had actually been drafted by the German government, was presented as the most comprehensive plan for monetary integration yet. It advocated for a 'parallelism' between monetary and economic integration. Since then, Germany's official position had gradually reverted to its earlier stance that full monetary integration could only follow a long period of economic convergence.[47] The Bundesbank, in particular, espoused this view time and again. As early as 1962, then President of the bank Karl Blessing had publicly declared in a radio interview that he was all in favour of European monetary integration, but that he could not see it happening: 'As a European, I would be ready to approve of European monetary union …; as a responsible central banking practitioner, and a realist, I cannot however avoid pointing out the difficulties'.[48] The Bundesbank carefully avoided opposing monetary integration outright or pinning down an explicit counter-argument against it. Rather, it cloaked its opposition in a set of conditions for integration that were hard if not impossible to fulfil. As much as these criteria represented a sincere economic belief, it is not improbable that they were in part also based on a strategic calculus to delay monetary integration to preserve the Bundesbank's own position as the leading central bank in Europe.[49]

The Genscher memorandum combined three important strategic decisions that proved consequential for establishing asymmetry. First, by claiming that monetary integration should serve as a 'catalyst' for a convergence in economic

[46] *cf* Thomas J Sargent and Neil Wallace, 'Some Unpleasant Monetarist Arithmetic' (1981) 5 *Federal Reserve Bank of Minneapolis Quarterly Review* 1; Eric M Leeper, 'Equilibria under "active" and "passive" monetary and fiscal policies' (1991) 27 *Journal of Monetary Economics* 129.

[47] Kaltenthaler, *Germany* 42; *cf* Werner Abelshauser, 'Deutsche Wirtschaftspolitik zwischen europäischer Integration und Weltmarktorientierung' in Werner Abelshauser et al (eds), *Wirtschaftspolitik in Deutschland 1917–1990* (München, De Gruyter, vol 4, 2016) 482–581.

[48] Cited in Marshall, *The Bank* 87.

[49] *cf* James, *Making the European Monetary Union* 207–36.

policy, Genscher charted a new path beyond the usual controversy between integrationists and proponents of the coronation theory. In what *sounded* like a nod to the integrationist position, Genscher essentially gave up on the condition of real economic convergence – without, however, embracing the political role of monetary policy that came with the integrationist position. Monetary integration would not require the national economies of potential member states to *actually* have similar per capita incomes, growth and inflation rates. Neither would monetary policy actively try to achieve that result as the integrationists had urged. Instead, in the second momentous strategic decision of his memorandum, Genscher suggested that a political consensus on economic policy would suffice for monetary integration to proceed. Consensus on policy could substitute convergence in hard economic facts. Potential member states of a monetary union should agree on what he called 'the magna charta' of economic policy. For which, unsurprisingly perhaps, German economic policy should serve as the role model. The third important strategic decision Genscher took in his memorandum was to advocate for an independent European central bank from the beginning. While he discarded the overall stance of the Bundesbank towards monetary integration, he took on board its main institutional demands. Despite the 'catalyst' function Genscher envisaged for monetary policy in the new currency union, it should be run by an independent central bank. The central bank should be made independent – 'autonomous' even – as the memorandum explained at some length. Its independence was to be guarded against member states as well as community institutions. They should exercise only 'well defined' and 'strictly limited' powers to appoint and remove governors of the central bank.

In combining these three strategic decisions, Genscher sketched out something that is not identical with, but reasonably close to the later AMU: a monetary union prior to economic convergence, with a strongly independent central bank but without a genuine economic government at the European level. For the time being, economic government was to be substituted by a consensus on economic policy, parts of which were later enshrined in rules. To be fair to Genscher, the memorandum also advocated for further economic integration. Genscher himself would probably have favoured a European federal state in some form, although he never formulated a clear vision of what European integration should ultimately lead to. Like many pro-European politicians of his generation, he was adamant in advocating that further integration was necessary. Just what kind of integration remained conspicuously unclear. But the crucial decision for the path forward which he made in his memorandum was to advocate for a monetary union on the one hard condition that it would have an independent central bank, but without at the same time making any specific proposals as to how economic and fiscal integration should proceed.

As a result, there was an imbalance between the monetary side on the one hand and the fiscal and economic side on the other hand in the Genscher memorandum that proved to be consequential for the negotiation process and ultimately the EMU. Asymmetry had been invented. At the end of his memorandum,

Genscher called for an 'expert committee' of '5–7 wise men' to work out the details.[50] They should be tasked with conceiving 'a principle for the development of a European currency area and the founding of a European central bank within a year'. Members of the committee, which would later become the Delors Committee, were to 'possess technical expertise and political authority and should be independent'. Notably, economic and fiscal matters were not things the wise men should consider. The mandate Genscher proposed for the committee as an annex to his memorandum was similarly limited. It was later adopted by the European Council during its meeting in Hanover in mid 1988 and tasked the committee with designing a statute for the future European central bank but did not include a similar mandate for the economic side of the Maastricht Treaty. From that moment on, the process had a lasting bias towards asymmetry. Just like the Genscher memorandum, the final Delors Report mentioned the need for further economic and fiscal integration 'in parallel advancement' but again remained vague and unspecific as to what this would entail in practice.[51]

2.3. Strategic Goals of a Foreign Minister

Why did Genscher publish his memorandum in February 1988? He knew that if an initiative for further integration should take shape through the German presidency of the European Council, it would likely have to result in a formal decision during the Council meeting in Hanover in June. In order to build momentum, he needed to launch his initiative at the beginning of the presidency. By then, Genscher had been foreign minister for 14 years. This time had seen him rise under three different Chancellors to become one of the most popular politicians in Germany.[52] He had started his career under the leader of the nationalist wing of his party, Erich Mende, before he quickly became indispensable as an organiser and integrating figure in his own right for the liberal democrats (FDP). Genscher prepared the progressive turn of his party to the left in the late 1960s as well as the later turn to the right in the early 1980s. In 1974, he rose to become party leader and came to the Foreign Office with little prior experience in European and foreign policy.[53] Eight years later, Genscher led the liberal democrats out of their coalition with the social democrats (SPD), orchestrating the downfall of Chancellor Helmut Schmidt to form a new government with the conservative Christian democrats

[50] Delors had already suggested a similar committee in 1987 to the European Council, see Heumann, *Hans-Dietrich Genscher* 219. Kohl later changed Genscher's plan and opted to appoint central bankers, see Fröhlich, *Helmut Kohl* 247.

[51] Committee for the Study of Economic and Monetary Union, 'Report on Economic and Monetary Union in the European Community' (1989) 28.

[52] For the following, see Heumann, *Hans-Dietrich Genscher*.

[53] Andrea Wiegeshoff, '"Nun wird er Außenminister, und Außenpolitik ist gewiß nicht seine erste Profession"' in Kerstin Brauckhoff and Irmgard Schwaetzer (eds), *Hans-Dietrich Genschers Außenpolitik* (Wiesbaden, Springer, 2015) 97–118.

(CDU) under Kohl. While this soothed the ordoliberal wing of his party which had soured on the economic policies of Schmidt's government, it brought the party to an existential crisis and paved the way for what appeared like a neoliberal turn in German politics for a while.

A lawyer by training, Genscher was generally considered a good tactician, energetic and pragmatic; constantly in motion even if it was not always apparent where to.[54] Over the years, many came to view him with suspicion for his seemingly opportunistic behaviour, which came to be known as 'Genscherism'.[55] As his hagio-biographer notes, Genscher always believed in the 'primacy of politics'.[56] This was especially true for European matters. 'We do not wish to nor can we build Europe solely on economics', he declared.[57] Unpopular in Washington, he enjoyed a particularly good rapport with his French counterpart, socialist politician Roland Dumas, who praised Genscher's 'finesse'.[58] Personally, Genscher had long taken the view that monetary integration in Europe was essential for further political integration.[59] The constant turmoil of realignments in the EMS was damaging to the whole process, he thought, especially due to the resentment which it caused in France towards the Bundesbank – and ultimately Germany.[60] Already in the early 1970s, Genscher had positioned the FDP to be strongly integrationist.[61] He believed that German reunification would only be possible within an integrated Europe and that Europe needed to become more independent internationally. It helped that German banks and exporters favoured economic and monetary integration. As early as 1972, the FDP had called monetary integration a 'logical continuation of economic integration and the same time the springboard for further political integration'.[62] Inflation and stagnation could no longer be dealt with by nation states. Under his leadership, the party adopted a programme that

[54] Gerhard A Ritter, 'Deutschland und Europa: Grundzüge der Außenpolitik Genschers 1989–1992' in Brauckhoff and Schwaetzer, *Hans-Dietrich Genschers Außenpolitik* 209–43.

[55] Eckart Conze, 'Das Geheimnis des "Genscherismus"' in Brauckhoff and Schwaetzer, *Hans-Dietrich Genschers Außenpolitik* 67–83, 68.

[56] Heumann, *Hans-Dietrich Genscher* 210.

[57] Cited in Hans-Dieter Lucas, 'Politik der kleinen Schritte – Genscher und die deutsche Europapolitik 1974–1983' in Hans-Dieter Lucas (ed), *Genscher, Deutschland und Europa* (Baden-Baden, Nomos, 2002) 85–114, 103.

[58] Heumann, *Hans-Dietrich Genscher* 15. Genscher was widely seen as the more international, less Teutonic figure than the Chancellor.

[59] For Genscher's European policies, see Ritter, 'Deutschland und Europa'; Lucas, 'Politik der kleinen Schritte'; Hans Werner Lautenschlager, 'Auf dem Wege zur Einheit Europas: ein Jahrzehnt entscheidender Weichenstellungen europäischer Integrationspolitik (1983–1992)' in Lucas, *Genscher, Deutschland und Europa* 297–322.

[60] Kaltenthaler, *Germany* 72; Loth, 'Between France and the Bundesbank' 334; Dyson and Featherstone, *The Road to Maastricht* 328.

[61] *cf* Andreas Moring, Die Europapolitik der FDP: Die Entwicklung der Europa-Programmatik in den Jahren 1949–1989 (Berlin, Köster, 2004); Lucas, 'Politik der kleinen Schritte'.

[62] 'Thesen des Bundesvorstands für eine liberale Europapolitik' (1972), reprinted in Günter Verheugen (ed), *Das Programm der Liberalen: 10 Jahre Programmarbeit der F.D.P.*, 2nd edn (Baden-Baden, Nomos, 1980) 160–62, 160.

called for a 'politically constituted' and 'federal' Europe.[63] Genscher pleaded for a more government-like structure of the community institutions and for European fundamental rights, and he pointed out that a European budget would need to take on a stabilising function. He would go on to fight the European election in 1989 with the slogan 'Liberal Europe pays off'.[64]

3. The Making of the Memorandum

3.1. A Focal Point for Integrationists

For some time, Genscher had been the focal point for integrationists in German politics. While official responsibility for monetary matters in Europe lay with the Treasury, the Foreign Office operated its own office for European monetary affairs to monitor what the Treasury and others were doing (*Spiegelreferat*).[65] Head of the office was a relatively junior staffer named Wilhelm Schönfelder, a 'calm, courteous, pro-European',[66] who later went on to become Germany's ambassador to the EU. It was Schönfelder who drafted the Genscher memorandum – the 'most important paper I wrote in my life'.[67] An economist by training, Schönfelder had not worked on monetary policy before.[68] Back from a stint at the embassy in Washington, he was originally placed in the USA office in Bonn, but he was already so well connected that he got an early promotion to head the small office for monetary matters. In his new role, he kept close track on discussions about monetary integration. The archived files of the office present a good overview of the various actors and initiatives at the time.[69] Genscher was lobbied by manufacturers eager to facilitate their exports through monetary union. Deutsche Bank, at the time the unofficial spokesperson of the German industrial sector, sent him speeches of board members calling for monetary integration. But academics and economists also lobbied him, each advocating their own vision of monetary integration.

[63] 'Leitlinien liberaler Europapolitik' (1975), reprinted in Verheugen, *Das Programm der Liberalen* 212–21; 'Zehn Thesen zur europäischen Einigung' (1984), reprinted in Freie Demokratische Partei (ed), *Das Programm der Liberalen* (Baden-Baden, Nomos, 1990) 235–37, 237 called for 'Federal States of Europe'. *cf* Moring, *Die Europapolitik der FDP* 120.

[64] 'Wahlaufruf zur Europawahl' (1989), reprinted in Freie Demokratische Partei, *Das Programm der Liberalen* 861–62, 862; Moring, *Die Europapolitik der FDP* 113.

[65] For ensuing conflicts, see Kaltenthaler, *Germany* 28.

[66] Marshall, *The Bank* 80.

[67] Genscher, *Erinnerungen* 388 acknowledged the role of his 'ausgezeichnete Vortragende Legationsrat'.

[68] Schönfelder holds a PhD in Economics from University of Cologne and wrote his dissertation on economic history, see Wilhelm Schönfelder, 'Die wirtschaftliche Entwicklung Kölns von 1370 bis 1513: Dargestellt mit linearen Trendfunktionen samt Analyse ihrer Bestimmungsfaktoren' (PhD thesis, Köln, Böhlau, 1970).

[69] They are kept at the political archive of the Foreign Office, see PA AA B 224-ZA/168727.

In the spring of 1987, Genscher was about to give a speech before ambassadors to the Community in Brussels.[70] Known to be media savvy, Genscher had a habit of repeating himself to get his message across.[71] This time was different. He tasked Schönfelder to write the speech for him with the explicit direction to say 'something new'. Schönfelder, still fresh to his new post, had not yet acquainted himself fully with monetary policy but included a sentence that 'institutional reform was not off the table'.[72] What exactly 'institutional reform' should entail, nobody knew, not even Schönfelder. The speech was never given, as Genscher liked to improvise. But the manuscript was later circulated and caused some uproar. Times clearly began to become more favourable for further monetary integration. Over the coming year, Schönfelder acquired a sense of possible coalitions that might support Genscher if he decided to put forward a proposal.

3.2. A Window of Opportunity

Genscher had become increasingly critical of the Bundesbank and what he saw as the hawkish coalition between orthodox ordoliberals at the Treasury and the Bundesbank.[73] Earlier than others, he had taken Gorbachev's promise of reform seriously.[74] He feared that with the possible end of the détente, the chances for European integration might vanish.[75] With the European Single Act agreed, calls for monetary integration became louder. Former Chancellor Helmut Schmidt had launched an initiative with former French President Valéry Giscard d'Estaing. Schönfelder reported to Genscher that the Treasury and the Bundesbank were both working on their own memoranda at the time.[76] He might therefore have been worried that they rather than himself would come to determine the government's position.

With the presidency approaching, a 'window of opportunity' seemed to open in the spring of 1988.[77] At the beginning of 1988, the French put forward their own proposal which called for a German answer.[78] Genscher's main opponent within

[70] Schönfelder and Thiel, *Ein Markt* 22.

[71] Richard Kiessler, 'Außenpolitik als "Public Diplomacy" – Hans-Dietrich Genscher und die Medien' in Lucas, *Genscher, Deutschland und Europa* 371–86.

[72] Institutional reform was a taboo word because the Treasury and the Bundesbank were both afraid it would cement a more 'politicised' form of monetary policy, see Eckart Gaddum, *Die deutsche Europapolitik in den 80er Jahren: Interessen, Konflikte und Entscheidungen der Regierung Kohl* (Paderborn, Schöningh, 1994) 301; Dyson and Featherstone, *The Road to Maastricht* 322.

[73] Dyson and Featherstone, *The Road to Maastricht* 327; Loth, 'Between France and the Bundesbank' 333.

[74] Marshall, *The Bank* 82; Dyson and Featherstone, *The Road to Maastricht* 328 note Genscher's early 'recognition that Gorbachev must be taken seriously as a Soviet reformer'.

[75] Marshall, *The Bank* 82.

[76] PA AA B 224-ZA/168727, Vorlage, 25 February 1988.

[77] Dyson and Featherstone, *The Road to Maastricht* 327.

[78] See N Piers Ludlow's chapter in this volume (ch 9); Bozo, 'In search of the Holy Grail' 301; Dyson and Featherstone, *The Road to Maastricht* 325.

the coalition government, finance minister Gerhard Stoltenberg from the CDU, was weakened after a botched tax reform and had become embroiled in a political scandal in his home state of Schleswig-Holstein.[79] Chancellor Kohl stayed his hand because he wanted to wait and see whether President François Mitterrand would be re-elected. In January, Genscher gave a speech to the European Parliament calling monetary union a 'logical' complement of a common market,[80] and in mid-February, the Council in Brussels finally resolved the long simmering budgetary conflict which had hampered any prospect for reform.[81]

3.3. Writing in Seclusion

In the second week of February, the CEO of Deutsche Bank, Alfred Herrhausen publicly called for a European central bank. He was joined by Lothar Späth, governor of the CDU stronghold Baden-Württemberg and the main intra-party rival of Chancellor Kohl. On 24 February, Genscher called Schönfelder and asked whether the memorandum was ready. Schönfelder was taken by surprise. He had spent the last year thinking about the matter and conferring with a confidant at the Bundesbank, but he had not prepared a memorandum. Schönfelder secluded himself and wrote a draft in two days which was considerably longer than the final version.[82] He drew on his own thoughts, which he had developed during the preceding year, but also on more incidental sources.[83]

It is evident from the files that Genscher himself was responsible for the final version of the memorandum. He redacted the initial draft with the green pencil that by convention only ministers are allowed to use. He then called Schönfelder from his car to let him know what needed to change. Genscher inserted headlines and shortened the memo considerably. He mainly cut out the more explicit and controversial parts. The second paragraph had originally stated that 'creating a European Central Bank goes at the heart of the sovereignty of member states'. Understandably, Genscher did not want to say this out loud, so he crossed out

[79] Fröhlich, *Helmut Kohl* 242; Dyson and Featherstone, *The Road to Maastricht* 329.

[80] Ungerer, *A Concise History* 197.

[81] Dyson and Featherstone, *The Road to Maastricht* 330; see Frank Schorkopf's chapter in this volume (ch 10).

[82] PA AA B 224-ZA/168727, Draft Memorandum, 25 February 1988. Dyson and Featherstone, *The Road to Maastricht* 330 in their otherwise excellent account suggest that it was two weeks. But the files indicate that Schönfelder was only tasked to write the memorandum on 24 February.

[83] Schönfelder reported to Genscher that in preparing the memorandum he had taken into account the agenda of the Committee for a European Monetary Union, the initiative established by Schmidt and Giscard, which had been published two days earlier; the public statements of 'Mr. Herrhausen and Mr. Christians', two board members of Deutsche Bank; the public statements of Ministerpräsident Späth; the statement of Chancellor Kohl before the select committee for foreign policy made on 23 February and a policy paper of the CDU 'Our responsibility in the world', see PA AA B 224-ZA/168727, Vorlage, 25 February 1988, 2.

the passage. 'On the one hand', the original text continued, 'this indicates that a European Central Bank should be the final stage or coronation of European integration'. Genscher deleted this reference to the coronation theory. He probably did not want to risk encumbering his proposal with a long-running controversy. To build a new coalition, it was advisable not to take sides and, crucially, to avoid provoking the Bundesbank explicitly. He also cut the next sentence of the draft: 'On the other hand, in many cases a beneficial pressure to harmonise has been exerted by the Community institutions. Strictly speaking, they likewise should have been instituted only at the end of the integration process.' Genscher did not want to be on record saying that to do things prematurely was just the nature of European integration.

The next paragraph also did not find Genscher's blessing. 'European integration', it read, 'has long been a question not solely of logic and reason but also of vision and the courage to make a first step'. Apparently, he did not want to concede outright that his proposal was based more on courage than on logic and reason. This deletion had the beneficial side-effect of cutting out lines that were taken from a speech given by Friedrich Wilhelm Christians, a board member of Deutsche Bank.[84] Genscher also cut a lengthy explanatory part about the state of the international financial system. He deleted the geostrategic goal to make the future European currency ('Europe/Africa') one of 'three blocks' next to the Dollar '(North-/South-America)' and the Yen '(Asia)'. Finally, Genscher made the memo less ambitious, at least outwardly. Schönfelder had suggested ending on the already cautious note that the Council in Hanover could not be expected to establish a European central bank but should at least commit to the goal. Genscher replaced this suggestion with a toned-down form that the Council should 'send a signal' for further monetary integration.

4. A Theory for Asymmetry?

The Genscher memorandum sought to avoid pitfalls, stake out a new path, and build a political coalition for monetary integration. In particular, Schönfelder tried to pre-empt opposition by the Bundesbank by adopting their main institutional demands. At first glance, it would thus appear that asymmetry was primarily based on political expediency.[85] In the year before the memorandum, Schönfelder had sought to recruit academic economists to support Genscher's potential initiative, but they had all declined. Was there an economic theory how the different pieces of the proposal would interact?

[84] PA AA B 224-ZA/168727, Speech 'Wir müssen vom Europa-Verständnis zum Europa-Gefühl kommen', 24 February 1988.

[85] Dyson and Featherstone, *The Road to Maastricht* 330.

4.1. Working with the Bundesbank

The intellectual mastermind behind the Genscher memorandum was an economist at the Bundesbank, Peter Wilhelm Schlüter. Schönfelder had met him a couple of years earlier at a routine meeting of civil servants. They developed a good rapport and later became friends. When Schönfelder began to delve into monetary integration in his new role, he turned to Schlüter, who was eight years his senior and whom he regarded as his 'intellectual mentor' on monetary policy.[86] Both men shared a deep conviction that European integration had to progress. Born in 1932, Schlüter went to school in occupied Poland, where his father worked as a factory director for the industrial conglomerate 'Reichwerke Hermann Göring', one of the main beneficiaries of enforced labourers from concentration camps.[87] Schlüter had started his career in the Ministry for Economic Affairs, before going on to work for the German Commissioner of the EEC, Hans von der Groeben. Rising through the ranks quickly, Schlüter went on to become head of the Bundesbank division for European monetary policy. Known to be strongly pro-European, he occupied an uneasy position within the bank. There was a group of younger staffers who did not share the hard-line scepticism of some of the board members. Schlüter was the most senior and most visible among them. His superiors were wary of his pro-European stance but tolerated it grudgingly, as long as he stayed within his remit.[88] When Genscher called for 'institutional reform' one year earlier, Schlüter certainly agreed. It is possible that he viewed Genscher's new initiative in early 1988 as a chance to outmanoeuvre the Bundesbank leadership.

4.2. Independence without Government

Shortly before the Genscher memorandum, Schlüter had written down his own thoughts on the chances of monetary integration for a talk he gave in Brussels.[89] The title already conveyed the main thesis: 'Central Bank Autonomy as a Prerequisite for a European Currency'. He later handed a copy to Schönfelder who kept it in his files at the Foreign Office.[90] Schlüter began on a sombre note. 'Since the failure of the Werner Plan', there could be 'no doubt that a European currency could not be the catalyst but only the result of an integration process encompassing the most

[86] ibid 331. Schönfelder later tried to install Schlüter as one of the secretaries of the 'Committee of wise men', see PA AA B 224-ZA/168727, Vorlage, 6 May 1988.

[87] *cf* August Meyer, *Hitlers Holding: Die Reichswerke "Hermann Göring"* (München, Europa-Verlag, 1999).

[88] His involvement in the Genscher memorandum caused some stir in the Bank, see Dyson and Featherstone, *The Road to Maastricht* 333.

[89] ibid 331.

[90] PA AA B 224-ZA/168727, Memorandum 'Notenbank-Autonomie als Voraussetzung für eine Europäische Währung'.

important parts of the economy'.[91] In line with orthodox Bundesbank thinking, Schlüter appeared to refute the instrumental use of monetary policy advocated by integrationists: 'All attempts to foster economic integration via technical improvements and new monetary mechanisms had quickly proven themselves to be insufficient'.[92] But far from quashing hopes for monetary integration any time soon, Schlüter's memorandum took a surprising turn. Monetary integration and a European central bank were 'no longer a taboo', he noted.[93] Only they could not come about in one big reform proposal, but instead they would need to advance piecemeal and step by step. This 'pragmatist' technique, however, had to be guided by 'fundamental principles' and a 'consensus' between all parties involved.[94] Schlüter then went on to identify the two guiding principles he deemed essential to make monetary integration a reality.

First, monetary integration required a consensus not only on monetary policy but also on the corresponding economic policies. There was no way round 'the relentless logic that the internal market, without which there can be no common currency area, can only be realised by way of a convergence of economic policy and economic development towards price stability'.[95] Monetary integration thus far had failed because of this 'inherent necessity' (*Sachzwang*). Second, monetary integration required institutional autonomy for a European central bank and all national counterparts.[96] For Schlüter, this argument combined good policy with useful politics. If monetary institutions in Europe were made independent from the beginning, the Bundesbank would be much less likely to object to the process.[97] He backed this tactical point up by a quote from President of the Bundesbank Karl Otto Pöhl who was on record saying that 'Central banks were more willing to adopt common rules for monetary policy if central banks in all member states enjoyed a status of autonomy'.[98]

[91] PA AA B 224-ZA/168727, Memorandum 'Notenbank-Autonomie als Voraussetzung für eine Europäische Währung', 1.

[92] ibid.

[93] ibid.

[94] ibid 1–2.

[95] ibid 1.

[96] ibid 2–3.

[97] Padoa-Schioppa had offered another rationale for the Bundesbank. In a speech given to the European University Institute (EUI) in February 1986 and later reprinted in the Economic Bulletin of the Banca d'Italia, he had argued that 'The scope for building a monetary authority at the European level, endowed with the same safeguards of strength and independence as the Bundesbank enjoys today in Germany, is much greater in the present state of incompleteness of the European construction than it might be at some later time when the political and institutional process of unifying Europe will have gone further', see 'Lessons from the European Monetary System' in *The Road to Monetary Union in Europe* 44–61, 60. Schlüter knew this speech. It is contained in a collection of quotes which he prepared for Schönfelder, see PA AA B 224-ZA/168727, 'Meinungsäußerungen zur europäischen Währungsintegration', 26 April 1988.

[98] PA AA B 224-ZA/168727, Memorandum 'Notenbank-Autonomie als Voraussetzung für eine Europäische Währung', 11.

But more importantly, Schlüter argued that autonomy was the right institutional policy for the governance of a supranational currency. 'If central bank autonomy for principled reasons provides the best basis for an optimal control of the money supply, which has been backed up by experience on a national level, the same must be true for a supranational monetary order'.[99] His principled reasons for this assumption were threefold. First, just empirically, the relation between autonomy and price stability was 'uncontroversial', he claimed.[100] Second, an autonomous central bank was needed to actively depoliticise the money supply. Schlüter recalled the assumption of classical equilibrium theory that money was a 'veil' only to discard it. 'No one doubts today that money is not neutral'.[101] But precisely because money was not neutral, monetary policy had to neutralise it. Economically, his argument was rooted in the 'conviction that a neutral supply of money freed from political influence is the best condition for economic equilibrium'.[102] Schlüter did not say so explicitly, but the sources of his memorandum reveal that his thinking was squarely based on monetarist thinking and the quantity theory of money. Even more important seems to have been another, more political argument. Only price stability came close to 'neutrality', as it did not involve redistribution by inflation, which was not 'politically mandated and hence arbitrary'.[103] Third, Schlüter claimed, price stability did not involve balancing the social welfare of different societal interests. Quoting monetarist economist Günther Engel, Schlüter argued that 'price stability has a relevance similar to legal certainty for long term decision making'.[104] Having the state 'oversee' both conditions was therefore 'beneficial to everyone'.[105]

4.3. The Force of Convergence

Schlüter, well versed in the monetarist theory of his time, relied on three standard arguments for central bank independence: (1) independent central banks had a better track record of low inflation; (2) low inflation was good for everyone; and (3) ordinary governments were unable to deliver low inflation because temptations to inflate were just too strong. It followed that central banks were only legitimate when they stuck to a narrow mandate of price stability. The way Schlüter employed these arguments for his stance on European integration was more unorthodox. He modified the Bundesbank theory in two key respects. First, monetary integration did not require full economic convergence but only a consensus

[99] ibid 10.
[100] ibid 2.
[101] ibid 3.
[102] ibid.
[103] ibid.
[104] Günther Engel, 'Verstetigung des Geldmengenwachstums und politische Unabhängigkeit der Zentralbank' (1984) 17 *Kredit und Kapital* 540.
[105] PA AA B 224-ZA/168727, Memorandum 'Notenbank-Autonomie als Voraussetzung für eine Europäische Währung', 3–4.

on economic policy focused on price stability which would then bring about convergence. Second, the key to integration was the institutional structure of monetary institutions, not the order of monetary and economic integration.

At the end of the 1980s, both points seemed closely intertwined. If the central bank was made autonomous, it would be able to pursue price stability unimpaired by political pressure. And if the bank carried out a disinflationary monetary policy, this would in turn have enormous consequences for the economic policy choices of member states. Having lost the ability to devaluate their currency and being bound by the fiscal rules of the Maastricht Treaty, they would essentially be left to supply-side reforms ('internal adjustments'). It was the dominance of the D-Mark within the EMS that among other things had ended the socialist policies of the early Mitterrand government. The 1980s had seen other member states grudgingly come around to the German position on monetary policy.[106] Based on that experience, it seemed likely that a system of fixed exchange rates would only reinforce this dynamic. If member states handed over monetary policy to a European central bank, it seemed, they would automatically be drawn towards convergent economic policies. Behind the ostensible call for consensus lay a strong undercurrent of force exercised by the autonomous central bank. It would help bring about convergence in economic policies if it actually followed through on its mandate.

Schlüter was hopeful, but he was also careful. The arrangements he had in mind raised democratic concerns and despite the potential power of an autonomous central bank the need for consensus was real. Ultimately, the public had to back the policy choices flowing from the primacy of price stability. Otherwise, it would not work. It was therefore 'imperative', he noted, 'to make the European monetary order democratically legitimate'.[107]

4.4. Helpful Ambiguity

Comparing the two memoranda, it is apparent that Schlüter's two central points found their way into the Genscher memorandum, while the more cautious point about democracy did not. It was Schlüter who provided Schönfelder with the two most important and consequential ideas for the Genscher memorandum. Schönfelder then rephrased Schlüter's theory of (forceful) convergence in terms of the integrationist language. Schlüter had explicitly started off on the assumption that a 'European currency could not be the catalyst' for further integration.

[106] Jeffry A Frieden, 'Making Commitments: France and Italy in the European Monetary System 1979–1985' in Barry Eichengreen and Jeffry A Frieden (eds), *The Political Economy of European Monetary Unification*, 2nd edn (Boulder, CO, Westview Press, 2001) 23–48. This point was stressed by Schönfelder as well as Bitterlich to Genscher and Kohl, see Dyson and Featherstone, *The Road to Maastricht* 328. For a contemporary view of the more problematic consequences, see Rüdiger Dornbusch, 'Money and Finance in European Integration' in EFTA (ed), *Money and Finance in European integration* (Geneva, EFTA, 1988) 9.

[107] PA AA B 224-ZA/168727, Memorandum 'Notenbank-Autonomie als Voraussetzung für eine Europäische Währung', 9.

The Genscher memorandum made it a 'catalyst for the necessary convergence of economic policy'. Although it sounded like a fundamental difference, the nod to the Werner Report was verbal only. In an internal document written sometime later which summarised the motivation and thinking behind the Genscher memorandum, Schönfelder mused that one might object that the time was not yet ripe for monetary union based on the memorandum's own criteria.[108] The necessary convergence of economic policies had yet to occur. 'We are hopeful', Schönfelder continued, that the conditions laid out in the memorandum would soon be met. This hope was based, he went on to explain, on the observation that under the Bundesbank dominance in the EMS, the economic policies of member states had already begun to converge over the last years.

If the use of word 'catalyst' could therefore pass as a political concession, the Genscher memorandum differed from Schlüter's in one other important respect. Genscher's praise of German economic policy which should serve as the role model for Europe was more ambiguous than one might have expected. Of course, the memorandum stated, it was important that member states should agree to prioritise price stability. What else the 'magna charta of economic policy' he called for would involve was much less clear. Despite his use of ordoliberal language, Genscher did not belong to the ordoliberal wing of his party and did not hold many firm economic views other than a deeply rooted disdain for socialism.[109] Much to the annoyance of the Bundesbank, the memorandum just referred to the economic stability law of 1967 (*Stabilitätsgesetz*) which obliged the government to pursue price stability, a high level of employment, economic growth, and a balanced trade account at the same time.[110] The law had codified the Keynesian consensus of the mid-1960s and seen inflation rise in the 1970s under the socio-liberal coalition. The stability law rested on the assumption that there was a genuine trade-off between inflation and other economic goals which could be maximised by the government. To reference the law, therefore, amounted to an implicit contradiction if not outright repudiation of the earlier call for prioritising price stability.

5. From the Memorandum to the Delors Committee

5.1. Shaping Government Policy

Initial public reaction to the Genscher memorandum was mildly positive.[111] The *Financial Times* discerned a 'firm proposal for progress' and aptly identified

[108] PA AA B 224-ZA/168727, Gesprächsvorlage, 25 April 1988.

[109] Heumann, *Hans-Dietrich Genscher* 24.

[110] Dyson and Featherstone, *The Road to Maastricht* 333. That was probably not to the Bundesbank's liking, as it would have involved constant and wide-ranging coordination. For the Bundesbank's role under the stability law, see Gunter Berger, 'Bundesbank und Stabilitätsgesetz' (PhD thesis, University of Cologne, 1977).

[111] The following newspaper articles are taken from the archived press review of the Foreign Office.

the main tactical point that Genscher's goal was to 'calm Bundesbank fears'.[112] That the Bundesbank should serve as the role model for Europe played well with most German commentators. The chairman of the board of Deutsche Bank, Wilfried Guth, was enthused and sent Genscher his own thoughts which were much the same as Schlüter's and later appeared in the conservative newspaper *Die Welt*.[113] Conservative newspapers remained sceptical.[114] The *Frankfurter Allgemeine Zeitung* (*FAZ*) commented that it was 'fair enough politically that Genscher was flying high, but he lost sight of reality'.[115] Swiss Newspaper *NZZ* only saw 'wishful thinking'.[116] A lobby group for 'German savers' found the proposal simply 'naïve'.[117] Otmar Issing called a European central bank 'a phantom' and Genscher's insistence on independence 'empty rhetoric'.[118]

More importantly though, the discussion had been set in motion. Genscher was content. Soon after his memorandum was published, 'diplomatic circles' – probably none other than Genscher's team – launched the rumour that Chancellor Kohl agreed with the memorandum, although he had not been consulted beforehand.[119] The Chancellor let it be known through his press secretary that 'of course' he had known in advance.[120] In his view, Genscher had done nothing more than 'to substantiate' his own ideas 'with details'.[121] But Kohl's spokesperson added that monetary union would take time. Less than two weeks after the memorandum was published, the *FAZ* reported that 'apparently' Chancellor Kohl had embraced Genscher's proposal.[122] At the same time, Lutz Stavenhagen, minister at the Chancellery, voiced concerns and scepticism.[123] Kohl remained ambivalent for the time being and sent mixed signals, keeping his options open.[124]

[112] Andrew Fisher, 'Genscher seeks EC currency, central bank' *Financial Times* (London, 27 February 1988).

[113] PA AA B 224-ZA/168727, Letter dated 29 February 1988. 'Die Bank von Europa steht am Ziel eines langen, goldenen Mittelweges' *Die Welt* (Berlin, 3 March 1988). Guth had initially planned to publish his article in the more liberal *Die Zeit*.

[114] 'Vorsicht – Kommission' *Welt* (Berlin, 27 February 1988).

[115] 'Genschers Höhenflug' *Frankfurter Allgemeine Zeitung* (Frankfurt am Main, 1 March 1988).

[116] 'Plädoyer Genschers für eine Europäische Zentralbank' *Neue Züricher Zeitung* (Zürich, 29 February 1988).

[117] PA AA B 224-ZA/168727, DPA press release 'Sparschützer halten Genschers Währungsplan für naiv', 1 March 1988.

[118] Otmar Issing, 'Europäische Notenbank – ein Phantom' *Frankfurter Allgemeine Zeitung* (Frankfurt am Main, 12 March 1988) 13.

[119] 'Genscher will in Hannover EG-Zentralbankpläne vorlegen' *Hannoversche Allgemeine Zeitung* (Hannover, 27 February 1988).

[120] PA AA B 224-ZA/168727, Press conference, 29 February 1988.

[121] Helmut Kohl, *Deutschlands Zukunft in Europa: Reden und Beiträge des Bundeskanzlers* (Herford, Busse & Seewald, 1990) 735.

[122] 'Trotz Bedenken Pöhls neue Pläne zur europäischen Zentralbank' *Frankfurter Allgemeine Zeitung* (Frankfurt am Main, 4 March 1988). Pöhl had been appointed by Chancellor Schmidt. For his ambivalent position, *cf* Harold James, 'Karl-Otto Pöhl: The Pole Position', in Dyson and Maes, *Architects of the Euro* 170–92, 172.

[123] PA AA B 224-ZA/168727, VWD report, 29 February 1988.

[124] Meyer, *Deutsche Europapolitik* 180. For the difficult political landscape Kohl was trying to navigate, see Stefan Fröhlich, 'Die innenpolitischen Kontroversen über die Europapolitik in der Regierung Kohl'

In a first reaction, President of the Bundesbank Pöhl was careful not to oppose the memorandum directly.[125] He did not want the Bundesbank to be perceived as the perpetual naysayer. Over the years, Genscher had tried to court him and to keep a good relationship despite their obvious differences. In line with the traditional Bundesbank stance never to oppose European integration outright, the President said in an informal talk with journalists that he 'welcomed' the memorandum 'in principle'. The memorandum forced other member states 'to put their cards on the table' and 'insofar' it was good. Only, he said, the problems were 'gigantic'. To further assess them, the Bundesbank publicly ordered an internal review. The result also found its way into Schönfelder's files at the Foreign Office.[126] Surprisingly, it noted that Genscher's memorandum was in large parts 'consistent with the principles for the further development of monetary cooperation that had always guided the Bundesbank': autonomy of the central bank and a consensus for 'stability'.[127]

It was likely Schlüter who reviewed the memorandum he himself had helped to inspire. The internal review was careful to mix downplaying the differences between the Genscher memorandum and the bank's position with targeted scepticism. It focused its critique on the peripheral idea of introducing the ECU as a parallel currency. The central point of contention whether a European central bank could serve as a 'catalyst' for convergence or whether it could only be established at the end of the process had become 'an open question'.[128] The review concluded the memorandum was a useful 'political initiative' that needed more expertise – which the Bundesbank should provide.[129] With some dissenting votes, the review was adopted during a meeting of the Bundesbank Council in early March 1988.[130] In mid-March, Ernst Albrecht, Ministerpräsident of Niedersachsen, a powerful figure within the CDU, endorsed Genscher's proposal.[131] As he saw that the memorandum was beginning to gain traction, Pöhl publicly warned that 'enthusiasm' for Europe should not lead to 'illusion'.[132]

in Hanns Jürgen Küsters (ed), *Deutsche Europapolitik Christlicher Demokraten* (Düsseldorf, Droste, 2014) 363–82, 366–70.

[125] PA AA B 224-ZA/168727, Vorlage 'Bundesbankpräsident Pöhl im Presseclub', 1 March 1988.

[126] PA AA B 224-ZA/168727, 'Betreff: Memorandum für die Schaffung eines europäischen Währungsraumes und einer Europäischen Zentralbank von Hans-Dietrich Genscher', undated.

[127] ibid 1.

[128] ibid 2–3.

[129] ibid 4.

[130] Meanwhile, member of the Bundesbank Council Günter Storch (FDP) privately wrote to Genscher to let him know that he disagreed with his colleagues. He found the proposal 'particularly suitable' and was eager to tell Genscher he had declared so publicly in a local party meeting, PA AA B 224-ZA/168727, Letter dated 29 March 1988.

[131] 'Albrecht lobt Genscher "Währungsunion nötig"' *Hannoversche Allgemeine Zeitung* (Hannover, 9 March 1988). Albrecht was the father of later President of the Commission Ursula von der Leyen.

[132] 'Pöhl warnt vor Europa-Illusionen' *Frankfurter Allgemeine Zeitung* (Frankfurt, 11 March 1988). Pöhl was in a difficult position, navigating different factions in the Bundesbank Council and trying to preserve the reputation of the Bank, see Gaddum, *Die deutsche Europapolitik in den 80er Jahren* 304.

Why was the Genscher memorandum not shot down by the Treasury? It was not for a lack of trying. In a frenzy, Treasury officials prepared their own memorandum for finance minister Stoltenberg. It was published two weeks later, on 15 March 1988.[133] The Stoltenberg memorandum, likely finalised by the then permanent secretary and later President of the Bundesbank Hans Tietmeyer who had a habit of controlling all documents to the comma, did not even mention the Genscher memorandum by name. It just referenced 'several proposals'. The rather lengthy memorandum listed the progress achieved over the last years. Monetary union was only for the 'long term'. It repeated Treasury orthodoxy but presented no alternative to Genscher's proposal. The opposition party SPD publicly rebuffed Stoltenberg and commended Genscher, who had sent Schönfelder to brief and lobby them.[134] Former Chancellor Schmidt assisted from the sidelines. In a long article in *Die Zeit* he launched a broadside against Stoltenberg and the Bundesbank.[135] He did not mince his words. According to Schmidt, the coronation theory was nothing but a distraction; central bankers had strongly opposed EMS at the start only to later appreciate its success; and monetary union was the only chance against unpredictable fluctuations of the dollar caused by an 'undisciplined fiscal and tax policy' in the United States. In addition, he claimed that Germany could hardly serve as a role model for Europe as it ran a continuous trade surplus for which, he predicted, it would one day pay a hefty political price. He settled some old scores, complaining that the Bundesbank was overstepping its territory and had developed into a 'fourth branch'. Europe was for politicians, not for monetary zealots.

Meanwhile, Stoltenberg failed to convince Kohl and the Cabinet to unequivocally endorse his memorandum.[136] The day after it was published, the *FAZ* already reported that the government was 'on Genscher's course'.[137] Kohl, the article noted, had expressed his tentative support for Genscher in a meeting with business leaders. His published speech was much more careful.[138] Germany and France would take a leading role in developing monetary integration further, he assured them.

For his later reflection on the process, see Pöhl, 'Der Delors-Bericht' 196–97: the Genscher memorandum 'caused astonishment, to put it mildly'.

[133] 'Zur weiteren Entwicklung der währungspolitischen Zusammenarbeit in Europa', reprinted in Krägenau and Wetter, *Europäische Wirtschafts- und Währungsunion* 310–12.

[134] PA AA B 224-ZA/168727, Press release of the SPD parliamentary party 'Weichenstellungen für Europäische Zentralbank und Europäische Währung', 6 April 1998, for Schönfelder's lobbying efforts, see Vorlage, 15 April 1988.

[135] 'Blockiert von Kleinmütigen' *Die Zeit* (Hamburg, 22 April 1988).

[136] Fröhlich, *Helmut Kohl* 244. 11 years later, Stoltenberg still chided Genscher for effectively vacating the long-held German position and giving up on price stability, see Stoltenberg's memoir *Wendepunkte* (Berlin, Siedler, 1997) 328–30.

[137] 'Auf Genscher-Kurs' *Frankfurter Allgemeine Zeitung* (Frankfurt, 16 March 1988).

[138] The published speech insisted on convergence and stated that it was 'still a long way to go'. It was therefore less important to talk about a European central bank than about 'how we want to get there', see Helmut Kohl, *Reden zu Fragen der Zukunft* (Bonn, Presse- und Informationsamt der Bundesregierung, 1989) 174. It is unclear whether the FAZ report misread Kohl's remarks or whether he went off script.

In a meeting on foreign policy in mid-April, he let his party know that close cooperation in monetary matters was essential, but that a central bank required 'great care'.[139] For a while, Kohl seemed to manoeuvre between both positions to manage the conflict in his cabinet.[140] Still in mid-May, Kohl once again declared there was 'no hurry' for a European central bank, probably to keep Stoltenberg and Pöhl in the dark.[141] However, when it was time to prepare the Council in Hanover, he had finally come around to Genscher's position.[142]

For Kohl, the Genscher memorandum had several advantages. He could no longer be outflanked by his intra-party rivals on European policy.[143] More importantly, he could regain control of the process, demonstrate statesmanship, and advance European integration strengthening the Franco-German alliance.[144] More than once, he had declared that it was part of Germany's 'raison d'état' to be the 'engine' of European integration.[145] Kohl so sincerely believed in this idea that he eschewed committing himself to any clear concept of what it meant.[146] The government had never formulated any detailed proposal for European policy.[147] As Dyson and Featherstone aptly observe, he was for the EMU 'in principle'.[148] In practice, he had long viewed it primarily as a tactical question of domestic politics.[149] In the early years of his chancellorship, Kohl usually sided with the Bundesbank and the Treasury on monetary matters.[150] Later on, his new adviser Joachim Bitterlich slowly convinced him to change course.[151] The changing tide in opinion helped. In the end, Kohl arranged a deal in early June 1988. In a conversation with French President Mitterrand, he conditioned his consent to monetary integration on the French agreeing to

[139] Fröhlich, *Helmut Kohl* 245.
[140] ibid 246.
[141] 'Keine Eile für Europa-Bank' *Rheinische Post* (Düsseldorf, 10 Mai 1988).
[142] Fröhlich, *Helmut Kohl* 246; Dyson and Featherstone, *The Road to Maastricht* 334–39.
[143] Dyson and Featherstone, *The Road to Maastricht* 337.
[144] ibid.
[145] Ulrich Lappenküper, 'Die deutsche Europapolitik zwischen der »Genscher-Colombo-Initiative« und der Verabschiedung der Einheitlichen Europäischen Akte (1981–1986)' (2003) 10 *Historisch-Politische Mitteilungen* 285. *cf* the collected speeches in Kohl, *Deutschlands Zukunft in Europa*; Meyer, *Deutsche Europapolitik* 174; Ulrike Kessler, 'Deutsche Europapolitik unter Helmut Kohl: Europäische Integration als "kategorischer Imperativ"?' in Gisela Müller-Brandeck-Bocquet (ed), *Deutsche Europapolitik von Konrad Adenauer bis Gerhard Schröder* (Opladen, Leske + Budrich, 2002) 115–66.
[146] Miriam Karama, *Struktur und Wandel der Legitimationsideen deutscher Europapolitik* (Bonn, Europa Union, 2001) 186 notes that Kohl talked interchangeably about 'European Union', 'Political Union', 'European federal state' and 'United States of Europe'. For a sceptical view whether there was any substance behind it, see Gaddum, *Die deutsche Europapolitik in den 80er Jahren* 221.
[147] Fröhlich, *Helmut Kohl* 240.
[148] Dyson and Featherstone, *The Road to Maastricht* 308.
[149] ibid.
[150] He had come into office with the view that further monetary integration was not 'opportune', see Gaddum, *Die deutsche Europapolitik in den 80er Jahren* 298.
[151] Fröhlich, *Helmut Kohl* 240.

capital liberalisation, which provided a political victory for Stoltenberg and the Treasury.[152]

5.2. European Reactions

The files at the Foreign Office offer a detailed account of how the Genscher memorandum was received in the capitals of Europe. Schönfelder ordered the embassies to send him any news report covering the memorandum.[153] There was quite a press storm in Germany – all dutifully collected by Schönfelder and sent up to his master – but European reactions were more muted and cautious. French newspaper *Le Quotidien* made Genscher 'homme du jour'.[154] The catholic *La Croix* warned against what it perceived as the newly found alliance between Genscher and Pöhl.[155] *Le Monde* reported in a mildly positive way.[156] Italian newspapers could not report about the memorandum at first because reporters were on strike.[157]

Former French Prime Minister Raymond Barre expressed scepticism in a private conversation with Willy Brandt's former chief of staff Horst Ehmke.[158] It was too early for a central bank, he thought. Current finance minister Édouard Balladur remarked that the Bundesbank could hardly serve as the role model for a European central bank as all other banks in Europe were organised like the Banque de France.[159] Behind this outward veil of scepticism, internal reactions were more enthusiastic. Pierre de Bouissieu, the Quai d'Orsay's head for economic cooperation, noted that the Genscher Memorandum was 'a present on a silver plate', one 'we have been waiting for … for five years'.[160]

Most governments remained cautious as long as it remained unclear whether the Genscher memorandum represented the new German position or just an initiative by the Foreign Minister. Only Her Majesty's Treasury made it known to the German embassy that it would have preferred to have been consulted in advance of such a major policy change[161] – all the more as the Memorandum clearly took a turn in the wrong direction in its view. The Community was not ready for monetary union, neither politically nor economically. Sensing danger for its control over the Bank of England, the UK Treasury remarked that the constitutional setting of national central banks was too divergent, and a European central bank was nothing more than 'a vision'. Dublin, Copenhagen, Athens and Rome initially did not react

[152] Bozo, 'In search of the Holy Grail' 303; Marshall, *The Bank* 83.
[153] PA AA B 224-ZA/168727, Letter, dated 29 February 1988.
[154] PA AA B 224-ZA/168727, Vorlage, 4 March 1988.
[155] PA AA B 224-ZA/168727, Telex Note of the German Embassy in Paris, 11 March 1988, 2.
[156] PA AA B 224-ZA/168727, Vorlage, 4 March 1988.
[157] PA AA B 224-ZA/168727, Telex Note of the German Embassy in Rome, 1 March 1988.
[158] PA AA B 224-ZA/168727, Telex Note of the German Embassy in Paris, 27 February 1988.
[159] PA AA B 224-ZA/168727, Vermerk, 15 April 1988.
[160] Cited in Bozo, 'In search of the Holy Grail' 302.
[161] PA AA B 224-ZA/168727, Telex Note of the German Embassy in London, 17 March 1988.

at all. Ireland later voiced scepticism,[162] arguing that the Genscher memorandum was premature, whereas Ireland had 'no problem' with Stoltenberg's position. Athens informed the German embassy that Greece supported the Memorandum 'in principle',[163] but the approach needed to be broadened to include financial assistance for member states such as, for instance, Greece.

In April, the *Handelsblatt* correspondent from Brussels reported that Genscher's initiative had won applause in Europe; the demarche of his junior minister Irmgard Adam-Schwaetzer who had called currency union a 'condition' for the common market was seen as 'revolutionary'.[164] President of the Luxembourg Institut monétaire Pierre Jaans, on the other hand, provided an early scathing critique of the Genscher memorandum to his interlocutor from the German embassy.[165] According to Jaans, a European central bank would not be able to bridge the North–South divide; German economic policy could hardly serve as a role model for Europe; and its unemployment numbers and a constant trade surplus were far from exemplary. He claimed that the independent Bundesbank was a specific product of the post-war situation, and even in Germany it would not be founded again in the same form today. To hold it out as a role model was therefore 'unfortunate'.

5.3. More than a Footnote?

In June, the European Council in Hanover adopted the mandate for a committee of experts along the lines proposed by Genscher. From that moment on, the process was underway. Negotiations for monetary union came close to falling apart more than once in the following years, but conceptually they never went beyond the basic parameters set out in the Genscher memorandum. Is the history of the memorandum worth more than just a footnote to the Delors Committee and the protracted negotiations of the Maastricht Treaty? If so, certainly not to eulogise a foreign minister who was not shy to sing the praise of his memorandum. In Genscher's memoir, the memorandum became the culmination of his European initiatives – a 'three-stage-rocket' starting with the Genscher-Colombo initiative in 1981, leading to the Single European Act and ultimately to monetary union.[166] Beyond this questionable teleological narrative,[167] it might still be worth thinking about the Genscher memorandum, since it indicates several core assumptions on which the founding of the EMU rested.

[162] PA AA B 224-ZA/168727, Letter of the German Embassy in Dublin, 5 Mai 1988.
[163] PA AA B 224-ZA/168727, Telex Note of the German Embassy in Athens, 23 May 1988.
[164] 'Hannover im Visier' *Handelsblatt* (Düsseldorf, 29 April 1988).
[165] PA AA B 224-ZA/168727, Telex Note of German Embassy in Luxembourg, 1 March 1988.
[166] Genscher, *Erinnerungen* 368.
[167] *cf* Kiran Klaus Patel and Hans Christian Röhl, *Transformation durch Recht: Geschichte und Jurisprudenz Europäischer Integration 1985–1992* (Tübingen, Mohr Siebeck, 2020) 37.

(1) The Genscher memorandum placed the central bank at the heart of monetary union, partly for tactical reasons, but mostly out of conviction. Not only was it to be made independent from government, for there was no European government, but 'autonomous' as the memorandum explicitly demanded. The memorandum seemed to assume that institutional arrangements similar to those of the Bundesbank would lead to similar policies, even though the European central bank would operate in a very different political and economic environment. Schlüter had seen this point and reasoned that 'criteria of independence do not conclusively indicate how a central bank will act'. Ultimately, the memorandum nevertheless operated on the assumption that replicating the Bundesbank would replicate its policies.

(2) Economic integration could be saved for a later day, but it would follow. In an opaque passage, the Genscher memorandum argued that monetary and economic union were 'closely linked'. Potential 'tensions' between the two areas could ultimately only be resolved through 'parallel progress in both domains'. Those who wrote the Genscher memorandum believed that their own pro-integrationist stance was a cross-party constant in German politics that would endure. They did not anticipate that the same tactical skilfulness they employed to force it through could lead future German politicians in a different direction. Asymmetry therefore had a strong tactical component. To make the institutional structure of the central bank front and centre sidelined the main internal opponent of monetary integration and was designed to assuage a public which trusted independent experts more than elected politicians. Asymmetry was not here to stay. It was not invented by the ordoliberal Eurosceptics who usually defend it in contemporary German politics. It was a structure invented by a group of strongly pro-European German officials, some with ordoliberal leanings, and fought through by pro-European politicians who believed in European integration to a degree that has become rare these days.

(3) The history of the Genscher memorandum underscores that asymmetry was not based on any elaborate economic theory. At most, there was an argument of how it might work. It assumed that the monetary policy of an autonomous central bank could ultimately force member states into the right economic policies and that it would do so because it was made independent from electoral politics.

(4) To assuage democratic concerns, monetary union had to – and could – be based on a 'consensus' on economic policy. Even without the benefit of hindsight, this was a peculiar political category to rely on, let alone in economic matters. Its central importance for the invention of an asymmetrical monetary union is at least partially explained by two factors. For one, it rested on the conviction that the German low-inflation economy was not so much a comparative advantage built on a highly specific economic model but an arrangement beneficial for everyone and adoptable everywhere. It also rested on the expectation that a 'consensus' would, if necessary, be brought about by

a forceful central bank with the upper hand – in much the same way that the Bundesbank had at times cajoled the German government into its preferred policies. Even then, the proclaimed need for consensus on economic policy was astonishing. If a monetary union were to work, on the Genscher memorandum's account, it required at least compatible policies of all member states in a broad field ranging from wage policy to taxing and spending. In effect, the memorandum stated that the structure it envisaged was dependent on a comprehensive agreement on national economic and fiscal policies, which should stand in for a common economic policy at the European level. Read this way, the Genscher memorandum listed a sweeping set of conditions for monetary union but weakened them from hard facts to a political agreement which could easily be expressed but was more difficult to follow through. This concept had two severe limitations. There was no clear idea which incentives would bring about the required consensus – other than a central bank. More importantly, it never asked the obvious question: whether the consensus on the German economic model would or even could work for all member states at the same time.

3

The Debate on the Revision of the European Fiscal Rules

Towards More Political Governance of the EMU?

CLAIRE MONGOUACHON

The European fiscal framework is currently subject to an intensive and wide-ranging debate. In February 2020, the European Commission launched a review of the EU economic governance.[1] Just one month later, the Covid-19 pandemic led to the activation of the 'general escape clause' in order to allow member states to support their economies. The review then restarted in October 2021 in a totally different environment.[2] In December 2021, the French president Emmanuel Macron announced his willingness to put on the table a revision of the budgetary rules, which would lead to 'a more political governance of the economic politics of the EU'.[3] This declaration was followed by a call for softer fiscal rules, jointly with the former Italian prime minister Mario Draghi. Here, it has been stressed that the fiscal rules 'should not prevent us from making all necessary investments' and that 'debt raised to finance such investments, which undeniably benefit the welfare of future generations and long-term growth, should be favoured by the fiscal rules'.[4] The idea that the fight against climate change requires more public investment

[1] European Commission, 'Commission presents review of EU economic governance and launches debate on its future' (*European Commission Website*, 5 February 2020) https://ec.europa.eu/commission/presscorner/detail/en/ip_20_170.

[2] Commission, 'Communication from the Commission to the European Parliament, the Council, the European Central Bank, the European economic and social committee, the Committee of the Regions – The EU economy after COVID-19: implications for economic governance' COM (2021) 662 final. The Commission invited stakeholders to reflect on the functioning of the EU economic governance framework and to present their views on how to enhance the framework's effectiveness.

[3] Eric Maurice, 'The Challenges of the French Presidency of the Council' (*Fondation Robert Schuman*, European Issue no 618, 10 January 2022) www.robert-schuman.eu/en/european-issues/0618-the-challenges-of-the-french-presidency-of-the-council.

[4] Emmanuel Macron and Mario Draghi, 'Op-ed by President Emmanuel Macron and Prime Minister Mario Draghi on EU Macroeconomic and Fiscal Strategy' (*Élysée*, 23 December 2021) www.elysee.

seems to be gaining ground. In its Communication on orientations for a reform of the EU economic framework from November 2022, the European Commission recognises that 'the green and digital transitions … will require sustained high levels of investment in the years to come'.[5] This finding has been confirmed in the proposal for a regulation from the Commission dated April 2023.[6]

The purpose of this chapter is to present the terms of this debate in light of the historic evolution of the fiscal framework and to highlight that these statements represent a paradigm shift. Whereas the fiscal legal framework results from different reforms that complexified the comprehension of fiscal rules in Europe, traditionally considered a technical field, it seems that the fiscal area is becoming more 'politicised'. The concept of politicisation, although not a legal concept, seems to be an appropriate concept for thinking about and questioning certain developments and proposals relating to the framework for the exercise of European budgetary rules. When referring to the current definition of the term,[7] a form of politicisation of the rules in the sense that the matter becomes a political issue can easily be observed, on the basis of the content of the discussions noted above. More precisely, political scientists characterise politicisation by three components: issue salience, actor expansion and polarisation.[8] Issue salience refers to the visibility of a given issue in public debate. Expansion refers to the mobilisation of actors becoming involved in a public debate. Polarisation refers to the intensity of conflict over the issue. Thus 'the more salient the issue, the more actors and people participate in the debate, the more positions are polarized, and the more politicized a decision or institution is'.[9] From a legal point of view, this results in the questioning of the degree to which the legal rule is open to political choices.

The theme of the politicisation of the European Union is currently receiving renewed interest in political science.[10] But work on questions of 'depoliticisation' has been carried out over the last 20 years in the field of European governance.

fr/en/emmanuel-macron/2021/12/23/op-ed-by-president-emmanuel-macron-and-prime-minister-mario-draghi-on-eu-macroeconomic-and-fiscal-strategy.

[5] Commission, 'Communication from the Commission to the European Parliament, the Council, The European Central Bank, the European economic and social committee, the Committee of the Regions – Communication on orientations for a reform of the EU economic governance framework' COM (2022) 583 final, 4.

[6] Commission, 'Proposal for a Regulation of the European Parliament and the Council on the effective coordination of economic policies and multilateral budgetary surveillance and repealing Council Regulation (EC) No 1466/97' COM(2023) 240 final, 2.

[7] The Cambridge Dictionary defines the term 'politicise' as follows: 'to make something or someone political, or more involved in or conscious of political matters' https://dictionary.cambridge.org/dictionary/english/politicize?q=politicise.

[8] Edgar Grande and Swen Hutter, 'Introduction: European integration and the challenge of politicisation' in Swen Hutter, Edgar Grande and Hanspeter Kriesi (eds), *Politicising Europe: Integration and Mass Politics* (Cambridge, Cambridge University Press, 2016) 3–31.

[9] Michael Zürn, 'Politicization Compared: at National, European, and Global Levels' (2019) 26 *Journal of European Public Policy* 977.

[10] Reinout Arthur Van Der Veer, 'Walking the Tightrope: Politicization and the Commission's Enforcement of the SGP' (2022), 60 *Journal of Common Market Studies* 81; Taru Haapala and Álvaro Oleart (eds), *Tracing the Politicisation of the EU: The Future of Europe Debates Before and After the 2019*

The term governance, which appeared in the early 2000s,[11] is deeply imbued with the idea of depoliticisation. Peter Burnham defines depoliticisation as 'the process of placing at one remove the political character of decision-making'.[12] The law has been a major tool for depoliticising budgetary matters, as will be demonstrated in the following developments. European budgetary rules, which were initially conceived as a condition for membership of the eurozone, have become a real constitutional constraint, in other words, a fully-fledged element of the financial constitution of the Union (and of the member states). This has had the effect of removing this fiscal issue or reducing fiscal policy flexibility from the hands of elected politicians. Authors have underlined that some international organisations such as the World Bank have played a role in the process of depoliticisation by deconstructing the political debate and presenting the policy choices as a neutral and a technical exercise based on expertise.[13] In the same vein, the influence of neoliberalism on the functioning of some economic policies exercised by the EU has been stressed many times.[14] The severe and controversial argument of 'Authoritarian Neoliberalism' has been used in the context of the eurozone crisis to criticise the supposed attempts of the institutions of the EU to insulate economic decision-making from democratic influence.[15] This will not be the approach defended in the present chapter.

Elections (Palgrave Macmillan, 2022); Anne-Marie Houde et al (eds), *The Politicization of the European Union: From Processes to Consequences*, 1st edn (Brussels, Editions de l'Université de Bruxelles, 2022). The authors analyse, from an empirical and normative perspective, the consequences of politicisation in different fields of European integration. Concerning the Euro Crisis, Ines Schäfer, 'Ever more politicized and Europeanized? Public debates over European integration in France and Germany' 107–27, 108 stresses that: 'While European integration issues are primarily politicized at the domestic level, instances of high domestic politicization can spill over to other European member states, thereby causing horizontal Europeanization'; Michael Zürn, 'Politicization Compared'; Tanja A Börzel and Thomas Risse, 'From the Euro to the Schengen Crises: European Integration Theories, Politicization, and Politics' (2018) 25 *Journal of European Public Policy* 83; Hutter, Grande and Kriesi, *Politicising Europe*; Pieter De Wilde, 'No Polity for Old Politics? A Framework for Analyzing the Politicization of European Integration' (2011) 33 *Journal of European Integration* 559 observed an 'increase in the polarization of opinions, interests or values and the extent to which they are publicly advanced towards the process of policy formulation within the European Union'.

[11] Commission, 'European Governance: A White Paper' COM (2001) 428; Matthew Flinders, 'Distributed Public Governance in the European Union' (2004) 11 *Journal of European Public Policy* 520.

[12] Peter Burnham, 'New Labour and the Politics of Depoliticisation' (2001) 3 *British Journal of Politics and International Relations* 127.

[13] eg Andy Storey, 'The World Bank, Neo-Liberalism and Power: Discourse Analysis and Implications for Campaigners' (2000) 10 *Development in Practice* 361.

[14] See Thomas Biebricher's chapter in this volume (ch 4).

[15] Agustín José Menéndez, 'Hermann Heller NOW' (2015) 21 *European Law Journal* 285; Werner Bonefeld, 'Human Economy and Social Policy: On Ordo-Liberalism and Political Authority' (2013) 26 *History of the Human Sciences* 106; Thomas Biebricher, *The political theory of neoliberalism* (Stanford, CA, Stanford University Press, 2018); more recently: Werner Bonefeld, 'Economic Constitution and Authoritarism: Carl Schmitt and the Idea of a Sound Economy' in Guillaume Grégoire and Xavier Miny (eds), *The Idea of Economic Constitution in Europe: Genealogy and Overview* (Leiden, Brill Nijhoff, 2022) 182–203; for further discussions: Vincent Valentin, 'Discussion L'idée de constitution économique et l'hypothèse du libéralisme autoritaire' in Grégoire and Miny, *The Idea of Economic Constitution in Europe* 237–58.

The elements of definition of the depoliticisation phenomenon will be taken as a guide to analyse the developments and discussions about the European budgetary framework from a legal perspective. In this respect, it is possible to distinguish between an institutional aspect and a substantive aspect of this process. Institutional depoliticisation operates by transferring the decision-making power to independent bodies or non-majoritarian institutions.[16] These bodies are designed to be released to some extent from short-term political considerations.[17] The substantial depoliticisation involves the adoption of a policy that builds explicit rules into the decision-making process constraining the need for political discretion. These analytical tools will allow us to examine the margin of discretion of the authorities responsible for the design and the enforcement of the European fiscal rules.

The response is dialectical and the proposed plan therefore follows a chronological path.

In the first part of this chapter, I shall return to the original budgetary framework and present the successive reforms that have been made to it. It will be shown that the Stability and Growth Pact (SGP) and the Treaty on Stability, Coordination and Governance (TSCG) illustrate a process of depoliticisation in the Economic and Monetary Union (EMU). Indeed, these reforms can be analysed as a kind of automatisation of the rules focused on financial stability and safe assets, depriving member states of broader political choices.

The second part of the chapter then gives an overview of the contestation of the rules and of recent proposals, and especially the 'greening' of the rules, formulated by institutions and academia. It thus illustrates a paradox associated with the phenomenon of depoliticisation. Political scientists have already shown that depoliticised governance, by moving decisions away from representative bodies, can have the unexpected effect of stimulating political debate more intensively than would be the case in an ordinary legislative framework.

The third part of the chapter analyses the recent proposal from the European Commission. The question of whether this text marks a phase of re-politicisation of fiscal governance will be answered in a nuanced way. Processes of depoliticisation and re-politicisation may actually take place concurrently. The chapter concludes by questioning the need to establish a new institutional framework to arbitrate between the different goals which will possibly guide the implementation of the EU fiscal rules in the future.

[16] Giandomenico Majone, 'Non-Majoritarian Institutions and the Limits of Democratic Governance: A Political Transaction-Cost Approach' (2001) 157 *Journal of Institutional and Theoretical Economics* 57; Giandomenico Majone, 'The Two Logics of Delegation: Agency and Fiduciary Relations in EU Governance' (2001) 2 *European Union Politics* 103, 106–07.

[17] Matthew Flinders and Jim Buller, 'Depoliticisation: Principles, Tactics and Tools' (2006) 1 *British Politics* 293, 295–96.

1. A Movement to Automate Budgetary Rules: Depoliticised Fiscal Governance?

While budgetary rules had an instrumental place in the Maastricht Treaty (see section 1.1), these rules were significantly strengthened during the latest reforms introduced following the euro crisis, and were meant to increase constraints on states (see section 1.2).

1.1. The Introduction of the Original Budgetary Constraints – The Result of a Political Compromise

1.1.1. The Unique Place of Budgetary Rules, between National Economic Sovereignty and Monetary Union

'Let us rediscover the Maastricht spirit – stability and growth can only go hand in hand', said the President of the European Commission, Ursula von der Leyen, in her State of the Union address in September 2022.[18] It seems essential to go back, at least briefly, to the context the Maastricht Treaty budgetary rules were introduced in, so as to assess the political role assigned to them. The political consensus[19] that was reached at the time of the Maastricht Treaty is well known. The decision to endow the European Community with a single currency was legally translated into transferring member states' monetary powers to a European system of central banks, whose essential prerogatives were entrusted to a supranational body: the European Central Bank (ECB). Monetary policy – one of the Community's exclusive competences – was in a way federalised at the European level, which was a major paradigm shift for member states. Deprived of any possibility of acting on exchange rates to deal with their national economic situations, states were deprived of a major economic intervention instrument. However, they were not prepared to surrender all of their economic sovereignty; they wished to hang on to the exercise of their own national economic policies, which is subject to mere intergovernmental coordination at the European level. This political consensus sealed what some authors have called the 'original asymmetry'[20] between monetary union and economic union.[21] From an economic point of view, this dissociation might be deemed totally artificial or even absurd. However, from a legal point of view, it leads to the identification of two areas of action governed by very distinct

[18] Ursula von der Leyen, State of the Union Address 2022 (*European Commission*) 11, https://state-of-the-union.ec.europa.eu/system/files/2022-09/SOTEU_2022_Address_EN.pdf.

[19] Francesco Martucci, *L'ordre économique et monétaire de l'Union européenne* (Brussels, Bruylant, 2015) note 42, 440, mentioning the Bruxelles consensus.

[20] The expression used by Jean-Louis Victor was 'systematic asymmetries', quoted by Martucci, *L'ordre économique et monétaire de l'UE* 439.

[21] See Christian Neumeier's and Paul Tucker's chapters in this volume (ch 2 and ch 1).

institutional mechanisms. The separation of monetary and economic competences has been greatly clarified by the Lisbon Treaty. On the one hand, Article 3(c) of the Treaty on the Functioning of the European Union (TFEU) grants exclusive competence to the Union for the conduct of 'monetary policy by Member States whose currency is the euro' – an area where the supranational integration rationale is fully operational. On the other hand, Article 5 TFEU grants the Union the specific competence to coordinate member states' economic policies – following a simple cooperation logic. Budgetary rules hold a unique place in this initial division, since they are at the heart of the asymmetry between monetary union and economic union – caught in tension as they stand between the two.

What exactly is the role of the European budgetary rules introduced in the Maastricht Treaty? Their purpose was not exactly to establish a fiscal union. Economic theory teaches that in a monetary union, loss of monetary independence can be partially counterbalanced by setting up a federal budget.[22] Hence, a fiscal policy must accompany the monetary union in order to guarantee one of the three traditional functions of a federal budget,[23] namely the monetary union's macroeconomic stabilisation, intended to mitigate cyclical fluctuations. Such a stabilisation function has not been thought of at the eurozone level. It remains with the states. This makes economic 'sense':[24] since the EMU is not an optimal monetary zone, national budgetary policies focus on asymmetric shocks, ie those affecting only national or sub-national territories. Meanwhile, the ECB's monetary policy makes it possible to absorb symmetric shocks, ie those affecting the entire eurozone, by acting on interest rates. It is therefore obvious that the budgetary rules set out in the Maastricht Treaty are not, as such, intended to fulfil one of fiscal policies' traditional functions.[25]

Rather, the Treaty simply establishes rules for coordinating national budgetary policies, which at that time were deemed essential for the monetary union's proper functioning. Although the famous 'Maastricht criteria' are most often associated with the need for budgetary discipline, these rules, which are purely instrumental, are above all in the service of monetary stability. Article 104 of the Treaty establishing the European Community (TEC) (now Article 126 TFEU) provides that member states shall avoid excessive government deficits. Criteria are defined in the protocol on the excessive deficit procedure, with reference values set at 3 per cent of GDP government deficit and 60 per cent of GDP government debt.

[22] Robert A Mundell, 'A Theory of Optimum Currency Areas' (1961) 51 *American Economic Review* 657.

[23] The three traditional functions of fiscal policy are: the financing of public goods; the transfer between regions to correct territorial inequalities; the stabilisation of the economy: Richard Musgrave and Peggy Musgrave, *Public Finance in Theory and Practice* (Tokyo, McGraw-Hill Kogakusha, 1989).

[24] Agnès Bénassy-Quéré, Xavier Ragot and Guntram Wolff, 'Quelle union budgétaire pour la zone euro ?' (2016) 2 *Notes du conseil d'analyse économique* 1, 3.

[25] Nevertheless, it can be noted that the stabilising function of national fiscal policies is only effective if public finances are sound. Bénassy-Quéré, Ragot and Wolff, 'Quelle union budgétaire pour la zone euro ?' 3.

These criteria correspond to the convergence criteria required for membership in the single currency, which points to their monetary function. They could easily be described as functional rules. On the one hand, this monetary stability would be threatened in the event of excessive budgetary imbalances, hence becoming a source of inflation.[26] On the other hand, for the ECB to be able to dedicate itself fully to its price stability objective, national fiscal policies must be conducted responsibly, through rules that impose compliance with sound public finances. Thus, budgetary rules are not in themselves one of EMU's objectives, but are a means to the end of achieving the euro's overarching monetary stability. Lacking any intrinsic rationality, the budgetary criteria have been harshly criticised for their arbitrary nature.[27] The 3 per cent ratio, which was also the average in France at the time, was adopted by Mitterrand on 9 June 1982, and was upheld during the Maastricht Treaty negotiations by Jean-Claude Trichet.

The monetary justification of budgetary rules is not devoid of consequences for the constraints they place on the conduct of national policies, given the primacy granted to the objective of monetary stability.

1.1.2. A Mild Legal Constraint on National Budgetary Policies

The objective of monetary stability, by virtue of its pre-eminent place in EMU, was bound to exert a constraint on governments' exercise of their budgetary policies. Because of the preponderance given to the imperative of monetary stability from the outset of EMU creation, the compromise reached in the Maastricht Treaty between the transfer of monetary policy and the preservation of states' budgetary competences was, in fact, fated to remain fictitious. The objective of budgetary discipline would necessarily result in a loss of national budgetary sovereignty. This is quite a telling example of the influence that a highly integrated policy has on the conduct of policies that remain under state jurisdiction. Considered as a regulatory policy,[28] the conduct of monetary policy has quite logically been removed from any political deliberation mechanism. Bound by Article 105 TEC (now Article 127(1) TFEU) to guarantee, in complete independence, price stability maintenance, the ECB is not accountable for its decisions before a political body. No doubt such an arrangement can be seen as an element of 'depoliticising' monetary union,[29] in line

[26] Franklin Dehousse, 'L'Union économique et monétaire' (1995) 20 *Courrier hebdomadaire du CRISP* 1, 8.

[27] See eg Willem Buiter et al, 'Excessive Deficits: Sense and Nonsense in the Treaty of Maastricht' (1993) 8 *Economic Policy* 57.

[28] Paul Magnette, *Le régime politique de l'Union Européenne*, 4th edn (Paris, Presses de Science Po, 2023).

[29] Fabian Amtenbrink, 'A Legal and Political Economy Mapping of European Economic Monetary Union' in Grégory Kalflèche, Thomas Perroud and Matthias Ruffert (eds), *L'avenir de l'Union économique et monétaire: une perspective franco-allemande* (Paris, LGDJ, 2018) 111–31, 115: 'In vesting the power to conduct monetary policy for the single currency area in a supranational central bank a deliberate choice has been made to (attempt to) depoliticize monetary policy'.

both with the dominant monetarist paradigm of the time and with the European integration theories.

For all this, the budgetary rules useful for the proper functioning of this monetary union do not follow this same depoliticised model. The desire to impose budgetary constraints on states does not stem from the legal framework itself.

On the one hand, budgetary discipline is guaranteed more by market logics than by the law. Accordingly, the Treaty provides for two rules to warrant that states will conduct a responsible budgetary policy: the prohibition on the Eurosystem buying back public debt instruments, set out in Article 101 TEC (now Article 123 TFEU); and the prohibition on both the Union and eurozone states being answerable for commitments by other states in the eurozone, set out in Article 103 TEC (now Article 125 TFEU). This is intended to prevent states from taking budgetary decisions whose financial cost would be borne by the ECB or by the other states. The law here enshrines the submission of national budgetary authorities to market rules.[30] It enshrines a financial constraint supposed to reduce the scope for budgetary deviation by states. As will be shown, this rule proved insufficient and needed to be strengthened.

On the other hand, the legal constraint on states' budgetary choices does not exclude exercising a marginal degree of political discretion, both at European and state levels. As for states, it is worth noting they are only subject to a relative constraint. First, the wording of Article 126(1) TFEU is not particularly restrictive, since it provides that states 'shall avoid' excessive government deficits. Secondly, states are only required to comply with a ceiling, set at 3 per cent, which allows them to retain a measure of financial sovereignty in the composition of their fiscal revenues and expenditures. National governments are not subject to any prescription as to how they are supposed to achieve this budgetary target. Nevertheless, it is worth noting that a medium-term budgetary framework has existed since the beginning of EMU. States must prepare annual convergence or stability programmes, which include budgetary and macroeconomic projections for the current year and the following three years, covering all budgetary aggregates.

As far as Community institutions are concerned, they are not dispossessed of political choice. Granted, it is sometimes stressed that the budgetary surveillance procedure involves independent bodies that issue forecasts and analyses and make recommendations. Article 126(1) TFEU provides that the European Commission shall adopt a report that takes into account the medium-term economic and budgetary position of those states that do not meet at least one of the two criteria. Eurostat provides the necessary statistical data for this purpose. However, the procedure is not depoliticised, since the final word is indeed given to a political body – a real decision-making body. According to Article 126(6), it is the Council

[30] On the distinction between discipline by the market and discipline by law, see Martucci, *L'ordre économique et monétaire de l'UE*; Herwig Hofmann, Katerina Pantazatou and Giovanni Zaccaroni, *The metamorphosis of the European economic constitution* (Cheltenham, Edward Elgar Publishing, 2019).

itself that 'decides' whether or not there is an excessive deficit. It is therefore a political institution, which enjoys indirect democratic legitimacy, that is responsible for the decision. This legal quirk seems to be linked to the wishes of the Monetary Committee of the European Community. In return for the above-mentioned reference values that were being proposed, it was intended to leave a certain role to public authorities, as opposed to a purely mechanical application of the criteria. The use of strict quantitative criteria was thereby counterbalanced by a degree of flexibility in the implementation process, leaving some room for political judgment.[31]

Overall, the budgetary framework established by the Maastricht Treaty reflects the unique place of budgetary rules: an embryonic constraint, necessary for the proper conduct of monetary policy, but also relative, because of its concern to preserve states' economic sovereignty.

It was the first reform of the Maastricht Treaty that paved the way for a system that more closely supervised budgetary policies – a process that was to be significantly amplified by the reforms introduced following the euro crisis.

1.2. The Attempt to Automate Budgetary Surveillance in the Wake of the Euro Crisis

1.2.1. The First Step Towards a Rule-Based System

While the Maastricht criteria were designed as a condition for states to join the eurozone, which could constitute a strong incentive to comply with them, the nature of the debate changed very quickly. The budgetary framework, considered insufficient, was the subject of two divergent positions, represented respectively by Germany and France.

Germany had long argued for stricter rules. As early as 1992, the Council of Wise Men had called for sanctions to be defined more precisely and enforced more strictly, a demand that was reiterated in 1995 in the form of a proposal for a 'budget pact'.[32] This preference for a rule-based system was widely supported by the Bundesbank, and by public opinion, which was increasingly negative about EMU because of the dangers to macroeconomic stability. France, on the other hand, insisted on the principle of economic government. It advocated the establishment of a political body as a counterpart to the ECB and rules more oriented towards growth and employment issues, but to no avail.[33] In the absence of a consensus to propose a revision of the Maastricht Treaty, the Community turned to legislative reform.

[31] Lorenzo Bini-Smaghi, Tommaso Padoa-Schioppa and Franceso Papadia, *The Transition to EMU in the Maastricht Treaty* (Princeton, NJ, Princeton Book Company, 1994).

[32] Martin Heipertz and Amy Verdun, 'The Stability and Growth Pact – Theorizing a Case in European Integration' (2005) 43 *Journal of Common Market Studies* 985.

[33] These proposals were not compatible with the German position. Heipertz and Verdun note that Germany had proposed the establishment of a Stability Council, but that this proposal was withdrawn

The purpose of the first reform of the Maastricht rules through the SGP was thus to strengthen economic stability and to establish budgetary discipline as an integral part of EMU (and no longer as a mere appendage to monetary union). Without getting into a detailed presentation of this pact, all that needs to be said is that it includes a preventive component (Council Regulation no 1466/97) that aims, through multilateral surveillance, to keep national public deficits below the 3 per cent threshold. States' stability programmes must contain a medium-term objective (MTO) of a position close to balance or in surplus, as well as an adjustment path that should make it possible to achieve this objective. In addition, a new criterion focusing on the level of public spending has been introduced: net spending may no longer grow beyond the reference rate for potential GDP growth in the medium term. It is therefore no longer only the results that are monitored, but also the means of achieving them. The coordination of budgetary policies is thus achieved through the inclusion of new budgetary constraints on states. The pact also includes a deterrent component (Regulation no 1467/97) that specifies a number of elements of the excessive deficit procedure. On the one hand, the notion of 'exceptional and temporary excess' of the 3 per cent public deficit was defined. On the other hand, the sanctions incurred are spelled out: in theory, the Commission and the Council can impose budgetary consolidation measures on the states concerned. All in all, the control of states' budgetary policies is undeniably reinforced.

However, this rule-based system does not remove all discretion from the authorities: the power to impose sanctions is vested in the Council and the Court of Justice has had occasion to specify that the exercise of this decision-making power is discretionary.[34]

In contrast, the latest reforms have tended towards a form of budgetary rules automation.

1.2.2. Distancing from Politics by Strengthening Budgetary Constraints

Following the 2008 financial crisis, the Union adopted a series of legislative texts that it is impossible to present in detail here. Let us simply note that the Six Pack, composed of six regulations adopted in 2011,[35] and the Two

because of the fear that this body would gradually be transformed into an economic government that could give instructions to the ECB. See Heipertz and Verdun, 'The Stability and Growth' 998.

[34] Case C-27/04 *Commission of the European Communities v Council of the European Union* ECLI:EU:C:2004:436.

[35] Regulation (EU) No 1174/2011 of the European Parliament and of the Council on enforcement to correct excessive macroeconomic imbalances in the euro [2011] OJ L306/8; Regulation (EU) No 1175/2011 of the European Parliament and of the Council amending Council Regulation (EC) No 1466/97 on the strengthening of the surveillance of budgetary positions and the surveillance and coordination of economic policies [2011] OJ L306/12; Regulation (EU) No 1176/2011 of the European

Pack,[36] approved in 2013, have very significantly limited the principle of national budgetary sovereignty.

On the one hand, budgetary objectives are more clearly defined, completing the rule-based system initiated with the SGP. With regard to the SGP preventive arm, a new public expenditure criterion has been introduced, which stipulates that, for countries that have not yet reached their MTO, public expenditure growth rate must not overshoot a reference rate for potential GDP growth in the medium term. The public debt criterion is subject to a numerical benchmark for assessing whether public debt is evolving at a satisfactory level, namely that the gap between the debt ratio and the 60 per cent value decreases by 1/20th per year, over an average of three years.

On the other hand, states experiencing difficulties in terms of budgetary stability are subject to increased surveillance by the Commission: Regulation 473/2013, in addition to subjecting eurozone states to a common budgetary timetable, requires states to communicate to the Commission the details of the measures they intend to implement to correct their excessive deficit. This may go as far as the presentation of an economic partnership programme detailing the structural reforms undertaken to remedy their excessive deficit.

In addition, the same regulation requires states to set up independent budgetary bodies to ensure better budgetary rules monitoring. In France, the High Council for Public Finance, attached to the Court of Auditors, was created in 2012, while, at the European level, the European Budget Committee was created in 2015 to evaluate the implementation of the EU budgetary framework.

Such tightening of the European budgetary framework is made all the more effective as it is intertwined with the more general framework of the Union's economic governance. For example, in 2010, the European Semester became an instrument for coordinating national economic and budgetary policies. States' macroeconomic measures must be consistent with the objectives and budgetary rules defined at the European level.

As a final point of this evolution, the Fiscal Compact was signed in 2012 to ensure better budgetary surveillance and coordination within the EU.[37] Although its budgetary part is relatively short and its legal contribution rather limited insofar as most of its provisions were already contained in the Six Pack and the Two Pack, it had the symbolic function of anchoring commitment to budgetary discipline.

Parliament and of the Council on the prevention and correction of macroeconomic imbalances [2011] OJ L306/25.

[36] Regulation (EU) No 472/2013 of the European Parliament of the Council on the strengthening of economic and budgetary surveillance of Member States in the euro area experiencing or threatened with serious difficulties with respect to their financial stability [2013] OJ L140/1; Regulation (EU) No 473/2013 of the European Parliament of the Council on common provisions for monitoring and assessing draft budgetary plans and ensuring the correction of excessive deficit of the Member States in the euro area [2013] OJ L140/11.

[37] Treaty on Stability, Coordination and Governance in the Economic and Monetary Union (Brussels, 2 March 2012).

Among the Treaty's contentious innovations, the first is the obligation for states to enshrine compliance with the SGP provisions in their national laws (if possible, at a constitutional level). This 'golden rule', a real brake on indebtedness,[38] stipulates public administrations' budgetary situations must be in balance or in surplus.[39] Second, the monitoring mechanisms, already tightened in the Six Pack, are further strengthened in the SGP. Sanctions are triggered on the Commission's recommendation, unless the Council, acting by a qualified majority, opposes them. This procedure's generalisation is supposed to confer on sanctions a degree of automaticity.

This is precisely what has triggered a major wave of protest.

2. Challenging European Budgetary Governance

Paradoxically, this depoliticisation process of budgetary rules has given rise to a wave of political protests, particularly in France (section 2.1). In recent years, it has been followed by a debate that opens the way towards taking into account not only budgetary but also political and social issues (section 2.2).

2.1. The Political Challenge to the Process of Budgetary Tightening

2.1.1. The Terms of the Challenge

There are countless analyses produced both in academic circles and in public debate that question the process of strengthening the European budgetary constraint. Following the financial crisis, a number of so-called budgetary austerity measures were passed, provoking a feeling of rejection of the entire European project on the part of some citizens. The economic reforms introduced may have had negative economic effects on growth and may have been perceived as a direct consequence of European budgetary surveillance.

The terms of the debate have often been ideologised insofar as some of the new fiscal governance key features have been used to support a demonstration of the EMU's allegedly ordoliberal character.[40] In Germany as well as in France, this

[38] Olivier Clerc and Pascal Kauffmann, *L'Union économique et monétaire européenne* (Paris, Editions Pedone, 2016) 202.

[39] This rule is considered to be respected if the structural deficit of a state does not exceed 0.5% of GDP, or 1% for states with a debt level of less than 60%. In addition, states must pursue a specific medium-term objective defined in terms of structural balance.

[40] On this renewed interest in ordoliberalism in the context of the euro crisis, see Josef Hien and Christian Joerges, 'Dead Man Walking: Current European Interest in the Ordoliberal Tradition' (2018) EUI Working Paper LAW 2018/03 http://cadmus.eui.eu/bitstream/handle/1814/51226/LAW_2018_03.

demonstration has led to critical academic positions against the authoritarian slide of European economic and financial governance.[41] Worse, in France, this ideologisation has led to extremely aggressive positions against Germany, which was suspected, particularly at the time of the Greek debt crisis, of imposing its rigorous economic views on all its European partners at the expense of democratic choice.[42]

It is worth noting that this vehement criticism of the European budgetary framework focuses precisely on the constituent elements of what we have called the depoliticisation process of budgetary rules. Some authors have questioned the budgetary constitutionalisation phenomenon reinforced by the TSCG: the ordoliberal doctrine was said to have been 'engraved in the marble of the treaties'.[43] The strengthening of the budgetary constraint has led to the claim that the European Union is a genuine 'iron cage'.[44] The Union was said to have confiscated states' political choice by imposing on them the pursuit of a single financial objective.[45]

The distancing of political bodies has also been decried. We are witnessing a new form of governance by numbers,[46] steered by technocratic authorities, devoid of any political legitimacy. The crisis in the eurozone was said to have radicalised budgetary discipline and accelerated what some authors have called 'tutelary federalism':[47] by submitting to budgetary rules tutelage, exercised in the form of automatic steering, states were said to have de facto relinquished the exercise of their powers in economic matters and lost the sovereignty they had wished to preserve at the time of the Maastricht Treaty.

pdf; Josef Hien and Christian Joerges (eds), *Ordoliberalism, Law and the Rule of Economics* (Oxford, Hart Publishing, 2017).

[41] Further to the reference mentioned above (*cf* n 12): Ulrich Beck, *Das deutsche Europa: Neue Machtlandschaften im Zeichen der Krise* (Berlin, Suhrkamp Verlag, 2012); Grégoire Chamayou, *La société ingouvernable: Une généalogie du libéralisme autoritaire* (Paris, La Fabrique, 2018); Nicolas Guillet, 'Les finances publiques contemporaines: surveiller et punir? De la norme démocratique à la norme disciplinaire' in Jacqueline Guittard, Émeric Nicolas and Cyril Sintez (eds), *Foucault face à la norme* (Paris, Mare et Martin, 2020) 87–106, the author advances that the state is put 'under market surveillance' by European budget discipline rules.

[42] Jean-Christophe Cambadélis, 'Lettre ouverte à un ami allemand' (*EURACTIV*, 16 July 2015) www.euractiv.fr/section/politique/opinion/lettre-ouverte-a-un-ami-allemand; Dominique Strauss-Kahn, 'Lettre ouverte à mes amis allemands' (*Huffington Post*, 18 July 2015) www.huffingtonpost.fr/actualites/article/dsk-partage-ses-pensees-sur-la-grece-dans-une-lettre-ouverte-a-ses-amis-allemands_59003.html.

[43] Frédéric Lordon, *La malfaçon: Monnaie européenne et souveraineté démocratique* (Arles, Actes Sud, 2015).

[44] Pierre Dardot and Christian Laval, *Ce cauchemar qui n'en finit pas: Comment le néolibéralisme défait la démocratie* (Paris, La Découverte, 2016).

[45] Robert Salais, *Le viol d'Europe: Enquête sur la disparition d'une idée* (Paris, PUF, 2013).

[46] Alain Supiot, *La gouvernance par les nombres: Cours au collège de France (2012-2014)* (Paris, Fayard, 2015).

[47] Michel Dévoluy, 'L'ordolibéralisme et la construction européenne' (2016) 3 *Revue Internationale et Stratégique* 26.

2.1.2. *The Reasons for the Dispute*

Strikingly, the handling of the Greek debt crisis gave rise to radically divergent controversies on both sides of the Rhine. This is not to say that challenges to budgetary discipline have not occurred in Germany, as has been indicated. Rather, the focus was more on the departures from the legal framework.[48] Creating the European Stability Mechanism (ESM), in exchange for which the TSCG was signed, was seen by some as a violation of the prohibition in Article 125 TFEU.[49] The unconventional measures taken by the ECB in return for abiding by specific budgetary guarantees were deemed to violate the prohibition of the non-bailout clause and public debts monetarisation. While German doctrine perceived these developments as a possible 'crisis of law',[50] French doctrine seemed reassured by these mechanisms, which can be analysed as intervention decisions – both financial and monetary.

These divergences can no doubt be attributed to traditional differences between these two countries: the weight of German *Ordnungspolitik*, ie great attachment to a policy subject to rules in Germany, versus a long tradition of economic interventionism in France.[51] There is, undoubtedly, more reluctance in France to accept that parliament, and especially the government in economic matters, should be limited as regards the exercise of their sovereign choices.

For whatever reasons, this protest movement, which has become polarised around the European budgetary framework, is akin to a process of budgetary issues politicisation. Fuelled by the Covid-19 crisis, this movement has generated, in a surprising reversal of fortune, a form of budgetary rules politicisation.

2.2. The Politicisation of the Debate

The second feature of the re-politicisation of budgetary rules lies in the current debate characteristics. This debate has not only intensified in recent years, but has also been broadly renewed to include imperatives that are less technical than political in nature.

[48] Matthias Ruffert, 'Mehr Europa – eine rechtswissenschaftliche Perspektive' (2013) *Zeitschrift für Gesetzgebung* 1, 5.

[49] Martin Seidel, 'Europäische Währungsunion und rule of law' (2012) ZEI Working Paper B05 2012 www.zei.uni-bonn.de/de/publikationen/medien/working-paper/wp2012_b05.pdf.

[50] Christian Callies, 'Nach der Krise ist vor der Krise: Integrationsstand und Reformperspektiven der Europäischen Union' in Jürgen Bröhmer (ed), *Europa und die Welt: Kolloquium zu aktuellen europa-, völker- und menschenrechtlichen Themen aus Anlass des 80. Geburtstages von Prof. Dr. Dr. h.c. mult. Georg Ress* (Baden-Baden, Nomos, 2016) 73–97.

[51] On this approach, see Kalflèche, Perroud and Ruffert, *L'avenir de l'Union économique et monétaire* 9.

2.2.1. *The Diversity of Proposals*

While initially European budgetary rules may have seemed immune to any discussion given their functional nature, as described above (they are designed as a tool for monetary union functioning), they have been criticised and proposals for reform have been made in very different ways since the end of the 2010s, particularly in the wake of the Covid-19 crisis. In general, there is a form of polarisation in the debate that makes it difficult to reach a consensus, at all levels. At a political level, this growing polarisation and fragmentation can be observed both within and between countries. While France – although it does not comply with the rules – and Italy as well are arguing for more flexibility,[52] other countries, such as the Netherlands and Germany, are calling for greater rigour.

At an academic level, the political divide is coupled with a debate fuelled by a wide variety of proposals from economists, beyond the shared observation that rules need streamlining. Among these proposals, Olivier Blanchard's suggestion has received much attention and deserves to be presented here.[53] Blanchard starts from the premise that the initial budgetary rules were economically unsatisfactory: the debt and deficit criteria could be easily met in prosperous economic times but, in contrast, could prove harmful in times of economic recession. Blanchard also notes that these initial rules were gradually made more complex, as a result of the reforms mentioned above: new criteria were added and flexibility clauses introduced. These rules have remained economically irrelevant and have been repeatedly breached, but these violations have never led to sanctions. Given these observations, Blanchard proposes replacing the current budgetary criteria (rules) with more general standards (principles) in order to obtain some flexibility in the determination of public finance objectives. The point is to examine each national situation to determine whether the debt is sustainable, which would not depend on debt and deficit criteria but on economic and political factors requiring specific analysis.

For all this, Blanchard's proposal does not lead to a more political governance of these budgetary 'principles' because the objectives would be set by independent institutions for each eurozone country. Therefore, the flexibility gained at the stage of defining the budgetary objectives assigned to states would be offset by strengthening the procedure for monitoring their enforcement. On the one hand, the Commission would be responsible for making recommendations to states, notably

[52] Emmanuel Macron and Mario Draghi, 'Op-ed by President Emmanuel Macron and Prime Minister Mario Draghi on EU Macroeconomic and Fiscal Strategy' (*Élysée*, 23 December 2021) www.elysee.fr/en/emmanuel-macron/2021/12/23/op-ed-by-president-emmanuel-macron-and-prime-minister-mario-draghi-on-eu-macroeconomic-and-fiscal-strategy.

[53] Olivier Blanchard, Alvaro Leandro and Jeromin Zettelmeyer, 'Redesigning EU fiscal rules: From rules to standards' (2021) Peterson Institute for International Economics Working Papers 21-1 www.piie.com/sites/default/files/documents/wp21-1.pdf.

concerning their primary balance trajectory, and these recommendations would no longer be subject to a decision by the Council of the Union. In the event that a state does not comply with the changes requested by the Commission, the latter could prevent the adoption of a budget. On the other hand, if the Commission's recommendation is opposed, the state concerned would have to appeal to the Court of Justice (through the creation of a specialised chamber capable of rendering a decision quickly) or to the European Budget Committee, whose decisions would be binding for the state concerned.

Other proposals consist in keeping only the 60 per cent debt ratio to the detriment of other existing procedural rules (MTO, flexibility clauses, etc). Therefore, the only operational rule would be an expenditure rule implying a downward trend in debt, while allowing the deficit to fluctuate according to cyclical revenue variations.[54] Finally, some proposals are looking at alternative operational rules (expenditure rule, revenue rule and balanced budget rules) linked to the debt anchoring to make enforcement and sanctions more automatic and less political.

2.2.2. The Debate's Political Reorientation

Beyond the technical modalities for revising budgetary rules, some proposals reflect a desire to rethink these rules' political scope in depth. The price stability and financial sustainability imperatives are sometimes relegated to the background. Many authors suggest European budgetary rules should be more protective of public investment, rather than focusing exclusively on debt-level issues.

This was the core of one of the proposals that was paid a lot of attention in the public debate. The authors of the manifesto for the democratisation of Europe,[55] which will be discussed below, renewed their proposal in the context of the Covid-19 crisis. They presented a reform of the SGP to notably increase public investment[56] thereby proposing a new kind of golden rule that would exclude investments from public deficit ratios. This proposal, which could have been viewed as quite radical before 2020, has gained credibility since the social changes brought about by the pandemic.

As has already been noted, the pandemic has raised new political and societal challenges. After the Covid-19 crisis, the European Union committed itself to an unprecedented form of fiscal support for national economies. The economic

[54] Zsolt Darvas, Grégory Claeys and Alvaro Leandro, 'A proposal to revive the European Fiscal Framework' (2016) *Bruegel Policy Contribution* Issue 2016/07; Agnès Bénassy-Quéré et al, 'Reconciling risk sharing with market discipline: A constructive approach to euro area reform' (2018) *CEPR Policy Insight* no 91; Zsolt Darvas, Philippe Martin and Xavier Ragot, 'European fiscal rules require a major overhaul' (2018) *Les notes du Conseil d'analyse économique* no 47; European Fiscal Board, 'Assessment of EU fiscal rules with a focus on the six and two-pack legislation' (11 September 2019).

[55] Stéphanie Hennette-Vauchez et al, *How to Democratize Europe* (Cambridge, MA, Harvard University Press, 2019).

[56] Manon Bouju et al, 'Face à la crise, construire l'Europe d'après le " consensus de Maastricht"' (*Le Grand Continent*, 18 December 2020) https://legrandcontinent.eu/fr/2020/12/18/construire-leurope-dapres.

rebound from the health crisis exposed the weaknesses of the energy supply system, which was further compounded by the war in Ukraine and the closure of the Nord Stream gas pipeline. This has led to heightened awareness towards these new challenges and the need for massive public investment by states.

In this context, the idea of a 'green' golden rule that excludes net 'green' public investment from the deficit and debt calculations has found a degree of support. This is, for example, the solution proposed by Zsolt Darvas and Guntram Wolff[57] which encourages governments to cut current expenditures rather than capital expenditures. Discussions thus show that the debate on European budgetary rules has changed in nature. The priority objective is no longer necessarily debt sustainability, which used to be the objective traditionally associated with budget rules. This objective has shifted to extra-budgetary considerations, more broadly integrating environmental concerns. Yet, these proposals entail formidable political arbitrage, if only to define which investments can be qualified as 'green'.

European authorities' margin of discretion would be further reinforced, which amounts precisely to a form of budgetary rules re-politicisation, whose features can already be observed in the case of the European Commission.

3. Towards a Politicisation of the European Commission's Role in European Budgetary Governance?

Sometimes presented as an independent body, the European Commission is above all a political institution. As such, it is capable of placing its budgetary surveillance function within the framework of a more general action integrating the Union's major political priorities (section 3.1), which does not fail to raise questions about the institutional arrangements for exercising budgetary governance (section 3.2).

3.1. The European Commission's Increasingly Political Budgetary Surveillance

3.1.1. The European Commission's Discretion Margin

The depoliticisation process highlighted above has, on the surface, been achieved through the rigidifying political bodies' decision-making power: the reverse voting procedure was intended to make it easier for the Council to comply with the Commission's recommendations. Now, the analysis needs refining with regard

[57] Zsolt Darvas and Guntram Wolff, 'A green fiscal pact: climate investment in times of budget consolidation' (2021) *Bruegel Policy Contribution* Issue no 18/21.

to the powers vested in the Commission. Indeed, once a body has a discretion margin – even though it is legally independent – it is driven to make choices that can be described as 'political'. This is the situation the European Commission finds itself in when exercising its budgetary rules supervision function.

Far from favouring a pure and hard application of budgetary rules, the European Commission has, on the contrary, contributed to the introduction of more flexibility in the period preceding the suspension of the SGP.[58] Breaches of fiscal rules have remained frequent in the euro area. According to a study by the European Budget Committee in 2019, the average compliance rate has been at 57 per cent since the introduction of the SGP.[59] In 2020, it was found that 10 member states did not comply with the criteria, the highest number since the 2011 reforms. Although some states may have been placed under surveillance because they did not meet the SGP criteria, no sanction procedure was triggered by the Commission. Rather than initiating the sanction procedure, the Commission engaged in bilateral negotiations with the states affected by their questionable public debt and deficits levels. Pierre Moscovici, then Minister of Economy and Finance in France (between 2012 and 2014), described how he was able to negotiate deadlines with the Commission to meet the 3 per cent public deficit criterion.[60]

The reason for this is that, despite the new sanctions introduced in 2011, the Commission has retained considerable leeway in implementing the rules. While some clarifications have been brought to budgetary indicators, many concepts remain vague. This is certainly true of potential growth and structural balance indicators, which 'lead to estimates that are very political in nature'.[61] Economists have pointed out that the Commission's budget analysis is based on unobservable variables, which can account for their frequent revisions.[62]

This margin of appreciation has been fully utilised by the Commission. Once appointed European Commissioner for Economic and Financial Affairs in the Juncker Commission, Moscovici was very open about promoting a 'more intelligent reading of budgetary rules'.[63] This more intelligent reading was

[58] Reinout Arthur Van der Veer, 'Walking the Tightrope: Politicization and the Commission's Enforcement of the SGP' (2022) 81 concludes in the same way that 'politization has gradually pushed the Commission towards increasingly flexible enforcement of EU fiscal rules'.

[59] European Fiscal Board, 'Assessment of EU fiscal rules with a focus on the six and two-pack legislation' 31.

[60] Hearing of Pierre Moscovici, reported in the French National Assembly's Information Report no 4990 presented by Caroline Janvier, 17 www.assemblee-nationale.fr/dyn/15/rapports/due/l15b4990_rapport-information.

[61] French National Assembly's Information Report no 4990, 23 www.assemblee-nationale.fr/dyn/15/rapports/due/l15b4990_rapport-information.

[62] Zsolt Darvas, Philippe Martin and Xavier Ragot, 'European fiscal rules require a major overhaul' (2018) *Les notes du Conseil d'analyse économique* no 47, quoted by Hamza Bennani et Baptiste Savatier, 'Le cadre budgétaire européen, son architecture institutionnelle et son évolution dans le temps' (2021) *Conseil d'analyse économique* no 056–2021, 6.

[63] Frédéric Mérand, *Un sociologue à la Commission européenne* (Paris, Presses de Sciences Po, 2021) 166.

very quickly translated into the adoption of a communication introducing more flexibility in the implementation of the SGP's preventive component on 13 January 2015.[64] The objective was to take into account the economic cycle fluctuations and to allow the states room for manoeuvre in implementing structural reforms and investments. A temporary deviation from the MTO, or from the path towards it, is allowed, so long as the proposed structural reforms or investments have a positive short-term fiscal impact and increase potential growth. In 2017, the Commission expressly recognised the exercise of 'some discretion when examining deviations from the budgetary adjustments implied by the matrix'.[65]

This 'more intelligent reading' of budgetary rules can be seen as a political reading of these rules. For the European Commissioner it has meant examining the political factors supposed to determine the conduct of each state's economic policy, as some fieldwork has shown.[66] In contrast to a mechanical budgetary rule implementation, the Commission's examination is shifting from the assessment of purely budgetary data to the relevance of more general economic measures. This way, Spain and Portugal – two countries likely to be sanctioned for their excessive deficits between 2015 and 2019 – have not been subject to any proposal for financial sanctions by the European Commission. It has been said that the Commission is nothing more than a 'dog without teeth'.[67]

Flexibility in fiscal rules' implementation has not failed to be reviled, particularly in Germany. For its part, the European Budget Committee denounced the bilateral nature of implementing rules, which resulted in opacity and less peer pressure.[68] Finally, in 2021, the Commission acknowledged that 'while elements of flexibility and discretion have been built into the current budgetary framework through a complex set of interpretative provisions, there is a need for transparency in the exercise of economic judgment within a rules-based framework'.[69] Despite its stated intention to place fiscal governance in a 'rules-based framework', the European Commission is nevertheless exercising a political role, which is manifested today in the reorientation of the objectives assigned to fiscal rules.

[64] Commission, 'Communication from the Commission to the European Parliament, the Council, the European Central Bank, the European Economic and Social Committee, the Committee of the Regions and the European Investment Bank on the review of the flexibility under the Stability and Growth Pact' COM (2018) 335 final.

[65] Commission, 'Communication from the Commission, 2017 Draft Budgetary Plans: Overall Assessment' COM (2016) 730 final.

[66] Frédéric Mérand, *Un sociologue à la Commission européenne* 166.

[67] Mihajlo Babin, Iva Ivanov and Milos Eric, 'The long-lasting post-covid symptom: the case for the EU fiscal rules reform?' (2022) 13 *Pravni Zapisi* 76, 85.

[68] European Fiscal Board, 'Assessment of EU fiscal rules with a focus on the six and two-pack legislation' 31.

[69] Commission, 'Communication from the Commission to the European Parliament, the Council, the European Central Bank, the European Economic and Social Committee, the Committee of the Regions, The EU economy after COVID-19: implications for economic governance' COM (2021) 662 final.

3.1.2. The European Commission's Reorientation of Budgetary Rules Purposes

Finally, it is time to examine the Commission's latest orientations, as developed in its Communication of 9 November 2022.[70] This text led to a package of proposals to replace the preventive[71] and corrective[72] arms of the SGP in order to move to a risk-based common EU surveillance framework. In the face of the diversity of suggestions made – sometimes in contradictory directions as mentioned above, and following the positions expressed in the public consultation launched by the Commission – these proposals seek a form of compromise. Following the SGP's temporary suspension, they attempt to return to a simplified and more operational supervisory framework. The Commission proposes to remain within the current reference values framework, namely the 60 per cent debt and 3 per cent deficit ceilings. In line with the original paradigm, the public debt sustainability imperative must remain the Commission's priority. It is 'the starting point for EU fiscal surveillance'.[73] So, it is not exactly a case of relaxing budgetary constraints on states, but rather of paying more attention to each state's specific situation. The national medium-term fiscal-structural plans would be the proposed revised framework's cornerstone, thereby allowing for differentiating between member states by taking into account their public debt challenges. Rather than requiring states to make similar adjustment efforts, more account would be taken of their respective debt levels, which can vary considerably from one state to another. While maintaining the requirement of public deficits below 3 per cent, the Commission would adapt debt indicators to states' respective budgetary situations. The Commission thus proposes abandoning the 1/20th reduction rule – 'which imposed a too demanding fiscal effort'[74] – in favour of a focus on departures from the net expenditure path. The Commission should put forward a trajectory for net expenditure ensuring that 'the public debt ratio is put or remains on a plausibly downward path, or stays at prudent levels'[75] while the public deficit is kept below 3 per cent over the medium term. Lastly, the Commission proposes to strengthen the enforcement of the rules relatively to the current framework. The procedure for breaching the 60 per cent criterion would focus on departures from

[70] Commission, 'Communication on orientations for a reform of the EU economic governance framework' COM (2022) 583 final.

[71] Commission, 'Proposal for a Regulation of the European Parliament and the Council on the effective coordination of economic policies and multilateral budgetary surveillance and repealing Council Regulation (EC) No 1466/97' COM(2023) 240 final.

[72] Commission, 'Proposal for a Council Regulation amending Regulation (EC) No 1467/97 on speeding up and clarifying the implementation of the excessive deficit procedure' COM(2023) 241 final.

[73] Commission, 'Communication on orientations for a reform of the EU economic governance framework' COM (2022) 583 final, 7.

[74] Commission, 'Proposal for a Regulation of the European Parliament and the Council on the effective coordination of economic policies and multilateral budgetary surveillance and repealing Council Regulation (EC) No 1466/97' COM(2023) 240 final, 3.

[75] ibid, Article 6.

the fiscal path set by the Council.[76] In case of an excessive deficit, the Council would require that the state implements a corrective net expenditure path corresponding to a minimal annual adjustment of at least 0.5% of GDP.[77]

Meanwhile, the Commission seems to be taking a more 'permissive' approach to public finances,[78] linked to the desire to preserve a number of non-exclusively fiscal imperatives. These imperatives are explicitly mentioned as 'common priorities of the Union' in the Annex VI of the proposal of the Commission.[79] While focusing on the debt sustainability objective, governments would be required to spell out the necessary reforms and investments responding to these main priorities. The commitments of the states to such reforms and investments could allow them to benefit from an additional adjustment period of up to three years.[80] As the Commission has already stated: 'Improving the quality of public finances and protecting public investment should be central elements of medium-term fiscal-structural plans, in light of the essential role of public investment and reforms in enhancing potential growth and addressing major systemic challenges such as the green and digital transitions'.[81] This new emphasis on investment is linked to the current political context. Here, the European Commission draws lessons from the Covid-19 crisis, which resulted in a significant increase in public- and private-sector debt ratios. 'The green and digital transitions, the need to ensure energy security, as well as social and economic resilience, and to build up defence capabilities will require sustained high levels of investment in the years to come.'[82] The Commission has underlined the need for 'higher public investment, backed by a good composition and quality of public finances'.[83] As indicated above, determining whether states' public finances are of good quality and composition implies a degree of appreciation margin for the European Commission. This requires determining whether states are indeed making the investments considered relevant.

[76] Commission, 'Proposal for a Council Regulation amending Regulation (EC) No 1467/97 on speeding up and clarifying the implementation of the excessive deficit procedure' COM(2023) 241 final, (10).

[77] ibid, Article 3.

[78] The Commission concludes that '[t]he necessary financing for the just transition … call[s] for fiscal rules that *allow* for strategic investment, while safeguarding fiscal sustainability' (emphasis added) in its Communication on orientations for a reform of the EU economic governance framework' COM (2022) 583 final, 20; and that 'the reformed framework should help *build* the green, digital and resilient European economy of the future' in its Proposal for a Regulation of the European Parliament and the Council on the effective coordination of economic policies and multilateral budgetary surveillance and repealing Council Regulation (EC) No 1466/97' COM(2023) 240 final, 2 (emphasis added).

[79] Commission, 'Proposal for a Regulation of the European Parliament and the Council on the effective coordination of economic policies and multilateral budgetary surveillance and repealing Council Regulation (EC) No 1466/97' COM(2023) 240 final, Annex VI.

[80] ibid, Article 13.

[81] Commission, 'Communication on orientations for a reform of the EU economic governance framework' COM (2022) 583 final, 8.

[82] ibid 4.

[83] ibid.

This shows the Commission's desire to link European budgetary surveillance directly to European issues of a strictly political nature. Ultimately, it is the European Union's political priorities that would determine national budget plans' relevance. I believe this illustrates a form of budgetary rules politicisation, insofar as budgetary surveillance would be exercised in light of objectives of a political nature. Such a process necessarily brings into question the framework for exercising the political choices underpinning fiscal governance.

3.2. Which Institutional Arrangements for Legitimate Fiscal Governance of the European Union?

3.2.1. Proposals for Parliamentarising the Eurozone

Different goals are now guiding the implementation of the EU fiscal rules. The sustainability of government debt was the principal objective intended for fiscal rules with the Maastricht Treaty. It has since then been completed by the goal of financial stability during the euro crisis. And now the green transition and climate protection are becoming a new objective. This diversity of the end purposes shows that the European fiscal framework cannot be disconnected from the political project of the EU as a whole. Fiscal rules are part of the EU's economic policy.

Indeed, Article 120 TFEU foresees: 'Member States shall conduct their economic policies with a view to contributing to the achievement of the objectives of the Union, as defined in Article 3 of the Treaty on European Union, and in the context of the broad guidelines referred to in Article 121(2).' And we know how broadly the objectives of the EU are defined in Article 3 of the Treaty on European Union (TEU), including for example sustainable development based on balanced economic growth and price stability, social market economy, full employment and social progress, improvement of the quality of the environment, and so on.

This plurality of goals raises the question of knowing which authority is legitimate to arbitrate between these different objectives.

When the goal is clear and can be objectively assessed, with numerical instruments, the rules-based system can devote the implementation of the fiscal rules to an independent authority. But this is more difficult in an environment where political issues have to be taken into account.

This is why a number of proposals have been made to democratise the functioning of EMU. In general, the French doctrine remains very attached to the idea of giving more powers to the European Parliament in order to reinforce EMU's democratic legitimacy.[84] In their famous proposal mentioned above,[85]

[84] Frédéric Allemand and Francesco Martucci, 'The Democratic Legitimacy of European Economic Governance: Change in the Role of Parliament' (2014) 134 *Revue de l'OFCE* 112.

[85] Hennette-Vauchez et al, *How to Democratize Europe*.

Stéphanie Hennette-Vauchez, Thomas Piketty, Guillaume Sacriste and Antoine Vauchez suggest creating a budget for democratisation which would be debated in and voted for by a sovereign European Assembly. The Democratisation Treaty anticipated that 80 per cent of the members of this Assembly should come from the national parliaments of the member states and that 20 per cent of its members should come from the European Parliament. The principal virtue of this proposition is to make new opportunities to deliberate in a democratic framework about questions that are currently debated by the Eurogroup in informal circles. But the need to create new institutions for this purpose can be questioned.

3.2.2. Conclusion: Which Space for Discussion in a Multi-Level Governance?

The fiscal budgetary framework must be rethought in a multi-level system of governance.

If we stick to the Commission communication presented above, it seems essential to distinguish between two decision-making levels.

The first one relates to the definition of the main political priorities that should guide budgetary rules implementation. As has been said, these priorities would be part of the European Union's common framework, as is already the case, in a way, with the European Semester. At this level, budgetary governance is not a matter that derogates from the functioning of the European Union. The European Commission itself is an increasingly politicised institution. Since Jean-Claude Juncker and also with von der Leyen, this institution establishes clear priorities for its term in office.[86] Von der Leyen set six priorities 2019–24 and these objectives are purposed to guide the European Commission's action. Climate and digital transitions are the core of NextGenerationEU and there is no reason that these two priorities will not be reflected in the future implementation of the European fiscal rules. Undoubtedly, these major priorities could be further debated, but this would imply strengthening the Union's parliamentary system: it is therefore a general issue that concerns the European Union's political functioning – not specifically European fiscal governance.

The second level concerns budgetary choices, ie the concrete measures to be implemented in order to abide by the European budgetary rules and the criteria defined at the European level. This decision-making level pertains to states' responsibility. In its Communication, the Commission particularly insists on this point, since by making medium-term budgetary plans – the new budgetary governance essential tool – it seeks to enhance member states' weight when designing their national budgetary trajectories. It would be up to national

[86] Robert Stüwe and Thomas Panayotopoulos (eds), *The Juncker Commission: Politizing EU Policies* (Baden-Baden, Nomos, 2020) 19: Juncker expressed the desire to establish a 'political commission' at the start of his mandate.

governments to commit themselves to a series of reforms and investments likely to bring their debt levels back onto a sustainable path. These trajectories would be discussed with the European Commission and adopted by the Council. This is why the Commission calls for 'a greater debate at national level and thus a higher degree of political buy-in and ownership of the medium-term plan'.[87]

It is probably somewhat ironical for some countries such as France to denounce the lack of parliamentarisation of economic and budgetary choices at the European level while, at the national level, parliamentary control over these choices remains relatively weak. In order for European fiscal governance to enjoy greater political legitimacy, adjustments should therefore be made at the national level. This means, on the one hand, increasing transparency on the reforms and investments proposed by member states in their budgetary plans and on the annual progress reports sent to the Commission. On the other hand, it requires the emergence of higher standards of national parliamentary scrutiny for the preparation of medium-term national budgetary and structural plans. If this condition were guaranteed, states' economic and social reforms could no longer be presented as constraints 'imposed by Brussels' but rather the expression of budgetary choices made by member states to achieve commonly shared objectives at the European level.

Without a doubt, the ability to develop mechanisms to make the European Union's major political priorities visible and to clarify the terms of the debate on budgetary choices for public opinion will be decisive for the future of the Union.

[87] Commission, 'Communication on orientations for a reform of the EU economic governance framework' COM (2022) 583 final, 10.

4

Covid-19, War and the End of Neoliberalism

THOMAS BIEBRICHER

1. Introduction – Neoliberalism's Nine Lives

Neoliberalism has been pronounced dead many times. Most notably, it was declared to be over in the midst of the banking crisis of 2008 that sparked the Great Recession and, in the European context, morphed into the eurozone crisis that kept most of the continent on its toes for the better part of the 2010s. Even politicians that seemed unlikely acquaintances with the very term 'neoliberalism' now distanced themselves from it, typically assimilating it to the world of finance and scandalising its presumed essence, ie the doctrine of a self-regulating market. From then Australian Prime Minister Kevin Rudd to then French President Nicolas Sarkozy, they all condemned neoliberal deregulation as the bane of today's economic world and vowed to move beyond it:

> The time has come to proclaim that the great neo-liberal experiment of the last 30 years has failed, that the emperor has no clothes. Neo-liberalism and the free-market fundamentalism it has produced, has been revealed to be little more than personal greed dressed up as an economic philosophy.[1]

In fact, even more considerate voices from the social sciences expressed their hope that the fiasco of the Great Recession might persuade political as well as economic actors to review the interplay of markets and political structures in order to consider alternatives to the status quo.[2]

It was only a few years later that commentators concluded that this hope had turned out to be futile.[3] Little had happened to recalibrate the political economy

[1] Kevin Rudd, 'The Global Financial Crisis' (*The Monthly*, 1 February 2009) www.themonthly.com.au/issue/2009/february/1319602475/kevin-rudd/global-financial-crisis#mtr.

[2] Joseph E Stiglitz, 'The End of Neo-liberalism?' (*Project Syndicate*, 7 July 2008) www.project-syndicate.org/commentary/the-end-of-neo-liberalism?barrier=true. 2008.

[3] Philip Mirowski, *Never Let a Serious Crisis go to Waste: How Neoliberalism survived the financial Meltdown* (London, Verso Books, 2013).

of the Organisation for Economic Co-operation and Development (OECD) world and while neoliberalism seemed to be intellectually bankrupt, it still lingered on, prompting some to speak of a zombie neoliberalism that continued to haunt the world.[4] Moreover, the eurozone crisis ushered in a regime of neoliberal austerity to be monitored and enforced through tightened economic governance structures.[5]

The second wave of obituaries appeared in the wake of what might be called the Great Regression in the wake of the election of Donald Trump in the United States and the successful Brexit referendum in the United Kingdom. The thesis that enjoyed wide approval on both sides of the Atlantic was that all the nefarious aspects of the rise of so-called right-wing populism aside, it was also going to bring down a neoliberal regime that relied on free trade and multilateralism, and was part and parcel of globalising processes that were the expressed target of those populist forces.[6] In some accounts, there was an added irony to this constellation because the rise of populism was in large part attributable to the continued hegemony of neoliberalism. The latter, thus, could be considered to have created its own gravediggers.[7] But these potential gravediggers had other things to do besides burying neoliberalism. To be sure, they were deeply averse to political liberalism, took issue with some aspects of multilateral trade regimes and were even prone to resorting to protectionist policies as in the case of the United States. Still, there was no sign of an outright departure from most other aspects of what is widely considered to be a typical neoliberal policy profile. The tax cuts delivered by the Trump administration were classical supply-side trickle-down economics in the tradition of Reaganomics, and even while they raged against Brussels, populist parties in Italy not only eventually gave in to the budgetary demands of the European Commission, they also (in the case of La Lega) pursued the project of a flat tax – a pet peeve of many in the neoliberal world, most prominently Milton Friedman.[8]

What we can conclude from this is that the verdict of an end to neoliberalism is not to be taken at face value but instead should be probed and investigated, which is what this chapter aims to do with respect to the latest rounds of neoliberal obituaries. They started to appear in the wake of the Covid-19 crisis and the resulting temporary breakdown of supply chains but also the precariousness

[4] Jamie Peck, 'Zombie Neoliberalism and the Ambidextrous State' (2010) 14 *Theoretical Criminology* 104.

[5] Mark Blyth, *Austerity: The History of a dangerous Idea* (Oxford, Oxford University Press, 2013).

[6] Cornel West, 'Goodbye, American neoliberalism. A new era is here' *The Guardian* (London, 17 November 2016) www.theguardian.com/commentisfree/2016/nov/17/american-neoliberalism-cornel-west-2016-election; Martin Jacques, 'The Death of Neoliberalism and the Crisis of Western Politics' *The Guardian* (London, 21 August 2016) www.theguardian.com/commentisfree/2016/aug/21/death-of-neoliberalism-crisis-in-western-politics.

[7] Chantal Mouffe, *The Return of the Political* (London, Verso Books, 2006).

[8] Thomas Biebricher, 'Neoliberalism and Authoritarianism' (2020) 1 *Global Perspectives* 11872, https://online.ucpress.edu/gp/article-abstract/1/1/11872/106236/Neoliberalism-and-Authoritarianism?redirectedFrom=fulltext.

of public services and the very shocking living conditions of significant parts of the population that were revealed during and also in between lockdowns – and one of them even came from the host of the World Economic Forum in Davos.[9] This was only intensified by the onset of the Ukraine war, which exacerbated the supply chain problems of global trade and not only gave rise to renewed calls for a re-nationalisation of certain strategically important parts of production (from computer chips to medicine) but also created an energy crisis of such dramatic proportions that, at the point of writing, even price caps feature among the weapons of choice to combat the energy shortage in combination with historically high inflation rates.

Here, I can only focus on some aspects of this constellation related to the Covid-19 crisis management of the European Union and, in particular, the NextGenerationEU fund (NGEU), in order to assess whether it may indeed signify a departure from neoliberal austerity. The chapter proceeds in three steps. Its obvious and unavoidable starting point is a conceptualisation of neoliberalism, which I derive from a historical-theoretical account that views it as problematic pertaining to the interaction of political and economic spheres, placing particular emphasis on the political infrastructure required for functioning markets. In a second step I will try to show that the economic governing structures of the European Union and the eurozone indeed provide some of these preconditions – at least to a certain degree – as they were formulated by neoliberal thinkers in their reflections on supranational federations. The final step then proceeds to assess whether and to what extent the introduction of NGEU can be considered to signify a departure from this structural set up with its neoliberal inflection. In the conclusion, I will recapitulate the findings and also explore how the Ukraine war figures in the context of NGEU and neoliberalism in Europe more generally.

2. Neoliberalism as a Problematic

As mentioned before, the curtain calls for neoliberalism over the last 15 years were mostly based upon a more or less explicitly stated assumption, namely that the essence of neoliberalism was an unwavering belief in the miraculous self-regulation of markets. For political actors this was not entirely inconvenient because it turned neoliberalism into a dogmatic and irrational belief system that was easy to vilify together with its presumed proponents, and it came with the added advantage that it moved the bar of reform as low as it could be. After all, if neoliberalism amounted to utterly self-regulating markets then even the slightest degree of state regulation qualified as a departure from it and decision makers, at least in appearance, could easily deliver on their promise to leave neoliberalism

[9] Klaus Schwab, 'Der Neoliberalismus hat ausgedient' *Die Zeit online* (21 September 2020) www.zeit.de/wirtschaft/2020-09/corona-kapitalismus-rezession-wef-neoliberalismus-klaus-schwab.

behind and make capitalism ethical again. To be sure, it was not just politicians who subscribed to such an understanding of neoliberalism and not exclusively due to strategic considerations. Any number of academic critics of neoliberalism were suggesting similar views, according to which neoliberalism was indeed the faulty creed of self-regulating markets that gave rise to the power of predatory corporations and bolstered attempts by economic elites to restore their income streams.[10] However, such a view of neoliberalism has not gone unchallenged, and as I will show in the following, there are good reasons to reconsider the notion of neoliberalism being synonymous with self-regulating markets, which turns out to be at least misleading if not false.[11]

In order to clarify the meaning of the term neoliberalism and the intellectual and political project attached to it, one promising starting point is to reconstruct the conditions of its emergence.[12] Still, while we tend to associate neoliberalism with Reaganomics and Thatcherism it was not in the 1970s and 1980s that it was born. It was conceived much earlier in the interwar years with its 'official birth' dating back to the so-called Walter Lippmann Colloquium that took place in Paris in August 1938 – at least it is in the records of that meeting that the term is mentioned for the first time as a label for the project the participants inaugurated during those August days.

This project can be reconstructed with view to the discussions taking place at the Colloquium[13] but also with reference to work that had been done before in various places. Neoliberalism was never one monolithic tradition and, before it was officially called into being at the Colloquium, scholars had been working in various places from Freiburg to Paris and from London to Chicago on various aspects of what was to become the neoliberal agenda broadly speaking. The pretext for the Colloquium was the publication of *The Good Society* by the American journalist and public intellectual Walter Lippmann the year before, which sparked the interest of both Friedrich August Hayek and Wilhelm Röpke, to name but two of the more prominent participants of the Colloquium.[14] They came up with the idea of bringing together academics committed to the embattled ideals of liberalism, and eventually the French philosopher Louis Rougier acted as the convener of the Colloque in Paris. Looking at the records of the meeting and also Lippmann's book, the main theme of the meeting was easy to identify: it was the crisis of liberalism and this crisis, thus, can also be seen as the overall context of the emergence of neoliberalism. Clearly, one component of the neoliberal project therefore was to rejuvenate a broadly liberal agenda in the

[10] Colin Crouch, *The Strange Non-Death of Neoliberalism* (Oxford, Oxford University Press, 2011).

[11] Bruno Amable, 'Morals and politics in the ideology of neo-liberalism' (2010) 9 *Socio-Economic Review* 3.

[12] Thomas Biebricher, *The Political Theory of Neoliberalism* (Stanford, CA, Stanford University Press, 2019).

[13] Jurgen Reinhoudt and Serge Audier, *The Walter Lippmann Colloquium: The Birth of Neo-Liberalism* (Cham, Springer/Palgrave Macmillan, 2018).

[14] Walter Lippmann, *The Good Society* (Boston, Little, Brown and Company, 1937).

midst of an era to which liberalism increasingly seemed anathema. Among the various aspects of the illiberal syndrome several stand out. There was of course the major impact of the Great Depression that had put classic economic liberals and their praise of markets on the defensive and, furthermore, had shifted social and economic responsibilities towards the state, which was most clearly on display in the New Deal legislation under the Roosevelt Administration in the United States – which had drawn Lippmann's express ire. Along with this came the slow but steady rise of 'interventionist' paradigms in economic policy making that corresponded to this marked shift in responsibilities, which had sent political actors searching for policy instruments and justificatory frameworks needed for a more robust economic and social policy. Keynesianism emerged as one of the most influential options in this regard and while the opinion on it at the Colloque was still divided, it would come to be seen as one of neoliberalism's main antagonist in the years and decades to come.[15] And, of course, there were the deeply anti-liberal forces on the rise ranging from Soviet Communism, which had been in power for a decade and showed no signs of collapsing as liberals had predicted, to European fascism and German National Socialism, all of which were united by hardly anything but their indelible enmity to liberalism. The participants of the Paris meeting included Röpke's fellow future ordoliberal Alexander Rüstow as well as liberal stalwart and Austrian School patron saint Ludwig von Mises, who represented the respective ends of the ideological spectrum present. All of the participants could easily agree on their opposition to the various forms of what they tended to call collectivism, from Communism to National Socialism, because what they were equally agreed on was the utter indispensability of a functioning price mechanism as the main allocator of resources in any political economy.[16] But this is where the more challenging part of the project began. How would liberalism be returned to a position where it could effectively challenge these new collectivist and interventionist philosophies? And as an even more vexing question: could it be that the ascent of these philosophies was not some development in complete independence of liberalism but also due to its own flawed trajectory over the past decades? Thus, the Colloquium embarked on a veritable liberal soul searching and a large majority of the participants– except for the archliberal holdout von Mises – came to share the diagnosis that, indeed, the question that was the title of the first Colloque session *Is the Decline of Liberalism Due to Endogenous Causes?* had to be answered in the affirmative. Significant strands of economic liberalism had degenerated into the simplistic maxim of laissez-faire with the corresponding demand for a minimal 'nightwatchman state' as Ferdinand Lasalle had once termed it sardonically. Such vulgar 'Manchesterim', as many participants called it, had not only ruined liberalism's reputation in the wake of the heavy toll of pauperisation and mass unemployment that capitalist economies exacted during crises – and in

[15] James Buchanan and Richard E Wagner, *Democracy in Deficit: The Political Legacy of Lord Keynes* (London, Academic Press, 1977).

[16] Reinhoudt and Audier, *The Walter Lippmann Colloquium*.

between them. It had also spelt intellectual bankruptcy for economic liberals who would throw their hands in the air amidst economic turmoil and submit exhortations to the elites and the general public that it would be best to ride out the crisis even if it hurt – which still used to be Hayek's position for the better part of the 1930s.[17] The conclusion to be drawn from this diagnosis was straightforward: in order to become an intellectual-political contender again, liberalism's renewal had to go beyond a return to the classic wisdom of Adam Smith. If it was to confront twentieth century collectivism and interventionism it had to modernise itself and this, crucially, involved a critical revision of the economic liberal agenda as it was handed down from the nineteenth century, which would also include abandoning obsolete or ill-informed notions. Laissez-faire and the minimal state were clearly at the top of the respective list.

This implies a number of important things. First, it means that contrary to conventional wisdom, the neoliberal paradigm was conceived of in direct opposition to what later came to be identified as its very essence, namely laissez-faire or the doctrine of self-regulating markets. Second, given that the option of laissez-faire with the corresponding call for a minimal state was no longer on the table, neoliberalism was bound to explore more nuanced and much more challenging approaches to understanding the workings of the economy that would put them into a position to contest the claims of collectivists and interventionists. Thus, the novel element in neoliberalism was to link the indispensable price mechanism on markets to certain sets of preconditions and, accordingly, view properly functioning markets as dependent on an infrastructure that would secure their continued existence. Third, this shift in the guiding question of its intellectual and political endeavours led to significant divergences within neoliberal thought with regard to what exactly constituted and encompassed that infrastructure and also how these preconditions of functioning markets could be brought about. Given the range of the respective positions, I suggest viewing neoliberalism as being held together only by the thin tie of a shared *problematic* regarding the preconditions of functioning markets. Finally, this meant that neoliberalism emerged as a body of thought that was not economistic as if the market existed in a vacuum but, on the contrary, highlighted the interactive effects between the economic and the political. And while there were indeed remarkably different answers to the question as to what preconditions were to be in place, all neoliberals concurred that the role of the state was of crucial importance in this regard: while it provided functions indispensable to setting up and maintaining markets it was, simultaneously, the greatest threat to the market order. It is no surprise that neoliberal thought is replete with reflections on the nature of existing statehood and designs of ideal statehood amongst which supranational statehood of a federative kind emerged as one of the more promising options.

[17] Angus Burgin, *The Great Persuasion: Reinventing Free Markets since the Depression* (Cambridge, MA, Harvard University Press, 2012).

3. Neoliberalism, Supranationalism and the European Union

Scanning the neoliberal classics on the proper role of the state, there are a number of different strands of thought that can be detected and distinguished from one another.[18] Prominently, there are those who emphasise the importance of putting the state in the position to be able to perform its desired functions and there are those who fret over the power of the state as a political monopolist that can resort to (legitimate) coercion and is thus capable of subverting and destroying market economies. Let us begin by distilling a somewhat stylised position from the first strand of thought that is based mostly on ordoliberal accounts but is echoed in many aspects in other quarters of neoliberal thought. To put it somewhat pointedly, the diagnosis of this first line of argument stated that the problem of contemporary nation states was they were mass democracies. In this way governmental policy and general and economic policy, in particular, became subject to the whims of a volatile electorate and also the power of interest groups, the combined effect of which being the inability of the state to engage in a 'rational' and market-sustaining policy to the extent that it was at odds with public sentiment or interests of particularistic actors.[19] In the ordoliberal framing this still has a highly conservative and somewhat old-fashioned ring to it but decades later, a rather similar argument would be formulated by those who merged public choice theory with neoliberalism. In their account, rational utility-maximising actors of all stripes had an incentive to demand some kind of special treatment from political actors and thus acquire 'rents'. And in a democratic setting these requests stood a good chance of being granted by politicians eager to secure or at least maximise their re-election chances.[20] Differing details aside, in both accounts it is a democratic stranglehold that prevents states from doing what they ought to and makes them stray into the realm of discretionary interventionism with all of its deleterious effects. Now, Walter Eucken, who was the spiritus rector of the ordoliberal Freiburg School, had little to offer when it came to the question of how to move beyond this deficient status quo but contended that it would have to involve the insulation of the state's will formation, decision-making and the enforcement of these decisions from the excessive influence of non-state actors and political parties.[21]

Moving to the other strand of thought identified above, among the various possibilities entertained by various neoliberals, there was one option that a significant number of them found to be promising. If the problem of the state was – at

[18] Biebricher, *The Political Theory of Neoliberalism*.

[19] Walter Eucken, 'Structural Transformations of the State and the Crisis of Capitalism' (1932) in Thomas Biebricher and Frieder Vogelmann (eds), *The Birth of Austerity: German Ordoliberalism and Contemporary Neoliberalism* (London, Rowman and Littlefield International, 2017); Werner Bonefeld, *The Strong State and the Free Economy* (London, Rowman and Littlefield International, 2017).

[20] James Buchanan, 'Public Choice: Politics without Romance' (2003) 19 *Policy* 13.

[21] Eucken, 'Structural Transformations'.

least to a significant degree – due to its power as a monopolist then one effective way of curtailing this power was to subject it to competition. Naturally, competition between states had been a given ever since the formation of nation states in early modernity. The challenge was to prevent this competition from descending into armed conflict and war and instead rein in the powers of each individual state so it would only be able to engage in desired forms of economic competition with others. The solution to this challenge was to embed nation states in supranational federations that would achieve two things simultaneously: creating not only a common political space but also an economic one. Such a federation would open up domestic economies to external competition and the same would apply to the respective nation states that would have to compete for capital but also human resources with other federation members and would be under constant threat of 'exit' from both. In such an open economic space certain options of interventionist economic policy, eg Keynesian demand management, but also certain fiscal regimes or certain worlds of welfare capitalism would become increasingly untenable – the nation state being deprived of some of its most 'dangerous' weapons in this arrangement. But what would keep supranational statehood then from developing into a nation state writ large with the same kind of interventionist and redistributive inclinations that the neoliberals observed in existing ones? Some, like Hayek put their faith in the unwillingness of populations and elites to entrust supranational entities with the competences and the resources to engage in such politics.[22] The Dutch, say, would simply not be willing to pay for the crises of the Italians – there was just not enough solidarity to go around beyond the nation state. Accordingly, the supranational level would only have to be endowed with the powers to maintain the market of jurisdictions and protect the rights of private actors across this common economic space – no harm could come from this. Others like James Buchanan had less faith in the continued lack of solidarity and sought other more reliable mechanisms that would ensure the circumscribed role of the supranational scale of statehood.[23] His solution was a specific distribution of the power to tax between the various levels of government that he summed up as 'reverse revenue sharing'.[24] While in existing nation states often the bulk of taxes is collected at the national level and then distributed to sub-state levels leaving the latter somewhat dependent upon the nation state, Buchanan proposed to reverse things in a supranational foundation, where the power to tax would be confined to the lower levels of government, ie sub-state and national level. They would act under the impact of the competition in such a common space and thus

[22] Friedrich August Hayek, *Individualism and the Economic Order* (Chicago, IL, University of Chicago Press, 1980).

[23] James Buchanan, 'Federalism As an Ideal Political Order and an Objective for Constitutional Reform' (1995) 25 *Publius* 19; James Buchanan, 'Federalism and individual Sovereignty' (1995) 15 *Cato Journal* 259.

[24] James Buchanan and Dwight R Lee, 'On a Fiscal Constitution for the European Union' (1994) 5 *Journal des Economistes et des Etudes Humaines* 219.

would be prevented from overtaxing the population and/or engaging in large-scale redistribution. While they would have the de jure power to do so, their de facto power would be significantly curtailed due to competitive pressures. Crucially, the supranational level should have no independent power to tax and therefore remain completely dependent on the lower levels of government for its revenue. Only if this condition was strictly adhered to could a transformation of the supranational level into another *Leviathan* of even bigger proportions and even bigger opportunities at exploitation through taxation, as Buchanan would put it, be prevented.

What I aim to show in the remainder of this section is that, if these two lines of argument are blended together, a picture emerges that – to a significant degree – resembles the structural set up of the European Union and the eurozone in particular.

From the beginning, the Europe of Maastricht was to be one where rules were supposed to reign supreme. The Germans, in particular, urged that the eurozone would have to display what they referred to as a 'culture of stability'. This meant that future members had to satisfy the so-called Maastricht criteria regarding inflation, public debt and other indicators in order to qualify for the Euro. And after they were accepted, members were still required to adhere to certain fiscal rules and also had to vow not to bail each other out, so as not to undermine the competitive pressures through some kind of redistributive scheme between member states or with the European Union as a supranational relay. What emerged was indeed a common economic space, in which the 'Four Freedoms' were enforced and bolstered by the European Court of Justice (ECJ) and thus served to discipline nation states in the way neoliberals had hoped they would.[25] And not only the Four Freedoms but also the common currency had the combined effect that policy-makers in member states found themselves deprived of a number of policy options they used to enjoy in the pre-Maastricht and Common Market world. And just as Hayek had hoped, these powers did not migrate upwards to the level of the European Union – they largely vanished. The EU simply lacked the competence to engage in any number of interventionist policies, instead it focused mostly on building the Common Market and enforcing the competition regime that had been put in place. Two points are worth mentioning here. First, it is striking that even before the most recent round of reforms, the crucial actors on the supranational level were institutions that could only claim a rather thin democratic legitimation, namely the already mentioned ECJ and also the European Commission. The latter, together with the European Central Bank (ECB), then emerged as the most important European actors over the course of the eurozone crisis.[26] This should provide

[25] Fritz Scharpf, 'The Asymmetry of European Integration, or, why the EU cannot be a "Social Market Economy"' (2010) 8 *Socio-Economic Review* 211.

[26] Michael Bauer and Stefan Becker, 'The unexpected Winner of the Crisis: the European Commission's strengthened Role in economic Governance' (2014) 36 *Journal of European Integration* 213; James Savage and Amy Verdun, 'Strengthening the European Commission's budgetary and economic surveillance capacity since Greece and the euro area crisis: a study of five Directorates-General' (2016) 23 *Journal of European Public Policy* 101.

significant consolation for all those neoliberals who were mainly concerned about economic policy being placed in the hands of democratically elected politicians prone to play the rent-seeking game and influenced by myriad interest groups, political parties and public opinion. The ECB, the ECJ and also the European Commission can be safely assumed to be one step removed from such democratic pressures – although of course the Commission is the target of significant lobbying activities. To be sure, national policy-makers remain subject to the democratic influencing some neoliberals feared but they enjoy much less leeway in their discretionary decision-making, their hands being tied by the effective disciplining of market forces as well as the sprawling sets of rules that have been introduced and tightened ever since the Stability and Growth Pact from 1997/98.

The second point concerns one of the reasons why the EU mainly focuses on enforcing the competition regime: money. Admittedly, there are cohesion funds and other resources that can be used for redistributive purposes and there is also, in principle, the commitment to a 'social dimension' of the Common Market. But, in reality, the volume of the respective funds is just too small to make a real difference. Of course, there are a number of reasons to explain this skewed policy profile but one of the main reasons is indeed that the EU budget is comparatively small and is exclusively financed through revenue coming from the member states. The EU, as Buchanan noted approvingly, has no independent source of financing itself and relies on funds channelled to it by the member states.[27] So one can see that some of the main concerns in neoliberal thought regarding the ambivalent role of the state are addressed in the setting of the European Union and the eurozone. It is a space where nation states are exposed to effective competition and also restrained by ever new and tightened rules regarding fiscal policy, macroeconomic imbalances and deficits, which may also affect any number of policy areas that the European Commission considers to be relevant for the respective targets in their regularly issued In-Depth Country Reports. The eurozone in the words of one critic had been turned into the 'iron cage of ordoliberalism'[28] – but, in a characteristic move, contemporary ordo- and neoliberals themselves were denying any resemblance between their ideal designs and the EU. We will see shortly on what grounds they did so.[29]

4. NGEU and the Future of Neoliberal Europe

While there is a considerable body of literature that paints the EU as an essentially neoliberal arrangement along the lines that were sketched in the preceding

[27] Buchanan and Lee, 'On a Fiscal Constitution'.

[28] Magnus Ryner, 'Europe's Ordoliberal Iron Cage: Critical Political Economy, the Euro Area Crisis and its Management' (2015) 22 *Journal of European Public Policy* 275.

[29] Brigitte Young, 'German Ordoliberalism as Agenda Setter for the Euro Crisis: Myth Trumps Reality' (2014) 22 *Journal of Contemporary European Studies* 276.

section, there are indeed those who claim – to the contrary – that the eurozone is not the dream but rather the nightmare of neo-/ordoliberal thought, with the introduction of NGEU only confirming and adding to that assessment. Let us take a look at this argument first, before we turn to the ambivalent impact of NGEU and various scenarios regarding how it may come to (re-)shape neoliberal Europe.

As already suggested, when the banking crisis morphed into the eurozone crisis and triggered a barrage of reforms from the Two-Pack to the Six-Pack and the Fiscal Pact, to name only the most important ones, critics railed against a regime of neoliberal austerity that was thus perfected, while those who preferred to refer to fiscal responsibility instead of austerity had a divergent point of view. When critics spoke of an ordoliberal iron cage of ever tighter rules their rebuttal highlighted how the authority of law had been hollowed out by the disregard for the no-bailout-clause through various 'hair cuts' etc to throw a lifeline to overleveraged countries, and, of course, the 'unorthodox' measures the ECB was pursuing that challenged the boundaries of its mandate and also violated the spirit of the no-bailout clause by helping ailing countries through targeted bond-buying. When critics spoke of neoliberal austerity that the Troika and the European Stability Mechanism (ESM) had been dealing out to countries on the verge of bankruptcy, the rebuttal drew attention to the extent to which any number of eurozone members were still overleveraged and lagging behind in the structural reforms that European authorities urged them to implement. And for those who problematised the vast toolbox at the disposal of the European Commission to monitor and even sanction member states for continued violation of the rules, the use of which had been explicitly facilitated through measures like the introduction of the reverse-majority principle in the council of ministers so that, for example, once an excessive deficit procedure was initiated, it was now to proceed unless there was a majority against it, their detractors pointed out the bluntness of these instruments. Ever since their introduction, instruments like the Macroeconomic Imbalance Procedure had not been activated a single time. When France continually failed to meet the deficit criteria in the 2010s, then President of the European Commission Jean-Claude Juncker responded to the question why an excessive deficit procedure had not been initiated by saying: 'Because it is France.' This summed up the concerns of those who already were of the opinion that, if anything, Europe needed more and real neoliberal austerity rather than less. What good was that box of instruments, if their use de facto was a matter of discretionary decision-making by a Commission, which did not view itself exclusively as the stoic rule enforcer that neoliberals have in mind when they think about an ideal state but rather a self-described 'political' body, as Juncker said on a different occasion. So we see that contemporary neoliberals – who would never call themselves that – did have significant misgivings with regard to what they considered to be at best an iron cage with massive holes, that remained unlocked most of the times, at least when it came to the more powerful animals it was supposed to house.

This impression of a deeply flawed arrangement that was miles away from neoliberal designs has been exacerbated by the introduction of NGEU. After all, while the current arrangement might not be perfect, at least the neoliberal perspective could claim to have won the debate over the narrative of the eurozone crisis and, while the reforms that were passed in this spirit still did not go far enough, they did at least aim in the right direction.

The debates over how to deal with the Covid-19 crisis, however, ended up following a different playbook. While in the eurozone crisis a narrative had prevailed that cast national governments that were living beyond their means as the main culprits, thus justifying an overall thrust in the crisis management that highlighted individual responsibility and saw no immediate obligation for solidarity, it only took a few months of Covid-19 lockdowns and an impassioned plea by those hardest hit by the first wave in Europe to put the crisis management on a different track. While some neoliberal voices pointed out that a more responsible fiscal policy in the past would have given countries like Italy or Spain more financial room to manoeuver and the ability to mitigate some of the adverse effects of the pandemic, it was obviously a non-starter to invoke the individual responsibility of each country to deal with a global pandemic. But still, while it was clear early on that there was a broad sense of solidarity, what was announced on 21 July 2020 in Brussels exceeded the hopes – and concerns – of most commentators. The NGEU recovery fund, with the Recovery and Resilience Facility at its centre was to distribute €750 billion, and over half of these were to be provided as non-repayable grants to EU member states. In order to finance this fund, the European Commission was authorised to raise money on financial markets on behalf of the European Union for the first time; then German finance minister Olaf Scholz even spoke of a 'Hamiltonian moment' with regard to this issuing of European debt, thus alluding to Alexander Hamilton's decision to 'nationalise' state debts, which was of major significance with regard to the formation of the United States. Clearly, this raised concerns that on top of the member states having to deal with massive debt burdens, now the supranational level would add to this with its own debt among those who lean towards fiscal discipline as the default course in finance policy and regard the resorting to debt as an illusionary remedy akin to a drug that, just like the devaluation of currencies, can only provide short term relief but in the long run only leads to even more dramatic crises. Another red flag that they noted was the suspension of the Stability and Growth Pact until at least 2022. Still, while NGEU was either hailed as a departure from the long-standing neoliberal script in Europe that had been reiterated and affirmed in the eurozone crisis, or condemned as the final nail in the coffin of Europe as a space of competition and fiscal responsibility under the banner of what was sometimes called 'corona socialism', we must investigate to what extent these are accurate assessments – with widely diverging normative conclusions.

The main point that would suggest that NGEU, in the short term, is anything but a departure from neoliberalism in general and not even from the course that was pursued in the eurozone crisis, can be summed up by the word *conditionality*.

After all, neither the credit lines nor the grants administered by the Recovery and Resilience Facility are instantly available to member states. Rather, they have to submit detailed recovery and resilience plans laying out how they aim to spend the money. Only if the plans are approved will the various tranches of money be transferred to the government in question. Now, in the public discussion the main criteria attracting most of the attention were investments in the digital infrastructure and the ecological transformation of national economies. However, if one takes a closer look at the EU documents that offer guidelines as to what the various plans ought to contain there is also another condition that must be met. Countries are expected to explain in detail how their investments address the Country-Specific Recommendations issued by the European Commission. In other words, the administration of the NGEU funds is tied into the European Semester and the entire apparatus built up in the wake of the eurozone crisis to monitor the economic behaviour of member states and push for more or less far-reaching structural reforms that are typically detailed in those Country-Specific Recommendations.[30] And as it turns out, this appears to make a real difference for a simple reason. As mentioned above, the problem with the instruments of the Commission which could have been used to effectively enforce compliant behaviour by member states was that they were too unwieldy and required the (political) will of the Commission to use them – which was not always the case, to say the least. This meant that delinquent governments had good reasons to hope that the Commission would not risk a showdown and actually activate a procedure – even in the case of Italy's populist government mentioned above the Commission held back until finally the government gave in. Even if the Commission did act, before a Macroeconomic Imbalance Procedure actually reached the point where financial sanctions would be issued against a member state in continued violation of the rules, many months if not years could potentially have passed. In the world of politics (and economics) where future effects are often discounted heavily – after all, one might not even be in office anymore – this took additional bite from those rules and instruments that turned out to be mostly bark. This has changed with the interlinking of NGEU and the European Semester. Now, countries who fail to meet the various requirements experience immediate repercussions in that the next tranche of NGEU funds might simply not be released. And the fact that the money is indeed not transferred once and for all but in tranches ensures that the pressure to conform to the various requirements is maintained. A task force called RECOVER has now been put in charge of monitoring the progress in the implementation of the Recovery and Resilience Plans, and whether the next tranche of money is released or withheld will depend on their assessment. To put it pointedly: NGEU has finally provided the lever needed to push for structural reforms and rule-adherence that eluded those reform packages passed in the wake of

[30] Martin Höpner, 'Die Kommission zeigt ihre neuen Waffen' (*Makroskop* 5, 30 December 2021) https://makroskop.eu/spotlight/das-war-2021-unter-dem-makroskop/die-kommission-zeigt-ihre-neuen-waffen2.

the eurozone crisis.[31] In other words, NGEU is not a departure from austerity neoliberalism but, arguably, its perfection.

But then again, nothing is 'perfect', and I must hasten to add two points. First, whether and to what extent the threat to withhold NGEU funds is an effective one depends crucially on how significant this money is in the overall context of a country's budgetary situation. For those who receive relatively smaller amount and/or enjoy considerable budgetary leeway anyway, the prospect of not receiving the next tranche is obviously far less dramatic than for those who, in contrast, rely heavily on NGEU money. Second, while this is a process that is even further depoliticised and more automatised than the Commission deciding to activate various instruments or procedures, there is an arguably ineradicable discretionary and political aspect to it. Withholding a tranche with reference to lack of progress in implementing a country's resilience plan would cause a major upstir and it would be naïve to assume that this would ever happen without express approval by the Commission, so there is still the potential to wave through governments even if they fall short on progress towards implementation.

Not only because of this but also with regard to the more long-term prospects for European neoliberalism that can be inferred from NGEU, one of the main sites of contestation over the years to come will be the various assessments of whether the Resilience plans were actually implemented. It is not hard to imagine that politicians might aim to channel funds into enterprises and projects that are non-conforming with the various requirements, including using the money to mend more or less significant holes in the national budget, and it can be assumed that a significant amount of budgetary creativity will flow into these endeavours. So there will in all likelihood be a considerable potential for controversy when it comes to taking stock in 2026, as by then the NGEU funds will have to be fully spent.

This is significant because the question of which narrative prevails will play a considerable role in deciding over the future beyond NGEU. If the dominant narrative turns out to be one that paints NGEU as a scheme that channelled billions of borrowed money to governments who misused significant portions of it, it is safe to assume that, all other things being equal, the Recovery Fund will remain what it was advertised at, namely an exception; a singular response to a crisis of epic proportions. It stands to reason that from a neoliberal perspective this would be the preferred outcome. After all, if an alternative narrative prevails that highlights the prudent investments and the ensuing productive effects made possible by NGEU money the obvious follow-up question will be: would it not be wise to establish this or something similar as a more permanent practice to be used in crisis situations? Neoliberals are likely to be alarmed by this prospect, not only because in their – not entirely mistaken view – once these instruments

[31] Thu Nguyen and Nils Redeker, 'How to make the marriage work: Wedding the Recovery and Resilience Facility and the European Semester' (Policy Brief, Berlin, Hertie School/Jacques Delors Centre, 31 January 2022) www.delorscentre.eu/en/publications/detail/publication/how-to-make-the-marriage-work.

are available, they tend to be used, even when a crisis might not be as severe as the Covid-19 crisis. Even more importantly, from an economic point of view, a political entity that regularly issues debt is practically a state. The only thing that is missing to qualify as one – again, economically speaking – is the right of taxation. And a permanent provision of debt-based funds would at least trigger a debate over how this debt ought to be repaid and whether this might to be done through EU taxes. Already the Commission has proposed new sources of funding in order to pay back NGEU debt through the revenues from a European Emissions Trading System and a so-called carbon border adjustment system. While these are not EU taxes, issuing debt as a permanent practice is still bound to raise the issue. This would be a worst-case scenario for neoliberals because the EU would gain an independent source of revenue in the form of taxation (aside from the other existing sources). This is exactly what economists like Buchanan wanted to see prevented from happening at all costs because in his view this would be tantamount to giving the EU the exact same instrument that turned most nation states into insatiable *Leviathans*. Moreover, an even more state-like EU that has the power to tax would raise the question of democratic deficits with even more urgency. And the result may well be a structural reform of the institutional ensemble of the EU to the effect that the Commission would no longer enjoy the semi-insulation from democratic pressures that neoliberals tended to value but would be turned into an executive with real accountability to parliament. Therefore, if they were to choose a future scenario, it is to be assumed that neoliberals would prefer an end to the practice of debt issuing and preventing it from being turned into a semi-permanent practice.

5. Conclusion

Let me briefly capitulate the main line of the argument in the preceding sections leading up to this conclusion before I explore somewhat tentatively the question as to what is added to this constellation by the war in Ukraine.

In this chapter, my main question was whether and to what extent the introduction of NGEU signifies a departure from a structural governance regime of the eurozone that is arguably skewed towards neoliberal austerity. My starting point was a conceptualisation of neoliberalism that rejects an understanding of it as the doctrine of self-regulating markets and instead opts for an interpretation that views neoliberalism as a problematic shared by all neoliberals in the proper sense of the word. A problematic pertaining to the question of which conditions have to be in place in order for markets to functioning properly. While the answers to this question vary significantly among neoliberals, they are all agreed that the state plays a crucial infrastructural role for functioning markets, being able to both maintain and destroy them. In the second step, I looked at two lines of neoliberal argument with regard to the state and its role: the first focusing on the problems caused by democracy for a market-maintaining politics, the second making the case for an embedding of nation states into supranational federations – not least to make them subject to effective (economic) competition. Finally, I tried to show in the same section that the set up and the institutional mechanisms of the European Union in combination with the Common Market and the eurozone tend to address both lines of argument as they remove much of the effective supranational decision-making from direct democratic influence and create a politico-economic space that forces nation states into competition with each other, with the respective competitive order, as Eucken would have called it, being enforced by European governance structures. In the final section, I have discussed the impact of NGEU in this context, which can be summed up in the following way: in the short term, while it may appear to be a departure from neoliberal austerity, NGEU, in fact, turns out to be a fairly effective lever to push nation states to implement those structural reforms and to adhere to those rules that are considered to be the hallmark of neoliberal austerity. Far from undermining this regime, NGEU – in a certain way – is its keystone. However, in the medium and long-term NGEU has a much more ambiguous potential, that is, if it turns from an exception into a semi-permanent practice. To be sure, it then continues to function as a more effective lever than what turned out to be rather unwieldy instruments such as the Macroeconomic Imbalance Procedure. However, other potential effects would also figure heavily in this scenario. Issuing debt on a permanent basis would undoubtedly trigger a debate over whether the EU should have – aside from its other sources of revenue – the right to levy taxes and, if this were the case, this would undoubtedly prompt renewed questions regarding an institutional restructuring of the EU in order to remedy its various democratic deficits. The end result could possibly be a supranational executive that has the right to tax and is democratically accountable to parliament – not the most desirable prospect from a neoliberal perspective.

While this may seem overly speculative and conjectural, there are already signs that suggest that debt issuing as a more permanent practice is indeed a realistic scenario, which brings us to the impact of the war in Ukraine. It is obviously too early for an informed assessment with regard to the long-term impact of the war, so I will restrict myself to two points. The first concerns the immediate link between NGEU as a debt financed funding scheme and the Ukraine war. In this regard, the concerns by (neoliberal-minded) observers that such instruments as NGEU, once they exist, acquire a dynamic of their own and have a tendency to become semi-permanent, have already been proven not to be entirely mistaken. The European Commission has already signalled that the envisaged reconstruction effort in Ukraine after the end of the war – whenever that may be – could be financed through a similar scheme. It was noted that such an effort should take into account the experience of the Recovery and Resilience Facility, so it is really not far-fetched to assume that NGEU may become a template for similar undertakings and the respective practices acquire some semi-permanence.

The second point is a much broader one pointing beyond NGEU and Europe pertaining to neoliberalism and its relation to war. The question here is to what extent conditions of war undermine the neoliberal project of economies based on markets and their pricing system. While this may not be a major issue in a short and limited armed conflict, the Ukraine war is unlikely to be short and, while military confrontations are – so far – concentrated on a limited terrain, the broader economic repercussions of the war are undeniable, from supply chain issues to energy shortages. Curiously, although neoliberal thought would soon cease to concern itself with matters of war – except for its cold version – at its inception on the eve of World War II and in the immediately following years, war and the respective questions with regard to a market-based economy figured prominently in the debates of the first generation of neoliberals. The Walter Lippmann Colloquium of 1938 even featured a session on Liberalism and Economic Nationalism and another on Liberalism and the War Economy. In the latter, the participants disagreed on any number of details but still concurred that even during a war, a political economy operating along liberal/neoliberal lines was still preferable – for governments and for populations – to a directed economy with rationing, price controls etc.[32] It will be interesting to see how contemporary neoliberals come to position themselves with regard to this issue and whether they follow the example of their forebearers at the Colloquium and maintain the superiority of the liberal model while possibly granting some concessions to planning based on tactical considerations, or whether an ongoing major armed conflict in combination with an energy crunch and high inflation will eventually come to reshape the profile of contemporary neoliberalism.

[32] Reinhoudt and Audier, *The Walter Lippmann Colloquium*.

PART 2

Innovative Law-Making on the Edge of Legality?

5

Follow the Money, Follow the Values

ALBERTO DE GREGORIO MERINO*

1. Introduction

The purpose of this chapter is to explore two of the most important recent developments of the European Union in constitutional terms: NextGenerationEU (NGEU) and the mechanism on a general regime of conditionality (rule of law) for the protection of the Union budget, enshrined in Regulation 2020/2092 on a general regime of conditionality for the protection of the Union budget. Both developments are closely related.

First, both were agreed on as part of the negotiations on the Multiannual Financial Framework (MFF) that took place between 2018 and 2020; negotiations the complexity of which was accentuated by the Covid-19 crisis.

Second, both developments show the fundamental integration value of the budget of the Union. The budget is not only a matter of complex and obscure financial rules; it is a field of EU law which carries with it principles of paramount constitutional value, the interpretation and application of which are key in shaping the paths for integration.

Third, both instruments, NGEU and the general regime of conditionality (rule of law), show the links between money and values. This contribution will explain the permeability between the Community of money and the Community of values on which the Union is founded. The discussion on values has come to the central stage of the Union in the last years, most notably the discussion concerning respect for the rule of law. Article 2 of the Treaty on European Union (TEU) is a provision with full normative value, the content of which is called to irrigate the policies and actions of the Union, including, of course, its budget. In a metaphorical manner one may say that values do also mint money.

This chapter aims to show an important aspect that has characterised the work of the EU legislator in relation to both developments and, more generally, EU action during the different crises since 2010: the EU Treaties are a living

* Director at the Council Legal Service. The views expressed by the author are personal and do not engage the institution for which he works.

document. Their interpretation through well-settled legal techniques allows the challenges of the times to be addressed. They are not a rigid text but lend themselves to a reading that contributes to the process of an 'ever-closer union' to which the preamble of the TEU refers. This evolutive interpretation does not amount to a blanket cheque for the legislator to break free of the Treaties, nor is it a recipe to twist them to accommodate the legislator's political preferences in an arbitrary manner. An evolutive interpretation of the Treaties allows legislation and societal choices to be factored in, as well articulating the different societal interests at stake.

2. NextGenerationEU

NGEU is the most important instrument established by the Union to tackle the financial consequences of the Covid-19 crisis. It comprises different Union programmes that provide funding through the Union borrowing in the markets. Its main features were agreed on at the European Council of 17–21 July 2020 after five days of lengthy negotiations.

NGEU is conceived on top of the normal MFF of the Union. It is endowed with €750 billion, a huge amount, ie about the 69 per cent of the total MFF ceiling for commitment appropriations in 2018 prices (€1074 billion). Of the €750 billion, €390 billion (52 per cent) are to be used as subsidies and €360 billion (48 per cent) as loans. NGEU is to be financed through the long-term issuance of debt in the markets by the Commission. It consists of long-term borrowings where the EU is held to pay off to the markets by the end of 2058. The legal commitments under NGEU are to be laid out for three years, ie before the end of 2023. Money is designated to finance a large number of programmes, most of which are cohesion related, linked to the Covid-19 crisis.

The most important of these programmes is the Recovery and Resilience Facility, endowed with €672 billion, the payment of which depends on compliance by the recipient member states with a plan of economic reforms submitted by them, and approved by the Council. The content of the Recovery and Resilience plans will adhere to the European Semester recommendations.

NGEU is composed of a plethora of legal acts, structured in three 'floors'. On the top floor lies the Own Resources Decision, which provides for an exceptional and temporary increase of the own resources ceiling by 0.6 per cent of the GNI of all the member states which is reserved up front for paying back the NGEU debt. The Own Resources Decision also empowers the Commission to borrow funds on capital markets on behalf of the Union. It provides for the overall volume of EU's liabilities, the part to be used as subsidies and as loans, and the essential financial conditions for repayment.[1] There is an intermediate floor, the Recovery

[1] See Arts 5(1) and 6 of the Own Resources Decision.

Instrument Regulation (founded on Article 122 of the Treaty on the Functioning of the European Union (TFEU)) which works as a 'control room' or channel that allocates the proceeds of borrowings in the markets to different measures and programmes that it identifies (including the recovery and resilience facility referred to previously). On the ground floor, we have the different programmes to which the resources are allocated – most notably cohesion based, as stated before – which lay down the rules for their implementation, including programming, eligibility and allocation criteria.

From a constitutional perspective, NGEU is a novel and unprecedented construction. Borrowing in the markets to finance EU actions has been a relatively common feature of financing by the Union for many years. Yet, until now, borrowing took place through back-to-back operations where the Union went to the markets to on-lend the proceeds to member states (for instance, the balance of payment facilities to assist non-euro area member states or the European Financial Stability Mechanism, created in 2010 to address the debt crisis affecting some member states). The recipient member states' commitment to repay was the asset which rendered the operation neutral on a budgetary level. However, never before the Union had resorted to borrowing for spending in such large amounts.

The budget of the Union is not a typical budget of a nation state. States finance themselves through, fundamentally, raising taxes and issuing debt. The budget of the Union does not have an autonomous capacity to raise taxes, nor it can finance expenditure through issuing bonds. It is financed by the so-called 'system of own resources', where member states are held to transfer revenue to the Union, up to a maximum limit determined in the Own Resources Decision itself. Now, for the first time the Union is endowed with the power to go to the markets to finance expenditure, thus incorporating a feature of financing of nation states.

This raised many concerns and reluctances from several member states, some of which were echoed at the video conferences of Heads of State or Government held at the outset of the pandemic, especially on 19 June 2020. Is NGEU a new European Treasury? Is borrowing for spending a change of budgetary paradigm through the back door? Can the EU finance today's actions on the basis of tomorrow's revenues? Is this a mutualisation of the national debt of member states – is this the birth of Eurobonds? Is the Union going beyond its conferred powers in the area of finance and budget?

These concerns were also the object of frenzied debates in some national parliaments. This is understandable. Not only for purely financial reasons linked to the appearance of a new, very large stock of public debt, the payment of which will eventually fall on the shoulders of member states. But most fundamentally because the creation of an EU Treasury may mark a new level of EU financial autonomy (beyond the system of own resources) with a potential federalisation strength. It may ultimately raise democratic legitimacy questions.

Thus, the question of compatibility of NGEU with the Treaties, and more especially with its budgetary principles, is not only one of budgetary technique but, most notably, a question of fundamental constitutional importance, at the bottom of which lies the principle of conferral and the financial-economic model on which the Union is founded.

The aforementioned questions of compatibility with the Treaties can be broken down into three essential points, that this chapter will examine in turn:

- The first question is whether NGEU, and more specifically the borrowing for spending on which it is based, is compatible with the principles of budgetary balance and discipline enshrined in Article 310 TFEU.
- The second question is whether NGEU is compatible with the system of own resources of the Treaties, as enshrined in Article 311 TFEU.
- The third question relates to the suitability of the legal basis on which NGEU is founded, in particular Article 122 TFEU, the crisis clause of the Treaties.

2.1. NGEU and the Principles of Budgetary Balance and Discipline

The third sentence of Article 310(1) TFEU sets out the principle of budgetary balance by stating that '[t]he revenue and expenditure shown in the budget shall be in balance'.

The principle of budgetary balance is at the core of the EU budgetary and financing system. In contrary to the national budgets, which can incur deficits (subject to the Stability and Growth Pact and national debt brakes), the EU budget must be in balance at the end of each year. It is one of the fundamental budgetary principles of the Union, together with the principles of unity, budgetary accuracy, annuality, universality, specification, sound financial management and transparency.[2]

Under the principle of budgetary balance, the Union is prohibited from adopting a budget in deficit. Eventual deficits must be carried over the next year and be financed through the own resources of the Union (see Article 7 of the Own Resources Decision). Any possible deficit that arises at the end of the year cannot be financed through the issuance of public debt.

Many have seen in Article 310(1) TFEU an uncontroversial and obvious prohibition on the Union for issuing debt to finance expenditure: according to these views, the revenue and the expenditure must be in balance, and any debt transaction by the Union is excluded. The Union should finance its expenditure from its revenue rather than by borrowing. *In claris non fit interpretatio*. Borrowing for spending is illegal. Period.[3]

[2] See Regulation (EU, Euratom) 2018/1046 of the European Parliament and of the Council on the financial rules applicable to the general budget of the Union, amending Regulations (EU) No 1296/2013, (EU) No 1301/2013, (EU) No 1303/2013, (EU) No 1304/2013, (EU) No 1309/2013, (EU) No 1316/2013, (EU) No 223/2014, (EU) No 283/2014, and Decision No 541/2014/EU and repealing Regulation (EU, Euratom) No 966/2012 [2018] OJ L193/1, Art 6.

[3] See in this sense Päivi Leino-Sandberg and Matthias Ruffert, 'Next Generation EU and Its Constitutional Ramifications: A Critical Assessment' (2022) 59 *CML Rev* 433, 450 ff.

But are things so clearly spelled out by primary law? Let us make both a literal and a finalistic reading of Article 310(1) TFEU. From a literal perspective this provision does not explicitly prohibit (or allow) financing by means of loans. Moreover, and this is a very important element, it refers to revenue and expenditure 'shown in the budget'.

However, proceeds from borrowings under NGEU consist of external assigned revenue: they do not finance EU expenditure in a general manner but are revenue earmarked to a specific purpose, namely, financing the Covid-19 relevant programmes. Yet, under the Financial Regulation, external assigned revenues consist of off-budget operations. They are not provided in the budget and are not decided upon the annual budget procedure. They are thus not 'shown in the budget' in the literal sense of Article 310(1) TFEU and thus by their very nature cannot jeopardise the budgetary balance.[4]

However, this examination cannot be confined to a literal or purely technical reading of Article 310(1) TFEU: otherwise, it would be very easy for the EU legislator to circumvent the principle of budgetary balance by simply establishing multiple programmes that provide funding through loans. This could ultimately lead to running an operating deficit, which is what the principle of budgetary balance is intended to avoid. A finalistic interpretation of that provision is also needed. Assessed overall and regarded from a multiannual perspective, the effects of borrowing for spending must be budgetarily neutral, for which borrowing should be duly counterbalanced by an asset that responds for that liability. As mentioned earlier, this has been the case in relation to back-to-back borrowing transactions undertaken by the Union, where the proceeds of borrowings in the markets were on-lent to member states or third countries. Here, the obligation for the recipient of the loan to pay it back constitutes the asset for the Union which permits to counterbalance its debt before the markets.

It is here where the yearly increase of the ceiling of the own resources of 0.6 per cent GNI of the EU is of essence (see Article 6 Own Resources Decision). Such an increase works as a closed compartment which is exclusively allocated to covering the NGEU borrowings. It is a credible and solid asset – a definitive, irrevocable and enforceable commitment of payment by member states – which ensures the budget neutrality of the operation and that, hence, guarantees that an operating deficit will not arise during the whole life cycle of borrowings. It should be underlined that this closed compartment earmarked for the payment of debt

[4] See Regulation (EU, Euratom) 2018/1046 of the European Parliament and of the Council on the financial rules applicable to the general budget of the Union, amending Regulations (EU) No 1296/2013, (EU) No 1301/2013, (EU) No 1303/2013, (EU) No 1304/2013, (EU) No 1309/2013, (EU) No 1316/2013, (EU) No 223/2014, (EU) No 283/2014, and Decision No 541/2014/EU and repealing Regulation (EU, Euratom) No 966/2012 [2018] OJ L193/1, Art 22, which provides that external assigned revenue shall only be reflected in the statements of revenue and of expenditure of the budget, *pro memoria*.

is fundamentally different to national debt issuance, where states do not create this kind of upfront guarantees of payment to the markets. In the case of member states, the guarantee of payment lies, fundamentally, in their creditworthiness.

2.2. NGEU and the Integrity of the Own Resources System

The second question is whether NGEU respects the integrity of the own resources system of the Union. The second subparagraph of Article 311 TFEU sets out that '[w]ithout prejudice to other revenue, the budget shall be financed wholly from own resources'.

This provision expresses another budgetary principle of the Union, namely the fact that its financing will preponderantly be led through the system of own resources. Of course, that system must ensure the necessary means to attain the Union's objectives through its policies (first subparagraph of Article 311 TFEU). But own resources are the quasi-exclusive means to fund Union's actions.

Now, the proceeds of borrowings cannot be regarded as own resources of the Union. By own resources one must understand irrevocable, definitive and enforceable payment rights to the benefit of the Union. Revenues obtained from the market are not irrevocable, definitive and enforceable payment rights in favour of the Union. Rather, they constitute a liability in front of the markets, which liability will, in turn, be financed by the own resources of the Union to be paid in by member states upon accrual of the relevant debt. Hence, proceeds from the issuance of debt must be regarded as 'other revenue' in the sense of the first subparagraph of Article 311 TFEU.

The question is evident. By establishing a mechanism of financing through the markets in such large amounts, is NGEU putting the integrity of the system of own resources of the Union (which, it is recalled, must be the preponderant source of finance of the EU budget) at jeopardy?

Again, this is not a mere question of budgetary technique but a constitutional one, which goes to the core of the financing system of the Union. The preponderance of the own resources as the quasi-exclusive source of finance of the Union is founded on the idea that the Union cannot itself decide on the manner of financing its actions as it sees fit. It is subject to a previous act of acceptance of each member state. The Own Resources Decision can only enter into force upon approval by all member states in accordance with their respective constitutional requirements (third subparagraph of Article 311 TFEU). This idea is, in turn, rooted in national budget sovereignty and, ultimately, on the principle of democracy of which such budget sovereignty is an expression. Remarkably, the Own Resources Decision is one of the few acts of secondary law whose entry into force depends on an act of further approval by member states – and this underlines its supra-legislative nature. The existence of a self-standing capacity of the Union to finance itself through the issuance of debt outside the system of own resources clearly threatens to deconstruct that system.

It is actually the idea of additionality and complementarity which is of utmost importance when examining this question. The second subparagraph of Article 311 TFEU recognises the existence of 'other revenues' outside the own resources system. Yet, those 'other revenues' must not call into question the preponderance of the own resources as source of finance of the Union's action. They must be additional or complementary to the general own resources system.

Whether NGEU is a funding scheme that can be regarded as additional or supplementary is not a question to be assessed only from a purely quantitative perspective– is €750 billion a top up in relation to the €1074 billion of the normal MFF financing for 2021–28? A qualitative examination of the specific economic circumstances, needs and context of the mechanism, as well as of the safeguards put in place to preserve the integrity of the EU own resources, is of essence.

In this respect, one can refer to the exceptional situation of the Covid-19 crisis and the ensuing urgent need for a swift recovery: NGEU is not a normal spending programme. It is an instrument to help economic recovery in a spirit of solidarity.

NGEU is accompanied by many guarantees which underscore its complementary nature and the respect for the integrity of the own resources system. Article 4 of the Own Resources Decision lays down the general principle that the Union shall not use funds borrowed on the capital market for the financing of operational expenditure. Under Article 5 of the Own Resources Decision, NGEU is an exception to this principle, whose use must be strictly limited to the sole purpose of addressing the consequences of the Covid-19 pandemic. It is a temporary and one-off mechanism. Borrowings are limited in time – until 2026 maximum. NGEU legal commitments are to be entered into within a maximum of three years. It is limited in size and duration to what is necessary to that end.

To sum up, borrowing for spending under NGEU comes with many guarantees which make it compatible with the Treaties, be they the principle of budgetary balance, or be they the integrity of the own resources system. It is designed to be budgetarily neutral and not to engender deficits. Bearing in mind its special characteristics and the very particular needs it intends to address, it can be regarded as complementary to the own resources system of the Union, and respectful of its integrity. NGEU does not constitute a new budgetary paradigm of the Union which is to be consolidated and continued indefinitely. Borrowing for spending cannot become a permanent feature of the EU budget to finance regular EU policies, unless the Treaties were to be changed. It is from this perspective that it must be concluded that we are not in a 'Hamiltonian moment' for the Union, which can be understood as a leap towards a common Treasury for the member states. NGEU is far away from constituting a genuine European Treasury.

2.3. The Legal Basis of NGEU: Recourse to Article 122 TFEU

As explained previously, NGEU is composed of a plethora of legal acts: the Own Resources Decision, founded on Article 311 TFEU, contains NGEU's fundamental regulatory principles; the EU Recovery Instrument (EURI), founded on Article 122 TFEU, specifies the main priorities for support, the rules on allocations of funds, including for the different priorities, and the fundamental rules of budgetary implementation; the sectorial programmes, most of which are founded on a legal basis for cohesion, such as Article 175(3) TFEU, set out the regulatory framework for each of the programmes where NGEU money will be spent, including on programming, eligibility, financing and control.

All the three legislative blocks work as a waterfall. The sectorial legislation must respect the rules and principles provided both in the Own Resources Decision and in the EURI Regulation; EURI follows the financial NGEU 'charter' that the Own Resources Decision lays down.

This contribution will now focus on one of the three elements, namely the use of Article 122 TFEU as the legal basis for the EU Recovery Instrument.

Article 122 TFEU corresponds to Chapter 1 (economic policy) of Title VIII (economic and monetary policy) TFEU. It reads as follows:

> 1. Without prejudice to any other procedures provided for in the Treaties, the Council, on a proposal from the Commission, may decide, in a spirit of solidarity between Member States, upon the measures appropriate to the economic situation, in particular if severe difficulties arise in the supply of certain products, notably in the area of energy.
> 2. Where a Member State is in difficulties or is seriously threatened with severe difficulties caused by natural disasters or exceptional occurrences beyond its control, the Council, on a proposal from the Commission, may grant, under certain conditions, Union financial assistance to the Member State concerned. The President of the Council shall inform the European Parliament of the decision taken.

The Recovery Instrument does not specify whether its legal basis is paragraph 1 or 2 of Article 122 TFEU, or whether the two paragraphs constitute the legal basis of the proposal at the same time. It is noted that Article 122(2) TFEU provides that the Council may, under certain conditions, grant Union financial assistance to member states. However, the Recovery Instrument does not grant financial assistance to the budget of member states. It lays down general arrangements for the use of the proceeds of the Union's borrowing in a number of Union programmes.

One can, therefore, conclude that the Recovery Instrument is based on paragraph 1 of Article 122 TFEU and not on paragraph 2 thereof. The wording used in paragraph 2, where it refers to the difficulties or the exceptional occurrences which may justify its use, helps, however, giving an indication of the sorts of exceptional circumstances that Article 122 TFEU as a whole is designed to address.

Article 122 TFEU was a kind of 'sleeping beauty' provision, which had hardly been used before the succession of crises that have afflicted the Union since 2010 – the financial crisis, the public debt crisis, the migration crisis, the Covid-19 crisis, and the war in Ukraine. Since then, the Union has relied on this provision as legal basis on six occasions: the adoption of the European Financial Stability Mechanism,[5] which aims at providing financial assistance to member states undergoing problems of budgetary liquidity or solvency; the adoption of the Emergency Support Instrument,[6] which initially aimed at providing financial support to member states that suffered most the consequences of the 2016 migration and refugee crisis and that eventually evolved towards supporting the public health consequences of the Covid-19 pandemic; the establishment of a European instrument for temporary support to mitigate unemployment risks (SURE)[7] following the Covid-19 outbreak; the establishment of the Health Emergency Preparedness and Response (HERA),[8] a new Commission's department that brings together experts from the Commission and member states' representatives and whose objective is to prevent, detect and rapidly respond to health emergencies; the adoption of the EU Recovery Instrument[9] which is focused on in this chapter; and, finally, at the date of publication of this chapter, the adoption of the Regulation on an emergency intervention to address high energy prices.[10]

Crisis clauses exist in most Constitutions. Typically, they allow for prompt action by the executive, which can rely on wide powers with limited parliamentary control. Moreover, their activation normally undergoes simplified, less burdensome procedures adapted to the gravity of the situation.

Yet, although recourse to crisis clauses is legitimate, their use must rely on principles of prudence and exceptionality. Otherwise, they risk becoming a vehicle that may erode a constitutional order on reasons of political convenience and opportunity. History is enlightening in this respect. One of the most telling examples relates to Article 48 of the Weimar Constitution, the emergency provision of that Constitution. It empowered the president of the Republic to enforce the Constitution against 'disobedient' *Länder* or to adopt the necessary measures, decrees, or orders, in case of serious disturbances or risks to public order and security. The president of the Republic undertook a widespread use of this article as from 1920 and most notably in years 1930 and 1931, both in quantitative and qualitative terms. That use went beyond security and public order issues

[5] Council Regulation (EU) No 407/2010 establishing a European financial stabilisation mechanism [2010] OJ L118/1.

[6] Council Regulation (EU) 2016/369 on the provision of emergency support within the Union [2016] OJ L70/1.

[7] Council Regulation (EU) 2020/672 on the establishment of a European instrument for temporary support to mitigate unemployment risks in an emergency (SURE) following the COVID-19 outbreak [2020] OJ L159/1.

[8] Commission, 'Proposal for a Council Regulation on a framework of urgent measures related to medical countermeasures in the event of a public health emergency at Union level' COM (2021) 577 final.

[9] Council Regulation (EU) 2020/2094 establishing a European Union Recovery Instrument to support the recovery in the aftermath of the COVID-19 crisis [2020] OJ LI 433/23.

[10] Council Regulation (EU) 2022/1854 on an emergency intervention to address high energy prices [2022] OJ LI 261/1.

and comprised decrees and orders in the financial and economic field.[11] The relentless use of Article 48 of the Weimar Constitution ultimately led to its mutation, to the creation of a parallel legal order detrimental to parliamentarism, and to the progressive transformation of the Weimar Republic into an authoritarian regime.

Of course, one should not dramatise the evolution of the law of the Union when it comes to Article 122 TFEU. The ghost of the Weimar Constitution does not risk haunting the Union legal order. Nevertheless, the evocation of the Weimar experience of exceptionality may be useful to warn against the dangers that an excessive use of exceptionality clauses, such as Article 122 TFEU, entails.

Arguably, the wording of Article 122(1) TFEU confers upon the Council a wide margin of discretion for its use. It empowers the Council to adopt the 'measures appropriate to the economic situation' in a 'spirit of solidarity', without specifying which are the situations which qualify for recourse to that provision, or the particular form, nature and content of the measures that may be adopted on its basis. Article 122(1) TFEU simply refers 'in particular' to severe difficulties in the supply of certain products, notably in the area of energy, but does not specify exhaustively either the kind of situations which may give rise to that provision or the specific measures that the Council is empowered to adopt. Despite this wide margin of discretion, and bearing in mind its expansive scope and strength, the use of Article 122 TFEU must be subject to strict limits – to an overall rule of prudence and of self-restraint – so that the legal fabric of the Union, founded on the principle of attribution of competences, is not affected. What are those limits?

First, Article 122 TFEU must be exclusively used in situations of exceptionality leading to severe difficulties in the economic situation of the member states which cannot be addressed by means of the ordinary Union measures.[12] Not any exceptional situation should qualify for the use of that provision. The bar is very high: the gravity of the situation must be especially serious. Situations where only a particular individual or specific sectors of the economy are affected would not be sufficient for its activation. It is necessary that the situation in question presents a systemic nature affecting, or threatening to affect, the fundamentals of the economy of the Union or of its member states in a generalised manner, in terms of, for instance, evolution of GDP and growth, unemployment rates, productivity and competitiveness indicators, or the financial stability, the solvency and the liquidity of the member states.

[11] Between 1920 and 1924, more than 100 presidential decrees were adopted on the basis of Article 48 of the Weimar Constitution. In 1932, 60 presidential decrees were adopted. See Josu de Miguel Bárcena and Javier Tajadura Tejada, *Kelsen versus Schmitt: Política y derecho en la crisis del constitutionalismo* (Madrid, Guillermo Escolar, 2018) 249 ff.

[12] The wording of Art 122(1) TFEU does not expressly mention the condition of urgency as is the case for Art 122(2). However, the two paragraphs need to be read jointly and on the basis of the specific purpose of Art 122 TFEU in the system of the Treaties: both contextual and systemic methods of interpretation therefore point to an 'emergency rationale' that applies to the whole provision.

Second, recourse to Article 122 TFEU must be temporary. It cannot be used for the purpose of regulating a matter on a permanent basis or to replace the ordinary financing of EU policies, since this would encroach on the relevant substantive legal bases provided for in the Treaties. The introductory words 'without prejudice to any other procedures provided for in the Treaties' underscore the exceptional and temporary nature of measures under Article 122(1) TFEU, as recourse to that provision may not undermine or circumvent the use of other legal bases laid down in the Treaties for use in 'normal times'.

Third, Article 122 TFEU belongs to Chapter 1 of Title VIII TFEU, which deals with economic policy. The objective and the content of measures adopted under Article 122(1) TFEU must therefore be economic in nature.

Fourth, Article 122 TFEU must be used for providing support to member states of the Union, and not as an instrument of external policy to the benefit of third countries. The competence set out in Article 122 TFEU is based on the particular *spirit of solidarity* between member states, which justifies taking exceptional action when member states experience situations of severe economic difficulty. The position of third countries in that regard is, in principle, fundamentally different. Article 122 TFEU cannot be used as an instrument of external policy.[13]

In my view, the EU Recovery Instrument (including the underlying sectorial programmes which it finances) fulfils all four conditions referred to above. Without doubt, the instrument responds to the exceptional circumstances engendered by the pandemic, the unprecedented character of the ensuing economic crisis, and to extraordinary size of its consequences. The instrument is temporary in nature bearing in mind the one-off nature of the budgetary construction explained above, as well as the fact that the rules on budgetary implementation of the EU Recovery Instrument set out a system of deadlines for concluding legal commitments related to the resources mobilised under the Recovery Instrument. The EU Recovery Instrument is clearly economic in nature since it finances a comprehensive set of measures for economic recovery, which are aimed at tackling tackle the economic consequences of the pandemic through measures related to the economic dimension of the crisis. Finally, its assistance is overall limited to the member states of the EU.

3. The Rule of Law Conditionality Mechanism

This contribution will now tackle the second major budgetary and constitutional development referred to in section 1, namely the budgetary conditionality rule

[13] The General Court has clarified that 'the spirit of solidarity between Member States that must inform the adoption by the Council of measures appropriate to the economic situation, within the meaning of Article 122 (1) TFEU, indicates that such measures must be founded on assistance between the Member States', Case T-450/12 *Alexios Anagnostakis v European Commission* ECLI:EU:T:2015:739, para 42. This finding has been confirmed by the Court of Justice on appeal, C-589/15 P *Alexios Anagnostakis v European Commission* ECLI:EU:C:2017:663, para 71.

of law mechanism enshrined in Regulation 2020/2092 on a general regime of conditionality for the protection of the Union budget (hereinafter, 'the conditionality rule of law Regulation').

As is the case regarding NGEU, the interest of this Regulation is not exhausted in its budgetary dimension. The conditionality rule of law Regulation is essentially an instrument of great constitutional and institutional value. It expresses fundamental principles of the EU legal order such as solidarity and mutual trust, and gives legislative translation to the values set out in Article 2 TEU, which include respect for the rule of law.

This chapter will briefly present the functioning of the mechanism and then the most important constitutional implications will be examined in turn in view of the judgments of the Court of Justice in two actions for annulment brought by Poland and Hungary against the conditionality rule of law Regulation.

3.1. Context and Content of the Conditionality Rule of Law Regulation

The Commission presented its proposal on the conditionality rule of law Regulation in May 2018.[14] The proposal was framed in a double context. On the one hand, it was part of the Commission's overall strategy to address the challenges to the rule of law that existed in some member states at the time of this proposal; on the other hand, the proposal is an integral part of the Commission's MFF legislative package for the period 2021–2027.

The negotiations for the current MFF revolved around three pillars: the MFF proposal; NGEU, which was explored above; and, finally, the conditionality rule of law proposal. The latter is therefore incorporated into the overall MFF and NGEU negotiations and cannot be politically understood outside that context.

The general conditionality mechanism aims at protecting the EU budget in case of breaches of the principles of the rule of law in the member states. It is based on the idea that member states can ensure the sound financial management of EU money only if their public authorities act in accordance with the law.[15] Its legal basis is Article 322(1)(a) TFEU, which allows for the adoption of financial rules on the procedure for establishing and implementing the budget.

Under Article 4(1) of the conditionality rule of law Regulation, the activation of the mechanism takes place under two circumstances: (i) a breach of the principles of the rule of law by a member state, which (ii) affects or seriously threatens to affect in a sufficiently direct manner the sound financial management

[14] Commission, 'Proposal for a Regulation of the European Parliament and of the Council on the protection of the Union's budget in case of generalised deficiencies as regards the rule of law in the Member States' COM (2018) 324 final.

[15] Recital 8 of the preamble to the conditionality rule of law Regulation.

of the Union budget or the protection of the financial interests of the Union. In this case, the Council, acting by a qualified majority on a proposal from the Commission, may adopt measures suspending or cancelling EU funding (Article 5(1) of the conditionality rule of law Regulation).

The volume of these measures is determined in accordance with proportionality criteria laid down under Article 6(1) of that Regulation. These criteria shall be primarily determined in light of the actual or potential impact of the breaches of the measures of the rule of law on the sound financial management of the Union budget or the financial interests of the Union. The nature, duration, gravity and scope of the breaches of the principles of the rule of law shall be duly taken into account.

The Regulation includes elements of definition aimed at ensuring that its application is as precise as possible. Among them, there is a definition of the concept of the rule of law, which incorporates elements stemming from the case-law of the Court (Article 2(a)), as well as the specification of several indications of the existence of a breach of the principles of the rule of law (Article 4(2)).

The mechanism is conceived as an instrument of a subsidiary nature, applicable where other budget protection procedures do not allow its protection more effectively (Article 6(1) of the conditionality rule of law Regulation).

The procedure – Article 6 of the Regulation – is divided into two stages. First, an instruction in which the Commission conducts a dialogue with the country concerned to establish the facts and the existence of the activation conditions. This dialogue can take up to six months. Second, there is a decision-making stage: if, based on its dialogue with the member state, the Commission considers that the circumstances for triggering the procedure are present, it is obliged to propose measures to the Council, which, in principle, has one month to decide on their adoption.

Finally, the Regulation provides for a procedure for reviewing and adapting or lifting measures imposed by the Council where the conditions which led to its application have evolved or disappeared (Article 7 of the Regulation).

At the time of drafting this chapter, the Commission has proposed the adoption of measures under the conditionality rule of law Regulation in relation to Hungary to the Council.[16]

3.2. Constitutional Meaning of the Conditionality Rule of Law Regulation: The Judgments of the Court of Justice in Cases C-156/21 and C-157/21

This chapter will now turn into the constitutional meaning of the rule of law conditionality Regulation, as spelled out in the judgments of the Court of Justice

[16] See Commission, 'Proposal for a Council Implementing Decision on measures for the protection of the Union budget against breaches of the principles of the rule of law in Hungary' COM (2022) 485 final.

of 16 February 2022 concerning the actions for annulment against that Regulation brought by Hungary and Poland in Cases C-156/21 and C-157/21.[17] The Court heard the two cases in full assembly.

3.2.1. *The Mechanism as Genuine Budgetary Conditionality*

Hungary and Poland focused their arguments on one main point, which had already been put forward during the legislative debate. The conditionality rule of law Regulation is a budgetary screen that hides the real purpose of enforcing the respect for the value of the rule of law through means less demanding in procedure than Article 7 TEU. Article 322(1)(a) TFEU would therefore be an incorrect legal basis. According to the applicants, Article 7 TEU constitutes the only remedy available to the Union to identify and put an end to potential breaches of the values laid down in Article 2 TEU.

In its judgments the Court rejected these arguments, concluding that the Regulation is a genuine instrument of budgetary conditionality, thus correctly founded on Article 322(1)(a) TFEU.

The Court came to this conclusion after examining a number of elements which prove the genuine budgetary character of the mechanism: For instance, the provision that requires a sufficient causal link between the breach of the principles of the rule of law and the actual or potential damage to the financial interests of the European Union – namely the fact that the breach must have a 'sufficiently direct' effect on the EU budget – is particularly relevant.[18] The criteria of proportionality laid down in the Regulation, whereby the volume of the measures (suspension or cancellation of funding) is determined primarily based on the damage to the budget, rather than on the basis of the seriousness of the breach of the rule of law, also underpin the genuine budgetary nature of the instrument.[19] In its reasoning as to the adequacy of the legal basis, the provisions of the Regulation on the lift and adaptation of measures imposed are also important. Indeed, such a lift or adaptation may take place when the damage to the budget has disappeared (or diminished), even if the breach of the rule of law is still ongoing.[20]

Because the instrument is one of genuine conditionality it does not overlap with Article 7 TEU. In accordance with its well-established case-law, the Court states that Article 7 TEU is not exhaustive in nature. The EU institutions may examine and, as the case may be, request to put an end to the possible breaches of the values under Article 2 TEU committed by a member state on the basis of other provisions of the Treaty, the effective implementation of which depends on compliance with those values. The Court refers to Article 19(1) TEU, which lays

[17] Case C-156/21 *Hungary v Parliament and Council* ECLI:EU:C:2022:97; Case C-157/21 *Poland v Parliament and Council* ECLI:EU:C:2022:98.

[18] See Case C-157/21 *Poland v Parliament and Council* ECLI:EU:C:2022:98, paras 125, 159, 165.

[19] See ibid para 128.

[20] See ibid para 127.

down the obligation for member states to provide remedies sufficient to ensure effective judicial protection in the fields covered by EU law, and which, as is well known, has served as the basis for the Court to verify the independence of the judicial systems of certain member states.[21]

3.2.2. The Conditionality Rule of Law Regulation and the Principles of Solidarity and Responsibility

Without doubt, the conditionality rule of law Regulation is an example of 'marriage' between the principles of solidarity and responsibility. Integration processes brought about by recent crises are founded on a trade-off of the two principles: The public debt crisis led to instruments such as the European Stability Mechanism (ESM), which may mobilise huge amounts of money to assist member states suffering liquidity or insolvency problems, in exchange for these states adopting measures of budgetary responsibility; in the face of the financial crisis, the Banking Union was created, in which the risks of banks are mutualised through a single resolution fund in exchange for a mutualisation of the control of those risks (through the Single Supervisory System which has been in the hands of the European Central Bank since 2014). The convergence of solidarity and of responsibility arises in other EU policies where member states share a common good – internal borders – such as asylum and immigration, and thus Article 80 TFEU reflects both principles on an equal footing.

The conditionality rule of law Regulation and the particular context in which it appears (the massive mobilisation of funding under MFF and NGEU) is another example of this interaction between solidarity and responsibility. As stated by Advocate General Campos Sánchez-Bordona, NGEU is possibly 'the largest solidarity effort launched by the Union in its history'.[22]

In its two judgments, the Court dwells on the relationship between the principles of solidarity and responsibility. It establishes a sort of 'super-conditionality', recalling that respect by the member states of the values set out in Article 2 TEU is a necessary condition for them to enjoy their rights under the Treaties.[23] It recalls that the Union budget is one of the main instruments that gives concrete form to the principle of solidarity. The principle of solidarity, in turn, presupposes the principle of mutual trust between the member states. There can be no solidarity, nor the mutual confidence that it presupposes, without respect by member states of the values of Article 2 TEU.[24] The Court concludes by recalling that respect for

[21] See ibid paras 194–99; See also Case C-619/18 *Commission v Poland* EU:C:2019:531, paras 58, 59 and Case C-192/18 *Commission v Poland* EU:C:2019:924, paras 106 f.

[22] See Case C-848/19 *Germany v Poland* ECLI:EU:C:2021:218, Opinion of AG Campos Sánchez-Bordona, fn 43.

[23] See Case C-157/21 *Poland v Parliament and Council* ECLI:EU:C:2022:98, para 114.

[24] See ibid para 147.

the rule of law, which presupposes judicial independence, is essential for the sound financial management and the protection of the Union's financial interests.[25]

Conditionality is the link between solidarity and responsibility. And, one should not forget, the negotiation of the last MFF as well as of the NGEU programme has been very much marked by the establishment of different budgetary conditionalities, aimed at ensuring a responsible execution of the huge solidarity effort at stake. It should suffice here to mention some of those conditionalities, such as environmental and climate conditionality; the conditionality based on respect for 'horizontal principles' relating to the protection of fundamental rights and compliance with the Charter of Fundamental Rights; or macroeconomic conditionality linking the provision and effectiveness of funds to the respect for budgetary obligations and sound economic governance.[26]

3.2.3. The Full Normative Character of the Values of Article 2 TEU as Identity of the EU Legal Order

The mechanism demonstrates the *structuring* function of the values referred to in Article 2 TEU. That article does not constitute a legal basis conferring competences on the Union. However, the values it mentions do not have a mere aspirational function. They are not a constitutional dead letter, Article 2 is not just constitutional iconography, in words of Joseph Weiler.[27] Article 2 TEU has full normative value, intended to provide underlying values running through EU legislation.

The two judgments of the Court confirm this. The Court repeatedly states that Article 2 TEU is legally binding on the member states. In particular, respect for the values of Article 2 TEU constitutes an obligation of result, in the sense that, while the member states have a margin of discretion for their internal organisation to ensure respect for the principles of the rule of law, each of them must ensure an equivalent and effective level of respect for the values.[28] Moreover, the obligation to respect the values of Article 2 TEU is subject to a principle of non-regression: such an obligation is not only a condition of accession to the European Union within the meaning of Article 49 TEU, but a requirement which must be complied with on a continuous basis once accession has taken place.[29]

[25] See ibid paras 148–51.

[26] These conditionality rules are laid down in Regulation (EU) 2021/1060 laying down common provisions on the European Regional Development Fund, the European Social Fund Plus, the Cohesion Fund, the Just Transition Fund and the European Maritime, Fisheries and Aquaculture Fund and financial rules for those and for the Asylum, Migration and Integration Fund, the Internal Security Fund and the Instrument for Financial Support for Border Management and Visa Policy [2021] OJ L231/159. Environmental conditionality is laid down in Art 6 and 9(4) thereof; respect for horizontal principles (as fundamental rights) in Art 9 thereof; macroeconomic conditionality in Art 19.

[27] Joseph HH Weiler, 'On the Power of the Word: Europe's Constitutional Iconography' [2005] 3 *International Journal of Constitutional Law* 173.

[28] See Case C-157/21 *Poland v Parliament and Council* ECLI:EU:C:2022:98, paras 142–45, 168, 169, 179, 263–65.

[29] See ibid paras 143, 144, 223.

And because Article 2 TEU has full normative value, its interpretation belongs to the European Union, and, ultimately, to the Court. These values are not an intangible part of the national constitutional identity but are at the core of what the Court calls the *European constitutional identity*. National constitutional identity cannot make the defence of the values under Article 2 TEU a task left to the sole discretion of each member state. The Union cannot outsource in full the definition, content and scope of these values to the member states. It is for the Union to define and defend them on the basis of the autonomy enjoyed by its legal order vis-à-vis the law of the member states.[30] And outside Article 7 TEU, which establishes a procedure subject to primarily political considerations, the monitoring of compliance by the EU institutions with the values of Article 2 TEU must be subject to legal criteria.[31]

According to the Court, respect for the values of Article 2 TEU is bound to penetrate legislative action. It is, in some way, a call on the legislature to incorporate into EU legislation – in so far as necessary for the attainment of the objectives of the act in question – conditionality rules linking EU acts to the respect for the value enshrined in Article 2 TEU. The rule of law budgetary conditionality is thus a model that could inspire similar constructions in other EU policies. Moreover, the Court refers to a kind of duty on the part of the EU legislator to pro-actively defend the values of Article 2.[32] It sends a message to Brussels: the Court should not bear the burden of enforcing respect for the values, notably of the rule of law, alone. The political institutions should also assume their responsibilities.[33]

4. Conclusions

NGEU and the rule of law conditionality Regulation constitute two extraordinary developments in constitutional terms. They prove the living nature of the Treaties, but also the awareness of the legislator that, together with large doses of creativity, it is necessary to incorporate guarantees that root those instruments within the boundaries of primary law. They are a telling example of the parallel paths of solidarity and responsibility. Solidarity presupposes mutual trust, which is in turn rooted in the effective and equivalent assumption by member states of their obligations under EU law, most notably respect for the values under Article 2 TEU. Both instruments show that the money is 'coloured' by the values of Article 2 TEU. These values are not relative concepts, the meaning and scope of which can be

[30] See ibid para 143.
[31] See ibid paras 200, 203.
[32] See ibid para 268.
[33] See in this sense Jean-Paul Jacqué, 'Le juge de l'Union saisi par la politique' [2021] 4 *Revue Trimestriel de Droit Européen* 799.

left to an *à la carte* determination of each member state. They constitute absolute targets, the normative content of which the Union is empowered to determine autonomously because they are part of its own constitutional identity. Article 2 TEU can be regarded as the substratum of a 'European Constitutional patriotism', borrowing the expression of Habermas.[34]

[34] Jürgen Habermas, *Between Facts and Norms: Contributions to a Discourse Theory of Law and Democracy* (William Rehg tr, Cambridge, MA, MIT Press, 1996) 507: 'a European constitutional patriotism would have to grow together from various nationally specific interpretations of the same universalist principles of law.' The origins of constitutional patriotism can be traced back to Carl Jaspers and his pupil Dolf Sternberger, see Jan-Werner Müller, *Constitutional Patriotism* (Princeton, NJ, Princeton University Press, 2007) 15–26, and has inspired further debates as European constitutional patriotism, 93–139.

6

When Size Matters

On the Legality of the Recovery Instrument 'Next Generation EU' in Light of its Unprecedented Volume

CLAUDIA WUTSCHER

1. *Iudex Non Calculat* – But Maybe He Ought To

The recovery instrument NextGenerationEU (NGEU) is 'part of a financial package of unprecedented volume'.[1] Together with the Multiannual Financial Framework (MFF) 2021–27,[2] a total of €2.018 trillion – in current prices[3] – contribute to 'a greener, more digital and more resilient Europe' in the coming years. NGEU alone comprises investments of up to more than €800 billion in current prices, disbursed until 2026, with the bulk allocated to loans and grants in the Recovery and Resilience Facility (RRF).[4] It is, however, not only huge, it is also special both in terms of financing and expenditure, as it is financed through debt incurred by the Union, and it operates outside the EU budget. To put its size

[1] European Commission, 'Presentation by Commissioner Johannes Hahn of the NextGenerationEU – Funding strategy to finance the Recovery Plan for Europe' (Speech/21/1743, Brussels, 14 April 2021) https://ec.europa.eu/commission/presscorner/detail/fr/speech_21_1743.

[2] Council Regulation (EU, Euratom) 2020/2093 laying down the multiannual financial framework for the years 2021 to 2027 [2020] OJ L433I/11; with total commitments of about €1.2 trillion in current prices.

[3] Council Decision (EU, Euratom) 2020/2053 on the system of own resources of the European Union and repealing Decision 2014/335/EU, Euratom [2020] OJ L424/1 (ORD), Art 5(1), (2) foresees a 'fixed deflator' of 2% per year to adjust the scale of admissible borrowing operations (€750 billion in 2018 prices). If, as is currently the case, inflation is higher than 2%, the available funds lose purchasing power.

[4] The announcement of May 2022 that more than a third of those investments could possibly be earmarked for the transition to more energy autonomy (*cf* the so-called REPowerEU proposal to amend, in particular, Regulation (EU) 2021/241, COM (2022) 231 final) was ultimately not implemented. Rather, the amending regulation to include REPowerEU Chapters in the recovery and

into perspective, the EU's annual budget for 2022 foresees total commitments of €169.5 billion and payments of €170.6 billion, so NGEU amounts to almost five yearly EU budgets (or about 5 per cent of the entire EU GDP[5]), which explains why the Commission advertises it as the 'largest stimulus package ever'.[6]

Yet, when assessing the legality of a measure against the backdrop of higher-ranking norms, lawyers are, in general, not too concerned with numbers. *Iudex non calculat* is taught to all law students in their first semester and many take pride in cultivating this preconception almost as a virtue. Thus, attempts to answer the question whether NGEU complies with primary law might look at whether the EU is, in general, competent to incur debt by issuing bonds and, if so, to what end and under which conditions; or they might assess whether the legal construction, on which NGEU is based, fulfils the prerequisites of Article 122 of the Treaty on the Functioning of the European Union (TFEU) (and Article 175(3) TFEU as regards RRF), is compatible with the no-bail-out-clause of Article 125 TFEU, with EU financial provisions,[7] and with the rules on the EU's own resources system (Article 311 TFEU).[8] From the perspective of national constitutional law, they might highlight the specifics of ratifying a new Own Resources Decision (ORD).[9]

It seems as though, however, the results of these legal assessments are usually not dependent on the volume of the assessed measure, or such dependency is at least not explicitly addressed. In other words, if the legal construction used for NGEU were compatible with primary law and member states' constitutional prerequisites, it would be just as compatible if its size was not €800 billion, but 'only' a tenth of its current volume, namely €80 billion, or, on the contrary, 10 times as much, meaning €8 trillion. Yet, such a conclusion is flawed. Rather, in this chapter I will use the assessment of NGEU to show why and to what extent the size of a measure is not only politically important, but also relevant for the legal assessment, both from the EU law perspective as well as from the perspective of member states' constitutional law.[10] I will focus on the EU law perspective and begin with a brief account of the legal set-up (section 2.1), which Frank Schorkopf called a 'master piece' and 'legal high-tech'.[11] Then, implications of NGEU's size for its legal assessment, namely in the interpretation of Treaty

resilience plans foresees an additional €20 billion from the Innovation Fund and ETS allowances; see Regulation (EU) 2023 1435 [2023] OJ L63/1.

[5] According to Eurostat, EU GDP in 2021 amounted to about €14.552 trillion, see Eurostat, 'GDP and main component (output, expenditure and income)' (NAMA_10_GDP) https://ec.europa.eu/eurostat/databrowser/view/NAMA_10_GDP/default/table?lang=en.

[6] *cf* the overview of NGEU on the Commission website, European Commission, 'Recovery plan for Europe' (*European Commission Website*) https://ec.europa.eu/info/strategy/recovery-plan-europe_en.

[7] Art 310(1) TFEU. Doubts regarding the compatibility of NGEU with the financial provisions pertain, in particular, to the principles of budgetary balance and discipline.

[8] eg Council Legal Service, Opinion, Council Doc 9062/20 (Brussels, 24 June 2020); Frank Schorkopf, 'Die Europäische Union auf dem Weg zur Fiskalunion' (2020) 73 *Neue Juristische Wochenschrift* 3085.

[9] eg Schorkopf, 'Auf dem Weg zur Fiskalunion' 3089 f paras 31 f.

[10] My considerations may apply mutatis mutandis to other measures taken, eg in connection with the war in Ukraine or the energy crisis.

[11] Schorkopf, 'Auf dem Weg zur Fiskalunion' 3087.

rules and the application of EU law principles, shall be addressed (section 2.2). The second part of this contribution will then briefly cover the constitutional law perspective (section 3) and show that size may also matter both for the applicable parliamentary procedure to be used for the approval of the Own Resources Decision (ORD) as well as for the assessment of its compatibility with parliaments' budgetary prerogatives.

2. The EU Law Perspective

2.1. The Legal Set-Up

NGEU's legal set-up is innovative[12] and has been ascribed to the 'grey zone between creative legal engineering and illegality'.[13] NGEU consists of several new legal acts as well as recasts of and changes to existing ones. Regarding expenditure, ie the distribution of the funds, Regulation (EU) 2020/2094 establishing a European Union Recovery Instrument to support the recovery in the aftermath of the COVID-19 crisis[14] (EURI Regulation) sets up the general regime and purpose, leaving implementation to the autonomous programmes, which the instrument finances. It is based on Article 122 TFEU, but although this provision contains two paragraphs with distinct prerequisites, it leaves open which of them specifically serves as the legal basis.[15] In any event, in order to comply with the no-bail-out clause of Article 125 TFEU as understood by the Court of Justice of the European Union (CJEU), the Recovery Instrument must not diminish the incentive to pursue a sound budgetary policy at the level of the member states, who should

[12] *cf* Päivi Leino-Sandberg and Matthias Ruffert, 'Next Generation EU and Its Constitutional Ramifications: A Critical Assessment' (2022) 59 *CML Rev* 433, 437; Frank Schorkopf, 'Auf dem Weg zur Fiskalunion' 3087; *cf* also Bruno de Witte, 'The European Union's COVID-19 Recovery Plan: The Legal Engineering of an Economic Policy Shift' (2021) 58 *CML Rev* 635, 635, who calls it 'a case of creative legal engineering'. Explicitly, as regards the RRF, Regulation (EU) 2021/241 of the European Parliament and of the Council establishing the Recovery and Resilience Facility [2021] OJ L 57/17, recital 8.

[13] Leino-Sandberg and Ruffert, 'Next Generation EU and Its Constitutional Ramifications' 439.

[14] OJ L433I/23.

[15] With its reference to difficulties caused by natural disasters or exceptional occurrences beyond member states' control, para 2 might seem to be the more fitting choice. However, the Recovery Instrument does not grant financial assistance, which would in any case also be limited to alleviating the consequences of the pandemic and require 'certain conditions' (*cf* Schorkopf, 'Auf dem Weg zur Fiskalunion' 3087 f paras 24 f wfr). Thus, the Legal Service of the Council considers para 1 as the proper legal basis for the EURI Regulation, while it suggests using para 2 as an 'indication on the sorts of exceptional circumstances that Article 122 as a whole is designed to address'; see Council Legal Service, Opinion, Council Doc 9062/20 (Brussels, 24 June 2020) para 119. *cf* Leino-Sandberg and Ruffert, 'Next Generation EU and Its Constitutional Ramifications' 446, who consider this omission 'intentional and instrumental'. Art 122 TFEU allows the Council to act without a veto right of the European Parliament on the EURI Regulation, while the RRF Regulation is based on Art 175(3) TFEU and thus adopted according to the ordinary legislative procedure; *cf* Schorkopf, 'Auf dem Weg zur Fiskalunion' 3086 para 10.

remain subject to the logic of the markets.[16] This is questionable when the funds are used for national reforms and public investments that would otherwise arguably be paid for from national budgets (especially when granted in the form of loans).[17]

Most of the NGEU funds[18] are distributed according to the rules laid down in Regulation (EU) 2021/241 establishing the Recovery and Resilience Facility[19] (RRF Regulation) in the form of loans on the one and grants on the other hand, with a maximum financial contribution calculated for each member state.[20] To access the funds, member states have drawn up national recovery and resilience plans (RRPs), setting out their reform and investment agenda,[21] which were assessed by the Commission and approved by the Council.[22] The distribution of RRF grants and loans, however, is based mostly on criteria not directly related to the Covid-19 crisis and used for objectives beyond merely compensating for Covid-19-related expenditure,[23] which further casts doubts on its justification as a crisis measure.[24] Although according to Eurostat[25] only the loans, not the grants, are included in the government deficit/debt for the purposes of Article 126 TFEU, by financing a

[16] Case C-370/12 *Thomas Pringle v Government of Ireland and Others* ECLI:EU:C:2012:756, paras 135 f.

[17] Leino-Sandberg and Ruffert, 'Next Generation EU and Its Constitutional Ramifications' 450, *cf* also 443; *cf* also Schorkopf, 'Auf dem Weg zur Fiskalunion' 3088 para 27.

[18] Namely €723.8 billion of NGEU's €806.9 billion in current prices.

[19] Regulation (EU) 2021/241 of the European Parliament and of the Council establishing the Recovery and Resilience Facility [2021] OJ L57/17.

[20] See Art 11 and annex IV RRF Regulation.

[21] See Art 18 RRF Regulation. The RRPs take into account the investment and reform priorities identified as part of the European Semester.

[22] Art 19, 20 RRF Regulation. A minimum of 37% of RRP has to contribute to the green transition ('climate target'), 20% to the digital transformation ('digital target'), see Art 18(4)(e) and f RRF Regulation. Commitments are entered into and loans and guarantees granted until the end of 2023 (see Art 3(4)–(6) EURI Regulation), payments made until the end of 2026 (Art 3(9) EURI Regulation, Art 24 RRF Regulation). The Commission thereby acts as a 'functional ministry of economy and finance', see Hanno Kube and Frank Schorkopf, 'Strukturveränderung der Wirtschafts- und Währungsunion' (2021) 74 *Neue Juristische Woschenschrift* 1650, 1655. Member states have an obligation to report on the progress in implementing the RRPs, with the possibility of payments being halted if milestones and targets indicated in the RRP are not met; *cf* Art 24 RRF Regulation.

[23] Rather, 'the general objective of the Facility shall be to promote the Union's economic, social and territorial cohesion by improving the resilience, crisis preparedness, adjustment capacity and growth potential of the member states, by mitigating the social and economic impact of that crisis, in particular on women, by contributing to the implementation of the European Pillar of Social Rights, by supporting the green transition, by contributing to the achievement of the Union's 2030 climate targets … and by complying with the objective of EU climate neutrality by 2050 and of the digital transition, thereby contributing to the upward economic and social convergence, restoring and promoting sustainable growth and the integration of the economies of the Union, fostering high quality employment creation, and contributing to the strategic autonomy of the Union alongside an open economy and generating European added value' (Art 4(1) RRF Regulation).

[24] *cf* Leino-Sandberg and Ruffert, 'Next Generation EU and Its Constitutional Ramifications' 450.

[25] *cf* Eurostat, 'Guidance note on the statistical recording of the recovery and resilience facility' (*Directorate D – Government Finance Statistics (GFS)*, Methodological note, September 2021) https://ec.europa.eu/eurostat/documents/10186/10693286/GFS-guidance-note-statistical-recording-recovery-resilience-facility.pdf/4117dec2-7840-a80d-7cb8-6d4f48c90a5a?t=1633505104650.

large variety of national measures in nearly all policy areas,[26] the RRF Regulation also pushes the limits of its legal basis, the cohesion policy flexibility clause of Article 175(3) TFEU.[27]

NGEU's 'innovative' design is particularly evident on the financing side, prompting Päivi Leino-Sandberg and Matthias Ruffert to stipulate that, with NGEU, 'the foundations of financing the European Union have been overturned'.[28] The money for NGEU's measures is EU money, more specifically, money *borrowed* by the Commission on behalf of the EU[29] and then channelled to the member states, in particular as grants and loans under the RRF. The empowerment to incur such high amounts of debt was included in the new ORD[30] and is therein limited to 'the sole purpose of addressing the consequences of the COVID-19 crisis through the Council Regulation establishing a European Union Recovery Instrument and the sectoral legislation referred to therein'. Even if the ORD repeatedly stresses that this empowerment and the corresponding increase of the own resources ceilings is 'extraordinary and temporary', the repayment of the funds borrowed is foreseen only from 2028 up until 2058 and with yet rather unspecified means.[31] Although the Union budget is primarily liable,[32] without future far-reaching changes to the

[26] *cf* the 'six pillars' under Art 3 RRF Regulation, for which financial support is granted: green transition, digital transformation, smart, sustainable and inclusive growth, social and territorial cohesion, health, and economic, social and institutional resilience, as well as policies for the next generation, children and the youth. According to the REPowerEU proposal, a significant proportion of the funds may be redistributed to contribute to energy autonomy.

[27] With this broad understanding of cohesion policy, virtually any distributive Union measure could be defined as 'leading to the strengthening of its economic, social and territorial cohesion' in the sense of Art 174 (1) TFEU; *cf* Leino-Sandberg and Ruffert, 'Next Generation EU and Its Constitutional Ramifications' 449 f.

[28] Leino-Sandberg and Ruffert, 'Next Generation EU and Its Constitutional Ramifications' 433.

[29] The funds are organised in a common funding pool for all NGEU programmes. According to the funding strategy of the Commission, it will borrow roughly €150 billion per year until 2026 at the latest. 30% of NGEU funds (amounting to up to €250 billion in current prices) shall be raised via green bonds according to the NGEU Green Bond Framework (Commission, 'Next Generation EU – Green Bond Framework (Commission staff working document)' SWD (2021) 242 final). *cf* in particular, Commission, 'Communication to the European parliament and the council on a new funding strategy to finance NextGenerationEU' COM (2021) 250 final; Commission Decision (EU) on the establishment of the primary dealer network and the definition of eligibility criteria for lead and co-lead mandates for syndicated transactions for the purposes of the borrowing activities by the Commission on behalf of the Union and of the European Atomic Energy Community C(2021) 2500 final; and Commission Decision on specific internal rules on the implementation of borrowing, debt management and lending operations and of the primary dealer network established by Commission Decision C (2021) 2500, C(2021) 2501; as well as Commission implementing decision establishing the necessary arrangements for the administration of the borrowing operations under Council Decision (EU, Euratom) 2020/2053 and for the lending operations related to loans granted in accordance with Article 15 of Regulation (EU) 2021/241 of the European Parliament and of the Council, C (2021) 2502; and Commission Implementing Decision (EU) 2021/1095 establishing the methodology for allocating costs related to borrowing and debt management operations under NextGenerationEU [2021] OJ L236/75; *cf* also the new Art 220a of the Financial Regulation (EU, Euratom) 2018/1046, as introduced by Regulation (EU, Euratom) 2022/2434 [2022] OJ L319/1, on the diversified funding strategy as a general borrowing method.

[30] Art 5 ORD.

[31] Art 5(2) ORD.

[32] See again Art 5(2) ORD. Since the Union uses own resources to pay back the money when the borrowing has reached maturity, it depends on the system and structure of own resources from

own resources system, which require unanimity and approval by member states, repayment will arguably have to be financed primarily by the member states (in particular: by way of the GNI-based contributions).[33] NGEU thus creates long-term liabilities for the member states, which may also be enforced by the Union.[34]

Compatibility of this legal set-up with EU financial provisions and the rules on own resources is, indeed, rather questionable. Article 310(1)(3) TFEU stipulates that revenue and expenditure shown in the budget shall be in balance, a rule which is generally understood and also defined in the Financial Regulation (FR)[35] in such a way as to preclude borrowing to finance current or operating expenses.[36] NGEU's otherwise obvious tension with this principle of budgetary balance is defused by treating the loans under the RRF, in line with established practice for back-to-back-lending operations, not as expenditure but as budget-neutral financial transactions[37] and by providing that the money used for grants

2028 onwards where the money for repayment comes from. *cf* also Eurostat, 'Guidance note on the statistical recording' para 42.

[33] *cf* Schorkopf, 'Auf dem Weg zur Fiskalunion' 3087 para 20. *cf* Case C-163/06 P *Finland v Commission* ECLI:EU:C:2007:371, paras 30–32 and 35, according to which the obligation for member states to make available own resources to the Union is founded directly on the own resources framework without requiring any additional act.

[34] Repayment is fully integrated into the system of own resources and based on conventional budgetary mechanisms; see Council Legal Service, Opinion, Council Doc 9062/20 (Brussels, 24 June 2020) para 31. Thus, future MFFs will foresee appropriations and revenue from own resources will be allocated up-front. The Council Legal Service however, sees the ORD as creating a 'claim against the Member States', resulting in an 'irrevocable, definitive and enforceable guarantee of payment' (Council Legal Service, Opinion, Council Doc 9062/20 (Brussels, 24 June 2020) para 43). Member states accordingly also have an obligation under the ORD to make the additional resources available to the Commission, where the authorised appropriations are not sufficient to meet repayment obligations (*cf* Art 9(4) ORD). While earlier drafts included a reference to Art 14 of the Making Available Regulation (Council Regulation (EU, Euratom) No 609/2014 on the methods and procedure for making available the traditional, VAT and GNI-based own resources and on the measures to meet cash requirements (Recast) [2014] OJ L168/39), according to which division among the member states in proportion to the estimated revenue from each of them was only foreseen 'as far as possible', this obligation is always only a *pro rata* obligation. The Council Legal Service suggested making it clear in the ORD that a member state's liability is limited in any event by the amount it has committed to transfer. See Council Legal Service, Opinion, Council Doc 9062/20 (Brussels, 24 June 2020) paras 107–113.

[35] Regulation (EU, Euratom) 2018/1046 of the European Parliament and of the Council on the financial rules applicable to the general budget of the Union, amending Regulations (EU) No 1296/2013, (EU) No 1301/2013, (EU) No 1303/2013, (EU) No 1304/2013, (EU) No 1309/2013, (EU) No 1316/2013, (EU) No 223/2014, (EU) No 283/2014, and Decision No 541/2014/EU and repealing Regulation (EU, Euratom) No 966/2012 [2018] OJ L193/1, Art 17 (2): 'The Union and the Union bodies referred to in Articles 70 and 71 shall not raise loans within the framework of the budget.' This is defined as the 'principle of equilibrium'.

[36] Council Legal Service, Opinion, Council Doc 9062/20 (Brussels, 24 June 2020) para 21 f wfr. *cf* also Päivi Leino-Sandberg, 'Who is ultra vires now? The EU's legal U-turn in interpreting Article 310 TFEU' (*Verfassungsblog*, 18 June 2020) https://verfassungsblog.de/who-is-ultra-vires-now-the-eus-legal-u-turn-in-interpreting-article-310-tfeu.

[37] The institutions consider that such operations of 'back-to-back-lending' are compatible with the Treaties, as they constitute 'neutral, off-budget operations' and create only 'contingent liabilities, ie liabilities which will only materialize in case of default on the loan', see Council Legal Service, Opinion, Council Doc 9062/20 (Brussels, 24 June 2020) para 24, 28. *cf* also Leino-Sandberg and Ruffert,

shall constitute external assigned revenue to the Union programmes.[38] This means it is not included in the budget, not voted upon in the annual budgetary procedure, not counted against the ceilings of the MFF, and last but not least, not an own resource but 'other revenue' as mentioned in Article 311(2) TFEU.[39]

The price for this ploy is a tension with the principles of unity and universality of the budget. Article 310(1) TFEU requires that '[a]ll items of revenue and expenditure of the Union shall be included in estimates to be drawn up for each financial year and shall be shown in the budget', thus limiting off-budget operations.[40] Universality means that all revenue shall finance all expenditure without distinction.[41] While the FR exceptionally allows that revenue also be assigned to specific items of expenditure,[42] such revenue has to be additional or complementary to the appropriations in the budget.[43] 'Other revenue' in the sense of Article 311(2) TFEU may thus not serve as a primary source of financing of the Union budget.[44] Borrowing that amounts to several times the general budget and while formally allocated to a 'recovery instrument' can be used for a wide variety of policy areas – in particular, but not exclusively, environmental, agricultural, and cohesion policies – is indeed difficult to reconcile with these prerequisites.[45]

The same holds true for the adherence to budgetary discipline and neutrality as stipulated in Article 310(4) TFEU, since the money borrowed will have to be paid back by the Union eventually. While this is less problematic for loans that are on-lent to the member states and are, thus, comparable to other forms of back-to-back-lending, creating only a contingent liability of the Union,[46] the repayment of the funds spent on grants is a different story. According to the Council Legal Service, their budget neutrality and thus, the necessary 'assurance' in the sense of Article 310(4) TFEU[47] is ensured by member states' commitment under the ORD, which creates an 'irrevocable, definitive and enforceable guarantee of payment that is given upfront by the Member States' as an asset counter-balancing the debt.[48]

'Next Generation EU and Its Constitutional Ramifications' 452, and Eurostat, 'Guidance note on the statistical recording', on the treatment of back-to-back lending under ESA 2010.

[38] Art 3(1) EURI Regulation. *cf* Art 21 FR.

[39] Council Legal Service, Opinion, Council Doc 9062/20 (Brussels, 24 June 2020) paras 31, 57.

[40] *cf* also Art 8(1) FR. The idea behind having a single document is to protect the budgetary prerogatives of the European Parliament and the Council (*cf* Art 14(1) and Art 16(1) TEU as well as Art 314 TFEU).

[41] Art 20 FR.

[42] Art 21(5) FR.

[43] Council Legal Service, Opinion, Council Doc 9062/20 (Brussels, 24 June 2020) para 59.

[44] *cf* the wording of Art 311(2) TFEU, according to which '[w]ithout prejudice to other revenue, the budget shall be financed *wholly* from own resources' (emphasis added).

[45] See also Schorkopf, 'Auf dem Weg zur Fiskalunion' 3088 para 30 and 3089 para 36.

[46] *cf* Art 2(15) FR.

[47] Art 310(4) TFEU stipulates that 'the Union shall not adopt any act which is likely to have appreciable implications for the budget without providing an *assurance* that the expenditure arising from such an act is capable of being financed within the limit of the Union's own resources and in compliance with the multiannual financial framework referred to in Article 312' (emphasis added).

[48] Council Legal Service, Opinion, Council Doc 9062/20 (Brussels, 24 June 2020) paras 43 ff.

Under Article 311 TFEU, however, amendment of the ORD is in the hands of the member states and has to be approved in accordance with their respective constitutional requirements.[49] Repayment of the funds borrowed will only start under the next MFF, making even the scarce provisions thereon in the ORD part of the leverage in the negotiations[50] regarding, inter alia, the introduction of EU taxes, which is why their irrevocability, definitiveness and enforceability is not as guaranteed as the Council Legal Service likes to make it sound.[51]

2.2. Why and how NGEU's Size Matters for the Legal Assessment

Against the backdrop of these manifold legal issues, this chapter will now turn to the question of why and how NGEU's size matters for its legal assessment. The terminology introduced by Ronald Dworkin will be used to differentiate between the importance of NGEU's unprecedented volume for the interpretation of rules on the one hand and for legal principles on the other. According to this terminology, rules are applicable in an all-or-nothing fashion and, if applicable, dictate a particular result, while principles, even if clearly applicable to a given case, only state a reason that argues in one direction, but do not necessitate a particular decision.[52]

2.2.1. Implications of NGEU's Size for the Interpretation of Rules

Many of the primary law provisions relevant for the assessment of NGEU's legality explicitly or implicitly take the size of a measure into account. Size is, thus, a factor to consider when determining whether the particular rule is applicable and prompts a particular result. Starting with the last point discussed in Section II, the provisions on the Union's own resources, size matters for the relationship between 'own resources' and 'other revenue'. When Article 311(2) TFEU stipulates that '[w]ithout prejudice to other revenue, the budget shall be financed wholly from own resources', it arguably presupposes that 'other revenue' is – also in quantitative terms – subordinate to the own resources, which otherwise 'wholly'[53] finance the budget. Size also matters for the safeguarding of budgetary discipline according

[49] Art 311 TFEU requires unanimity in the Council and approval by member states in accordance with their respective constitutional requirements.

[50] *cf* Eurostat, 'Guidance note on the statistical recording' para 36: 'it is common that the own resources ceilings are raised or reviewed to accommodate the EU budget needs'.

[51] It was thus suggested that functionally the debts were *pro rata* member states' debts, which were, however, not included in the government debt quota; see Schorkopf, 'Auf dem Weg zur Fiskalunion' 3090 para 40.

[52] See Ronald Dworkin, *Taking Rights Seriously* (Cambridge, MA, Harvard University Press, 1977) 22 ff.

[53] In the French version 'intégralement'; in German 'vollständig'.

to Article 310(4) TFEU, which only requires 'an assurance' for acts likely to have 'appreciable implications for the budget'. Despite there being no further definition of when implications are 'appreciable', this arguably means that minor implications for the budget do not prompt the need for an assurance that the expenditure arising is capable of being financed within the limit of the Union's own resources and in compliance with the MFF.

That size matters is also rather obvious for the prohibition of excessive government deficits in Article 126 TFEU in combination with Protocol (No 12), containing the actual 'reference criteria' and thus, quantitative limits, for deficit and debt in relation to GDP.[54] Considering that the prohibition of bailouts aims at ensuring that member states' public finances remain subject to the logic of the markets when they enter into debt,[55] and Article 122 TFEU provides only an exemption to this rule for cases of difficulties, size also matters, however, for the compatibility with Article 122 in combination with Article 125 TFEU. It would thus seem that the bigger the instrument based on Article 122 TFEU, the less likely it is to comply with Article 125 TFEU, or, put differently, the more likely it is to diminish the incentive for recipient member states to conduct a sound budgetary policy.[56] On the other hand, it seems that below a certain threshold, there would not be an appreciable implication on member states' budgetary policies.

What all of these provisions have in common is that when size matters, it is *relative* not absolute size that can be identified as a crucial factor for the legality of a measure. An instrument's size thus matters only in relation to a frame of reference, which is subject to change over the course of time. Regarding Article 122 in combination with Article 125 TFEU, it is member states' yearly budgets that provide the frame of reference; regarding Article 126 TFEU in combination with Protocol (No 12), it is member states' GDP at market prices. As for Article 310(4) TFEU, the Union budget provides the frame of reference, and for Article 311(2) TFEU it is the total amount of own resources accrued by the Union. Admittedly, unless clearly specified in primary law – as is the case for the reference criteria for government deficit and debt in Protocol (No 12) – it is rather difficult to determine a specific materiality threshold in relation to the relevant frame of reference. Since any such threshold is dependent on the particular provision and can arguably only be determined by approximation, the (Union) legislator has a wide margin of manoeuvre, in spite of being subject to review by the CJEU. Even when considering this wide margin of manoeuvre, arguing for NGEU's legality arguably requires contortions when interpreting primary law rules – and this is partly owed to its unprecedented volume.

[54] These reference criteria are 3% for the ratio of the planned or actual government deficit to GDP at market prices and 60% for the ratio of government debt to gross domestic product at market prices, see Protocol (No 12) on the excessive deficit procedure [2008] OJ L115/279, Art 1.

[55] *cf Pringle v Ireland* para 135.

[56] ibid para 136.

2.2.2. Implications of NGEU's Size on EU Law Principles

Size also matters as a factor for the interpretation of Union law principles, which provide arguments for or against the compatibility with EU law without mandating a particular outcome. The natural starting point for this hypothesis is Article 5 of the Treaty on European Union (TEU), containing the principles of conferral, subsidiarity and proportionality. The principle of conferral, which stipulates that 'the Union shall act only within the limits of the competences conferred upon it by the Member States in the Treaties to attain the objectives set out therein', only requires size to be taken account of when the respective competence used by the Union does so. As we have seen regarding NGEU, this is the case for both Article 122 in combination with Article 125 TFEU as well as for Article 310(4) and Article 311 TFEU. The principles of subsidiarity and proportionality, however, warrant further consideration. Both are principles governing the *exercise* of Union competences.

Subsidiarity means that 'the Union shall act only if and in so far as the objectives of the proposed action cannot be sufficiently achieved by the Member States, … but can rather, by reason of the scale or effects of the proposed action, be better achieved at Union level'. Already the wording suggests that the 'scale … of the proposed action' matters in determining whether an action may be better achieved at Union level. It seems that in this case, however, larger size does not mean that member state action is sufficient. On the contrary, the fact that an action is large scale might even serve as an argument in favour of Union action. With the Treaty of Lisbon, a scrutiny mechanism was established allowing national parliaments to file a 'reasoned opinion' when they consider the principle of subsidiarity violated by a draft legislative act.[57] Such a reasoned opinion was issued by the Swedish Riksdag on the draft of the ORD containing the empowerment of the Union to borrow for spending,[58] as it considered the measures too extensive to achieve the objectives of the proposal, and a clear justification as to why the borrowing should occur at EU level was missing.[59] In its reply, the Commission indeed used the large size of NGEU as an argument in favour of its compliance with the principle of subsidiarity.[60]

The principle of proportionality, on the other hand, provides arguments for limiting the size of a measure at Union level. Under this principle, 'the content and form of Union action shall not exceed what is necessary to achieve

[57] A reasoned opinion cannot prevent the adoption of a legal act. However, if reasoned opinions represent at least one third of the votes allocated to the national parliaments (there is one vote per chamber for a bicameral parliamentary system and two votes for a unicameral system), the Commission must review the draft (so-called 'yellow card').

[58] Sveriges Riksdag, 'Subsidiaritetsprövning av kommissionens ändrade förslag till beslut om Europeiska unionens egna medel' (Finansutskottets utlåtande, 2019/20:FiU63, Stockholm, 22 June 2020).

[59] Commission, 'Annual Report 2020 on the Application of the Principles of Subsidiarity and Proportionality and on Relations with National Parliaments' (Report) COM (2021) 417 final, 12.

[60] ibid.

the objectives of the Treaties'. Any Union action is thus limited by its objective, also in quantitative terms. When such an objective is defined as 'addressing the consequences of the COVID-19 crisis', a large-scale distributive programme which goes beyond alleviating the problems caused by the pandemic becomes hard to justify. Such an orientation towards what is actually needed, and, therefore, a limitation for a measure's size, may also be considered as part of a Union law principle of solidarity, which the CJEU has recognised as one of the fundamental principles of EU law.[61]

Finally, Union law is based on the principle of member states' responsibility for their budgets as well as their fiscal autonomy, a principle which was also maintained after the establishment of the Economic and Monetary Union (EMU). This is expressed, for instance, in the obligation to avoid excessive public deficits or in the prohibition of bail-out, but is generally entailed in the concept of a Union comprised of 'Member States',[62] with an EMU based on stability.[63] Respect for member states' national identities and their essential state functions, which arguably include budgetary powers and decisions on revenue and expenditure, is also enshrined in Article 4(2) TEU. EU law therefore generally presupposes the budgetary autonomy of its member states. The scale of payment obligations and/or transfers of funds to/from member states caused by a measure can call into question their freedom to generally decide on public revenue and expenditure. Thus, the principles of budgetary and fiscal autonomy may suggest a limitation to the size of a measure.

3. The Constitutional Law Perspective

Turning now briefly to the constitutional law perspective, NGEU's legal set-up entails a new ORD, which can only 'enter into force [once] it is approved by the Member States in accordance with their respective constitutional requirements'.[64] According to these constitutional requirements, the approval is generally in the hands of national parliaments, although in some member states[65] the government is responsible. Depending on the assessment of the substance of the decision, some member states require a qualified majority. In Finland, the Constitutional

[61] *cf*, recently, Case C-157/21 *Poland v EP/Council* ECLI:EU:C:2022:98 para 147 with further references; Case C-156/21 *Hungary v EP/Council* ECLI:EU:C:2022:97 para 129.

[62] In its seminal *Maastricht* judgment, the German Federal Constitutional Court followed Paul Kirchhof in describing the then European Community as a compound of member states ('Staatenverbund'); see BVerfGE 89, 155 <205>.

[63] The German Federal Constitutional Court coined the term 'Stabilitätsgemeinschaft' (stability union) to describe the relationship of the member states within EMU; see BVerfGE 89, 155 <205>. The provisions binding member states in their fiscal and economic policies therein also form the basis for the credibility of the common currency.

[64] Art 311(3) TFEU.

[65] Namely SLO, SK, MT, LV, CY, IE, CZ.

Law Committee concluded that NGEU's approval required a qualified majority, arguing essentially that it would change the nature of the Union and the relationship between the EU and its member states, affecting not only the overall control of risks but also Finnish budgetary sovereignty.[66] Although this view was not shared by the Austrian parliament itself, I believe that as the Federal Constitutional Law requires a two-thirds majority whenever an ORD introduces 'new categories of own resources of the European Union'[67] there would have been ample reason to argue for a two-thirds majority also in the Austrian national assembly.[68] In Germany, the Federal Constitutional Court rejected a preliminary injunction against the ratification of NGEU,[69] paving the way for its entry into force in June last year, after all member states notified approval. However, the Court will still have to issue its final decision on NGEU's constitutionality, in particular its compliance with the integration barriers of Article 79(3) in combination with Article 20 of the Basic Law (GG).[70]

Without being able to go into detail here, size may matter from a constitutional law perspective for the assessment of which parliamentary procedure has to be used for the approval of the ORD, but also generally for the constitutional assessment of the expenditure side of NGEU. Several member states assert constitutional barriers for European integration as protection of their national identities or against acts that are ultra vires. While the CJEU considers that EU law will take primacy even before structural principles of national constitutional law,[71] in order to achieve such an effect, member states argue, their legal systems must have opened up to EU law accordingly. The basis for the application of Union law, thus, lies in national constitutional law. Consequently, by monitoring the inviolability of those national constitutional principles, which are constitutive for democracy and the rule of law, national constitutional courts legitimately act as guardians of these principles in the respective member states.[72] National constitutional courts are, admittedly, rather reluctant to use these instruments, given the open opposition otherwise created towards the CJEU. However, budgetary prerogatives and, in particular, the overall budgetary responsibility of (a federal) parliament

[66] See further Päivi Leino-Sandberg, 'Between European Commitment and "Taking the Law Seriously"': The EU Own Resources Decision in Finland' (*Verfassungsblog*, 29 April 2021), https://verfassungsblog.de/between-european-commitment-and-taking-the-law-seriously.

[67] Art 23i(3) Federal Constitutional Law (B-VG).

[68] Claudia Wutscher, *Budgethoheit* (forthcoming 2024).

[69] BVerfGE 157, 332 (English language version available at www.bundesverfassungsgericht.de/SharedDocs/Entscheidungen/EN/2021/04/rs20210415_2bvr054721en.html).

[70] For an overview of the topics addressed during the oral hearing see Ruth Weber, 'Karlsruher Türsteher: Das Bundesverfassungsgericht verhandelt das Eigenmittelbeschluss-Ratifizierungsgesetz' (*Verfassungsblog*, 29 July 2022), https://verfassungsblog.de/karlsruher-tursteher/.

[71] See Case 11/70 *Internationale Handelsgesellschaft v Einfuhr- und Vorratsstelle* ECLI:EU:C:1970:114, para 3.

[72] *cf* Jürgen Habermas, 'Die Krise der Europäischen Union im Lichte einer Konstitutionalisierung des Völkerrechts' in Claudio Franzius, Franz C Mayer and Jürgen Neyer (eds), *Grenzen der europäischen Integration: Herausforderungen für Recht und Politik* (Baden-Baden, Nomos, 2014) 61–92, 75.

are among the areas where such a verdict is conceivable, as famously advanced by the German Federal Constitutional Court.[73] This is also, though not exclusively, because 'sovereign statehood is … not possible without sufficient and secure financial resources".[74] The conclusion reached in section 2.2, namely that member states' budgetary autonomy entails quantitative limitations for Union action, is, consequently, also relevant from a constitutional law perspective.

Without budgetary autonomy, it would seem, no effective and independent state power can come into being, because the exercise of *any state power* requires the authority to decide on the procurement and allocation of the resources required for this purpose. Budgetary autonomy may thus be qualified as a necessary, though not sufficient, condition of statehood.[75] This is relevant under EU law as well, as the Treaties presuppose the existence of member states, which arguably (and not only for a possible application of the excessive deficit procedure, but also for the term 'member state' to make sense) must be states responsible for their public finances. If the fulfilment of any government task requires financial resources, it also becomes clear why budgetary autonomy can also be understood as a financial manifestation of the constitutional principle of democracy recognised in many member states.[76] Democratic self-determination in the understanding of modern constitutional states thus requires budgetary autonomy, both in the material sense of being able to dispose of public revenue and expenditure, as well as in the formal sense of an elected parliamentary authority periodically deciding on a comprehensive budget.

However, the threshold is rather high. NGEU requires member states to request grants and loans for concrete reforms and investments, leaving it in member states' hands to decide whether and for what projects or measures they request funds from the recovery instrument. Moreover, transfers to individual member states amount to a lower single-digit percentage range in relation to the particular member states' GDP. Both factors suggest that member states' budgetary autonomy is not yet at risk from NGEU in its current form.[77] This conclusion would be different, however, if a significant part of member states' budgets were to be transferred to and then distributed at EU level, especially if done without further involvement of national parliaments as to what the funds are ultimately used for. Such significance is once again determined in relation to member states' total budgets as a frame of reference.

[73] *cf* eg BVerfGE 123, 267 <359>; and BVerfGE 129, 124 <177>.

[74] Michael Schaper and Michael Philipp, 'Währungsstabilität und Staatsfinanzen bei Jean Bodin' in Michael Philipp (ed), *Debatten um die Souveränität* (Baden-Baden, Nomos, 2016) 99–122, 99.

[75] I have first advanced and elaborated this argument further in Claudia Wutscher, 'Budgethoheit als konstitutives Element der Staatlichkeit?' in Lisa Heschl et al (eds) *L'État' c'est quoi? Staatsgewalt im Wandel* (Baden-Baden, Nomos, 2015) 175–92, 175.

[76] *cf* eg Christian Waldhoff, 'Finanzautonomie und Finanzverflechtung in gestuften Rechtsordnungen' in Vereinigung der Deutschen Staatsrechtslehrer, *Bundesstaat und Europäische Union zwischen Konflikt und Kooperation* (Berlin, VVDStRL 66, 2007) 216–76, 238.

[77] *cf* Schorkopf, 'Auf dem Weg zur Fiskalunion' 3089 f para 31 f, para 42.

4. Concluding Remarks

In conclusion, NGEU's design is indeed innovative, but its compliance with primary law is questionable. This concerns, in particular, the compatibility of the EURI Regulation with Articles 122 and 125 TFEU as well as the compatibility of the empowerment in the ORD to borrow on the markets with Articles 310 and 311 TFEU. It was argued that when assessing such compliance, size, not in absolute terms but in relation to a specific frame of reference, is a crucial factor for determining the legality of NGEU. Size has to be taken into account in the interpretation of concrete rules, such as the provisions just mentioned, as well as in the application of EU law principles such as subsidiarity, proportionality and member states' budgetary autonomy. Size also matters from the constitutional perspective, both for the assessment of the relevant procedure for approval of the ORD as well as for determining whether member states' constitutional prerogatives are respected. In particular, these prerogatives also entail budgetary autonomy as the financial manifestation of democratic self-determination.

7

The Solidarity Framework

Towards a New Pillar of the EMU?

FRANCESCO MARTUCCI

'This is European solidarity in action', said Ursula von der Leyen in her speech about the State of the Union.[1] The President of the European Commission was not only talking about solidarity with Ukraine, but also about budgetary matters, energy, migration, etc.

According to the European Court of Justice (ECJ) the principle of solidarity is indeed 'one of the fundamental principles of EU law'.[2] Several provisions of the Treaties refer to the principle of solidarity.

> As regards the EU Treaty, in the preamble thereto, the Member States declare that, by establishing the European Union, they intend 'to deepen the solidarity between their peoples'. Solidarity is also mentioned in Article 2 TEU, as one of the characteristics of a society founded on the values common to the Member States, and in the third subparagraph of Article 3(3) TEU, according to which the European Union is to promote, inter alia, solidarity among Member States.[3]

The solidarity principle is not absent from the Economic and Monetary Union (EMU).[4] In accordance with Article 122(1) of the Treaty on the Functioning of the European Union (TFEU), the Council 'may decide, in a spirit of solidarity between Member States, upon the measures appropriate to the economic situation'. However, this legal basis had not been used within the EMU until the sovereign

[1] Ursula von der Leyen, State of the Union Address 2022 (European Commission) 11, https://state-of-the-union.ec.europa.eu/system/files/2022-09/SOTEU_2022_Address_EN.pdf.

[2] Case C-848/19 P *Germany v Poland* ECLI:EU:C:2021:598, para 38. See Christian Tomuschat, 'Solidarität in Europa' in Francesco Capotorti, Claus-Dieter Ehlermann and Jochen Frowein (eds), *Du droit international au droit de l'intégration: liber amicorum Pierre Pescatore* (Baden-Baden, Nomos Verlag, 1987) 729–57. See also Ramona Coman, Louise Fromont and Anne Weyembergh (eds), *Les solidarités européennes: Entre enjeux, tensions et reconfigurations* (Bruylant, Bruxelles, 2019).

[3] Case C-848/19 P *Germany v Poland* ECLI:EU:C:2021:598, para 39.

[4] See Fabian Amtenbrink, Christoph Herrmann and René Repasi (eds), *The EU Law of Economic and Monetary Union* (Oxford, Oxford University Press, 2020). Jean-Victor Louis, *L'Union européenne et sa monnaie* (Bruxelles, Éditions de l'ULB, 2010).

debt crisis. The reason for this is that the EMU was grounded on the following disciplinary paradigm: as the single currency, the euro was supposed to guarantee the prosperity of the eurozone through the two principles of price stability and fiscal discipline. The Treaty of Maastricht was based on the premise that member states whose currency is the euro would not need any financial assistance. But the financial crisis and the sovereign debt crisis showed the limits of this disciplinary paradigm. The mechanisms put in place to remedy the sovereign debt crisis, however, were based on a logic of conditionality in line with the paradigm of discipline.

The real change came with the Covid-19 crisis. Real solidarity mechanisms based on debt mutualisation have emerged since. As the Advocate General Campos Sánchez-Bordona said:

> The adoption at the European Council of 10 and 11 December 2020 of the Multiannual Financial Framework 2021-2027 and the European Union Recovery Facility (Next Generation EU) is arguably the biggest step forward in terms of solidarity which the European Union has taken in its history. For the first time, the European Union is going to borrow by raising money on the capital markets in order to finance, through large-scale grants and loans, the economic recovery of the Member States, depending on how badly they have been affected by COVID-19.[5]

Insofar as the regulation establishing the Recovery and Resilience Facility (RFF) is based on Article 122 TFEU,[6] NextGenerationEU (NGEU) is an integral part of the EMU. Did the Covid-19 pandemic promote a new framework of the EMU? After decades of discipline, the time of solidarity finally came.[7] At least, this is what the introduction of new mechanisms to overcome crises suggests. This chapter aims to show the progress of solidarity in the EMU and argues that the framework of discipline has been complemented by that of solidarity.

1. Fiscal Discipline

Since the introduction of the single currency, the Economic Union has relied on a discipline framework organised by the Treaties. While monetary policy is an exclusive competence of the EU, economic and fiscal policies remain national

[5] Case C-848/19 P *Germany v Poland* ECLI:EU:C:2021:598 Opinion of AG Campos Sánchez-Bordona, fn 44.

[6] Regulation (EU) 2021/241 of the European Parliament and of the Council establishing the Recovery and Resilience Facility [2012] OJ L57/17.

[7] On solidarity before the Covid-19 crisis, see Christian Calliess, 'Perspektiven des Euro zwischen Solidarität und Recht – Eine rechtliche Analyse der Griechenlandhilfe und des Rettungsschirms' (2011) 14 *Zeitschrift für europarechtliche Studien* 213. Jean-Victor Louis, 'Solidarité budgétaire et financière dans l'Union européenne' in Chahira Boutayeb (ed), *La solidarité dans l'Union européenne: Éléments constitutionnels et matériels* (Paris, Dalloz, 2011) 107–24. Francesco Martucci, 'Stabilité et solidarité dans la zone euro' in Estelle Brosset, Rostane Mehdi and Nathalie Rubio (eds), *Solidarité et droit de l'Union européenne: Un principe à l'épreuve* (Aix-en-Provence, DICE Éditions, 2021) 137–50.

competences. Therefore, since the Treaty of Maastricht, member states have implemented their fiscal and economy policies in the legal framework enshrined in the primary law and established by the secondary law. The so-called 'discipline framework' refers to the fiscal rules applied to the member states.

On the one hand, the market discipline of fiscal policies relies on three provisions. Article 123 TFEU prohibits monetary financing, ie the European Central Bank (ECB) and the national central banks (NCB) may not grant overdraft facilities or any other type of credit facility to the member states. Therefore, member states are to ensure their capacity to finance themselves on the financial markets. According to Article 124 TFEU, any measure establishing privileged access by member states to financial institutions shall be prohibited. Article 125 TFEU enshrines the no-bail-out clause: neither the Union nor the member states shall be liable for or assume the commitments of another member state. These three provisions enable financial discipline by the market. Member states ensure sustainability of public finances in order to borrow on the financial markets at convenient conditions. Financial operators are to apply the risk premium to member states whose public finances are not sound. Thus, the spread rises when the state is in financial difficulties. Greece's crisis is the most remarkable example of such a situation. When in 2009 the Greek government published the real situation of its public finances, the spread increased.

On the other hand, Article 126 TFEU prohibits the member states from having an excessive deficit. The compliance with budgetary discipline is examined on the basis of two criteria. The ratio of the public debt to gross domestic product shall not exceed the reference value of 60 per cent while the ratio of the public deficit to gross domestic product shall not exceed the reference value of 3 per cent. On the basis of Articles 121 and 126 TFEU, the EU legislator adopted the Stability Growth Pact (SGP) in order to enforce these fiscal rules. The SGP relies on three pillars: preventive, corrective and repressive. The member states shall prevent the occurrence of an excessive deficit by respecting the medium-term objective for the budgetary position of close to balance or in surplus. When the Council decides that an excessive deficit exists, the procedure becomes corrective. If a member state fails to comply with this decision taken, the Council may decide to apply financial sanctions. Up until now, no sanctions have been decided by the Council.[8] Fiscal discipline is, rather, based on the assessment that the Commission and the Council exert pressure on member states, the extent of which depends on the sustainability of national public finances. As long as the member states comply with the fiscal rules, they remain within the disciplinary framework. If there is

[8] Except for one case: Portugal and Spain had been sanctioned for failure to take effective action in response to the Council recommendation, but finally the Council decided to cancel the fines. Council Implementing Decision (EU) 2017/2350 on imposing a fine on Portugal for failure to take effective action to address an excessive deficit [2017] OJ L336/24; Council Implementing Decision (EU) 2017/2351 on imposing a fine on Spain for failure to take effective action to address an excessive deficit [2017] OJ L336/27.

a risk of an excessive deficit in a member state, European institutions address an opinion to the national government. When the Council decides that an excessive deficit exists, recommendations are addressed to the member states.

In practice, fiscal governance is determined by procedures more than by rules. According to Article 126 TFEU, the member states shall respect the rules of avoiding excessive deficit. The EU legislator has adopted the rules for the objective medium-term objective of a budget close to balance or in surplus. Along with the EU law, the Fiscal Compact had been concluded by member states as *inter se* Treaty: pursuant to Article 3 of the Treaty on Stability, Coordination and Growth (TSCG), the rule that the budgetary position of the state shall be balanced or in surplus, shall take effect in the national law through provisions of binding force and permanent character, preferably constitutional, or otherwise guaranteed to be fully respected and adhered to throughout the national budgetary processes. However, these fiscal rules are a kind of soft law in so far as they are not binding for the member states. More precisely, courts are not competent to sanction the breach of fiscal rules.[9] In accordance with Articles 121 and 126 TFEU, the EU legislator has provided procedures which permit the European Commission and the Council to survey the economic and fiscal policies of the member states in the framework of the European Semester. Every year, national governments must submit programmes to the EU institutions which prepare reports and address opinions and recommendation to member states. Thus, in the eurozone, the national government is to address the stability programme, the national reform programme and the draft budgetary plan to the Commission. If the Council, acting under Article 126(6) TFEU, decides that an excessive deficit exists in a member state, the member state concerned must present an economic partnership programme. The European Commission and the Council examine whether the programmes submitted by the member states are in accordance with the fiscal rules. To sum up, where there is divergence, recommendations are addressed to the concerned member states. Fiscal surveillance is based more on the logic of political pressure than legal constraint. As long as the state respects the limits of the framework, it is free to conduct its economic policy as it wishes. Once it steps outside the framework, pressure is exerted to bring it back within the limits.

Before the Covid-19 crisis, the procedures of fiscal discipline had already been implemented. In 2003, the Council adopted decisions on the existence of a public deficit in France and Germany. The European Commission recommended the adoption of a decision establishing inadequate action and a decision to give notice, pursuant to Article 126(8) and (9) TFEU. However, the Council decided, in breach of SGP, to suspend the process as stated by the ECJ.[10] Finally, the decision on the existence of an excessive deficit was abrogated in 2007. Due to the financial

[9] Art 126(10) TFEU.

[10] Case C-27/04 Commission of the European Communities v Council of the European Union ECLI:EU:C:2004:436.

crisis in 2009, excessive deficit procedures had been implemented for all member states, except for Estonia and Sweden. For instance, France was subject to a deficit procedure until 2018, while the procedure concerning Germany was closed in 2012. When the Commission proposed to make 'the best use of the flexibility within the existing rules of the stability and growth' since 2015,[11] the Covid-19 crisis marks a paradigm shift in the implementation of deficit excessive procedures. For the first time, the European Commission activated the general escape clause of the SGP in March 2020 allowing member states to react swiftly and adopt emergency measures to mitigate the economic and social impact of the pandemic. In March 2021, the Commission clarified:

> the decision to deactivate the general escape clause should be taken based on an overall assessment of the state of the economy based on quantitative criteria, with the level of economic activity in the EU compared to pre-crisis levels as the key quantitative criterion.[12]

The general escape clause continued to be applied in 2022 and is expected to be deactivated in 2023. To be precise, it does not suspend the procedures of the SGP. 'It will allow the Commission and the Council to undertake the necessary policy coordination measures within the framework of the Pact, while departing from the budgetary requirements that would normally apply.'[13] The Covid-19 crisis could explain the Commission's proposals to reform the EMU by introducing more flexibility to assess fiscal discipline.[14]

2. Assistance Mechanisms and Financial Stability

The drafters of the Maastricht Treaty were not mindful of the need for such a financial assistance mechanism within the eurozone.[15] This explains why the European institutions and the member states were unable to manage the Greek

[11] Commission, 'Communication from the Commission to the European Parliament, the Council, the European Central Bank, the Economic and Social Committee, the Committee of the regions and the European Investment Bank, Making the best use of the flexibility within the existing rules of the stability and growth pact' COM (2015) 012 final.

[12] European Commission, 'European Semester Spring Package: Paving the way for a strong and sustainable recovery' (*European Commission Website*, 2 June 2021) https://ec.europa.eu/commission/presscorner/detail/en/ip_22_3182.

[13] Commission, 'Communication from the Commission to the Council on the activation of the general escape clause of the Stability and Growth Pact' COM (2020) 123 final.

[14] Commission, 'Communication from the Commission to the European Parliament, the Council, the European Central Bank, the European Economic and Social Committee and the Committee of the Regions on orientations for a reform of the EU economic governance framework' COM (2022) 583 final.

[15] Päivi Leino-Sandberg and Tuomas Saarenheimo, 'Fiscal Stabilisation for EMU: Managing Incompleteness' (2018) 43 *EL Rev* 623.

sovereign debt crisis that started in 2009.[16] Paradoxically, during the financial crisis, financial assistance had been granted to Hungary, Latvia and Romania, all of which did not participate in the single currency (the states with a derogation regarding Articles 139 and 140 TFEU). Pursuant to Article 143 TFEU, the EU shall grant mutual assistance to a member state with a derogation that is in difficulties or is seriously threatened with difficulties as regards its balance of payments. The procedures applicable to the mutual assistance facility provided for in Article 143 TFEU are established by the Council Regulation 332/2002 of 18 February 2002 establishing a facility providing medium-term financial assistance for member states' balance of payments.[17]

After a few months of hesitation, the European institutions and the member states of the eurozone decided to grant loans to Greece and to establish a package of measures to rescue member states, whose currency is the euro, dealing with financial difficulties.[18] In May 2010, the first rescue mechanism had been adopted which was made up of two key elements.[19] On the one hand, adopted on the basis of Article 122 TFEU, Regulation 407/2010 of 11 May 2010 established the European Financial Stabilisation Mechanism (EFSM).[20] The EFSM grants loans to a member state which is experiencing, or is seriously threatened with, a severe economic or financial disturbance caused by exceptional occurrences beyond its control. These loans are guaranteed by the general budget of the European Union. Therefore, due the structural weakness of the EU budget, the EFSM has the authority to raise up to €60 billion.[21] On the other hand, the member states of the eurozone set up the European Financial Stability Facility (EFSF). The EFSF was incorporated as a *société anonyme* under Luxembourg law, whose shareholders are the euro area member states.[22] The euro area member states and the EFSF concluded a Framework Agreement which sets out the terms and conditions upon

[16] See Annamaria Viterbo and Roberto Cisotta, 'La crisi della Grecia, l'attacco speculativo all'euro e le risposte dell'Unione europea' (2010) 4 *Il Diritto dell'Union europea* 961.

[17] Council Regulation (EC) No 332/2002 establishing a facility providing medium-term financial assistance for Member States' balances of payments [2002] OJ L53/1. Amended by Council Regulation (EC) No 431/2009 amending Regulation (EC) No 332/2002 establishing a facility providing medium-term financial assistance for Member States' balances of payments [2009] OJ L128/1.

[18] Council Regulation (EU) No 407/2010 establishing a European financial stabilisation mechanism [2010] OJ L118/1.

[19] See Alberto de Gregorio Merino, 'Legal Developments in the Economic and Monetary Union During the Debt Crisis: The Mechanisms of Financial Assistance' (2012) 49 *CML Rev* 1613.

[20] Council Regulation (EU) No 407/2010 establishing a European financial stabilisation mechanism [2010] OJ L118/1.

[21] Commission, 'Communication from the Commission to the Council and the Economic and Financial Committee on the European Financial Stabilisation Mechanism' COM (2010) 713 final, 4: 'At the time of the adoption of the Regulation, it was estimated that, with careful management of the repayment schedules, a volume of up to EUR 60 billion for the EFSM could be accommodated below the ceiling in addition to the volume of EUR 35 billion which remains available under the Balance of Payments facility'.

[22] EFSF, Société anonyme, statuts coordonnés au 23 avril 2014, www.esm.europa.eu/sites/default/files/efsf_status_coordonnes_23avrl2014.pdf.

which the EFSF may grant financial assistance.[23] The loans of the EFSF were guaranteed by the euro area member states, explaining that this fund was able to issue bonds for an amount of €460 billion. During the sovereign debt crisis of the eurozone, Greece, Ireland and Portugal in 2010 and Cyprus and Spain in 2012 received financial assistance, essentially from the EFSF.

While the EFSM was based on Article 122 TFEU, the EFSF was a pure private law tool which relied on intergovernmental grounds. Therefore, doubts arose as to whether the temporary financial assistance within the eurozone infringed the so-called 'no bail out clause'. Indeed, according to Article 125 TFEU, neither the Union nor the member states shall be liable for or assume the commitments of a member state. Therefore, from a political point of view, it had become apparent that member states needed to establish a permanent crisis mechanism to safeguard the financial stability of the euro area as a whole without appealing to the International Monetary Fund (IMF). Finally, the European Stability Mechanism (ESM) was set up in October 2012 at the height of the crisis as a permanent mechanism replacing the EFSM and the EFSF from 1 July 2013 onwards.[24] Criticised as a 'Legal Monster',[25] the ESM has been enshrined as an international organisation by a Treaty concluded between the member states whose currency is the euro. From my point of view, it is an illustration of the 'Union Method' defined by Angela Merkel as 'coordinated action in a spirit of solidarity – each of [the European institutions and member states] in the area for which we are responsible but all working towards the same goal'.[26]

The ESM raised a number of questions on compatibility with EU law.[27] However, since the ECJ's *Pringle* judgment,[28] it is clear that the member states

[23] EFSF framework agreement, www.esm.europa.eu/sites/default/files/20111019_efsf_framework_agreement_en.pdf.

[24] Treaty establishing the European Stability Mechanism, Recital (1): the 'European Stability Mechanism ("ESM") will assume the tasks currently fulfilled by the European Financial Stability Facility ("EFSF"") and the European Financial Stabilisation Mechanism ("EFSM") in providing, where needed, financial assistance to euro area Member States'.

[25] Loïc Azoulai et al, 'Another Legal Monster? An EUI Debate on the Fiscal Compact Treaty' (2012) EUI Working Paper Law 2012/9.

[26] Angela Merkel, 'Speech by Federal Chancellor Angela Merkel at the opening ceremony of the 61st academic year of the College of Europe in Bruges' (2 November 2010) www.coleurope.eu/sites/default/files/speech-files/europakolleg_brugge_mitschrift_englisch_0.pdf.

[27] See Claire Kilpatrick, 'On the Rule of Law and Economic Emergency: The Degradation of Basic Legal Values in Europe's Bailouts' (2015) 35 *OJLS* 325. Franz-Christoph Zeitler, 'The European Public Debt Crisis and the Institutional Framework of the Monetary Union: Experience and Adjustments' in Peter Huber and Wolf-Georg Ringe (eds), *Legal Challenges in the Global Financial Crisis: Bail-Outs, the Euro and Regulation* (Oxford, Hart Publishing, 2013) 245–48. Edoardo Chiti and Pedro Gustavo Teixeira, 'The Constitutional Implications of the European Responses to the Financial and Public Debt Crisis' (2013) 50 *CML Rev* 683. Georgios Maris and Pantelis Sklias, 'Intergovernmentalism and the New Framework of EMU Governance' in Federico Fabbrini, Ernst Hirsch Ballin and Han Somsen (eds), *What Form of Government for the European Union and the Eurozone?* (Oxford, Bloomsbury, 2015) 57–75.

[28] Case C-370/12 *Thomas Pringle v Government of Ireland and Others* ECLI:EU:C:2012:756.

may grant financial assistance within the eurozone if the conditions of Article 125 TFEU are fulfilled. The ECJ interpreted this provision as follows:

> 135. The prohibition laid down in Article 125 TFEU ensures that the Member States remain subject to the logic of the market when they enter into debt, since that ought to prompt them to maintain budgetary discipline. Compliance with such discipline contributes at Union level to the attainment of a higher objective, namely maintaining the financial stability of the monetary union.
>
> 136. Given that that is the objective pursued by Article 125 TFEU, it must be held that that provision prohibits the Union and the Member States from granting financial assistance as a result of which the incentive of the recipient Member State to conduct a sound budgetary policy is diminished.[29]

In order to maintain the financial stability of the eurozone, Article 136(3) TFEU lays down the condition of 'strict conditionality' which must be interpreted in a restrictive sense. In other words, the financial assistance is attached to the necessity to safeguard the financial stability of the euro area as a whole. Therefore, the purpose of Article 136(3) TFEU is not to promote solidarity between the member states, but to re-establish the macroeconomic stability required by the market. For this reason, the conditionality must contain a range of austerity measures.[30] According to the ESM Treaty, the European Commission is mandated by the ESM to negotiate the Memorandum of Understanding (MoU) with the concerned member state, which provides the conditionality.[31] Greece is a perfect example of the impact of conditionality on the economy and the society of a member state.[32]

The Covid-19 crisis brought about a substantial change in the conditionality. In May 2020, the ESM created the Pandemic Crisis Support instrument, which was available until the end of 2022. The ESM Pandemic Crisis Support was intended to provide loans to support member states in the financing of healthcare costs related to the Covid-19 crisis. According to the Eurogroup,

> the only requirement to access the credit line will be that euro area Member States requesting support would commit to use this credit line to support domestic financing of direct and indirect healthcare, cure and prevention related costs due to the Covid-19 crisis. This commitment will be detailed in an individual Pandemic Response Plan to be prepared on the basis of a template, for any facility granted under the Pandemic Crisis Support.[33]

[29] ibid para 135 f.

[30] See Ulrich Forsthoff and Nathalie Lauer, 'Public Conditionality Attached to the ESM Financial Assistance' in Amtenbrink, Herrmann and Repasi, *The EU Law of Economic and Monetary Union* 878–919.

[31] See Alberto de Gregorio Merino, 'Memoranda of understanding: a critical taxonomy' in ECB Legal Conference 2019, *Building bridges: central banking law in an interconnected world* (Frankfurt, ECB, 2020) 253–62.

[32] Francesco Martucci, 'La Grèce et la crise de dette souveraine: En attendant Godot, allons voir Godeau' (2015) 29 *JCP Edition Générale* 1604.

[33] Council, 'Eurogroup Statement on the Pandemic Crisis Support' (*Council Website*, 8 May 2020) para 4 www.consilium.europa.eu/en/press/press-releases/2020/05/08/eurogroup-statement-on-the-pandemic-crisis-support.

Therefore, the conditionality was designed to be purely health related. Despite the fact that no austerity measure was required, no member state applied for the ESM Pandemic Crisis Support. On the one hand, governments could borrow at very low rates. On the other hand, there was a fear that assistance would nevertheless involve austerity. In the event, the Pandemic Crisis Support played a useful role during the pandemic crisis by calming and reassuring financial markets that euro area countries could quickly gain access to emergency financing if needed. This shows a balance between conditionality and solidarity.

3. NextGenerationEU

The Covid-19 crisis brought with it a milestone for financial solidarity. 'A Hamiltonian moment for the European Union?', asked Otmar Issing, among others.[34] To address the Covid-19 crisis, the European Commission proposed a €750 billion recovery plan – NextGenerationEU (NGEU) – which consists of three pillars.[35] The first pillar includes the European Recovery and Resilience Facility, anchored in the European Semester, taking the form of grants and loans provided under member states' recovery and resilience plans (€560 billion, composed of €310 billion for grants and €250 billion for loans). The Facility was established by a regulation adopted by the EU legislator on the basis of Article 175 TFEU as part of the economic, social and territorial cohesion policy.[36] Additionally, there is the REACT-EU instrument, supporting recovery for Europe's cohesion and territories, consisting of grants to municipalities, hospitals and businesses through the managing authorities of the member states (€55 billion of additional funding under the cohesion policy between 2020 and 2022).[37] The second pillar includes the reinforced InvestEU programme, consisting of a Strategic Investment Facility in the form of an EU budgetary guarantee to finance investment projects through the EIB Group and national development banks (€15.3 billion for

[34] Otmar Issing, 'The COVID-19 Crisis: A Hamilton Moment for the European Union?' (2020) 23 *International Finance* 340. See Leino-Sandberg and Saarenheimo, 'Fiscal Stabilisation for EMU'. This refers to Alexander Hamilton's role in the formation of the United States.

[35] Commission, 'Communication from the Commission to the European Parliament, the European Council, the Council, the European Economic and Social Committee and the Committee of the Regions, Europe's moment: Repair and Prepare for the Next Generation' COM (2020) 456 final. See Bruno De Witte, 'The European Union's COVID-19 recovery plan: The legal engineering of an economic policy shift' (2021) 58 *CML Rev* 635.

[36] Regulation (EU) 2021/241 of the European Parliament and of the Council establishing the Recovery and Resilience Facility [2012] OJ L57/17.

[37] Regulation (EU) 2020/2221 of the European Parliament and of the Council amending Regulation (EU) No 1303/2013 as regards additional resources and implementing arrangements to provide assistance for fostering crisis repair in the context of the COVID-19 pandemic and its social consequences and for preparing a green, digital and resilient recovery of the economy (REACT-EU) [2020] OJ L437/30.

InvestEU and €15 billion for the new Strategic Investment Facility).[38] The third pillar consists of the creation of a new health programme entitled 'EU for Health' to strengthen health security and prepare for future health crises (€9.4 billion), on the basis of Article 168(5) TFEU, ie under health policy.[39] Finally, there are tools to enable 'a rapid, flexible and coordinated Union response to crises' by deploying resources through the Union Solidarity Fund, the European Globalisation Adjustment Fund and the Solidarity and Emergency Aid Reserve.[40]

In order to organise the whole package, the European Commission proposed the adoption of a regulation to establish the EU Recovery Instrument.[41] Based on Article 122 TFEU, this regulation sets out all the measures designed to remedy the economic consequences of the pandemic. The NGEU plan is remarkable for the amount of funding it provides. It has two novel features that are particularly significant for the EU and the member states. First, there are two types of funding for the member states. On the one hand, €360 billion is granted in the classic form of loans under the European Recovery and Resilience Facility. On the other hand, and this is the real innovation, there are 'grants' of €312.5 billion, so that the Union is moving towards a logic of pure transfers without any counterpart – except that of the allocation of funds – in order to contribute 'to alleviating the burden on the budgets of the member states at a time when public finances are under strong pressure'.[42] This marks a remarkable advance in financial solidarity in the European Union, as the choice of the legal basis of Article 122 TFEU shows. Second, once the Union resorts to the instrument of grants, the question of the sources of financing arises, especially since, under Article 310 TFEU, the Union budget must be balanced in terms of expenditure and revenue. The EU budget cannot therefore be financed by borrowing, which would increase the deficit, breaking with decades of budgetary discipline dogma.[43]

Thus, two financing logics coexist. In the short term, it is planned that the Union has been authorised until 31 December 2024 to borrow on the markets the sums necessary to finance the European Recovery and Resilience Facility.[44] For the loans granted to the member states, the idea of borrowing and lending

[38] Regulation (EU) 2021/523 of the European Parliament and of the Council establishing the InvestEU Programme and amending Regulation (EU) 2015/1017 [2021] OJ L107/30.

[39] Regulation (EU) 2021/522 of the European Parliament and of the Council establishing a Programme for the Union's action in the field of health ('EU4Health Programme') for the period 2021–2027, and repealing Regulation (EU) No 282/2014 [2021] OJ L107/1.

[40] Commission, 'Communication from the Commission to the European Parliament, the European Council, the Council, the European Economic and Social Committee and the Committee of the Regions, Europe's moment: Repair and Prepare for the Next Generation' COM (2020) 456 final, 18.

[41] Council Regulation (EU) 2020/2094 establishing a European Union Recovery Instrument to support the recovery in the aftermath of the COVID-19 crisis [2020] OJ LI 433/23.

[42] Commission, 'Communication from the Commission, The EU budget powering the recovery plan for Europe' COM (2020) 442 final, 16.

[43] European Council Meeting at Fontainebleau, Conclusions of the Presidency (25 and 26 June 1984) www.consilium.europa.eu/media/20673/1984_june_-_fontainebleau__eng_.pdf.

[44] Regulation (EU) 2021/241 of the European Parliament and of the Council establishing the Recovery and Resilience Facility [2012] OJ L57/17, Arts 12 and 13.

operations, whereby the EU lends money borrowed on the capital markets to third parties, is repeated. In this way, the Union, which has an excellent reputation on the markets, can give the states the benefit of loans on very favourable terms which are then repaid. In contrast, for grants to member states, one has to take a long-term perspective and, in the absence of repayment by the member states, the mechanism of borrowing and lending operations is not relevant. In order to repay the EU loans, the European institutions work towards introducing sufficient new own resources, with a view to covering an amount corresponding to the expected expenditure related to the repayment of NGEU. As the European Commission argues, the only way out is through a fundamental reform of the Union's own resources system.[45] The broad lines of such a reform are presented in the Communication entitled 'The EU budget: Driving the European recovery plan'.[46] The European Commission has proposed new own resources that would complement the traditional own resources, like for instance taxes on the activities of large companies or on digital technology.[47] This brings us back to the recurring question of a European tax, as the Commission is considering lowering member states' contributions in the Multiannual Financial Framework (MFF) for 2021–27. In accordance with Article 311 TFEU, which implies unanimity in the Council and the approval of the decision by all the member states, each in accordance with their constitutional rules, a new decision on own resources has been adopted.[48] Finally, the Own Resources Decision (ORD) of 14 December 2020 provides for a new category of own resources which is a national contribution on the basis of the quantity of non-recycled plastic packaging waste, with a uniform call rate of €0.80 per kilogram.[49] In addition, the Council and the European Parliament have reached an agreement of a provisional and conditional nature on the Carbon Border Adjustment Mechanism (CBAM).[50]

The European Recovery and Resilience Facility is also based on a logic of conditionality.[51] Member states submit national plans that are assessed by the EU institutions before loan or grant financing is provided. The plan must contain reforms and investments to achieve the six objectives of the facility. Loans and grants are then disbursed on the basis of the achievement of the reforms and

[45] Commission, 'Communication from the Commission, The EU budget powering the recovery plan for Europe' COM (2020) 442 final, 16.

[46] ibid 16–17.

[47] Commission, 'Communication from the Commission, The EU budget powering the recovery plan for Europe' COM (2020) 442 final, 17.

[48] Council Decision (EU, Euratom) 2020/2053 on the system of own resources of the European Union and repealing Decision 2014/335/EU, Euratom [2020] OJ L424/1, Art 2. See Christian Neumeier, 'Political Own Resources: Towards a legal framework' (2023) 60 *CML Rev* 319.

[49] Council Decision (EU, Euratom) 2020/2053 on the system of own resources of the European Union and repealing Decision 2014/335/EU, Euratom [2020] OJ L424/1.

[50] Commission, 'Proposal for a Regulation of the European Parliament and of the Council establishing a carbon border adjustment mechanism' COM (2021) 564 final.

[51] Regulation (EU) 2021/241 of the European Parliament and of the Council establishing the Recovery and Resilience Facility [2012] OJ L57/17.

investments. Conditionality is thus not intended to promote fiscal discipline, but to promote national economic investment policies, particularly in the fields of climate and digitalisation. While NGEU is a significant step towards solidarity within the EU, it raises legal issues for the constitutional system of EU law.[52]

4. Energy Crisis

The war in Ukraine has led to increased solidarity in the European Union. Faced with an energy crisis, the European Union and the member states reacted with a whole series of measures, the adoption of which depended on political interests, revealing the strengths and weaknesses of the Union's energy policy. Energy policy, which is a competence shared between the European Union and the member states,[53] is defined by the objectives set out in Article 194 TFEU, the spirit of which is summed up in the first paragraph: first, to ensure the functioning of the internal energy market, and second, to guarantee energy supply in the Union, the promotion of energy efficiency and energy saving, and the development of new and renewable energy sources.[54] The energy crisis has led to a rebalancing of these objectives since, according to the Council, the EU's response is designed to ensure affordable and competitive energy for EU consumers, to increase the EU's energy security and preparedness in the event of emergencies, and to strengthen the energy resilience and autonomy of member states. The European Union and the member states are therefore implementing actions intended to limit excessively high gas prices, to improve solidarity and to share supplies, to cut energy costs for households and businesses, to reduce the EU's energy dependencies, to secure gas supplies, and to accelerate the green transition.[55] European energy policy thus oscillates between tensions on the market and solidarity, and between security of supply and energy transition.

While the completion of the internal energy market was for a long time the dominant dogma, energy solidarity is progressing as a result of crises. On the one hand, it has been elevated by a ruling of the ECJ to the rank of a specific expression of the principle of solidarity, which 'is itself one of the fundamental principles of EU law'.[56] This principle 'cannot, as such, produce binding legal effect on the Member States and institutions of the European Union'.[57] The European judges nevertheless underpin 'all of the objectives of the European Union's

[52] See Päivi Leino-Sandberg and Matthias Ruffert, 'Next Generation EU and Its Constitutional Ramifications: A Critical Assessment' (2022) 59 *CML Rev* 433.

[53] Art 4(2)(i) TFEU.

[54] Council of the European Union, 'Energy prices and security of supply' (*Council Website*) www.consilium.europa.eu/fr/policies/energy-prices-and-security-of-supply.

[55] ibid.

[56] Case C-848/19 P *Germany v Poland* ECLI:EU:C:2021:598, para 38.

[57] ibid para 43.

energy policy, serving as the thread that brings them together and gives them coherence'.[58] Both

> the EU institutions and the Member States must take account of the principle of energy solidarity referred to in Article 194 TFEU, in the context of the establishment and functioning of the internal market and, in particular, the internal market in natural gas, by ensuring security of energy supply in the European Union, which means not only dealing with emergencies when they arise, but also adopting measures to prevent crisis situations.[59]

At the normative level, all acts adopted by the EU institutions, including under energy policy, 'must be interpreted, and their legality assessed, in the light of the principle of energy solidarity'.[60]

On the other hand, the 'solidarity clause' of Article 122(1) TFEU, which has long remained virtually unused, has been implemented with a view to adopting four regulations in the last quarter of 2022,[61] one of which will be of particular relevance to the discussion in this chapter as it includes the emergency intervention mechanism to deal with high energy prices.[62] This normative push is explained by the war of aggression waged by Russia against Ukraine, which has shown how gas supply remains a major geopolitical instrument, especially in a 'hybrid war'.[63] The EU legislator underlines

> the disruption of the energy market, caused by one of the main market players which has artificially reduced the supply of gas in the context of Russia's war of aggression against Ukraine, and the hybrid war which is thereby being carried out, have created a crisis situation which requires the adoption of a set of urgent, temporary and exceptional measures of an economic nature to address the unbearable effects on consumers and companies. If not addressed rapidly, the crisis situation may have severe detrimental effects on inflation, on the liquidity of market operators and on the economy as a whole.[64]

Thus, the interaction between security and solidarity leads to a further tempering of the market reference point on which European energy policy is based. Guaranteeing energy supply is thus just as important as ensuring the functioning of the internal market.

In EU law, a new and original instrument has been enshrined, in that it consists of imposing on companies the payment of contributions intended to finance aid

[58] ibid.
[59] ibid para 69.
[60] ibid para 44.
[61] Council Regulation (EU) 2022/2576 enhancing solidarity through better coordination of gas purchases, reliable price benchmarks and exchanges of gas across borders [2022] OJ L335/1; Council Regulation (EU) 2022/2577 laying down a framework to accelerate the deployment of renewable energy [2022] OJ L335/36; Council Regulation (EU) 2022/2578 establishing a market correction mechanism to protect Union citizens and the economy against excessively high prices [2022] OJ L335/45.
[62] Council Regulation (EU) 2022/1854 on an emergency intervention to address high energy prices [2022] OJ LI 261/1.
[63] ibid Recital (8).
[64] ibid.

to consumers. This is the European response to the debate on the 'superprofits tax scheme' of the oil and gas industries, which has polarised the French public arena since the beginning of the energy crisis.[65]

Regulation (EU) 2022/1854 mentioned above provided for the creation of a 'solidarity contribution'.[66] It is defined as:

> a temporary measure intended to address surplus profits of Union companies and permanent establishments with activities in the crude petroleum, natural gas, coal and refinery sectors to mitigate exceptional price developments in the energy markets for Member States, consumers and companies.[67]

Recital 14 of Regulation (EU) 2022/1854 explains that the contribution 'is an appropriate means to tackle surplus profits, in the event of unforeseen circumstance'. In essence, companies in the oil and gas sector have made profits that

> do not correspond to any regular profit that Union companies or permanent establishments with activities in the crude petroleum, natural gas, coal and refinery sectors would or could have expected to obtain under normal circumstances, had the unpredictable events in the energy markets not have taken place.

The purpose of the contribution is therefore to correct market failures, 'in a spirit of solidarity', in order

> to provide financial support to households and companies heavily affected by the soaring energy prices, while ensuring a level playing field across the Union. It should be applied in parallel to the regular corporate taxes levied by each Member State on the companies concerned.

Thus, it 'should act as a redistributing measure to ensure that the companies concerned which have earned surplus profits as a result of the unexpected circumstances, contribute in proportion to the improvement of the energy crisis in the internal market'.[68] Indeed, the Regulation provides that the contribution should be used for

> i) financial support measures to final energy customers, and in particular vulnerable households, to mitigate the effects of high energy prices; ii) financial support measures to help reducing the energy consumption; iii) financial support measures to support companies in energy intensive industries; and iv) financial support measures to develop the energy autonomy of the Union.[69]

Secondly, Section 2 of Chapter II of Regulation (EU) 2022/1854 introduced a cap on market revenues and distribution of surplus revenues and surplus congestion

[65] Théo Bourgery-Gonse, 'MPs report on "superprofit" tax scheme, disagree on recommendations' (*EURACTIV*, 5 October 2022) www.euractiv.com/section/all/short_news/mps-report-on-superprofit-tax-scheme-disagree-on-recommendations.

[66] Council Regulation (EU) 2022/1854 on an emergency intervention to address high energy prices [2022] OJ LI 261/1.

[67] ibid Art 2(19).

[68] ibid Recital (51).

[69] ibid Recital (56).

income revenues to final electricity customers. The market revenues of producers obtained from the generation of electricity shall be capped by the member states to a maximum of €180 per MWh of electricity produced. Once again, this mechanism is intended to correct the disruption of the energy market, that has led electricity producers to generate revenues that do not reflect their production costs to any real extent. Member states shall ensure that all surplus revenues resulting from the application of the cap on market revenues are used to finance measures in support of final electricity customers that mitigate the impact of high electricity prices on those customers, in a targeted manner.

The question therefore arises as to the extent to which the state will finance these support schemes and the extent to which energy companies contribute to this financing. Solidarity and redistribution – both the solidarity contribution and the cap on the infra-marginal income of electricity producers – mark a remarkable advance in EU law, since it involves financing aid intended for consumers by means of a form of taxation on companies. However, the legality of Regulation (EU) 2022/1854 under EU primary law is hardly apodictic. The contribution and the cap could be of a fiscal nature, which raises the question of the Union exceeding its attributed competences at a time when the threat of ultra vires is taken seriously in a renewed dialogue of judges. It is undeniable that the Union does not have competence in the field of direct taxation.[70] However, Regulation (EU) 2022/1854 is based on Article 122(1) TFEU, which empowers the Council to decide 'in a spirit of solidarity between Member States, upon the measures appropriate to the economic situation, in particular if severe difficulties arise in the supply of certain products, notably in the area of energy'. According to a first interpretation, this legal basis is relevant for the Council to impose the enactment of a measure such as the solidarity contribution on member states. The Union does not exercise fiscal competence directly; it requires states to exercise fiscal competence in order to 'ensure the full application of the solidarity contribution'.[71]

By analogy, the reasoning in the environmental criminal law cases in which the ECJ accepted that the European Community could require member states to exercise their criminal jurisdiction to punish violations of European environmental law is similar.[72] In these cases, however, the primacy of Union law was ensured since the state had to sanction violations of Community law. In the case of the solidarity contribution, the Council of the Union requires positive action by member states to correct malfunctions in the internal energy market, the establishment and functioning of which is governed by Union law. In this respect,

[70] See Alexandre Maitrot de la Motte, Souveraineté fiscale et construction communautaire: Recherche sur les impôts directs (Paris, LGDJ, 2005).

[71] Council Regulation (EU) 2022/1854 on an emergency intervention to address high energy prices [2022] OJ LI 261/1, Recital (55).

[72] Case C-176/03 *Commission v Conseil* ECLI:EU:C:2005:542; Case C-440/05 *Commission v Conseil* ECLI:EU:C:2007:625.

the Regulation stresses the risks of 'fragmentation of the internal market' caused by the exorbitant benefits of the competitive operation of the market.[73] According to a second interpretation, the Union encroaches on state competence in the field of direct taxation. The legal basis of Article 122(1) TFEU is therefore inappropriate, as the Council acts unanimously. Recourse to Article 352 TFEU would be necessary to adopt such a measure. This flexibility clause makes it possible to compensate for the silence of the Treaty by adopting appropriate provisions if Union action is necessary to attain one of the objectives of the Treaty. However, Article 352 TFEU requires unanimity in the Council and the approval of the European Parliament. The energy crisis has thus infused the internal energy market with a dose of solidarity that is not only inter-state, but also inter-individual.

Energy companies have brought actions before of the General Court for annulment of the Regulation (EU) 2022/1854. The applicants argued that this regulation was incorrectly adopted on the basis of Article 122(1) TFEU insofar as it contains fiscal measures. They also put forward pleas alleging that the Regulation constitutes a violation of fundamental rights, especially the right to property as enshrined in Article 17 of the Charter of Fundamental Rights of the EU, as well as the EU principles of legality and legal certainty.[74]

5. Conclusion

Thanks to the crises, the EMU now has a solidarity framework that interacts with the disciplinary framework. It shows in a more comprehensive way that solidarity has become not only one of the fundamental principles of EU law, but also a political objective to be achieved by European institutions and member states. This is another manifestation of the Community method. The European Union is indeed moving forward thanks to crises that allow for deeper integration. As Pierre Pescatore wrote, 'the progressive strengthening of links between Member States within the Community should undoubtedly make it possible to give greater prominence to the idea of solidarity in its various expressions, both in reality and in legal reasoning'.[75]

[73] Council Regulation (EU) 2022/1854 on an emergency intervention to address high energy prices [2022] OJ LI 261/1, Recital (57): 'In the absence of a Union measure such as a solidarity contribution, there is a high risk of disruption and further fragmentation of the internal market, which would be detrimental to all Member States, given the integration of energy markets and of value chains'.

[74] Case T-795/22 *Vermilion Exploration and Production Ireland and Vermilion Energy Ireland v Council*; T-775/22 *Vermilion Energy Netherlands e.a. v Council*; Case T-802/22 *ExxonMobil Producing Netherlands and Mobil Erdgas-Erdöl v Council*; Case T-803/22 *Petrogas E&P Netherlands v Council*; Case T-759/22 *Electrawinds Shabla South v Council*.

[75] Pierre Pescatore, 'Les objectifs de la Communauté européenne comme principes d'interprétation dans la jurisprudence de la Cour de justice' in W J Ganshof van der Meersch (ed), *Miscellanea* (Bruxelles, Bruylant, vol 2, 1972) 325–63, 359: 'le resserrement progressif des liens entre États membres au sein de la Communauté devrait permettre, dans la réalité des faits autant que dans les raisonnements juridiques, de mettre davantage en valeur cette idée de solidarité dans ses diverses expressions'.

8

Constitutional Imaginaries of Solidarity

Framing Fiscal Integration Post-NGEU

PÄIVI LEINO-SANDBERG*

1. Introduction

What are the key ingredients of a fiscal union? In the EU, the answer is strong institutional ambition, a suitable crisis or two, and a sprinkling of legal creativity building on a constitutional imaginary of solidarity.

The EU has always been shaped by crises, and the past 10 years or so have continued the pattern in the area of fiscal integration. Events tend to follow a predictable pattern: the expediency of the crisis creates a battering ram which makes long-standing national objections crumble. The institutions – and the large member states that are able to use institutions for their own purposes – act quickly and push for the realisation of their long-term ambitions under a 'normativity of distress', which is

> manifest in the unheeded exhortation that 'something needs to be done', regardless by whom and how. The poignant exhortative tone reveals a built-in preference for quick action over deliberation. A society seized by anxiety experiences itself to be under Handlungszwang. Since the justification for action lies in its responsiveness to exigency it would not even make sense for it to stay within pre-established constraints. Wherever jurisdictional boundaries exist – be they officially classified as emergency powers or not – they are likely to be extended and transgressed.[1]

* Professor of Transnational European Law, University of Helsinki. This publication results from the NORFACE project 'Separation of powers for 21st century Europe (SepaRope)' under the 'NORFACE Democratic Governance in a Turbulent Age' programme. I thank Jan Komarek, Peter Lindseth, Sakari Melander, Urška Šadl and Tuomas Saarenheimo for comments on an earlier draft.

[1] Alexander Somek, *Individualism: An Essay on the Authority of the European Union* (Oxford, Oxford University Press, 2008) 233–34.

When facing the inevitable, some national parliaments cheer, others find their backs against the wall, and, in a flurry of events, EU fiscal relations get rearranged with little democratic debate and contemplation of the long-term consequences. The majority of EU scholars rejoice, as more integration and stronger institutional presence are believed to be a good thing.[2] While justified with reference to the ongoing crisis, every new innovation becomes a permanent part of the toolbox; the ratchet of EU fiscal integration only moves to one direction.

Many of the crisis responses have been found in legally grey areas and build on solutions that would have been *considered* illegal just a while ago.[3] I say 'considered', because what counts as illegal is ultimately in the hands of the European Court of Justice (ECJ), which may or may not have a say after the acute crisis is over and measures are already implemented. Until then, setting the limits of legal and illegal action is a question of framing,[4] which is largely conducted by the legal advisers working in the EU institutions. This offers the EU institutions broad leeway,[5] thus turning crises into 'a grey hole':

> A grey hole is a legal space in which there are some legal constraints on executive action – it is not a lawless void – but the constraints are so insubstantial that they pretty well permit government to do as it pleases.[6]

This does not mean that the law is irrelevant. It provides a frame within which the EU institutions and their legal advisers argue about the legality of envisaged measures. Therefore, what can plausibly be claimed as legal under the Treaty framework tends to dictate the design of measures. Often this means that functional design takes the back seat and the end result may not be best suited for the intended purpose.

One consequence of this crisis-driven method of integration is that it favours the executive at the expense of the legislator. It is a general phenomenon that during crises executives tend to be strengthened. '[S]upreme emergency risks fostering a discursive process in which politicians and officials construct and dramatize threats as justifying exceptional supra-national discretionary action.'[7] The euro crisis, the Covid-19 crisis, the rule of law crisis – and, as I will seek to

[2] Päivi Leino-Sandberg, 'Enchantment and Critical Distance in EU Legal Scholarship: What Role for Institutional Lawyers?' (2022) 1 *European Law Open* 231.

[3] For this argument in greater length, see Päivi Leino-Sandberg and Matthias Ruffert, 'Next Generation EU and Its Constitutional Ramifications: a Critical Assessment' (2022) 59 *CML Rev* 433.

[4] On this, see also Matthew Windsor, 'Expertise As Framing' in Emilia Korkea-aho and Päivi Leino-Sandberg (eds), *Law, Legal Expertise and EU Policy Making* (Cambridge, Cambridge University Press, 2022) 43–54.

[5] On this, see Päivi Leino-Sandberg, *The Politics of Legal Expertise in EU Policy Making* (Cambridge, Cambridge University Press, 2021).

[6] David Dyzenhaus, *The Constitution of Law: Legality in a Time of Emergency* (Cambridge, Cambridge University Press, 2006) 42.

[7] Kenneth Dyson, 'Sworn to Grim Necessity? Imperfections of European Economic Governance, Normative Political Theory, and Supreme Emergency' (2013) 35 *Journal of European Integration* 207, 214.

demonstrate, even the more recent crises (climate and the EU's reaction to Russia's war in Ukraine) – have all required a new legal framing under the EU Treaties. Each of them has also strengthened the executive in relation to both the European Parliament and national parliaments.[8] While some design failures of the earlier crisis models have been corrected, new ones have emerged.

Overall, the European Parliament's power to steer Union expenditure has steadily eroded in relation to the EU's multiple executives. There has been a loss of parallelism between budgetary and legislative power in the EU. Budgetary democracy has been replaced by technocratic executive action, which, however noble in its intentions, necessarily ends up limiting the effect of democratic politics. This is not an accident but a result by design, which has so far merited little debate. And when a crisis ends, there should be return to normalcy. However, as Kenneth Dyson suggests, incentives exist to 'construct the Euro Area as in a state of semi-permanent emergency. In these circumstances, exceptional measures become the new normality'.[9] This takes place largely without democratic debate and without parliamentary control. The fiscal union emerging from EU measures does not seem to me as particularly stable or democratically sustainable.

This chapter tracks the movement towards deeper fiscal integration against broader political and constitutional arguments. I do not aim to question the need for fiscal integration. I believe it is necessary, but I also believe that the process should be respectful of constitutional fundamentals rather than an opportunistic exercise guided by institutional ambition. The chapter starts by discussing the significance of budgetary power in democratic life. It argues that a nation's budget is not merely another aspect of public policy but rather the very heart of its democratic decision-making, the financial embodiment of political will and a key object of democratic accountability. The chapter then looks into the evolution of EU fiscal policy measures and their effect on the exercise of budgetary powers over the course of the successive crises of the last decade and a half.

Finally, the chapter looks into the arguments used to defend the recent moves and sees them as reflections of constitutional imaginary. The emerging 'solidarity' discourse is an attempt to dress up, in 'as if' constitutionalist terms to use Peter Lindseth's vocabulary,[10] a form of national-supranational and executive-technocratic governance taking over the legislature's core task of mobilising and redistributing fiscal resources. I argue that the way in which this has happened is profoundly disruptive of the national legislatures' traditional 'reserve' over budgets and abuses forms of administrative governance to achieve this clearly constitutionalising step, which is now being legitimised through a process of sedimentation and self-referencing by key actors in the institutional sphere. The development raises

[8] On this, see also Päivi Leino-Sandberg and Tapio Raunio, 'Learning from the Crises? Towards a Democratically More Legitimate Fiscal Union' *Government & Opposition* (forthcoming).

[9] Dyson, 'Sworn to Grim Necessity?' 213–14.

[10] See Peter L Lindseth, 'The Perils of "As If" European Constitutionalism' (2016) 22 *European Law Journal* 696.

fundamental questions of constitutionality, separation of powers, and democratic control in the EU. What is at stake is the essence of democratic decision-making – nothing more, nothing less.

2. What is Budgetary Power?

2.1. Budgetary Power in States and Federations

Democracy has grown out of the demand of taxpayers to decide on how their money should be collected and spent ('no taxation without representation'). Even today, at the heart of the 'modern notion of democratic self-government is the legitimate capacity to extract and redirect fiscal and human resources on a societal scale'.[11] These processes involve political choices and a responsibility for overall budgeting. Yet, it has been fairly little thought what this means for fiscal integration in the EU.

Budgetary powers are exercised in constitutional democracies through the formal and informal rules governing the drafting of the budget law, its passage through the legislature and its implementation.[12] Budget law is undoubtedly the single most important expression of political will on the legislative calendar, and having the representatives of the people decide on it is one of the cornerstones of any democratic system.[13] Budgets are 'the lifeblood of government, the financial reflection of what government does and intends to do'.[14] Parliaments exercise supreme financial power and steer society through their power of taxation and budgetary power, including decisions on sovereign debt and state guarantees. When exercising these powers, a parliament sets legal limits to and scrutinises the actions of the executive. The Bundesverfassungsgericht (German Federal Constitutional Court) has emphasised that 'the right to decide on the budget serves as an instrument of comprehensive parliamentary monitoring of the government', which offers 'the elected parliament … a paramount constitutional position'. In this setting, the budget

> is not merely an economic plan, but at the same time a sovereign act of government in the form of a statute. It is subject to a time-limit and task-related. The state functions are presented in the budget as expenses which must be covered by revenue under the principle of compensation. The extent and structure of the budget thus reflect overall

[11] ibid 707.

[12] Mark Hallerberg, Rolf Strauch and Jürgen von Hagen, 'The Design of Fiscal Rules and Forms of Governance in European Union Countries' (2007) 23 *European Journal of Political Economy* 338, 340.

[13] eg Jonathan Kahn, *Budgeting Democracy: State Building and Citizenship in America 1890-1928* (Ithaca, NY, Cornell University Press, 1997).

[14] Aaron Wildavsky, 'Political Implications of Budgetary Reform' (1961) 21 *Public Administration Review* 183, 184; Paul L Posner, 'Federalist No. 30: What Is to Be Done About the Federal Budget?' (2011) 71 *Public Administration Review* 53.

> government policy. At the same time, the revenue achievable restricts the latitude to exercise state functions resulting in expenditure. Budget sovereignty is the place of conceptual political decisions on the correlation of economic burdens and privileges granted by the state. Therefore the parliamentary debate on the budget, including the extent of public debt, is regarded as a general debate on policy.[15]

While parliamentary involvement is essential for ownership, it often leads to weakening fiscal discipline.[16] For this reason, it is important that parliaments get to decide both income and expenses of the state, with a view to ensuring a balanced state budget. The practice of channelling funding into expenses outside the normal budget reduces budgetary transparency and undermines the normal budgetary procedures and the usefulness of debt brakes, deficit and debt rules. For this reason, International Monetary Fund (IMF) good practices advise against authorising off-budget spending or tax expenditures outside the normal budget cycle,[17] as they tend to create ways to add new expenditure to existing ones with little substantive debate about priorities.

Living in a federation does not mean that budgetary powers become less. Instead, they are exercised at two different levels, each with their own executives and parliaments, and with their own checks and balances and channels of accountability. The classic thinking on fiscal federalism derives from the United States, in particular the Federalist Papers, which stress that decisions regarding taxation and expenditure should be made in the most representative of institutions.[18] Federal states have established rules on the use of federal and state funds and normally can build on decades of political integration and strong institutions. Their emphasis is on providing common public goods such as security or environmental protection. Dyson explains how '[l]iving in a state and sharing a collective identity imply the willingness, if conditional, to equalize living conditions, to provide collective insurance, and to share burdens through tax burdens'. However, the scale and implications of such 'collective assistance constitute a potentially explosive issue area in domestic politics' and create tensions and conflicts that could threaten the very cohesion of states, which is often premised on 'implicit grand bargains'.[19] The wish to prevent conflicts is also why federations have constitutional provisions on debt issuance and the means to pay back the debt. To the extent politically sensitive intra-state transfers take place, they form a part of a clearly defined constitutional settlement that the federation builds on.[20]

[15] BVerfGE 123, 267 <361> paras 121–24; BVerfGE 55, 274 <302–03>.

[16] Ian Lienert, 'Role of the Legislature in Budget Processes' (*International Monetary Fund*, April 2010) www.imf.org/external/pubs/ft/tnm/2010/tnm1004.pdf.

[17] ibid.

[18] On this, see also Abner J Mikva, 'The Congress, The Purse, The Purpose, and The Power' (Sibley Lecture Series, 1986) 57 https://digitalcommons.law.uga.edu/lectures_pre_arch_lectures_sibley/57.

[19] Kenneth Dyson, *States, Debt, and Power: 'Saints' and 'Sinners' in European History and Integration* (Oxford, Oxford University Press, 2014) 512.

[20] Päivi Leino-Sandberg and Tuomas Saarenheimo, 'Fiscal Stabilisation for EMU: Managing Incompleteness' (2018) 43 *EL Rev* 623.

Therefore, moves towards greater fiscal federalism do not mean that competence limitations or checks and balances become less important – experience from established federations suggests exactly the opposite.

2.2. Budgetary Powers in the EU

Against this background, how are budgetary matters then arranged in the EU? Like fiscal federations, the EU has rules and procedures concerning fiscal procedures and institutions at both central and member state level, even though in the Treaties matters falling under national competence and concerning national budgets are largely left to the member states to regulate. The EU Treaties emphasise member states' national responsibility for fiscal policy and its outcomes, building on a principle of 'no bailout'. The same applies to the broader economic policies, where the Treaty leaves the responsibility for substantive choices with the member states. As the ECJ acknowledged in its *Pringle* ruling, 'Articles 2(3) and 5(1) TFEU restrict the role of the Union in the area of economic policy to the adoption of coordinating measures'.[21] This said, due to the design of the Economic and Monetary Union (EMU), national decision-making on these issues must take into account implications for the whole EU. This tension has been addressed through the several incarnations of the Stability and Growth Pact since the creation of the Euro.[22]

As is logical, the Treaties are more concerned with the EU budget. The ECJ has emphasised that 'in a democratic society, taxpayers and public opinion generally have the right to be kept informed of the use of public revenues',[23] though in reality, the line of accountability for the use of EU funds towards the people of Europe has always run in a rather indirect and opaque manner.[24] Approval of EU measures with budgetary implications requires two separate decision-making processes: one for the budget by the budgetary authority, and a second one for the legislative frame decided by the legislative authority:[25]

> implementation of Community expenditure relating to any significant Community action presupposes not only the entry of the relevant appropriation in the budget of the Community, which is a matter for the budgetary authority, but in addition the prior

[21] Case C-370/12 *Thomas Pringle* v *Government of Ireland and Others* ECLI:EU:C:2012:756, para 64.

[22] These are discussed in detail in Päivi Leino-Sandberg and Fernando Losada Fraga, 'How to make the European Semester more effective and legitimate?' (*Economic Governance Support Unit at the Directorate-General for Internal Policies of the European Parliament*, PE 651.365, July 2020) requested by the ECON Committee.

[23] Joined Cases C-465/00, C-138/01 and C-139/01 *Rechnungshof v Österreichischer Rundfunk* ECLI:EU:C:2003:294, para 85.

[24] Koen Lenaerts and Amaryllis Verhoeven, 'Institutional Balance as a Guarantee for Democracy in EU Governance' in Christian Joerges and Renaud Dehousse (eds), *Good Governance in Europe's Integrated Market* (Oxford, Oxford University Press, 2002) 34–88, 36, 79.

[25] Case C-16/88 *Commission v Council* ECLI:EU:C:2012:756, para 17.

> adoption of a basic act authorising that expenditure, which is a matter for the legislative authority.[26]

Approval of such an act in the EU legislative institutions presumes substantive competence allocation for the purpose in the EU Treaties. Following the same logic, policies falling under the competence of national parliaments' legislative powers have been funded from national budgets.

The ceiling to EU expenditure is set in the Multiannual Financial Framework (MFF), which the Council approves unanimously with the Parliament's consent (Article 312 TFEU). Article 310(1) TFEU establishes that all Union items of revenue and expenditure 'shall be shown in the budget' and that the 'revenue and expenditure shown in the budget shall be in balance'. Until 2020, these provisions were read as prohibiting the EU from borrowing to fund its policies.[27] There were understandable reasons for such a limitation. Borrowing for a Treaty-based entity such as the EU, without an autonomous capacity to raise income, is different from borrowing by a state, which is the master of its own future incomes and where the required balance between revenue and payment can hence be filled by incurring debt.

As indicated above, unity and universality are central among the generally accepted principles of good government budgeting, and they are also clearly spelled out in Article 310 TFEU. Under the principle of universality, 'total revenue shall cover total payment appropriations' and 'all revenue and expenditure shall be entered in the budget in full without any adjustment against each other'.[28] External assigned revenue and internal assigned revenue, used to finance specific items of expenditure, are an exception to normal budgetary procedure.

An attempt has been made to create a direct link between EU revenue and the policies it funds through the system of own resources. The Council may establish new categories of own resources by acting unanimously and after consulting the European Parliament. The provision in Article 311(3) TFEU is remarkably open and includes no limitations as to what such own resources could be. This is balanced by the requirement that the Own Resources Decision will 'not enter into force until it is approved by the Member States in accordance with their respective constitutional requirements'. The system has seldom worked as intended; there has been a persistent and 'significant shortfall in revenue from the own resources compared to ever-increasing expenditure needs'.[29] Ultimately, the EU budget relies on contributions from the member states according to their Gross National Income shares. In this way, the EU lacks a key element of a constitutional entity in its own right: 'an autonomous political capacity to

[26] Case C-106/96 *United Kingdom v Commission* ECLI:EU:C:1998:218, para 26.

[27] See in more detail Leino-Sandberg and Ruffert 'Next Generation EU'.

[28] Regulation (EU, Euratom) 2018/1046 of the European Parliament and of the Council on the financial rules applicable to the general budget of the Union, Art 20.

[29] Richard Crowe, 'An EU Budget of States and Citizens' (2020) 26 *European Law Journal* 331, 334.

extract and redirect (ie "mobilise") fiscal and human resources in a legitimate and compulsory fashion in pursuit of collective ends'.[30]

The general pattern of Treaty reforms over the years has been to compensate the loss of national parliaments' budgetary powers by increasing the budgetary powers of the European Parliament.[31] Its role is strongest in the approval of the annual budget (Article 314 TFEU), where it can even have its amendments approved against the will of the Council and grants discharge to the Commission (Article 319 TFEU). The ECJ has emphasised how

> the exercise by the Parliament of its budgetary powers in plenary sitting is of particular importance for the transparency and democratic legitimacy of actions of the European Union based on its annual budget [… and] constitutes a fundamental event in the democratic life of the European Union and requires, inter alia, a public debate in plenary sitting enabling the citizens of the European Union to acquaint themselves with the various political orientations expressed and, as a result, to form a political opinion on the European Union's actions. Furthermore, the transparency afforded by a parliamentary debate in a plenary sitting is likely to strengthen the democratic legitimacy of the budgetary procedure in the eyes of citizens of the European Union and the credibility of the latter's actions.[32]

The annual budget is adopted by the President of the Parliament, which endows it binding force vis-à-vis both the institutions and the member states.[33]

However, not everybody shares the ECJ's belief in the legitimising power of the European Parliament. The Bundesverfassungsgericht, the most active authoritative body to discuss the constitutional limits of EU fiscal integration,[34] agrees that decisions on public revenue and public expenditure form a fundamental part of the ability of a constitutional entity to democratically shape itself and bring about a specific responsibility to the people and therefore belong to parliamentary procedures.[35] Yet, for the Bundesverfassungsgericht, the European Parliament is not where the political representation of the European people is expressed and, therefore, it cannot completely fill the gap between the extent of the decision-making power of the EU institutions and the citizens' democratic rights in the member states.[36] The Bundesverfassungsgericht also treats the European Council and the Commission as non-majoritarian bodies of a supernational organisation. For the Bundesverfassungsgericht, the provisions of the EU Treaties presuppose national budget autonomy as an essential competence, which national parliaments cannot relinquish. Strict compliance with it guarantees that the acts of the bodies

[30] Lindseth, 'European, The Perils' 700.
[31] Lenaerts and Verhoeven, 'Institutional Balance' 36, 79.
[32] Case C-73/17 *France v Parliament* ECLI:EU:C:2018:787, para 35.
[33] Case C-77/11 *Council v Parliament* (budget signature) ECLI:EU:C:2013:559, para 51.
[34] BVerfGE 123, 267 <351> para 237.
[35] BVerfGE 123, 267 <359>.
[36] BVerfGE 123, 267 <362–63> paras 258–60.

of the EU in and for Germany have sufficient democratic legitimation.[37] This means that the German Bundestag must make decisions on revenue and expenditure with responsibility to the people.[38]

Similar elements can also be found in the practice of the Constitutional Law Committee of the Finnish Eduskunta, which has repeatedly emphasised budgetary sovereignty and the need to uphold the prerogatives of the Eduskunta in relation to various crisis arrangements of EU origin.[39] In addition, various constitutional courts in the programme states after the euro crisis (Greece, Portugal and Cyprus) have addressed the constitutional questions involved in the rescue packages and needed to adjust the intensity of constitutional review to the economic needs of their states.[40] These constitutional analyses demonstrate differences between net contributor and net beneficiary states whose democratic concerns differ fundamentally, and predate the Covid-19 crisis. Therefore, no comprehensive constitutional analysis on the moves towards deeper fiscal integration and the effects of growing executive dominance on the powers of national parliaments exists yet. As the next section seeks to demonstrate, the impact of the later measures on parliamentary powers has been considerable.

3. Developing Through Crises – Deepening Fiscal Integration in the EU

3.1. Euro Crisis Legacy

Initially, EU economic policy coordination took place through non-binding (country specific) recommendations. During the past decade, this coordination has evolved far from the initial competence division in the EU Treaties and changed the role of several EU institutions.[41] The development builds on what Kaarlo Tuori calls 'the strategy of de-politicisation': economic and fiscal policies are reframed as fields of non-political expertise where decisions are grounded on objectively given economic parameters, thus negating their need for democratic input legitimation.[42]

[37] BVerfGE 89, 155 <199 ff>; BVerfGE 97, 350 <373>.

[38] BVerfGE 70, 324 <355–56>; BVerfGE 79, 311 <329>; see also BVerfGE 129, 124 <128–86> paras 1–142.

[39] Päivi Leino-Sandberg and Janne Salminen, 'The Euro Crisis and Its Constitutional Consequences for Finland: Is There Room for National Politics in EU Decision-Making?' (2013) 9 *European Constitutional Law Review* 451.

[40] Constantinos Kombos, 'Constitutional Review and the Economic Crisis: In the Courts We Trust? – Part Two' (2019) 25 *European Public Law* 229.

[41] Discussed in Päivi Leino-Sandberg and Tuomas Saarenheimo, 'Sovereignty and Subordination: On the Limits of EU Economic Policy Coordination' (2017) 42 *EL Rev* 166.

[42] Kaarlo Tuori, *European Constitutionalism* (Cambridge, Cambridge University Press, 2015) 220.

The euro crisis evolved around the euro area states. Solving it relied on various intergovernmental solutions that allocated key roles to the Commission, the European Central Bank (ECB) and the Eurogroup.[43] Most of the important decisions from bailouts to subsequent temporary and permanent crisis mechanisms were taken swiftly in the European Council (or Euro Summit), leaving little time for scrutiny and debate by national parliaments. The European Parliament, for its part, was essentially just kept informed. The adjustment programmes were formally political contracts between the creditors and the recipient country, in which the latter committed to budgetary austerity and reforms in exchange for periodical disbursement of loans. Bailouts and strong conditionality led to poor ownership of reform agendas, political polarisation and often strong national resistance in the programme countries.

Another legacy of the euro crisis was an overhaul of the EU economic governance framework, aimed at imposing a more holistic centralised oversight of member states' economic policies by the EU, so as to prevent policy mistakes before they happen.[44] As a result of the changes, the (EU) executive is expected to guide member states' budgetary policies at every stage of the budgetary cycle and offers Country-Specific Recommendations (CSRs) in various policy areas including areas falling under national competence, backed up by the possibility to impose sanctions on disobedient states. While national parliaments retain formal budgetary powers, they are treated more as agents of the supranational bodies.[45] While the latter is perhaps a slight exaggeration, the 'result is a system that is all about regulatory discipline',[46] aimed at controlling democratic position building at the national level.

Unsurprisingly, this too has led to poor 'ownership' by national actors and low levels of implementation of CSRs. The reforms have not helped to ensure euro area stability. In practice, the Commission has occasionally used its broad discretion by barking but backing out before matters escalated into a direct conflict with member state parliaments.[47] The new sanctions have proved politically difficult to apply. Two conclusions can be drawn: first, the framework has not been particularly efficient,[48] and second, no matter how fiscal policies are framed, the operation of the framework is a deeply political exercise.[49] However, instead of reconsidering direction, the EU has persistently continued on the same path. Poor ownership has been a permanent source of institutional concern, but there

[43] See Leino-Sandberg and Raunio, 'Learning from the Crises?'.

[44] Discussed in Leino-Sandberg and Saarenheimo, 'Sovereignty and Subordination'; Leino-Sandberg and Losada Fraga, 'European Semester'.

[45] Tuori, *European Constitutionalism* 195.

[46] Lindseth, 'European, The Perils' 701.

[47] See, Päivi Leino-Sandberg and Tuomas Saarenheimo, 'Discretion, Economic Governance and the (New) Political Commission' in Joana Mendes (ed), *EU Executive Discretion and the Limits of Law* (Oxford, Oxford University Press, 2019) 132–56, 132.

[48] For a summary of criticisms, see Leino-Sandberg and Losada Fraga, 'European Semester'.

[49] Leino-Sandberg and Saarenheimo, 'Discretion' 132.

has been little discussion of how this might relate to the redistributive effects of fiscal and economic policy. However, as Tuori writes, 'legitimacy expectations cannot be manipulated at will from above'.[50]

A recent attempt to tackle poor ownership is the introduction of 'positive incentives', ie monetary incentives to support CSRs. The idea was first suggested by the Commission in its proposal for the Reform Delivery Tool (RDF),[51] which later evolved into a Budgetary Instrument for Competitiveness and Convergence (BICC)[52] and finally into the Recovery and Resilience Facility (see below). This is a powerful innovation, the legal construct of which has not received the attention it deserves. It has offered the EU powerful tools to direct member state policies in all policy areas, without need to worry about competences, as cohesion policy is now reframed to cover anything that the EU funds, irrespective of who exercises legislative competence in the area.[53] This has broadened the scope of EU action considerably and broken the old parallelism between legislative and budgetary power. As Max Steinbeis has noted: 'Governing by financial incentives is a very efficient technique of exercising power and as such can cause major constitutional issues.'[54] So far, these constitutional issues have not been debated in the EU, nor has the efficiency of such policies for ensuring EU objectives been thoroughly studied.

While many EMU scholars were thrilled about these developments,[55] there were also more critical voices who saw the developments described above as representing a pattern that 'threaten[s] national parliaments with the loss of a key prerogative – the power of decision over spending and indebtedness – which some observers hope will shift to supranational bodies or otherwise be denationalized in some way'.[56] While Koen Lenaerts already in 1990 argued that the EU may exercise its specific, implied or non-specific powers to the fullest, without running into any inherent limitation set to these powers as a result of the sovereignty of member states,[57] critical observers pointed to 'the domain(s) of normative authority that must remain with the member states in order to preserve their historically-recognizable democratic and constitutional character'.[58] Lindseth argued,

[50] Tuori, *European Constitutionalism* 220, 221.

[51] Commission, 'Proposal for a Regulation of the European Parliament and of the Council on the establishment of the Reform Support Programme' COM (2018) 391 final.

[52] See Commission, 'Proposal for a Regulation of the European Parliament and of the Council on a governance framework for the budgetary instrument for convergence and competitiveness for the euro area' COM (2019) 354 final.

[53] On this in more detail, see Leino-Sandberg and Ruffert, 'Next Generation EU'.

[54] Maximilian Steinbeis, 'Follow the Money' (*Verfassungsblog*, 10 June 2022) https://verfassungsblog.de/follow-the-money. In greater detail, see Leino-Sandberg and Saarenheimo, 'Fiscal Stabilisation for EMU'.

[55] See in more detail Leino-Sandberg and Ruffert, 'Next Generation EU'.

[56] Peter L Lindseth, 'Author's Reply: "Outstripping", or the Question of "Legitimate for What?" in EU Governance' (2012) 8 *European Constitutional Law Review* 153, 159.

[57] Koen Lenaerts, 'Constitutionalism and the Many Faces of Federalism' (1990) 38 *American Journal of Comparative Law* 205, 220.

[58] ibid.

> Europe simply can't go there, unless it is prepared to fundamentally alter understandings of what democratic self-government on the national level means … like any form of essentially administrative governance, supranational governance in the EU is legitimate for certain purposes but not others – unless, again, Europeans are prepared to change fundamentally their understanding of what democratic self-government means, or where it is located. Whenever we talk about the legitimacy of integration, we must always ask the question 'legitimate for what?' It is one thing for a member state to delegate authority to a supranational process to harmonize regulatory standards in various domains (important a task though that may be). It is quite another to denationalize the power over the national purse in an indeterminate way. … any shifts in authority to the EU must still be reconciled with historical understandings of democratic self-government on the national level, in precisely the way that the history of administrative governance teaches us. This reconciliation is grounded in the concept of delegation; it is operationalized through mediated legitimacy; and it (sometimes) requires the imposition of delegation constraints to preserve the democratic and constitutional character of the state.[59]

Yet, the direction has not changed, as 'the strategy of de-politicisation' has spread to new areas.

3.2. Covid-19 Pandemic

The NextGenerationEU (NGEU) package was born out of the outbreak of the Covid-19 pandemic. It coincided with the negotiations of the EU's new MFF and had a profound impact on it, and was shaped by the EU's rule of law crisis, which strengthened calls for stronger budgetary conditionality. The Covid-19 crisis created new funding needs and a political unity in face of a shared threat. As a result, the universally held conviction that the EU cannot borrow to fund its policies changed nearly overnight. NGEU was legally structured as an 'extra-budgetary' fund. The 750 billion it raises from the markets were agreed to be channelled to the EU budget as external assigned revenues, thus, in a remarkable legal sleight of hand, transforming the borrowed funds into revenues which counterbalance the expenditures for NGEU and thus fulfil the legal requirement of balanced budget.[60] On the expenditure side, the Recovery package entails massive use of EU funds to 'incentivise' national legislative programming and reform in the member states. Unlike the euro-crisis measures earlier, NGEU was placed within the EU institutional structure and is managed by and for the EU-27. A genuine effort was made to place political ownership more firmly in the hands of the member states whose governments prepare and sign the national reform plans. Compared to the euro-crisis approach, NGEU fixes some problems and creates some new ones.

[59] Lindseth (n 56) 160.
[60] See Leino-Sandberg and Ruffert, 'Next Generation EU'.

Through NGEU, the EU issues debt to provide grants and loans to member states to be spent during the next few years. The package amounts to €750 billion (in 2018 prices), most of which is allocated to the Recovery and Resilience Facility (RRF) (€724 billion). As to its scope, NGEU goes far beyond the EU's traditional redistributive instruments. Compared with the relatively restrictive way that normal EU spending programmes target the funds, NGEU provides remarkably few limits to how the money is used. The RRF finances a very wide variety of measures with no connection to the Covid-19 pandemic, spanning nearly all sectors of public policy in the member states.[61] This emphasis also makes NGEU remarkably different from established fiscal unions, which exist to provide common public goods. It builds on country-specific allocation of money, which is largely foreign to established federations and reinforces the cleavage between net payers and beneficiaries of the EU budget.

The substantive spending plans are refined in confidential negotiations with the Commission prior to the formal submission of the National Recovery and Resilience Plans (NRRPs). The Commission explains that its negotiations with member states last

> several months and are carried out in conditions of strict confidentiality, which is necessary in order to make progress on a document of technical and political complexity. The components of the plan and their implementation are the object of regular discussions between Member States and the European Commission, at every stage of the decision-making process.[62]

The Commission has resisted requests for information about these engagements, on the basis that

> disclosure of the internal and preliminary considerations laid down in … these documents would undermine the climate of mutual trust with the Member State concerned and seriously undermine the required independence and objectivity of the ongoing decision-making process. Disclosing these details would discourage the Commission officials and members of the [Member State] administration from having free and open discussions on the national plan without interference.[63]

A similar method is used for assessing disbursements: a member state submits a payment request, documenting completion of milestones and targets. After the Commission's preliminary assessment, the Economic and Financial Committee submits an opinion, followed by Commission assessment in comitology.

Altogether, the preparation and submission of NRRPs and the monitoring of their implementation is procedurally and technically heavy and subject to

[61] Regulation (EU) 2021/241 of the European Parliament and of the Council establishing the Recovery and Resilience Facility [2021] OJ L57/17, Arts 3 and 4.

[62] Decision of the European Commission pursuant to Article 4 of the Implementing rules to Regulation No (EC) 1049/2001, Brussels, 22.08.2022 C(2022) 6154 final (on file with author).

[63] ibid.

frequent consultation with the Commission. Particularly in the preparation of the plans, this effectively limits domestic consultations and weakens the practical possibilities of domestic legislatures to direct the outcomes. The extent to which national parliaments have a say on their national plans depends also on national practices; in some member states, the plan is purely the government's document and is never subjected to parliamentary approval.[64] Even in the countries where the parliament has a role, the opaque and bilateral and confidential nature of the negotiations between the government and the Commission inevitably emphasises the role of the governments and makes it more difficult (or even impossible) for national parliaments to fulfil their normal budgetary roles. As a result, national parliaments tend to find themselves squeezed towards the dystopian nightmare painted earlier by the Bundesverfassungsgericht, in which a parliament's role shrinks into one 'of mere subsequent enforcement and [it can] no longer exercise its overall budgetary responsibility as part of its right to decide on the budget'.[65] The myth of 'conditionality' is used to disguise an executive coercion of the legislature, where technocratic governance is using a crisis to take over the legislature's core task of mobilising and redistributing fiscal resources. In practice, member state governments can use the EU money for their own pet projects, subject only to a confidential oversight process by the Commission. A cursory look into the national recovery plans confirms their wide reach: traditional investments in infrastructure and energy; IT projects in a variety of different fields; reforms of budgetary planning, judicial systems, insolvency systems, taxation, pension systems, labour markets, measures in the field of education, social policies and housing. Only security and defence and financial market policies seem to be absent.[66]

While technically placed in the EU constitutional structure, the role of the European Parliament is minimal. Following the July 2020 European Council, the European Parliament was involved in fine-tuning the high-level criteria for the RRF as part of the ordinary legislative procedure. Considering the scope and ambition of the programme, more detailed EU-level legislative guidance would be difficult to provide, as the details of the measures to be funded fall under national competence. For reasons of institutional balance and separation of powers, it would be equally difficult to grant the European Parliament any role in executing the legal framework. Therefore, the European Parliament is left with

[64] A recent study by Follow the Money substantiates this concern by demonstrating how 'several parliaments across Europe hardly had any say in the drafting of the plans or had little opportunity to propose amendments'. See Lise Witteman and Peter Teffer, 'The Recovery Files: scrutinising the billions from Brussels' (*Follow the Money*, 3 November 2021) www.ftm.eu/articles/corona-recovery-fund-europe.

[65] See BVerfGE 132, 195 <197–207> paras 1–24.

[66] The national plans can be found at European Commission, 'The Recovery and Resilience Facility' (*European Commission Website*) www.ec.europa.eu/info/business-economy-euro/recovery-coronavirus/recovery-and-resilience-facility_en#national-recovery-and-resilience-plans.

an ad hoc committee[67] where its role is reduced to holding a rather mysterious 'recovery and resilience dialogue' with the EU executive.[68] This process is a far cry from Crowe's ideal model for the EU budget where

> every euro collected from citizen-taxpayers to pursue Union policy objectives should be processed through procedures that involve clearly-defined roles for the institutional actors concerned, and which ensure respect for certain uniform European standards of transparency, accountability and budgetary control.[69]

NGEU also weakens the European Parliament's role as the EU's budgetary authority. As noted above, it builds on external assigned revenue and as such, it escapes the annual budgetary negotiations between the Council and the Parliament and is only subject to the annual discharge procedure. Therefore, the arrangement is clearly problematic for the institutional roles under the Treaties. The Council Legal Service stressed in its 2020 legal opinion that

> recourse to external assigned revenue is subject to important restrictions which aim, in particular, at preserving the inter-institutional balance by protecting the prerogatives, including the budgetary ones, of the European Parliament and the Council. External assigned revenue must, therefore, remain additional or complementary in nature in order to avoid deconstructing the system of own resources and the regular budgetary mechanisms, in circumvention of the applicable procedures.[70]

The European Parliament may have accepted its weak role as the price to be paid for avoiding intergovernmental models and for securing progress towards a permanent borrowing and redistributive mechanism for the EU. Yet, NGEU clearly dilutes its democratic powers and, as a model for future fiscal integration, is deeply flawed from the perspective of parliamentary participation and the possibilities of ensuring political accountability for how the funds are spent. In a solid fiscal union structure, the EU funds would be spent on purposes where the European Parliament can exercise both budgetary and legislative powers. In the NGEU structure, EU funding is directed to national policy objectives on which the EU legislature cannot legislate beyond the broad frame of funding instruments, and which presume a great deal of national legislation to be achieved. This creates a permanent tension.

Therefore, while NGEU addresses some of the shortcomings of the euro-crisis assistance programmes, it does little to remedy the lack of parliamentary

[67] Interinstitutional Agreement between the European Parliament, the Council of the European Union and the European Commission on budgetary discipline, on cooperation in budgetary matters and on sound financial management, as well as on new own resources, including a roadmap towards the introduction of new own resources [2020] OJ LI433/28.

[68] Cristina Dias, 'European Parliament involvement in scrutinizing the Recovery and Resilience Facility' (*Economic Governance Support Unit at the Directorate-General for Internal Policies of the European Parliament*, PE 659.627, October 2022).

[69] Richard Crowe, 'The European Budgetary Galaxy' (2017) 13 *European Constitutional Law Review* 428, 451.

[70] Council Legal Service, Opinion, Council Doc. 9062/20 (Brussels, 24 June 2021) para 62.

oversight. It continues to transfer a great deal of budgetary powers from the legislator to the executive, particularly at the EU level but also at the national level. It directs the EU towards a 'fiscal union' that is institutionally and legally fragile, compared with established federal states. The result is a system that builds on executive dominance and where democratic debate is structurally almost impossible. It is simply a bad structure for allocating money and flawed in ways that are difficult to address. These broader implications of NGEU have received little attention.

In 2020, NGEU was framed as 'an exceptional response to those temporary but extreme circumstances', which would not be 'used for any purpose other than tackling the direct economic and social consequences of the Covid-19 pandemic'.[71] It was explained by institutional lawyers that 'NGEU does not constitute a new budgetary paradigm of the EU called to be consolidated throughout time. Borrowing for spending cannot become a permanent feature of the EU budget to finance regular EU policies, unless the Treaties were to be changed.'[72] Despite these assurances, one did not need the powers of an oracle to predict that NGEU will not remain exceptional but will pave the way for new similar solutions. This requires forgetting the old frame of Covid-19 exceptionalism, and creating a new one.

3.3. The EU's New Crises

Russia's war in Ukraine has led to fundamental changes in the EU. First, the EU's strong potential competence in defence and security will remain largely unused.[73] Instead, the EU has authorised financing of military assistance to Ukraine through the European Peace Facility. This is another off-budget funding mechanism, which emerged from a legal battle on the interpretation of Article 41(2) TEU, which forbids the use of the EU budget to finance military expenditure.[74] Second, in the area of energy, the Commission's REPowerEU Communication indicates various new policy measures that will add to Union expenditure.[75] In practice, the EU rechannels unspent Covid-19 funds to freeing Europe from

[71] Council, 'Amended proposal for a Council decision on the system of Own Resources of the European Union' COM (2020) 445 final.

[72] Alberto de Gregorio Merino, 'The Recovery Plan: Solidarity and the living constitution' (*EU law live*, 6 March 2021) 9–10. The same view is repeated by Crowe from the European Parliament's Legal Service in Crowe, 'An EU Budget' 342.

[73] Päivi Leino-Sandberg and Hanna Ojanen, 'Time for Military Integration in the EU? Armed aggression and the scope of Article 42 TEU' (*Verfassungsblog*, 3 March 2022) https://verfassungsblog.de/time-for-military-integration-in-the-eu.

[74] On this, see Leino-Sandberg, *The Politics of Legal Expertise* 66–67.

[75] Commission, 'Communication from the Commission to the European Parliament, the European Council, the Council, the European Economic and Social Committee and the Committee of the Regions' COM (2022) 108 final.

its dependence on Russian oil and gas.[76] While not difficult to justify as a matter of common sense and logic, the measures clearly undermine the uniqueness and single-purpose nature of NGEU that was so instrumental to its legal structure and the political agreement enabling its creation.

Finally, there is no agreement on how the debt will be paid back beyond the political agreement that the process would pave the way for new own resources, which 'could, over time, lead to highly acrimonious and destabilising budgetary disputes between Member States'.[77] Russia's war in Ukraine has led to debate about the issuance of new debt to deal with the consequences of the war. While there is yet no sign of this debate materialising into anything concrete, it is evident that EU debt issuance is now part of the supranational toolbox, and the possibility and temptation of making common debt a permanent feature of EU fiscal integration will henceforth always be there.[78]

The European Council agreed in July 2020 to reform the own resources system and to use the proceeds of the new own resources introduced after 2021 for early repayment of NGEU borrowing.[79] The new own resources, introduced under the shadow of multiple crises and through the Conclusions of the European Council,[80] mark a significant change in how the EU is funded. The Commission Fit for 55 package of July 2021 aiming to fight climate change includes various proposals that affect this system, as further elaborated in the Commission proposal for a new Own Resources Decision.[81] An important part of the Commission proposals is a new Social Climate Fund, which supports measures and investments that reduce emissions in road transport and buildings sectors. The new fund would be financed by the own resources of the Union budget, including those related to the emissions trading – in other words, the same new own funds which the European Council agreed in July 2020 to use to repay the funds raised by the EU to finance the grant component of NGEU.

Under the current Treaties, the introduction of new own resources is not a legal problem, presuming that the member states approve them. While the Own Resources Decision is approved unanimously, the secondary legislation defining

[76] European Commission, 'REPowerEU: A plan to rapidly reduce dependence on Russian fossil fuels and fast forward the green transition' (*European Commission Website*, 18 May 2022) https://ec.europa.eu/commission/presscorner/detail/en/IP_22_3131.

[77] Crowe, 'An EU Budget' 333.

[78] The IMF recently repeated its proposal for a new EU Fiscal Capacity. See Vitor Gaspar, Alfred Kammer and Ceyla Pazarbasioglu, 'European Fiscal Governance A Proposal from the IMF' (*IMF*, 5 September 2022) 22 www.imf.org/en/Publications/Departmental-Papers-Policy-Papers/Issues/2022/08/31/Reforming-the-EU-Fiscal-Framework-Strengthening-the-Fiscal-Rules-and-Institutions-The-EUs-518388.

[79] European Council conclusions, EUCO 10/20 (Brussels, 21 July 2020).

[80] See also the Interinstitutional Agreement on budgetary discipline, on cooperation in budgetary matters and on sound financial management, as well as on new own resources, including a roadmap towards the introduction of new own resources [2020] OJ LI433/28.

[81] See Commission, 'Proposal for a Council Decision amending Decision (EU, Euratom) 2020/2053 on the system of own resources of the European Union' COM (2021) 570 final.

the use of the new funds will be adopted in the ordinary legislative procedure, which gives the European Parliament a strong legislative role. However, like the grants under the RRF, many of the more recent proposals – such as the innovation fund attached to the Emissions Trading System (ETS), the sanctions from the FuelEU Maritime Regulation, and the proposal for renewable air fuels – are structured as external assigned revenue. Just as common debt, external assigned revenues were in the NGEU context initially framed for a single-use purpose in a highly exceptional case. Their use seems to be well on its way to become a permanent feature of the EU budgetary practice, affecting parliamentary prerogatives in a fundamental manner.

The Social Climate Fund is interesting also from a competence perspective. In certain respects, it can be explained as a measure falling under environmental and climate policy. But it can just as easily be seen as social policy in climate disguise, as the 'specific objective of the Fund is to support vulnerable households, vulnerable micro-enterprises and vulnerable transport users through temporary direct income support.' As such, the proposal is a paradigm shift, apparently intended to provide substance to the Commission's long-aspired social pillar that has so far remained nearly empty. The link to environmental objectives is indirect at best: conceivably, it may act as a sweetener that paves the way for political acceptance of the Fit for 55 package and its emissions trading system. However, as a class of public expenditure, it looks very much like social policies – something that so far has been considered falling under national competence.[82] Social security is also a core element in the Commission's September 2022 proposal for a Council regulation on an emergency intervention to address high energy prices, which mentions the word 'solidarity' 94 times. It provides for a 'temporary solidarity contribution' (carefully framed as something different from taxation, which would require unanimous decision-making in the Council) applying to the profits of businesses active in the oil, gas, coal and refinery sectors, which the member states should use to 'provide support to households and companies and to mitigate the effects of high energy prices'.[83]

When the Treaty of Lisbon was drafted, the relevant Working Group discussed ways to clarify that the Union respects certain core responsibilities of the member states when exercising its competences, including their system of social welfare benefits.[84] This competence division has been justified with reference to

> democratic legitimacy and the boundedness of solidarity; cultural, ideological, and economic differences among Member States; and the fiscal resources that welfare policies presuppose.

[82] Art 153 TFEU specifically enshrines the primacy of the national welfare state.

[83] Commission, 'Proposal for a Council regulation on an emergency intervention to address high energy prices' COM (2022) 473 final.

[84] The Secretariat of Working Group V on Complimentary Competences, The European Convention (Brussels, 4 November 2002) CONV 375/1/02 REV 1, 11, namely '*Basic public policy choices and social*

> Social policy, especially in the key areas of social security and health care, is about redistribution based on value choices, and such redistribution entails an enhanced need for democratic legitimacy. … Redistributive social policy draws on and presupposes solidarity among the members of the polity.[85]

The new proposal illustrates well how many of the claims used to defend crisis solutions are inherently problematic 'in the absence of a federal state structure, founded on independent democratic legitimacy for a "transfer union"'.[86] Changing the paradigm of social policy and welfare benefits is yet another fundamental change in how the EU is governed. Its aims are laudable, no doubt, but actually making it work would presume strong grassroot-level solidarity – something that, in the absence of a genuine European political community, remains a constitutional imaginary.

4. EMU Law as a 'Living Constitution' – Framing Solidarity as a New General Principle

The developments described above have affected the very fundamentals of our democratic societies. But they also affect the understanding of where EU law comes from and how competence is transferred. I have argued elsewhere that NGEU represents a constitutional change without a constitutional change.[87] Rather than invoking the formal procedure for Treaty amendment, the change has taken place through a re-framing of existing key Treaty provisions; a process now known as the EU's 'living constitution', which builds on

> a dynamic reading of the relevant provisions of the Treaties – especially those that relate to the EU budget – [which make it] possible to cater for the dramatic social and economic contingencies of Covid-19. That dynamic reading, which informs the Recovery plan, is fuelled by the principles of solidarity and responsibility.[88]

For Bruno De Witte, the EMU developments demonstrate how

> constitutional change does not only happen, in the European Union, by means of formal changes in the text of primarily law, but also by means of changing *judicial*

values of a Member State e.g., (a) policy for distribution of income; (b) imposition and collection of personal taxes; (c) *system of social welfare benefits*; (d) educational system; (e) public health care system; (f) cultural preservation and development; (g) compulsory military or community service' (emphasis added).

[85] Tuori, *European Constitutionalism* 232.

[86] Dyson, *States, Debt, and Power* 220–21.

[87] Päivi Leino-Sandberg, 'Next Generation EU – A Constitutional Change without Constitutional Change' (*Reconnect*, 13 January 2021) https://reconnect-europe.eu/blog/new-generation-eu-a-constitutional-change-without-constitutional-change.

[88] de Gregorio Merino, 'The Recovery Plan' 2.

> *interpretation* of the norms of primary law, or by *institutional practice* that transforms the significance or effect of written norms of primary EU law.[89]

Therefore, we are to understand that the EU constitutional system has evolved so as to allow the EU institutions to expand their own competence basis through their own decisions – this is the core of the 'living constitution' argument. The only constraint on EU action is a political one: what the institutions can agree on.

This understanding is in direct contradiction with the traditional reading of the principle of conferral,[90] which has certainly allowed new interpretations but still insisted that new competence is shifted through Treaty change – a hazy border, which has also been debated before. In the context of such debates, the Bundesverfassungsgericht has stressed that

> faith in the constructive force of the mechanism of integration cannot be unlimited. If in the process of European integration primary law is amended, or expansively interpreted by institutions, a constitutionally important tension will arise with the principle of conferral and with the individual Member State's constitutional responsibility for integration. … if the institutions are permitted to re-define expansively, fill lacunae or factually extend competences, they risk transgressing the predetermined integration programme and acting beyond the powers granted to them.[91]

It follows that the EU can 'not simply take away competences from the Member States at will. The same holds true for interpreting the Treaties: The EU may only interpret the competences conferred upon it; it may not create new ones.'[92]

Control of the EU legislative and executive branches is exercised, in particular, by the ECJ. The Court has traditionally approached the EU's legislative work more through questions of legal basis and the correct legislative procedure, protecting, in particular, the Parliament's institutional prerogatives, rather than limiting the substantive choices of the legislature. Historically, the ECJ's review powers have permitted the Court to fill a void created by political impasses. However, as Treaty changes have gradually expanded EU competence, the Court has become more withdrawn and more focused on procedural review of formal requirements, leaving substantive choices to the legislature and allowing broad executive discretion. Bold interference in the will-formation processes has in more recent years been limited to issues where EU law is still in a developing stage, such as fundamental rights matters.[93] While crisis measures have been repeatedly settled by the

[89] Bruno De Witte, 'EMU as Constitutional Law' in Fabian Amtenbrink, Christoph Herrman and René Repasi (eds), *The EU Law of Economic and Monetary Union* (Oxford, Oxford University Press, 2020) 278–92, 291.

[90] See Consolidated versions of the Treaty on the European Union and the Treaty on the Functioning of the European Union [2012] OJ C 326/03, Art 4 (1) TEU and Art 5 TEU.

[91] BVerfGE 123, 267 <351–52> para 237–38.

[92] Dieter Grimm, 'A Long Time Coming' (2020) 21 *German Law Journal* 944, 945.

[93] Leino-Sandberg, The Politics of Legal Expertise.

European Council (or the European Central Bank), it is difficult to think of a case where the Court would have intervened.

Yet, as a matter of constitutional law, there may be cases where it should intervene. The EU policy-making process remains of a highly executive and technocratic character. The EU institutions have increasingly reached into politically sensitive areas and enjoyed the unveiling support of their constitutional court. However, the latter also faces a legitimacy challenge – less based on 'its hermeneutics (a good outcome based on a questionable interpretation) but quite the opposite – an unassailable interpretation but an outcome which underpins, supports, and "legitimates" a highly problematic decisional process'.[94] Critics claim that through such interpretations the Court 'has eroded the principle of conferral – the basis of the entire European order'.[95] As a result,

> [t]he CJEU is deeply involved in this political struggle. With growing divisions between EU lawmakers and the ensuing gridlock, space opens up for the CJEU to pursue its integration goals. Many worry this may threaten the maintenance of a politically acceptable balance between European Union competences and national competences. Constitutionally, the erosion of the principle of conferral subverts the EU's foundation, which is the consensual but limited grant of competence by the Member States.[96]

The EU's constitutional imaginary has always relied on a strong interplay between academics, judges and institutional lawyers.[97] Today, we are witnessing how 'the principle of solidarity' is being framed as a new general principle of law that can be used to justify derogating from the EU Treaties and thus expanding EU competence. The Commission Legal Service argued, the RFF constitutes

> extraordinary measures in situations of crisis as an expression of solidarity among Member States. Recourse to that legal basis is necessary for derogating from standard Treaty rules, which would not allow the financing of such large amounts in addition to the Union's budget and outside of the annual budgetary procedure. This is justified only in the circumstances of the current crisis.[98]

The Council Legal Service stresses that NGEU is an 'exceptional, temporary and one-off instrument to help economic recovery in a spirit of solidarity' and that '[s]olidarity is a core principle underlying the Treaties'.[99] A Council Legal Service

[94] Joseph HH Weiler, 'Europe in Crisis: On "Political Messianism", "Legitimacy" and the "Rule of Law"' (2012) *Singapore Journal of Legal Studies* 248, 265.

[95] Grimm, 'A Long Time Coming' 945–46.

[96] Ulrich Haltern, 'Revolutions, Real Contradictions, and the Method of Resolving Them: The Relationship Between the Court of Justice of the European Union and the German Federal Constitutional Court' (2021) 19 *International Journal of Constitutional Law* 208.

[97] See eg Antoine Vauchez, *Brokering Europe: Euro-Lawyers and the Making of a Transnational Polity* (Cambridge, Cambridge University Press, 2015) 87.

[98] European Commission, 'Questions and answers, Q&A: Next Generation EU – Legal Construction' (*European Commission Website*, 9 June 2020) https://ec.europa.eu/commission/presscorner/detail/en/QANDA_20_1024.

[99] Council Legal Service, Opinion, Council Doc. 9062/20 (Brussels, 24 June 2021) para 64.

lawyer further stresses in an academic article how 'the NGEU is a construction at the core of which lies the value of solidarity'.[100] A European Parliament lawyer writes,

> [o]verall, the agreement on NGEU represents an important signal of solidarity between states and citizens in times of crisis. Admittedly, the bulk of NGEU funds will be allocated along national lines under the RRF. … Nevertheless, the symbolism of issuing joint debt in a spirit of solidarity in response to a major health and economic crisis that affects all Member States and citizens cannot be ignored.[101]

As a recent *Common Market Law Review* editorial notes, this is an example of how '[c]lassic principles of EU law are used to provide a normative justification for new constructions. Legally, the interregnum assumes a special shape: old forms are embedded in new ones'.[102] Since many of the EU's values and general objectives and principles have a generally *communautaire* flavour and direction, they can be used to justify an expansive rather than a restrictive interpretation of its powers and the scope of Union law.[103] Solidarity is well suited for such a purpose. It has always had an existence in EU legal vocabulary.[104] As the Court emphasised in *Wightman*, a matter may be examined 'in the light of the Treaties taken as a whole'; thus, the 'interpretation of a provision of EU law requires that account be taken not only of its wording and the objectives it pursues, but also of its context and the provisions of EU law as a whole'.[105] Such a meta-teleological reading builds on identifying ends on the highest level of generality while ignoring the contestability of the extent of legal integration, and replaces the member states as the EU's constituent power by autonomous EU institutional action.[106]

In the context of NGEU, the emphasis on solidarity did not stay at the EU's political institutions and their servants, but has also received significant support in the extra-judicial writings of the Court's President Koen Lenaerts and Stanislas Adam, a member of his Cabinet, who stressed the importance of the spirit of solidarity between member states for the viability of the European project as a truly federating principle. The timing of the article was curious, as it was published

[100] de Gregorio Merino, 'The Recovery Plan' 10. The article refers to a single article written by a colleague in the Council Legal Service preceding the adoption of NGEU, Jeno Czuczai, 'The principle of solidarity in the EU legal order – some practical examples after Lisbon' in Jeno Czuczai and Fredrik Naert (eds), *The EU as a Global Actor – Bridging Legal Theory and Practice* (Leiden, Brill Nijhoff, 2017) 145–65.

[101] Crowe, 'An EU Budget' 340.

[102] Editorial Comments (2022) 59 *CML Rev* 957, 958.

[103] Gunnar Beck, *The Legal Reasoning of the Court of Justice of the EU* (Oxford, Hart, 2012) 316.

[104] See Art 2 TEU, Art 3 TEU, Art 194 TFEU, Art 67 (2) TFEU and Art 122 TFEU. The Court's case-law is summarised in Case C-848/19 P *Germany v Poland* ECLI:EU:C:2021:598 para 41.

[105] Case C-621/18 Wightman and Others v Secretary of State for Exiting the European Union ECLI:EU:C:2018:999 paras 46–47.

[106] For a critique, see Gerard Conway, *The Limits of Legal Reasoning and the European Court of Justice* (Cambridge, Cambridge University Press, 2021) 274.

at a time when it was already known that a challenge concerning the NGEU construction was pending before the Bundesverfassungsgericht, with the prospect that the matter would be referred to the ECJ for a preliminary ruling. In the article, Lenaerts and Adam stress that inter-state solidarity is protected, promoted or even required in many of the Union's policies.[107] While recognising that solidarity has not been intended to constitute a general principle of EU law and must be reconciled with the principle of attribution of competences, they underline its programmatic character. And as regards NGEU in particular, they define solidarity as the 'true functional matrix of integration' and a 'part of the very DNA of the Union' and argue,

> [t]he agreement reached in 2020 on the Next Generation EU is in this respect a completely fundamental for the deepening of the bonds of solidarity woven between Member States and all their citizens, on the way to a Union more resilient in the face of crises and the challenges of globalization.[108]

I see this 'academic contribution',[109] together with the institutional contributions quoted above, as an example of a doctrine-building that Tuori calls 'sedimentation':

> [T]o accomplish a major change in the general doctrines of a certain field of law, it is not enough that an individual legal scholar introduces a new set of concepts and principles as an alternative to the prevailing doctrines. Only when her proposal receives support from other scholars and when it is resorted to in adjudication, possibly even in lawmaking, can we speak of sedimentation, which leads to the inclusion of the new doctrines in the legal culture.[110]

The Court soon received the chance to sediment solidarity in a case involving Article 194 TFEU in a case concerning energy supply in a context of external dependence. For the Court, 'the spirit of solidarity between Member States, mentioned in that provision, constitutes a specific expression, in the field of energy, *of the principle of solidarity, which is itself one of the fundamental principles of EU law*' (emphasis added).[111] This could soon be developed further when Hungary and Poland raised challenges against the new regulation on budgetary conditionality. In his opinion in the Hungarian case, Advocate General Campos Sánchez-Bordona noted, the 'budget is the instrument of EU law which, each year, translates the principle of solidarity … into financial terms and it is of constitutional importance'.[112] The only reference provided for the

[107] Koen Lenaerts and Stanislas Adam, 'La solidarité, valeur commune aux États membres et principe fédératif de l'Union européenne' (2021) 57 *Cahiers de droit européen* 307.

[108] ibid (translation my own).

[109] For a critical analysis of the academic functions of institutional lawyers and their effect on EU legal scholarship, see Päivi Leino-Sandberg, 'Enchantment and Critical Distance'.

[110] Kaarlo Tuori, *Critical Legal Positivism* (London, Routledge, 2017) 201.

[111] Case C-848/19 P *Germany v Poland* ECLI:EU:C:2021:598, para 38.

[112] Case C-156/21 *Hungary v Parliament and Council* ECLI:EU:C:2022:97 Opinion of AG Campos Sánchez-Bordona, para 96.

latter argument (in footnote 56) was none other than the article by Lenaerts and Adams quoted above. Building an argument like this on a single source deriving from inside the Court represents 'self-referentiality' which affects what we know[113] as views of a single (institutional) author come to represent what is a 'generally accepted' interpretation, or how the interpretation proposed is 'consistent with the mainstream thought'.[114] The ECJ subsequently observed, with reference to its ruling in the energy supply case quoted above, that 'the Union budget is one of the principal instruments for giving practical effect, in the Union's policies and activities, to the principle of solidarity, mentioned in Article 2 TEU, which is itself one of the fundamental principles of EU law'.[115] An identical paragraph can be found in the ruling concerning the Polish appeal[116] even though the Opinion by the (same) Advocate General lacks any discussion of the principle of solidarity.[117]

Like many times before, 'the justificatory arguments of the Court are found in its own previous decisions, which are cited out of their immediate context (legal and factual), and repeated in subsequent novel situations almost at random'. Šadl argues, 'What holds the cases, which are cited in support of the Court's argument, together, is language (the Court's rhetoric)'.[118] Solidarity works ideally as such rhetoric. However, solidarity also escapes any specific meaning and would require political choices in order to be able to guide policies. What kind of solidarity, by whom, and under what conditions? It is one thing to argue that EU states should 'act jointly in a spirit of solidarity if a Member State is the object of a terrorist attack or the victim of a natural or man-made disaster' (Article 222 TFEU). It is something else to suggest that the principle of solidarity also creates an obligation for states to provide transfers to fund new IT systems for the Italian judiciary or the Dutch Ministry of Defence or electric cars for social workers in Porto, or an obligation for Swedish taxpayers to contribute to the high gas bills of German taxpayers. All of these are divisive and highly political questions. A meta-teleological reading may also place a great emphasis on broad principles, and use them to bypass inconvenient Treaty articles. Such articles may have been historically introduced as limits to integration to safeguard parliamentary democracy or national constitutional purposes. When institutional documents on EMU development are examined, there is a silence on questions relating to whether

[113] Lianne J M Boer, '"The Greater Part of Jurisconsults:" On Consensus Claims and Their Footnotes in Legal Scholarship' (2016) 29 *Leiden Journal of International Law* 1021, 1023–24.
[114] ibid.
[115] Case C-156/21 *Hungary v Parliament and Council* ECLI:EU:C:2022:97, para 129.
[116] Case C-157/21 *Poland v Parliament and Council* ECLI:EU:C:2021:978, para 147.
[117] Case C-157/21 *Poland v Parliament and Council* ECLI:EU:C:2021:978 Opinion of AG Campos Sánchez-Bordona.
[118] Urška Šadl, 'Case – Case-Law – Law: Ruiz Zambrano as an Illustration of How the Court of Justice of the European Union Constructs Its Legal Arguments' (2013) 9 *European Constitutional Law Review* 205, 229.

certain types of powers can appropriately be delegated to supranational executive bodies.[119] Instead, the goals promoted by solidarity are presented as 'all win' – there are no costs and no losers.

When the key actors are deeply engaged in integrationist objectives, there seems to be limited space and time for an open debate of the effects of the measures that they promote. In the EU, constitutional discourse largely takes place between EU judges, lawyers and legal scholars for whom the constitutional character of EU law is often a 'predetermined' article of faith.[120] Arguments for respecting existing readings on competence or giving national parliaments a say in the process are easily treated as Eurosceptic political bias. The EU is 'special'; therefore the 'EU model of democracy cannot be measured by reference to traditional nation-State standards' and 'democracy is a dynamic concept which evolves hand in hand with societal change';[121] therefore, one should be careful when criticising the EU's effect on democratic decision-making, as the principle of democracy must be adapted 'to alternative methods of policy making'.[122] The 'special' nature of the EU allows ends to justify means; therefore, the EU does not need to care about the democratic anchoring of its policies, prioritisation, balanced budget rules, competence divisions, or a deep political community that elsewhere have been considered vital for a stable and successful fiscal union. After all, the EU's autonomous regulatory power is believed to offer it an autonomous constitutional legitimacy,[123] as 'EU politics likes to pretend it operates within an environment of dense political community'.[124] This thinking represents a dominant constitutional imaginary, or what Lindseth calls an aspirational 'as if' constitutionalism,[125] which fails to recognise 'a crucial fault line between the EU's primarily regulatory (ie "administrative") character as opposed to its potential 'constitutional' future. This state of affairs has a whole range of implications for the nature of EU law as well as for what European integration can realistically achieve.[126] The EU is far from developing into a constitutional regime:

> at this historical juncture, regardless of how the ECJ or other legal actors may conceive of the EU legally, European governance has not gone through this phase transition to become an autonomous 'constitutional' regime in its own right.[127]

Instead of institutional agendas led from Brussels, 'what is perhaps most needed right now is a wider, pan-European conversation, extending beyond the confines of the Brussels institutional bubble, on what the Union budget is for and how it

[119] For a review, see Leino-Sandberg and Losada Fraga, 'European Semester'.
[120] Lindseth, 'European, The Perils'. See also Leino-Sandberg, 'Enchantment and Critical Distance'.
[121] Koen Lenaerts, 'The Principle of Democracy in the Case Law of the European Court of Justice' (2013) 62 *ICLQ* 271.
[122] ibid 313.
[123] See Lindseth, 'Author's Reply' 154.
[124] Haltern, 'Revolutions'.
[125] Lindseth, 'European, The Perils' 700.
[126] ibid.
[127] ibid.

should function'.[128] Overall, there is little analysis of citizen opinions that could be used to back up such constitutional imaginary.[129] Lindseth reminds us of the need to ask 'legitimate for what?', referring to a linkage between the nature of a legal or political order and the scope of power that it can successfully exercise. The potential of the EU in this respect remains highly limited when compared with 'the socio-political and socio-cultural demos-based legitimacy that supports compulsory mobilisation powers in national constitutional law'.[130] He points out how

> [n]ational institutions are increasingly constrained in the exercise of their constitutional authority but supranational institutions cannot fill the void because they are unable to transition to genuine constitutionalism – that is the autonomous capacity to mobilise fiscal and human resources in a compulsory fashion. The EU lacks this essential capacity not because of the lack of the right kind of institutional engineering (e.g., through more power for the EP). Rather, it lacks it because, on a deeper socio-historical level, the EU also lacks the demos-based constitutional legitimacy needed to attain it.[131]

He warns against confusing regulatory power with democratic and constitutional legitimacy in EU governance: 'The absence of legitimate mobilisation capacities at the EU level suggests that EU judges, lawyers and their scholarly allies are engaging in an aspirational power play'.[132] Instead, he proposes: 'Policing the boundaries of competences conferred on the EU with much greater rigour, in recognition that these sorts of constraints … must be enforced in the interest of democracy.'[133] Self-referencing a general principle of solidarity would seem to represent 'as if' constitutionalism in its most blatant form, and also contributes to the de-legitimation of the ECJ in the eyes of national apex courts, whose support is vital in light of the polycentric constitutional character of European integration.

When the EU institutions promote fiscal integration in the abstract name of solidarity, they in fact engage in a deeply political discussion that affects democratic choice in a foundational manner. Their consistent agenda over the past decade has been to replace democratic institutions with their own supranational technocratic decision-making that specifically aims at neutralising national politics. When democratic institutions are eliminated, who is then left to settle

[128] Richard Crowe, 'The European Council and the Multiannual Financial Framework' (2016) 18 *Cambridge Yearbook of European Legal Studies* 69, 91.

[129] For a limited survey supporting the current division of powers, see Constantin Schäfer, Bernd Schlipphak, and Oliver Treib, 'The ideal setting of the EU in the mind of European citizens' (*Reconnect*, 22 April 2021) Work Package 9 – Deliverable 2, https://reconnect-europe.eu/wp-content/uploads/2021/04/D9.2.pdf.

[130] Lindseth, 'European, The Perils' 709.

[131] ibid 701.

[132] ibid 711.

[133] ibid 717.

priorities and conduct political debate? In this way, no matter how it is framed, debate about the future orientation of fiscal integration represents an 'epic battle for nothing less than the control Member States exercise over both the integration process and their own self-governance. It is not just about power, but about democracy and legitimacy'.[134] The questions involved demand an answer that is rooted in something else than constitutional imaginary.

5. More or Less Democracy – And Does it Really Matter?

This chapter has argued that a proper basis for a fiscal union requires more than just an accumulation of crisis mechanisms. Bypassing foundational questions is not a solid method of constitutional development. 'Constitutional change should appear unbiased, stand public scrutiny, and hold also beyond the ongoing or imminent crisis.'[135] The permanent crisis mode in which the decisions of the last decade have been taken has led to a technocratic governance model in matters forming the core of national democratic policies. It has taken both the EU and the member states far from democratic governance, where decisions on revenue and expenditure are a central element of development of informed opinion and taken with responsibility to the people. In an article published in 2013, the President of the ECJ assured that the 'transfer of powers from the Member States to the EU must not adversely affect national democracies. On the contrary, the EU decision-making process must be accommodated so as to create "more democracy", be that at national or at EU level'.[136] In today's EU economic and fiscal policies, there is no question of 'more democracy' – it is a model of 'less democracy' at all levels. Along the way, the objective of creating a fiscal union that actually benefits all Europeans through provision of European public goods has been lost. The model that is currently being consolidated as a permanent construction is fundamentally twisted and relies on a constitutional imaginary of solidarity rather than tangible progress towards a political community that would be vital for constructing and buttressing such solidarity. Not only would the involvement of parliaments need to be ensured but there would also need to be some explicit choices about the constitutional scope of EU spending.

It is no secret that the EU is genetically a paternalistic project; it was about the elites leading the masses, not the other way around. Its (noble) original reason for existing was to tie member states together with thousands of small ties, so that they would be forced to spend their days bickering about mundane things of everyday

[134] Haltern, 'Revolutions'.
[135] Leino-Sandberg and Ruffert 'Next Generation EU'.
[136] Lenaerts, 'The Principle of Democracy' 312.

policy rather than shooting at each other. As the citizens were not ready to just voluntarily walk into an ever-closer embrace, a certain degree of well-intentioned deception was necessary and justified to achieve this. This is what is still hardcoded into the Union's institutional DNA. The EU's living constitution keeps evolving, not through formal Treaty changes, nor as a response to a broader cultural evolution in European societies, but rather in a strategically directed endless cycle of framing and re-framing, interpreting and re-interpreting, which gradually and almost invisibly shifts competences from member states to the Union, at a pace that keeps member states in a constant state of discomfort but still mostly remains below the threshold of unbearable pain.

One could ask whether this really is still necessary, whether the Union still needs to make use of every crisis to bring about constitutional evolution. Could it be that the ties that have grown over years are now strong enough so that the Union could finally allow a good crisis to go to waste, and be ready to graduate into a more deliberative and organised method of federal evolution?

PART 3

Integration Through Financial Constitution?

9

Budgeting for Success

How a Series of Budgetary Breakthroughs Underpinned the EC/EU's 1980s Boom

N PIERS LUDLOW

The current standard explanation of the remarkable revival or *relance* of the European Community (EC) in the latter half of the 1980s – a transformative moment that paved the way for the establishment of today's European Union in the early 1990s – highlights institutional reform and emerging policy consensus as the two main drivers of process. Different authors, it is true, highlight somewhat different causal links and identify different individuals as the key protagonists. Some accounts are hence more supranational in focus, singling out the role of the incoming European Commission President Jacques Delors in particular, while others adopt a more intergovernmental approach, emphasising the importance of key actors amongst the member states, and the vital significance of an emerging consensus amongst the national governments about what the Community should do.[1] But virtually all construct an explanation that centres on the adoption by the European Economic Community (EEC) of the Single Market programme in 1985, and the decision, also taken that year, to convene an intergovernmental conference (IGC), which would lead to the first major new European treaty since the Treaty of Rome: the 1986 Single European Act.[2] This last, it is widely claimed, had a transformative effect on the manner in which the Community functioned, thereby making it much better able to attain its bold new policy target of constructing a

[1] For a Delors-focused account see eg Ken Endo, *The Presidency of the European Commission under Jacques Delors: The Politics of Shared Leadership* (Basingstoke, Macmillan, 1999). A newer, but equally Commission-centred version, is in Nicolas Jabko, *Playing the Market: A Political Strategy for Uniting Europe, 1985–2005* (Ithaca, NY, Cornell University Press, 2006). The classic intergovernmental case remains Andrew Moravcsik, 'Negotiating the Single European Act: National Interests and Conventional Statecraft in the European Community' (1991) 45 *International Organization* 19.

[2] The first concerted attempt by historians to explain these developments is constituted by Michael Gehler and Wilfried Loth (eds), *Reshaping Europe: Towards a Political, Economic and Monetary Union, 1984–1989* (Baden-Baden, Nomos, 2020).

truly functioning internal market by the end of 1992.[3] A new sense of purpose and a new manner of operating thus lie at the heart of the 1980s *relance*.

Budgetary matters, by contrast, do not loom large in the traditional account. To the extent that they figure at all, it is usually to argue that the 1984 resolution of the divisive and controversial row over the British budgetary contribution constituted a precondition for the subsequent revival. A few studies also note the wider budgetary problems that the Community faced in the early 1980s, with the massive and volatile expenditure on the Common Agricultural Policy threatening to outstrip the EEC income from the so-called 'own resources', ie the sources of revenue which automatically accrued to the Community.[4] But while this budgetary noose and the deadlock over Britain's share of Community expenditure are presented as symptoms of the EEC's malaise in the first half of the 1980s, little detailed scholarship has been devoted to the manner in which these problems were overcome. Instead the focus of most of the literature shifts elsewhere as the 1985 acceleration began.[5]

The purpose of this chapter will be to suggest that this neglect of the budgetary dimension is a mistake. To be sure, this is not the same as claiming that neither the renewed policy consensus, centred initially around the creation of a Single Market then later on Economic and Monetary Union (EMU) nor the institutional revolution brought about by the Single European Act were important. They clearly both were. But it is to suggest that the budgetary breakthroughs not just of 1984 but still more that of 1988 were absolutely crucial components in the revival of Community fortunes. There is, to put it differently, a really important budgetary dimension to the 1980s *relance*, and the intention of this chapter is to bring it back into focus.

1. The Problem

At the heart of the Community's budgetary difficulties in early 1980s – and indeed at the heart of its wider problems during this most crucial of decades – was the fundamental mismatch between the largely undynamic income from the so-called 'own resources' and the all too dynamic expenditure, centred on the Common

[3] See eg the comments by Riccardo Perissich, the Commission official responsible for the Internal Market programme, in Vincent Dujardin et al (eds), *The European Commission 1986–2000: Histories and Memories of an Institution* (Luxembourg, Publications Office of the European Union, 2019) 193–94.

[4] Dinan does acknowledge the wider problem, although the British Budgetary Question (BBQ) is presented as the core obstacle to progress. Desmond Dinan, *Europe Recast: A History of the European Union* (Boulder, Lynne Rienner Publishers, 2014) 177–80.

[5] Moravcsik is typical of this tendency, moving straight from the negotiation of the Single European Act to the push for Monetary Union and the road to the Maastricht Treaty. Andrew Moravcsik, *The Choice for Europe: Social Purpose and State Power from Messina to Maastricht* (London, UCL Press, 1999) chs 5, 6.

Agricultural Policy (CAP).[6] In an EEC that was obliged by Article 199 of the Treaty of Rome to run a balanced budget, this mismatch quickly became a serious brake on the Community's ability to grow and develop. On the income side neither of the first two own resources that the Community received from 1971 onwards, customs receipts and agricultural levies, seemed likely to grow substantially. In fact in the early 1980s the amount coming in from the latter shrank as often as it rose – a reflection of the way in which the EEC grew ever more of its own food and hence imported less. As a result, the EEC budget became progressively more reliant on the 1 per cent slice of national Value Added Tax (VAT) takes that it had begun to be paid from 1979 onwards. By 1982, just three years after it had started to receive this source of revenue, over half (54.3 per cent) of the Community's income came from VAT.[7] The 1 per cent ceiling on such income could only be raised, however, with the unanimous consent of all member states – something that could not easily be obtained. Expenditure, by contrast, was all too prone to rise. Although by the early 1980s the total spent on the CAP had fallen somewhat from the peaks it had reached in the previous decade, it still consumed the bulk of the Community's budget. It was 68.6 per cent of the total in 1980; 59.7 per cent the following year; and back up to 68.4 per cent in 1985.[8] As these figures rather emphasise, furthermore, the exact sums needed each year for the CAP were extremely hard to predict, given the vagaries of both agricultural prices and production levels. There was hence little room for other Community policies to grow, despite the professed intention to increase EEC expenditure on structural policies and research. Instead, the Community found itself in an increasingly restrictive financial straitjacket, uncertain of being able to meet its existing commitments, let alone take on any substantial new ones.

This budgetary squeeze had a number of damaging knock-on effects. First, it led to a severe deterioration of intra-institutional relations within the European Community. The new directly-elected European Parliament was already keen to exploit the leverage that it enjoyed through the budgetary process to pursue its quest for additional powers. This was something that had become apparent with its rejection of the budget in December 1979, for instance. But it also showed mounting annoyance at the way in which the obligatory nature of CAP expenditure, over which it could exercise no control whatsoever, all but squeezed out any spending priorities favoured by parliamentarians. The limitations of Strasbourg's ability to shape the Community's expenditure thus became yet another example of the powerlessness to which the newly elected members of the European Parliament

[6] Roy Jenkins had used this formula when having his final conversation with Valéry Giscard d'Estaing as Commission President. Tickell Papers, All Souls College, Oxford, File 18, 'Record of a conversation between the President of the European Commission and the President of the French Republic, Elysée', 26 November 1980.

[7] European Commission, *The Community Budget in Facts and Figures* (Brussels, European Commission, 1994) 38.

[8] ibid 31–32.

objected so strongly.[9] The Commission meanwhile was always the first affected by the unreliability of the budgetary decision-making process, restricted in its ability to plan ahead, constrained in engaging new staff on long-term contracts, and obliged to resort to ever more questionable accounting techniques to honour its existing spending commitments.[10] And the Council itself saw budgetary disagreement worsen the pre-existing log-jam of draft legislation. The increasingly tetchy relationship between the Commission, Parliament and Council that characterised the first half of the 1980s revealed much about the Community's malaise.

Second, the wider budget problem aggravated the ongoing row amongst the Community member states about national contributions and receipts from the EEC budget. This dispute is of course most famously associated with Margaret Thatcher's vociferous campaign during 1979 and early 1980s 'to get her money back' from the EEC.[11] But alongside the high-profile British assault on what they perceived as the unfairness of EEC financing, there was also lower-key but still potentially hazardous grumbling on the part of the Germans and Italians too.[12] Other member states, by contrast, regarded any attempt to alter the Community's budgetary system as a dangerous retreat from an important part of the *acquis Communautaire*. The British case for change, seen from such a viewpoint, risked introducing the dangerous notion of *juste retour*, or the idea that member states' receipts from the EEC budget had to remain fully in line with each country's contribution. Accepting this principle would strip the Community budget of any redistributive capacity and seriously limit the range of common policies which could be pursued. Resisting Thatcher's demands was thus not simply a way of protecting a budgetary system that worked well for some member states; it was also a way of protecting the idea and the potential of a genuinely common budget. Bridging this divide of both financial interest and underlying philosophy would be no easy task. Deep-seated disagreement about how the budget should function was certainly not the only source of division and discord amongst the Ten in the early 1980s, but it was a significant contributing factor.

[9] For an insider's view of the Parliament's struggle to assert itself within the EEC's budgetary process, see Julian Priestley, *Six Battles That Shaped Europe's Parliament* (London, John Harper, 2008) 6–22.

[10] For a discussion of Commission staffing trends in this period, which makes it clear that numbers could grow only slowly, despite the enlargement towards Greece, see Éric Bussière et al, *The European Commission 1973–86: History and Memories of an Institution* (Luxembourg, Publications Office of the European Union, 2014) 63–65.

[11] For a detailed look at Thatcher's motivations and underlying approach, see Charles Moore, *Margaret Thatcher: The Authorized Biography*, vol 1 (London, Allen Lane, 2013) 485–95. And for an exploration of why the problem had arisen and why it was so difficult to resolve, see N Piers Ludlow, *Roy Jenkins and the European Commission Presidency 1976–1980: At the Heart of Europe* (Basingstoke, Palgrave Macmillan, 2016) 207–16.

[12] The lingering Italian discontent at the budgetary situation was very apparent in the conversation between Franco Maria Malfatti, the Italian foreign minister, and Roy Jenkins, the President of the European Commission. Tickell Papers, 'Record of a Conversation between the President of the European Community [*sic*] and the Italian Foreign Minister, Villa Madama, Rome', 9 September 1979.

Third and perhaps most seriously, the budgetary impasse cast doubt over the Community's ability to expand either its activities or its membership. In the early 1980s there was no shortage of ideas about how the integration process could be further developed. Landmarks like the 1983 Stuttgart Solemn Declaration on European Union suggested furthermore that the Ten were edging towards the required level of intergovernmental consensus about the need for greater integration.[13] But fine words could only be followed up with new policies if the budgetary constraints were overcome. Nor was the planned expansion of Community membership to include Spain and Portugal likely to be possible under existing budgetary provisions. Both of the Iberian countries were certain to become major net beneficiaries of the EEC budget rather than contributors, with Spanish agricultural production likely to be especially expensive to subsidise on a par with the farmers of the existing member states.[14] There was hence absolutely no prospect of the Community being able to honour its promise to admit both applicants without a budgetary breakthrough being achieved.

2. The Breakthroughs

The first double step towards resolving this situation was taken in 1984. Crucially, it involved both a resolution of the British budgetary problem *and* a more general financial settlement, even though this last would prove only to be a short-term solution. The higher profile of the two – and the longer lasting – was the Fontainebleau deal on the UK budgetary rebate, an accord that would bring to an end the long-lasting and deeply damaging row over Britain's contribution to the Community budget. The details of what was agreed and how so acrimonious a dispute was eventually resolved need not detain us here.[15] But what mattered is that an issue that had been poisoning debate within the EEC, and especially perhaps at European Council level where Thatcher had pursued her objective in particularly abrasive fashion, had at last been cleared away.[16] Equally crucial was the wider budgetary advance, with agreement reached to raise the slice of VAT returns that accrued to the Community from 1 per cent to 1.4 per cent. This at a stroke ended

[13] The text of the declaration is available at www.cvce.eu/en/obj/solemn_declaration_on_european_union_stuttgart_19_june_1983-en-a2e74239-a12b-4efc-b4ce-cd3dee9cf71d.html (*Centre Virtuel de la Connaissance sur l'Europe*, 18 December 2013).

[14] For a revisionist take on the path to Spanish membership see Marta Alorda Carreras, 'Europeanisation à la Carte: Negotiating Spanish Accession to the European Community, 1979–1985' (PhD thesis, Florence, European University Institute, 2022).

[15] For my own analysis of how the deal was reached, N Piers Ludlow, 'A Double-Edged Victory: Fontainebleau and the Resolution of the British Budgetary Problem, 1983–1984' in Gehler and Loth, *Reshaping Europe* 45–71.

[16] François Mitterrand used the terminology of poisoning in his May 1984 meeting with Helmut Kohl, Daniela Taschler and Tim Szatkowski (eds), *Akten zur Auswärtigen Politik des Bundesrepublik Deutschland 1984* (Berlin, De Gruyter Oldenbourg, vol 1, 2015) 705.

the imminent budgetary crisis within the EEC of which the European Commission had been warning. And this too gave Europe's leaders valuable breathing space to begin to think about more generalised European advance.[17]

Importantly the two agreements were linked, politically as well as chronologically. For one of the key difficulties confronting Britain's leaders in their campaign to get the budgetary redress that they believed themselves to deserve, had been persuading their partners, upon whom the costs of any British rebate would fall, to recognise the urgency of the problem and the need to act. In 1980 and again in 1982 they had tried to do this by linking progress on the British budgetary question to the annual setting of CAP prices. Without progress on the former, UK ministers would not permit the much-needed price agreement to be finalised.[18] On the second occasion that this tactic had been tried, however, British threats to veto the CAP prices as they were agreed had been overridden, the nine other countries disputing the UK's claim that its vital interests were in play and that the Luxembourg Compromise thus applied. With the UK in midst of an actual war with Argentina over the Falkland Islands, and keen to preserve the Community economic sanctions that had been imposed upon General Galtieri's regime, the British government had been compelled to accept this reverse.[19] But this left it requiring a new lever with which to force its fellow member states to address the issue of Britain's budgetary contribution. And this in turn made the Community's wider budgetary problems absolutely crucial, since in order to resolve the general lack of money and to raise the VAT ceiling, unanimity amongst member states would be required. Britain could therefore make its assent to the proposed 1.4 per cent VAT limit conditional on a deal also being struck on its own budgetary problem. This is what happened at Fontainebleau.

Also of importance was the fact that the increase of the VAT ceiling to 1.4 per cent was nothing more than a temporary fix. Even so, it was still of great political significance, since it would provide the Community's leaders with the budgetary headroom to take the first crucial decisions of what we now refer to as the *relance*. The push for a Single Market and the IGC leading to the Single European Act would thus take place during a period when the Community was not greatly preoccupied with its budget.[20] It also meant that Spain and Portugal could take their place around the Community table in 1986 without immediately

[17] This was the aspect emphasised most by Mitterrand in his post-summit press conference. See www.cvce.eu/en/obj/press_conference_by_francois_mitterrand_fontainebleau_26_june_1984-en-b28bbf91-7fd4-4274-a7a1-49f8576cfff8.html (*Centre Virtuel de la Connaissance sur l'Europe*, 8 November 2016).

[18] The 1982 decision is outlined in Stephen Wall, *The Official History of Britain and the European Community*, vol 3 (Abingdon, Routledge, 2019) 216.

[19] Michael Butler, *Europe: More than a Continent* (London, Heinemann, 1986) 99–100. On the intersection between the Falklands War and British European policy, see N Piers Ludlow, 'Solidarity, Sanctions and Misunderstanding: The European Dimension of the Falklands Crisis' (2021) 43 *The International History Review* 508.

[20] For the latest historical research on the *relance*, see Gehler and Loth, *Reshaping Europe*.

bankrupting the EEC. But given the inexorable rise of Community expenditure, even without enlargement or the new policy priorities that the ambitious Delors Commission was beginning to set, it was entirely predictable that a new round of budgetary negotiations would be necessary. Indeed the temporary nature of the wider budgetary deal agreed in 1984 almost certainly made it much easier to settle the British budgetary rebate too, since most of the UK's partners, in agreeing to cut Britain's contribution to the budget, (wrongly) assumed that they were doing so only for four or five years, and would be able to revisit the issue once a new budgetary settlement was required.[21] Had they known that they were in effect allowing an arrangement for the UK which would endure, more or less unscathed, until Britain's departure from the EU in 2020, it is much less likely that they would have granted so generous a deal. But British diplomats and politicians would prove highly adept over the years and decades ahead at preventing a reopening of the British budgetary question. Unpleasant memories of how disruptive an issue it had been, meant moreover that few of the other member states were inclined to try too hard to revisit the issue. There was always a better time to discuss this question.

No such stay of execution applied to the general Community budget however. In fact by 1987 the Community was facing a budgetary squeeze even more daunting than that of the early 1980s. It was a 1987 Commission report, after all, that opened with the blunt observation: 'The Community is a present faced with a budgetary situation which can only be characterised as being on the brink of bankruptcy.'[22] A key part of maintaining the Community's new momentum hence became the identification of a new budgetary deal. This would become the Delors I package of 1988.[23]

The key to this second and much more transformative budgetary breakthrough was the combination of ambition and the favourable context. Jacques Delors, the President of the Commission and the main architect of the plan, was certainly ambitious. But then so too had his predecessor Gaston Thorn been in his attempts to respond to the May 1980 mandate and to initiate a budgetary revolution seven years earlier.[24] What made the difference in the late 1980s was the dramatic change in the mood of nearly all senior European decision makers, whether in the Commission or in the member state governments. Whereas in 1981 the backdrop had been highly gloomy, with many doubting Europe's capacity to succeed, the atmosphere in 1987–88 was much more positive, the economic and

[21] Mitterrand was very clear on this point: www.cvce.eu/en/obj/press_conference_by_francois_mitterrand_fontainebleau_26_june_1984-en-b28bbf91-7fd4-4274-a7a1-49f8576cfff8.html (*Centre Virtuel de la Connaissance sur l'Europe*, 8 November 2016).

[22] Commission, 'Report by the Commission to the Council and Parliament on the financing of the Community budget' European Commission Historical Archives, Brussels (henceforward ECHA) COM (87) 101 final.

[23] Michael Shackleton, *Financing the European Community* (London, Pinter, 1990) 9–22.

[24] It is usually argued that Thorn's over-ambition on the budgetary settlement contributed to his lack of success as a Commission president. Klaus Schwabe, 'Gaston Thorn (1981–1985): A Forgotten President' in Jan van der Harst and Gerrit Voerman (eds), *An Impossible Job? The Presidents of the European Commission, 1958–2014* (London, John Harper Publishing, 2015) 151–72.

political context significantly more benign. Therefore while reaching agreement proved difficult, with a failed summit at Copenhagen in December 1987 underlining the risks still involved, this time, unlike in the early 1980s, a deal was reached.[25] Furthermore Delors' determination to hold fast to his ambitious plans, despite failure at Copenhagen, enhanced his growing reputation – a stark contrast with Thorn whose reputation had never really recovered from the failure of his 1981 budgetary scheme.[26]

In substantive terms furthermore, the 1988 package was much more significant than the 1984 accord had been. This time it was not simply a matter of raising the VAT ceiling further. Instead, the package agreed had four main elements which cumulatively transformed the budgetary process and politics of the EEC.[27] The first was a move away from self-standing annual budgets towards five (and later seven) year Multiannual Financial Frameworks. The second, was a doubling of the structural funds, designed to boost the redistributive functions of the Community budget and help the poorer regions of the EEC prepare themselves for the completion of the Single Market in 1992. Third, this new expenditure would be in part covered by a newly introduced 'fourth resource': a new member state contribution to the Community budget linked to each country's gross national product (GNP), and designed to increase as the budget itself increased. And fourth, the Delors I package included a series of so-called 'stabiliser mechanisms' designed to rein in CAP expenditure. These last highlighted the Commission's intention to use its new revenue streams responsibly. But the other three mechanisms between them would revolutionise the Community's budgetary process – and with it clear the way for the most productive period of the integration process.

3. A Transformed Budgetary Landscape

So what had changed? And what justifies claiming that the budgetary alterations brought about by the 1988 Delors I package were as vital for the Community's successes of the late 1980s and early 1990s as the much better-known institutional and policy related breakthroughs had been? This chapter will point to three vital consequences of the new budgetary procedure, and then flag the way in which the deal reached and the manner in which it was secured, point to a fourth fundamental

[25] Dujardin et al, *The European Commission* 212–15.

[26] Ross lists the Delors I package alongside the Single Market programme, the Single European Act and EMU, as the key examples of the Commission President's 'astounding success', George Ross, *Jacques Delors and European Integration* (Oxford, Oxford University Press, 1995) 12.

[27] For the text of the agreement, see www.cvce.eu/en/obj/conclusions_of_the_brussels_european_council_extract_concerning_own_resources_budgetary_discipline_and_budget_management_11_13_february_1988-en-eeec6f42-3251-44b0-9749-0dcc4bf64931.html (*Centre Virtuel de la Connaissance sur l'Europe*, 6 September 2012).

evolution in the political leadership of the Community. Taken together these four changes were essential components of the EC's golden years.

The first and the most basic consequence of the Delors I package was that the Community, and later the European Union, could press forward without regularly encountering a financial ceiling on its ambitions. The great merit of the fourth resource introduced in 1988 was that it was flexible and could adjust upwards as and when EC/EU expenditure rose. As a result, the Community and then Union was able to embark upon a period of extremely rapid development, involving both a significant widening of its policy agenda, and, somewhat more slowly but ultimately even more impressively, a huge increase in its membership without periodically finding its progress restricted by the danger of imminent bankruptcy. To put some figures on this change, in 1988, the last budgetary year before the new regime came into force, total EU expenditure had been €42495.2 million; by 1992 this had risen to €60844.1 million; and by 2000 it had more than doubled at €92253.6 million (a rise of 117 per cent).[28] A comparable rise in an earlier period with a finite set of own resources would have necessitated a succession of decisions – almost certainly fraught decisions at 'crisis' summits given the usual politics that surround any EC/EU decision about money – to raise the expenditure ceiling. But the new fourth resource had been able to expand automatically to accommodate the new costs, in the process becoming the single biggest source of EU income. By 2000 42.3 per cent of the overall budget came from this revenue stream, compared to 38.1 per cent from VAT, and 15.3 per cent from the two original 'own resources' (ie agricultural levies and customs receipts) combined.[29] Given that the new fourth resource was directly tied to each member state's share of EU GNP, this new financial regime also made much less likely any recurrence of the type of problem that had lain at the heart of the British budgetary question, namely the significant mismatch between the UK's status in the early 1980s as one of the biggest net contributors to the Community budget, and its position as a country with a per capita GNP that was significantly below the then Community average.[30]

This loosening of the financial strait jacket within which the Community had previously been obliged to operate also allowed the Community and then Union institutions themselves to expand as their duties broadened. The inability to hire significant number of new staff had been one of the more insidious effects of the previous regime. That same 1987 report which had spoken of the EEC being on 'the brink of bankruptcy' had also denounced the staffing level consequences.[31] It was therefore important that over the 1988–2000 period Commission staff numbers

[28] European Commission, *The Community Budget* 30–31.

[29] ibid 42–43.

[30] Britain's subsequent strong economic growth during the mid-to-late 1980s means that this aspect of the British budgetary question is often forgotten, but in 1979, when the Thatcher government began agitating about the issue, only Ireland and Italy had lower per capita GNP amongst the then nine member states.

[31] Commission, 'Report by the Commission to the Council and Parliament on the financing of the Community budget' ECHA COM (87) 101 final.

would rise from just over 14000 to 21729, with the other structures within the EC/EU institutional system enjoying comparable increases.[32] The expansion of Europe's new duties could thus be accompanied by a commensurate expansion in the numbers of those tasked with implementing the new activities – although as the scandals that would befall the Santer Commission as the twentieth century drew to its close would demonstrate, it would take some time for the European Commission fully to develop the administrative and management structures needed to oversee its significantly larger work force.[33]

The second major change was the way in which the move to Multiannual Financial Frameworks (MFFs) made the use of the EC/EU budget for long-term transformative expenditure much easier. Both structural funds and the Community's research budget, it is true, predated the move to MFFs. Both had indeed been amongst the fastest growing spending priorities of the early to mid-1980s.[34] But the effectiveness of each had been somewhat held in check by the delays and uncertainty that surrounded each round of annual budgetary bargaining between the Commission, Parliament and Council. This was all the more so because one of the features of the 1979–88 period had been the frequency of breakdowns in this bargaining process, with knock-on effects on all Community expenditure. As that same 1987 report noted, none of the preceding three budgets had been agreed in the normal time frame.[35] So any form of EEC expenditure that required financial commitments that stretched over a period longer than 12 months was constantly at the mercy of the ill-tempered and crisis-prone negotiating process that surrounded each annual budget.

Under the new system, by contrast, there was much less drama and uncertainty, and far more chance of European moneys being used to effect long-term change. This mattered greatly given the way in which the fastest growing categories of Community/Union expenditure over the subsequent period would continue to be structural spending and research, as well as external action, each of which depended upon the predictable and steady flow of funding to the projects earmarked for development.[36] Structural funds indeed would grow so significantly during the subsequent period that they would begin to challenge agricultural subsidies as the biggest category of EC/EU expenditure. By 2000, the European Agricultural Guarantee and Guidance Fund (EAGGF)'s share of the total budget had fallen to 45 per cent (compared to the 60–70 per cent of the total which had been the norm in the 1970s and 1980s), whereas structural funds now accounted for 34.6 per cent.[37] The trend towards the toppling of the CAP as the Union's most

[32] Dujardin et al, *The European Commission* 113.
[33] ibid 97–106.
[34] European Commission, *The Community Budget* 37.
[35] Commission, 'Report by the Commission to the Council and Parliament on the financing of the Community budget' ECHA COM (87) 101 final.
[36] European Commission, *The Community Budget* 37.
[37] ibid 33–36.

expensive policy was unmistakeable. And in this context the avoidance of major controversy each year over the EU budget made this new distribution of expenditure much more effective than it might otherwise have been.

The third consequence, also closely connected to the move away from annual budgets and towards MFFs, was the improvement of inter-institutional relations. This of course was a much broader phenomenon than just the alteration of the budgetary procedure. Multiple other factors fed into the easier rapport between the Commission, the Parliament and the Council, including the changed voting rules brought in by the Single European Act, the rediscovery of shared purpose around the objective of establishing a working internal market by 1992, and the virtuous circle of high expectations and tangible results.[38] In the late 1980s those discussing European integration did so with a real belief that the process could deliver that had been notable by its absence only a few years before. Such self-belief and the expectation of success, then made it much easier to succeed, since all of those involved in the policy-making process adjusted their tactics and approach for an advancing Community rather than travelling to Brussels with negative instructions designed to protect national positions come what may.[39] Similarly institutional change helped create an environment where further institutional change could more easily be contemplated. It could in fact be argued that the European Parliament would only have been prepared to surrender its annual hold over the other two partners in the budgetary process in a context where it was beginning finally to be granted the additional powers it had longed for and was hence able to demonstrate some trust in the European Commission in particular. But it remains the case that had the budgetary process continued in its pattern of acrimonious and time-consuming confrontations each year, this would have constituted a significant brake on the growth of trust between the three main European institutions and a major distraction from the torrent of other legislation that needed to be processed were the ambitious targets that the Community had set itself to be attained. Removing this source of annual tension was thus another important ingredient in the Community's most successful period.

Finally, the budgetary breakthrough also highlighted a major change in the political dynamics of leadership within the EC which would be central to Community politics for several years to come. The central factor in allowing the Brussels summit of February 1988 to succeed in reaching a deal on the budget, where the Copenhagen Council of December 1987 had failed, was the willingness of German Chancellor Helmut Kohl to accept that the Federal Republic would need to accept an increase of its budgetary contributions.[40] It was hence the first of what would become an important sequence of Community breakthroughs linked to Kohl's readiness to get out his chequebook at crucial moments. This constituted

[38] Dujardin et al, *The European Commission* 183–210.
[39] See the comments by Riccardo Perrisich cited in Dujardin et al, *The European Commission* 193–94.
[40] Ross, *Jacques Delors* 42.

a vital change. One of the surprises, to me at least, of several recent pieces of historical research done on the Community in the early to mid-1980s, is the way in which Kohl's government was initially associated by its partners not with budgetary largesse but instead with a penny-pinching attitude more in line with the UK than with his later reputation. Kohl's pro-European rhetoric was not, in other words, initially matched with a readiness to accept the costs of more Europe. This in turn led both the French and Italian governments to harbour serious doubts as to whether Germany could be fully trusted to work for greater integration. Instead, both Paris and Rome, grumbled to each other about the seeming emergence of a London–Bonn axis designed to minimise Community expenditure and choke off any policy advantage that cost money.[41] This would be a feature not just of the difficult first years of Kohl's Chancellorship, ie 1982–84 when the whole Community was struggling somewhat, but also of 1985–86 as the deadlock in Brussels appeared to ease. Kohl's change of heart in 1988 and his willingness to rescue Delors' budgetary package by accepting that Germany would need to shoulder a significant portion of the additional costs thus represented a really important change of direction.

It was a change furthermore with huge implications for the pattern of EC politics over the next half-decade or so. For a start, it helped cement the personal rapport between Kohl and Delors that would lie at the heart of so much of the Community's dynamism – and the dynamics of the European Council itself – in the years ahead. The Commission President acknowledges the vital importance of Kohl's changed position in his memoirs, drawing a particular contrast between the manner in which agreement on the budgetary package at Copenhagen had been sunk by German opposition, and the altered circumstances two months later in Brussels.[42] Even more importantly it would confirm Kohl's personal centrality to the workings of Europe's top decision-making body, the European Council, and the centrality of his country to virtually all of the key advances that would follow over the subsequent four or five years. Germany's new position was not of course something that all were entirely comfortable with. Indeed the politics of the European Community in the run-up to 1992 would be impossible to understand without the realisation that virtually all of the Federal Republic's partners had misgivings about German power.[43] But it is also the case that the confirmation that the Federal Republic was fully committed to the integration process, and prepared to dig into its own pockets to see it advance, became a highly positive

[41] Giovanni Lella, 'La Francia di Mitterrand, l'Italia e il rilancio della costruzione Europea (1981–1986)' (PhD thesis, Rome, La Sapienza/Université Sorbonne Nouvelle, 2022); Alorda Carreras, *Europeanisation à la Carte*.

[42] Jacques Delors, *Mémoires* (Paris, Plon, 2004) 238–41.

[43] French misgivings, but also the way in which the French turned these misgivings into a spur for closer Franco-German and European cooperation, are central themes of Frédéric Bozo's analysis. See Frédéric Bozo, *Mitterrand, La Fin de La Guerre Froide et l'unification Allemande: De Yalta à Maastricht* (Paris, O. Jacob, 2005); Frédéric Bozo, 'In Search of the Holy Grail: France and European Monetary Unification, 1984–1989' in Gehler and Loth, *Reshaping Europe* 283–330.

factor in the years that followed. Kohl would use his and his country's centrality to push Europe forward rather than hold it back.[44] And to the extent that France and many of the other member states were worried about German dominance, their response tended to be to seek to strengthen the European framework within which Germany could best be contained. The European politics that would surround the unification process in 1989–90 would underline this important reality.[45] The one leader who bucked this trend – Margaret Thatcher who liked the idea of more Europe even less than she liked the idea of more Germany – would eventually lose her job in large part because this stance made her so isolated as to be largely ineffective in collective European decision-making.[46] And the importance of a Germany that was committed to Europe and willing to pay for the privilege would be further underlined by the rather changed fortunes that the integration process would experience in the post-1992 period, when the costs of German unification seriously sapped the willingness of Germany and its Chancellor to resort to the same type of cheque book diplomacy which had been so important in the late 1980s.

All four of the consequences of the budgetary deal identified were hence of real importance to the development of the European Community during the late 1980s. The budgetary dynamic did not eclipse the institutional and policy agenda level changes that loom so large in most existing accounts of the period. But they were a vitally significant complement to these changes. The conclusion of the Delors I package in particular therefore merits a place alongside the start of the Single Market Programme or the signature of the Single European Act in the list of major milestones in the making of Europe's most dynamic decade. There is thus a major budgetary component in the European revival of the mid-1980s.

[44] Hans-Peter Schwarz, *Helmut Kohl: eine politische Biographie* (München, Deutsche Verlags-Anstalt, 2012) 397–419.

[45] N Piers Ludlow, 'Not a Wholly New Europe. How the Integration Framework Shaped the End of the Cold War in Europe' in Frédéric Bozo, Andreas Rödder, and Mary Elise Sarotte (eds), *German Reunification: A Multinational History* (Abingdon, Routledge, 2017) 133–52.

[46] For a fairly charitable analysis of Thatcher's position, Patrick Salmon, 'The United Kingdom and German Unification' in Frédéric Bozo et al (eds), *Europe and the End of the Cold War. A Reappraisal* (Abingdon, Routledge, 2008) 177–90. A rather less generous view is given by George Robert Urban, *Diplomacy and Disillusion at the Court of Margaret Thatcher: An Insider's View* (London, I.B. Tauris, 1996) 118–59.

10

The Integration Surplus of the EU's Budgetary Law – Or 'No Representation without Taxation'?

FRANK SCHORKOPF*

1. Power of the Purse from Two Perspectives

In March 1965, Walter Hallstein and Sicco Mansholt opted for the grand solution. When the Commission submitted the new regulation on financing the Common Agricultural Policy (CAP) to the Council, the powers of the European Parliament were to be strengthened at the same time. This meant that the planned conversion of Community financing to own resources was to be matched with giving the Parliament budgetary authority, thereby deepening European integration.[1]

Although not as a primary goal, Hallstein and Mansholt also thought in terms of European constitutional history. This constitutional historical dimension was based on the idea of budgetary powers as the 'royal prerogative', in German literally *Königsrecht*, of Parliament. In earlier centuries, parliamentarians had won budgetary powers for their institution in long battles with monarchs and executives. During the eighteenth century, budgetary powers had been reallocated to Parliaments.[2] Hallstein wanted to shape the European federation accordingly. Above all, from the constitutionalists' point of view, the parliamentarisation of the Community budget was intended to strengthen supranationality.[3]

* I am grateful to Antonia Craven for her mother-tongue review of the manuscript for publication and to Ruth Weber for further suggestions.

[1] Commission, 'Financing the common agricultural policy – independent revenue for the Community – wider powers for the European Parliament' (Commission Proposals to the Council) COM (65) 150.

[2] Werner Daum, 'Finanzen' in Werner Daum (ed), *Handbuch der europäischen Verfassungsgeschichte im 19. Jahrhundert* (Bonn, Dietz, vol 3, 2020) 130.

[3] Hans Herbert Götz, 'Die Krise 1965/66' in Wilfried Loth, William Wallace and Wolfgang Wessels (eds), *Walter Hallstein – der vergessene Europäer?* (Europäische Schriften des Instituts für Europäische Politik 73, Bonn, Europa Union Verlag, 1995) 189–202, 193, on the three speeches in which Hallstein set out his philosophy of the unification process; see Thomas Oppermann (ed), *Europäische Reden* (Stuttgart, Deutsche Verlags-Anstalt, 1979) 55, 58, 59.

But Hallstein's and Mansholt's ambitious plan famously failed. On the contrary, the Commission laid one of the ground stones for the conflict between France and the other five founding member states arising in 1965–1966. This conflict has gone down in integration history as the 'empty chair crisis'. Only the 'Luxembourg Compromise' of 1966 made a return to joint action in the Council of Ministers possible, forcing Hallstein out of office as Commission President after a grace period.

This dimension of one of the major crises of European integration introduces the main argument of this chapter: Superficially, the European budgetary and financial constitution is about technical questions. Where does the money come from? How is it spent? Who is responsible for the revenue and who controls the expenditure? But what is more, in the European Union, as in the member states and any other organisation, the budget formulates a political programme in numbers. The budget is the place where 'politics and law, … by means of the indicator money' touch each other and 'an overall coordination of policy' takes place.[4] Different political priorities, as for example the identity-forming role of the CAP within the EU, are translated into figures according to procedural rules.

In the European budgetary and financial constitution, the allocation of powers was and still is negotiated along with deepening of integration. Budgetary and financial issues – as will be argued in this chapter – are a resource of an indirect integration surplus of the EU. In allusion to the formative school of thought 'integration through law', one could speak of 'integration through money'. Also in the European context, Parliament's budgetary power – its 'power of the purse' – is the point of departure for further democratic legitimisation of revenues and expenditures. In the European Union the iconic phrase 'no taxation without representation', which explained and justified the North American Revolution at the end of the eighteenth century, seems to apply in reverse: 'no representation without taxation'.[5]

The argument of an integration surplus of the EU's budgetary law can be viewed through the lens of a comparison. First, this chapter goes back to the 1970s, when the system of own resources was introduced by two financial treaties. The debate linked the budget dossier to the universal suffrage of the European Parliament. In the second step, the chapter will turn to the current debates regarding the Fiscal Union and its manifestation through NextGenerationEU (NGEU).

[4] Christian Waldhoff, 'Überforderung nationaler Parlamente durch die Globalisierung? Grenzen am Beispiel der Budgetverantwortung' in Claudio Franzius, Franz C Mayer and Jürgen Neyer (eds), *Modelle des Parlamentarismus im 21. Jahrhundert* (Baden-Baden, Nomos, 2015), 109–34, with reference to Paul Kirchhof, 'Die Steuerung des Verwaltungshandelns durch Haushaltsrecht und Haushaltskontrolle' (1983) 9 *Neue Zeitschrift für Verwaltungsrecht* 505.

[5] Giacinto della Cananea, 'No Representation without Taxation in the European Union' in Lina Papadopoulou, Ingolf Pernice and Joseph HH Weiler (eds), *Legitimacy Issues of the European Union in the Face of the Crisis – Dimitris Tsatsos in memoriam* (Baden-Baden, Nomos, 2017) 95–112; Alessandro Isoni, 'No representation without taxation: For a history of budgetary control in the European Union' in Luca Zamparini and Ubaldo Villani-Lubelli (eds), *Features and Challenges of EU Budget* (Cheltenham, Edward Elgar Publishing, 2019) 44–59.

2. Introducing Parliament's Budgetary Powers in the 1970s

2.1. Turning Point: The Hague Summit in 1969

The Commission's 'grand solution' failed in 1965. France wanted permanent agricultural funding, but neither an increase in competence for the Parliament nor a main political role for the Commission. As a result of the 'empty chair crisis', the dossier on CAP financing with parliamentary involvement and own resources was closed. The CAP received further provisional financing for the time being.

A new political opportunity for change emerged at the end of the 1960s for various reasons. Most importantly, the 12-year transitional period for the establishment of the Common Market approached its end and the French President Charles de Gaulle resigned in April 1969. In the late 1960s, the Commission took the coming into force of the customs union on 1 July 1968 as an opportunity to project an economic union. It emphasised its commitment to a political union and presented an action programme. The reconciliation of the European nations thus was achieved. Now the moment had come 'to call the young and creative forces of Europe to union, action and hope'.[6] The European Parliament seconded that only unification into an 'economically and politically federal entity' would enable the peoples of Europe to assert themselves in the world of today and tomorrow in peace, freedom and security, in independence and prosperity.[7] With the end of the transition period for the establishment of the Common Market approaching, the question arose as to which next steps should be taken on the way to a European federation. Issues such as a monetary union, the harmonisation of national economic policies, new issues such as social and regional affairs, technology and industry, and a European foreign and defence policy were on the agenda. At the same time, the Communities found themselves in a crisis. Although the Luxembourg deal brought a working compromise, the second French veto of 1967 against British accession had considerably upset the 'friendly five'.[8] Their government representatives discussed how to organise a rapprochement with the accession aspirants outside the treaties. The undecided accession dossier also hampered the development of the Communities.

After de Gaulle's resignation from the French presidency, the European policy framework changed fundamentally. This was associated with the general expectation of a change in French European policy. The enlargement of the

[6] Commission, 'Declaration of 1.7.1968', Bulletin of the European Communities 1/1968, No 7, 5, reprinted in Heinrich Siegler (ed), *Europäische Politische Einigung II. 1968–1973* (Bonn, Siegler Verlag für Zeitarchive, 1973) 7.

[7] European Parliament, 'Resolution of 3.7.1968' [1968] OJ C72/37, point 26 (own translation).

[8] N Piers Ludlow, The European Community and the Crisis of the 1960s: Negotiating the Gaullist Challenge (London, Routledge, 2006) 158.

Communities now seemed achievable. The Commission additionally pushed for institutional reform, ie for strengthening of the Commission, for the abolition of the veto, majority decisions in the Council, and for universal suffrage of the European Parliament. Furthermore, the upcoming decision on the permanent CAP financing gave reason to readdress the failed budget reform.[9] Finally, in May 1969, the Commission published a revised version of its original proposal formulated in 1965.

These developments converged at the Summit of Heads of State and Government in The Hague in early December 1969. The summit committed itself as follows:

> [The Heads of State and Government] agreed, within the framework of these financial arrangements and taking into account all the interests at stake, to gradually replace the contributions of the Member States by their own revenue, in accordance with the procedure laid down in Article 201 of the EEC Treaty, with the aim of achieving full financing of the budgets of the Communities within the time limits laid down; they also agreed to strengthen the budgetary powers of the European Parliament.[10]

Taking this into account, as early as April 1970, the governments agreed on the amendment of the Communities' budgetary law. This meant a minor treaty change requiring ratification.[11]

While dealing with these questions, the summit postponed another pending question regarding universal suffrage of Parliament. The Council of Ministers was to deal with it. While at first glance appearing to be two different dossiers, budgetary law and universal suffrage were actually closely related. The budgetary powers were in fact a new, substantial competence of the Parliament. It was supposed to reduce the democratic deficit of the Communities and increase the likelihood of universal suffrage. At the beginning of the 1960s, in the context of the deliberations on provisional CAP financing, the European Parliament already viewed budgetary law as a suitable lever to increase its significance in the institutional architecture of the Communities.[12] In 1965, the Hallstein Commission, supported by some member states, attempted to link the aforementioned financial

[9] European Commission, COM (65) 150; Commission, 'Communication concerning the replacement of Member States' financial contributions by their own resources and the strengthening of the budgetary powers of the European Parliament' (Communication to the Council) COM (69) 700.

[10] Communiqué of the Conference of Heads of State or Government of the Member States of the European Communities held in The Hague on 1 and 2 December 1969, Bulletin of the European Economic Community 2/1970, No 1, point 5.

[11] Treaty amending certain budgetary provisions of the Treaties establishing the European Communities and of the Treaty establishing a Single Council and a Single Commission of the European Communities [1971] OJ L2/1; BT-Drs 6/879, 3.

[12] Berthold Rittberger, *Building Europe's Parliament: Democratic Representation Beyond the Nation State* (Oxford, Oxford University Press, 2005) 116–23; Ann-Christina L Knudsen, 'Delegation as a political process: The case of the inter-institutional debate over the Budget Treaty' in Wolfram Kaiser, Brigitte Leucht and Morten Rasmussen (eds), *The History of the European Union* (London, Routledge, 2009) 167–88, 170–74; esp European Parliament, 'Session Documents 1962–63' (Deringer Report), Doc 74, paras 152–59.

reform of the Communities, ie the changeover to a system of own resources, with parliamentary budgetary powers.

2.2. Luxembourg Treaty of 1970

The Treaty of Luxembourg introduced Parliament's budgetary authority in 1970. With regards to the revenue, the financing of the Communities was gradually switched from financial contributions by the member states to the own resources already envisaged in the Treaty establishing the European Economic Community (EEC Treaty). These were levies on food imports from third countries, customs duties, and part of the national VAT revenue. Subsequently, the Council adopted the initial Own Resources Decision. With regards to expenditure, Parliament received the power to oppose the Council on a certain part of the expenditure, the so-called 'non-compulsory expenditure'. It was able to prevent the adoption of this part of the budget, though this was essentially only the administrative expenditure of the Communities, accounting for not more than about 10 per cent of the total budget. Ninety per cent, of the budget was declared compulsory expenditure. Regarding this part of the budget, Parliament was able to have its say. The Council, however, retained the last word. The treaty provisions thus presented a momentous minimum consensus.

The parliamentarians remained dissatisfied. They had articulated much greater pro-integration and pro-parliament positions. The budget should have been subject to their approval, not to mere consultation. New own resources were to be introduced by a two-thirds majority in the Parliament, after approval by the Council and without member states' participation. The European Parliament resolution of 1969 explicitly mentioned a 'tax basis'. And finally – and this is particularly interesting – the Communities were to be given the right to debt.[13] Moreover, in the counterfactual self-confidence typical of the European Parliament, it derived from the rules of the new Luxemburg Treaty the competence to reject the entire draft budget – a daring interpretation rejected by the Council but supported by the Commission.

In a spirit of 'friendly cooperation', the European Parliament also brought its position on the 'important problem of the institutional rights of parliaments in the budgetary sector' to the attention of the national parliaments. It claimed that it should participate in the budget preparation and demanded the final decision-making power on the allocation of funds. In the ratification debates on the Luxembourg Treaty, the national parliaments were supposed to work towards

[13] European Commission, 'Proposal for provisions adopted pursuant to Article 173 of the EAEC Treaty and Article 201 of the EEC Treaty concerning the replacement of Member States' financial contributions by their own resources' [1969] OJ C123/24, 26 and OJ C152/32. European Parliament, 'Resolution of 10.12.1969' [1970] OJ C2/15. Summary in Giacomo Benedetto, 'Institutions and the Route to Reform of the European Union's Budget Revenue, 1970–2017' (2017) 44 *Empirica* 615, 619.

'guaranteeing genuine parliamentary control over Community funds', for which the national parliaments would henceforth no longer be responsible.[14] In these national ratification debates, in addition to the European Parliament's claim to have the right to reject the entire draft budget the unfulfilled expectation of its universal suffrage received attention.

2.3. Connecting Universal Suffrage

The universal suffrage of the European Parliament was anything but a new issue. The issue was directly related to the existence and competences of a parliamentary body in the Communities. The inclusion of an assembly in the institutional architecture, first of the Coal and Steel Community and later of the Economic Communities, was based on a compromise. On the one hand, there was the principal rejection of supranational parliamentarism, which was essentially based on the idea that the model of parliamentary democracy was contrary to the efficiency of supranational integration. On the other hand, the proponents pointed to the need for a political constituent of European citizenship, or at least a European representation of peoples, which was to create the federation democratically.[15] According to the compromise, the Parliament was only a 'consultative assembly', comparable to other international organisations. Its members were delegated from the national parliaments and its competences were limited to the right to be consulted and to discuss European issues, supplemented by the possibility of a vote of no confidence on the Commission.[16] The Treaties of Rome then authorised the Assembly to draw up 'proposals for elections by direct universal suffrage in accordance with a uniform procedure in all member states'. Such a draft was to be adopted by the Council unanimously and submitted to the member states for ratification.[17]

The European Parliament[18] had already seized the opportunity for its universal suffrage immediately after its constituent session in 1958. The Committee on Political and Institutional Affairs had mandated a working group chaired by the 'European saint', Fernand Dehousse, to fully discuss the issues. After extensive

[14] European Parliament, 'Resolution of 13.5.1970' [1970] OJ C65/32, point 11.

[15] Hans-Peter Schwarz, 'Ansätze zur Parlamentarisierung des europäischen Zusammenschlusses: Eine entwicklungsgeschichtliche Skizze' in Ernst-Joachim Mestmäcker, Hans Möller and Hans-Peter Schwarz (eds), *Eine Ordnungspolitik für Europa: Festschrift für Hans von der Groeben zu seinem 80. Geburtstag* (Baden-Baden, Nomos, 1987) 360–90, 373.

[16] Art 21(1) of the Treaty establishing the European Coal and Steel Community (ECSC Treaty).

[17] Art 138(3) EEC Treaty; Art 108(3) of the Treaty on the European Atomic Energy Community (EAEC Treaty); Art 2(2) of the Agreement on Common Institutions for the European Communities amended the Montan Treaty accordingly.

[18] European Parliament, 'Decision of 30.3.1962' [1962] OJ No 31, 1045; in German and Dutch the de facto renaming had already taken place in the Constituent Session on 20/21 March 1958 as a corresponding translation of the official French name 'Assemblée parlementaire européenne', Verhandlungen, No 1, 96–97, 100. Nestor Schumacher, *Der Wortschatz der europäischen Integration* (Düsseldorf, Pädagogischer Verlag Schwann, 1976) 266.

preparatory work, the committee had presented a package that was adopted by the plenary in May 1960 and handed over to the Council of Ministers.[19]

The internal parliamentary debates had revealed a fundamental disagreement. The question was whether parliamentary competences and universal suffrage should be thought of together or separately. Some MEPs saw an increase in competences as the decisive preliminary question for direct elections. A directly elected Parliament with limited scope for action could ultimately damage the European idea through unfulfilled expectations on the part of the electorate. According to the German Social Democrat and co-rapporteur Ludwig Metzger, 'it cannot be good in the long run for hundreds of men and women with political brains and will to come together and only make speeches, but otherwise have nothing to decide'.[20]

The ad hoc group set up in 1972 by the Commission to examine the question of extending the powers of the European Parliament, the so-called Groupe Vedel, explicitly took up and rejected this argument in its report. According to the group of legal experts, it was based on a logical fallacy and led to a vicious circle. If a parliament endowed with real powers was already inconceivable as long as it did not emerge from direct universal suffrage, then general direct suffrage for a parliament not endowed with broad powers was inconceivable. Thus, two equally desirable goals held each other in check.[21] In this regard, the advisory group was in line with Dehousse. According to him, direct elections could be a 'salutary shock' for the European electorate, spurring them to turn more strongly to the work on Europe that had so far been done by only a few.[22]

2.4. Political Participation Improved Through Budgetary Powers

During the conclusion of the Luxembourg Treaty, member states, Parliament and the Commission had already agreed to discuss additional parliamentary budgetary powers within two years. Moreover, the Council had promised the Parliament to communicate the reasons for its deviation from the parliamentary position and to enter into an informal budget dialogue.[23] This promise of renegotiation was

[19] European Parliament, 'Resolutions of 17.5.1960' (Protocol) [1960] OJ C 37/834, 860.

[20] European Parliament, 'Session of May 1960, Session of 11.5.1960' (Negotiations) 43–48, quote 46.

[21] Report of the ad hoc group to examine the question of an extension of the powers of the European Parliament ('Vedel Report') of 25.3.1972, Bulletin of the European Economic Community 1972, Supplement No 4.

[22] Umberto Tulli, 'Which democracy for the European Economic Community? Fernand Dehousse versus Charles de Gaulle' (2017) 37 *Parliaments, Estates and Representation* 301, 308; European Parliament, 'Decision of 30.3.1962' [1962] OJ No 31, 1045; see statements by van Dijk and Rubinacci in European Parliament, 'Session of May 1960, Session of 11.5.1960' (Negotiations), 72 and 76 respectively.

[23] John Forman, 'The Conciliation Procedure' (1979) 16 *CML Rev* 77, 79–82.

fulfilled only hesitantly. In 1973, Parliament even filed – for the first time ever – a motion of censure against the Commission for failing to make a proposal.[24] Finally, after tough negotiations, the second financial treaty of 1975 was reached.[25] This Brussels Treaty gave Parliament the right to reject the Commission's entire draft budget for good cause and to demand the submission of a new draft. In the case of compulsory expenditure, the Council could only overrule any parliamentary opposition by a qualified majority. Council and Parliament postponed an answer to the question of whether member states should continue to participate in financing decisions or whether the Council alone should be responsible for this with parliamentary participation. Parliament had again wanted to assign this decision to the Community institutions, as it also demanded a right to debt. The member states rejected this competence and provided for a unanimous Council decision and ratification by the national parliaments for the Own Resources Decision. So: *neither representation nor taxation.*

The system of own resources, the budgetary procedure and the two financial treaties are noteworthy landmarks in their own right. However, the treaties had wider implications.

In connection with the Brussels Treaty of 1975, the Council, Parliament and the Commission agreed by means of an inter-institutional agreement on joint decision-making on legal acts with 'significant financial implications'. With this conciliation procedure, Parliament succeeded for the first time in establishing a participation procedure in lawmaking along with the toothless right of consultation. It is the nucleus for the subsequent co-decision procedure.[26] In the event of an emerging disagreement on financially effective legal acts, the procedure served to reach a consensus position of the Council and Parliament within a maximum of three months through the mediation of the Commission.[27] By this time, the member states had already agreed on the Act concerning the election of the representatives of the Assembly by direct universal suffrage (Electoral Act). The budgetary powers thus entailed improved political participation, although not enshrined as primary law yet.

The steps taken in the 1970s were the source of considerable conflict between Parliament and Council. The size of the budget, the procedure for drawing it up, political priorities, the distributive effect, and the definition of compulsory and non-compulsory expenditure were at stake. With the argument of the 'power of the purse' behind it, Parliament tried to further improve its institutional position and shake off the existing restrictions. The Council was still able to legally

[24] Roland Bieber, 'Das parlamentarischer Mißtrauensvotum in den Europäischen Gemeinschaften' (1973) 10 *Neue Juristische Wochenschrift* 405.

[25] Treaty amending certain financial provisions of the Treaties establishing the European Communities and of the Treaty establishing a Single Council and a Single Commission of the European Communities of 22 July 1975 [1977] OJ L359/1; BT-Drs 7/4684, 7.

[26] Yves Mény, *Building a Parliament: 50 Years History of the European Parliament (1958–2008)* (Luxembourg, Office for Official Publications of the European Communities, 2009) 153.

[27] The English term 'conciliation' emphasises the mediation element, see Forman, 'The Conciliation Procedure' 77.

assert itself over the Parliament. However, political dissent delayed decisions and put additional pressure on the Council to justify itself. The parliamentary rejection of the draft budget for 1980 works as a historical example. Parliament self-confidently claimed a say not only in the technical drafting of the budget, but also in the monetary shaping of policies, like the paramount CAP.[28]

Even though the Parliament had not formally received any new competences by the end of the 1970s, due to its universal suffrage it could now claim to legitimise European public power, if not primarily, then at least alongside the Council. With universal suffrage, albeit without a common electoral system and with national seat allocations, the Parliament came roughly on an equal footing with national parliamentary systems. The continuing inadequacies of democratic legitimacy could be justified with future steps of parliamentarisation – constitutionalism's success story since the late eighteenth century could be invoked as a paragon for this. At the beginning of the 1970s, the Vedel Report had still attested that Parliament had the 'representativeness … of the ivory tower'. Its debates and work barely resonated in the press, in the public sphere, and in the life of the political parties.[29] With universal suffrage, the architecture of the institutional triangle of Commission, Council and Parliament changed. This had already been foreshadowed by the budgetary powers of the 1970s. Additionally, this underpinned the hope that the new 'power of the purse' in the budgetary procedure and the conciliation procedure would also improve representativeness. Universal suffrage took away the utopian dimension of Parliament's aspiration to speak for a European citizenry. For the time being, the Council and the member states refused to accept the principle of 'no representation without taxation'. Therefore, the decision on taxation remained with the member states. The introduction of the conciliation procedure, nevertheless, clearly proves that the changes to the budgetary and financial constitution produced an integration surplus.

3. Special Budget – NextGenerationEU

Budgetary law deepens integration – this is the thesis that emerges from my historical analysis. In the second step, I now turn to the major political projects of the present budgetary and fiscal constitution – NextGenerationEU and the Fiscal Union. Is there also an integration surplus in these more recent developments? And will this possibly lead to a democratic empowerment of the Parliament?

[28] European Parliament, 'Resolutions of 13.12.1979' [1980] OJ C 4/36-38; Siegfried Magiera, 'Die Haushaltsbefugnisse des Europäischen Parlaments – Ansatz zur parlamentarischen Mitregierung auf Gemeinschaftsebene?' in Ingo von Münch (ed), *Staatsrecht – Völkerrecht – Europarecht: Festschrift für Hans-Jürgen Schlochauer zum 75. Geburtstag am 28. März 1981* (Berlin, de Gruyter, 1981) 829–54, 846.

[29] Vedel Report.

3.1. Alterations on the Budget's Expenditure Side

After five days of negotiations, in July 2020 the European Council agreed on financial assistance in response to the Covid-19 pandemic through a €750 billion special budget[30] and a new Multiannual Financial Framework totalling €1074 billion.[31] From the special budget, €360 billion can be granted as loans to member states and €390 billion is available for non-repayable financial aid.[32]

Several dimensions shaped the context of the European Council meeting. For some time already, discussion of future budgetary planning had been controversial. Brexit had caused a significant hole in the financing of the EU's budget.[33] The EU and the member states were struggling to find a common understanding of values. The Economic and Monetary Union had been in crisis for a decade, and the introduction of a fiscal policy with distributive effects was being debated as a possible solution.[34] Additionally, the hard impact of the Covid-19 pandemic was damaging the EU's economies and causing member states' tax revenues to collapse. When it came to the question of distributing European funds in reaction to this crisis, the European Parliament insisted on a full say in their use. Furthermore, EU bodies had, for many years, been discussing the introduction of new own resources to make the Union's financing less dependent on the member states.[35] Indirectly, this debate stood for an admittance in disguise that the own resources based on VAT and gross national income (GNI) were basically contributions from the member states.

The special budget resulting from the European Council meeting is distinguished by one novelty: its financing. The European Union is authorised to issue bonds on capital markets, which are secured by the EU budget. To this end, the Council amended its Own Resources Decision. It now provides for a significantly increased own resources ceiling (2 per cent GNI). Under current conditions, the

[30] The overall approach is explained in Commission, 'The EU Budget as the Engine of European Recovery' (Communication) COM (2020) 442.

[31] European Council conclusions, EUCO 10/20 (Brussels, 21 July 2020).

[32] In this section I follow, partly verbatim, the considerations published in an article co-authored with Hanno Kube, see Hanno Kube and Frank Schorkopf, 'Strukturveränderung der Wirtschafts- und Währungsunion' (2021) 74 *Neue Juristische Wochenschrift* 1650.

[33] Peter Becker, 'Der Brexit und die Folgen für den Europäischen Haushalt' A-Drs 18(21)101 www.swp-berlin.org/publications/products/sonstiges/Brexit_Stellungnahme_Peter_Becker.pdf (Written statement in the context of the public hearing of the Committee on the Affairs of the European Union of the German Bundestag on 24 April 2017); Ewa Chomicz, *EU budget post-Brexit: Confronting reality, exploring viable solutions* (Discussion Paper, Brussels, European Policy Center, 2017); Margit Schratzenstaller, 'Brexit and the EU Budget' in Zamparini and Villani-Lubelli, *Features and Challenges* 180–204, 185.

[34] Frank Schorkopf, *Der Europäische Weg. Geschichte und Gegenwart der Europäischen Union*, 3rd ed (Tübingen, Mohr Siebeck, 2020) 101–16.

[35] Commission, 'Future Financing of the EU: Final report and recommendations of the High Level Group on Own Resources' (1 April 2017) 36; Commission, 'Future of EU Finances (Reflection Paper)' COM (2017) 358, 27. The German Council Presidency submitted a reform proposal of 29 July 2020, Council Doc No 110025/20.

non-repayable financial aid to individual member states must be repaid through increased national contributions to the EU budget over 30 years. It is up to the member states and their national budgets how they will raise these increased contributions. Ultimately, an increased share of national revenue must be allocated for EU membership.

Since not only the amount of national financial contributions as such, but at the same time the net contributions of some member states will continue to rise, the overall consensus is moving towards the imposition of EU taxes. In this case, genuine EU levies and taxes are to generate financial resources from which the loans are to be repaid. The European Council mentions taxes and levies such as a carbon dioxide levy, a plastics levy, the extension of the Emissions Trading Scheme, a financial transaction tax, and a digital levy.[36]

Taking into account the historical meaning of budgetary powers, the democratic legitimacy of the special budget needs to be examined. As in the 1970s, the Own Resources Decision continues to be adopted unanimously by the Council without depending on a parliamentary vote and must be ratified by the national parliaments, thereby justifying the transfer of resources. European Parliament only has the right to be heard in this procedure. The revenue side therefore remains firmly in the hands of the Council. In other words, politically the member states decide on the financial volume and the sources of funding.

On the expenditure side of the budget, the institutional setting is different. When adopting the Multiannual Financial Framework, the Council acts unanimously after obtaining the consent of the Parliament. Parliament therefore has a veto. The Regulation on the Reconstruction and Resilience Facility, which is central to the distribution of the special budget, was adopted in the ordinary legislative procedure. However, the Council alone adopts the corresponding national reconstruction and resilience plans after proposal by the Commission. Parliament has been given extensive information and participation rights in the implementation of the plans, but it has no voting power on their content.

3.2. Confrontation with Political Reality

This doctrinal view certainly has to be confronted with political reality. First, the Rule of Law Conditionality Regulation showed that Parliament used its veto position in one area to impose substantive demands in other dossiers. Parliament hinged its approval of the Multiannual Financial Framework on the adoption of

[36] European Council conclusions, EUCO 10/20 (Brussels, 21 July 2020), point A 29, 146–50. The proposal for a financial transaction tax is already included in Commission, 'Proposal for a Council Decision on the European Union's own resources system' COM (2018) 325; the Commission has adapted its amendment proposal for the Own Resources Decision to NGEU, see Commission, 'Amended proposal for a Council Decision on the system of Own Resources of the European Union' COM (2020) 445; see also Commission, 'The EU Budget as the Engine of European Recovery' (Communication) COM (2020) 442.

the conditionality regulation, even though this legislation was also most welcome to many member states. From this perspective, the package as a whole is crucial.

Second, it is important to keep in mind that NextGenerationEU has an extremely complicated structure – it is legal high-tech. Behind this construction stood certain predispositions. Debt borrowing was to be neutral for the national debt ratios. At the same time, the regular EU budget was not to be permanently increased and the primary law was to be respected.

Even without a formal treaty change, the recent developments have structurally changed the previous parameters of the budgetary and financial constitution: With NextGenerationEU, and already with the temporary support scheme against unemployment (SURE),[37] the European Union has abandoned the principle of a materially balanced budget. The European Union itself now has significant indebtedness. Under the law in force, the Union is allowed to borrow more than two-thirds of the Union's annual budget. To repay it, the member states' own resources obligations have been significantly extended. The member states have also assumed default guarantees for each other, so that one national budget guarantees for the creditworthiness of the other. The long maturity of the loans exceeds the Multiannual Financial Framework. This medium-term span of seven years – although limited in time – opens up the possibility of adjusting the member states' financial burdens of European integration to the economic strength of the member states. In addition, the financing of the EU budget from member states' tax revenues is subject to democratic legitimisation and control by the national Parliaments at regular intervals. The intergenerational maturity of the loans reshuffles these dependencies. Ultimately, while the temporary and crisis-related character of NextGenerationEU is put on political display, some perceive a 'Hamilton moment' in the first time that Union debt has existed and see a true fiscal union on the horizon.[38]

The financial burdens postponed to the future will push the member states to introduce genuine EU taxes. The European Parliament, in particular, has been repeatedly demanding EU taxes.[39] The revenue from genuine EU taxes would, in fact, reduce member states' own resources payments. It is debatable whether

[37] Council Regulation (EU) 2020/672 establishing a European instrument for temporary support to unemployment risk reduction in emergency situations (SURE) following the COVID-19 outbreak [2020] OJ L159/1.

[38] On the Hamilton moment, ie Alexander Hamilton's role as Secretary of Finance in the formation of the United States, see Funke-Mediengruppe, Interview with Olaf Scholz, Federal Finance Minister, Germany (21 August 2020) https://bit.ly/3inwpOd; ECB President Christine Lagarde (Balazs Koranyi, 'Europe must not delay cash to crisis-hit economies, Lagarde tells Le Monde' (*Reuters*, 19 October 2020) https://reut.rs/3diDfUV) and EP President David Sassoli (Alberto d'Argenio, 'Die Regierungen im Norden werden ihre Meinung ändern' (*WELT*, 18 November 2020) https://bit.ly/32aHUSy) have spoken out in favour of a continuation. *cf* also Federal Court of Auditors, report pursuant to § 99 BHO of 11 March 2021, 4, 18.

[39] See in particular Commission, 'Future Financing of the EU: Final report and recommendations of the High Level Group on Own Resources' (Luxembourg, Publications Office of the European Union, 2017).

primary law would already allow such EU taxes to be introduced today – the better reasons argue against it. Apart from these technical legal questions, it is of greater importance that there are no substantive standards for freedom- and equality-oriented taxation by the Union. Moreover, such standards would only be sustainable and legitimate if they were decided at least with the decisive participation of the European Parliament. It is difficult to conceive taxation by the Union without the European Parliament involved on the revenue side.

Finally, the most recent development outlined here leads to a federal financial equalisation. The EU funds have always led to net contributor and net recipient positions amongst member states. Limited financial transfers associated with these positions have always existed. They can either be seen as a solidarity-based moment of integration or based on a reciprocity postulate of market opening and market opportunities.[40] The justification for the current EU recovery plan was provided by the Covid-19 pandemic. However, the distribution principles governing it are reminiscent of the criteria known from the traditional funds. This is especially true since they are only in parts directly linked to pandemic-related losses and damages and are to be used for the digital and green transformation of the EU's economy. It is foreseeable that genuine EU tax funds would be distributed in a similar way. The purchase of government bonds by the European Central Bank (ECB) also has horizontal redistribution effects.[41] The shape and extent of these cannot be estimated more precisely due to the complexity of the interrelationships and the long-term nature of the issues. However, the considerable redistribution effects in favour of real property, which can clearly be assumed in the meantime, raise profound problems of legitimacy and questions of social cohesion. These questions and problems should be discussed and solved before union taxation is put into place.

3.3. NGEU's Integration Surplus

Coming to the question of legitimacy, which is linked to my hypothesis of 'no representation without taxation', then at first glance NextGenerationEU does not pose a severe problem. Member states continue to hold the reins. The ratification of the Own Resources Decision is secured and the participation of the European Parliament on the revenue side is limited. But, at second glance, things look different.

The fundamental problem of democratic legitimacy is illustrated by the Own Resources Decision. Clearly, the Own Resources Decision, in conjunction with the

[40] Schorkopf, *Der Europäische Weg* 67; Ubaldo Villani-Lubelli, 'The EU budget and the European integration process' in Zamparini and Villani-Lubelli, *Features and Challenges* 12–29, 17.

[41] Gunther Schnabl, 'Die Verteilungseffekte der Geldpolitik und deren Einfluss auf die politische Stabilität' in Pierre Bessard and Olivier Kessler (eds), *Explosive Geldpolitik: Wie Zentralbanken wiederkehrende Krisen verursachen* (Zürich, Liberales Institut, 2019); Deutsche Bundesbank, 'Distributional effects of monetary policy' (Monthly Report, September 2016) 15 www.bundesbank.de/resource/blob/667166/eaaf80cf3f98df384b5a2ad216414272/mL/2016-09-effects-data.pdf.

EU recovery plan, is union crisis legislation. It officially concerns the management of the pandemic consequences in the member states. In principle, crisis legislation is both justified and reasonable in the EU. The current case, however, is problematic because this crisis legislation took place with a normative surplus. In the case of the decisions taken, it can therefore be asked why the own resources ceiling has been raised unduly and the loans for NGEU are significantly over-secured as a result.[42] Why, despite low interest rates, is the repayment stretched to 30 years over the next generation and over at least six election periods? Why does the project introduce the own resources category of a new, genuine EU tax on a precarious legal competence?

Questions also arise on the expenditure side. For example, the special budget's main part will be spent on member states' projects that are intended to promote economic structural change and bring about modernisation: digitalisation, research, 'fair climate change', climate protection, agricultural and cohesion policy, protection of biodiversity, and gender equality.[43] These are all political goals worth striving for. But they are only to a lesser extent related to damage caused by the pandemic. The Commission exerts considerable influence on the content of national recovery and resilience plans – with the aim of imposing its economic policy ideas on member states.

Since the guarantee of national budgetary discipline via the Stability and Growth Pact has not been successful in the long run, it is becoming apparent that the Commission is shifting its focus to supervising the conditions under which financial resources are allocated to the member states. This evasive movement is obvious and understandable. However, it is only an imperfect surrogate for the deficit procedure and the complementary instruments of control over member states' economic policies. Action on the revenue side can also be understood as an evasive movement. As the intergovernmental financial institutions – such as the European Stability Mechanism – had already been set up as hybrid entities to receive and pass on funds, the current Union debt is based on a complex legal construction.[44] It stands alongside the regular budget of the Union and thus seeks a formal distance from the traditional standards and limits of Union financing.

The EU institutions are thus reacting to the problem of a de facto petrification of an EU law that is in political need of development. The petrification is caused by a lack of political consensus and burdensome procedures that make formal treaty changes unlikely in the eyes of politicians. On top of that, such changes would

[42] Friedrich Heinemann, 'Die Überdeckung der Next Generation EU-Schulden im Entwurf des neuen EU-Eigenmittelbeschlusses: Ausmaß und Haftungskonsequenzen' A-Drs 19(21)112 www.bundestag.de/resource/blob/800870/2a19d54c782dc9d7bc60ce8fdd34fcd1/heinemann-data.pdf (Written statement in the context of the hearing of the Committee on the Affairs of the European Union of the German Bundestag on 26 October 2020).

[43] European Commission, 'Europäischer Aufbauplan' (*European Commission Website*) https://ec.europa.eu/info/strategy/recovery-plan-europe_de.

[44] See Claudia Wutscher's chapter in this volume (ch 6).

lead to incalculable ratification risks. The Court of Justice of the European Union covers the implicit treaty changes and enables the informal change of the normative framework in order to keep the EU as a whole capable of politics. Nonetheless, these developments are to be judged from a legal point of view. Irrespective of how these questions are to be assessed, the large-scale project NextGenerationEU with its major impact on EU's budgetary and financial constitution causes a considerable integration surplus.

4. Conclusion

The two reference points of my reflections on the significance of the Union's budgetary and financial constitution present an ambivalent picture. In the 1970s, the member states kept the decisive levers for the revenue and the expenditure side of the budget in their hands. The proposals of constitutionalists such as Dehousse to endow Parliament with more competences, framed as a 'salutary shock', remained unnoticed as long as the European Parliament did not have sufficient democratic legitimacy. Parliament's call for a right to debt and taxation went unheard. But, with the introduction of budgetary powers to Parliament, the supporters of deeper European integration immediately intended to establish a right to more influence on the political programme. In practice, notably this led to the introduction of the conciliation procedure. It was the starting point of Parliament's – so far unfinished – expansion of competences in the institutional architecture of the European Union.

With NextGenerationEU the member states and the EU institutions – in a moment of crisis – jointly took a step towards a Fiscal Union based on loans. The political decisions were made within the framework of the treaties in force. Parts of the package gained the consent of the European Parliament; parts needed ratification by national parliaments. However, with the acceptance of an EU right to debt and the fundamental decision for at least one genuine EU tax, the member states put into action a systemic change of the budgetary and financial constitution. This alone is a considerable deepening of integration. The dynamics of integration fuelled by this step pose the question of representation anew. What share of fiscal resources will be distributed to whom and for which purpose? And how should one define the benefit for the public good in the European Union?

It is not unlikely that the present developments amplifying the 'power of the purse' will demand more substance of parliamentary justification so that the phrase 'no representation without taxation' fits unreservedly. Hallstein's parallel to European constitutional history could still come to fruition.

11

Integration Through Funding

The Union's Finances as Policy Instrument

BRUNO DE WITTE

1. Introduction

The European Union does not have an army or a police force. Its budget is small. It achieves its integration aims mainly by regulating – by making laws that apply throughout Europe. It is often noted that 'what the EU lacks in terms of material capacity, it partly compensates for by regulation'.[1] This contrasts with federal systems where the 'power of the purse' of the federal state plays an important role in governance, in two different ways: by operating direct transfers to the member states for their general use; and by funding the member states or local authorities for specific purposes decided at the federal level. The latter is often described as the 'federal spending power'. By spending money, the federal level exercises power, in that it can force or at least encourage the member states or local authorities to pursue the policy preferences set at the federal level. In the European Union, general financial transfers from the European to the member state level do not exist (quite the opposite, in fact); however, there are various ways in which the European Union uses its 'spending power' to try and steer the policy choices made at the national or local level. Such integration through funding forms the object of this chapter. As is the case with European-level law-making, the question whether a given policy requires spending at EU level depends on an assessment of the added value compared to action taken by national governments alone.[2] However, public expenditure by the EU is not only subject to such a subsidiarity test. It is also subject to other constraints of EU constitutional law that will be discussed in the next sections: it should remain within the limits of the competences conferred

[1] Philipp Genschel and Markus Jachtenfuchs, 'More Integration, Less Federation: The European Integration of Core State Powers' (2016) 23 *Journal of European Public Policy* 42, 45.

[2] Gabriele Cipriani, 'The EU Budget' in Nikolaos Zahariadis and Laurie Buonanno (eds), *The Routledge Handbook of European Public Policy* (London, Routledge, 2018) 142–54, 142.

on the Union by the Treaties (section 2); and it must respect the rules and limits imposed by EU public finance law (section 3). After that, section 4 will give a general overview of the main policy areas in which integration through funding is happening. Section 5 will explore the way in which instruments for emergency funding have recently been turned into instruments to achieve the EU's general policy goals, and section 6 will show how cohesion policy has now become the institutional seat of broadly based integration-through-funding mechanisms.

2. The Legal Basis Requirement

The legal basis requirement permeates the institutional life of the European Union. Under the principle of conferral of competences, every EU legal measure must be connected directly, or via an intermediate act, to a Treaty article (the legal basis) allowing the Union to act in a particular domain, for a particular purpose and in a particular manner. Since almost all EU legislation is proposed by the Commission, that institution takes the initiative of choosing the appropriate legal basis for whichever policy objectives it seeks to achieve with the legislation, and the other institutions usually follow the Commission's lead when adopting the act. The preamble of the legislative act is normally used to justify the choice of the legal basis; that is, to explain how the content and objectives of the proposed act fall within the scope of the chosen legal basis.

There was a time, in the 1970s and 1980s, when the annual EU budget set aside some money for what were called pilot actions, that is policies which the budgetary authorities (especially the European Parliament) wanted to support even in the absence of a clear EU competence. The Court of Justice put an end to that in a judgment from the 1990s.[3] Since then, the EU's Financial Regulation states that every item on the EU budget must refer to a 'basic act',[4] which is defined in its Article 2 as 'a legal act, other than a recommendation or an opinion, which provides a legal basis for an action and for the implementation of the corresponding expenditure entered in the budget'.[5] That basic act must in turn have a legal basis in the Treaties, that is, it must fall within the scope of a competence conferred on the EU.

In the many legal basis provisions spread all across the Treaties, the use of funds is either denied, expressly permitted, implicitly permitted or simply not

[3] Case C-106/96 *United Kingdom v Commission* ECLI:EU:C:1998:218.

[4] Regulation (EU, Euratom) 2018/1046 of the European Parliament and of the Council on the financial rules applicable to the general budget of the Union, amending Regulations (EU) No 1296/2013, (EU) No 1301/2013, (EU) No 1303/2013, (EU) No 1304/2013, (EU) No 1309/2013, (EU) No 1316/2013, (EU) No 223/2014, (EU) No 283/2014, and Decision No 541/2014/EU and repealing Regulation (EU, Euratom) No 966/2012 [2018] OJ L193/1, Art 58(1): 'Appropriations entered in the budget for an Union action shall only be used if a basic act has been adopted.' Paragraphs 2 to 5 of the same Article contain some exceptions to this rule.

[5] The key content of that provision is repeated in Art 310(3) TFEU, which makes it into a true constitutional requirement.

envisaged. The first of these four categories comprises legal bases specifying that the Union should only act by means of 'rules' or by means of directives,[6] which excludes the adoption of EU funding measures. The second category consists of legal bases where financial expenditure is expressly named as one of the policy tools that is available for the EU institutions. Examples include Article 40(3) of the Treaty on the Functioning of the European Union (TFEU) allowing for setting up 'one or more agricultural guidance and guarantee funds' and, in the domain of external relations, Article 212 TFEU allowing for financial assistance to third countries. The third category comprises those Treaty articles that imply the use of funds by stating that the Union is able to 'support' member state action in a given policy domain, or to adopt 'incentive measures' for a particular purpose. Thus, Article 196 TFEU states that the Union shall 'support and complement' member state action in the field of civil protection, and this article could thus serve as a basis for the adoption of a Union Civil Protection Mechanism with a financial expenditure component.[7] Several legal bases allow for the European Union to adopt 'incentive measures' – a generic term which has been interpreted consistently as allowing for the adoption of funding programmes in fields such as education and culture.[8] The fourth category consists of the many legal basis provisions that refer generically to the adoption of 'measures', 'actions' or 'provisions' by the EU institutions. This generic description leaves open the possibility to adopt funding measures alongside regulatory measures. The generic wording has, in EU institutional practice, served as a sufficient basis for funding mechanisms in the field of the environment, energy policy, and asylum and migration policy, to name just the more prominent examples.

As any EU legislation must have a legal basis in the Treaties, and as these legal bases define a limited set of objectives, it is questionable whether the EU legislator may pursue other objectives 'on the side', beyond those defined in the legal basis. The 'mainstreaming clauses' or 'integration principles', mostly contained in the Articles 8 to 13 TFEU, help to remove such doubts; they clarify, beyond discussion, that it is perfectly legitimate for agricultural policy measures to include an environmental dimension, or for migration policy measures to have a gender equality dimension, to give just some examples of such mainstreaming.[9] Apart from the application of these mainstreaming clauses, EU legislation can also pursue other policy objectives laid down elsewhere in the Treaties, as long as those other objectives are ancillary to the main objectives that correspond to the chosen legal basis. If those other objectives are more than ancillary, they should be reflected by adding

[6] eg Art 16(2) TFEU on data protection ('rules') or Art 23 TFEU on diplomatic protection ('directives').

[7] The basis act creating the Mechanism was last amended by Regulation (EU) 2021/836 of the European Parliament and of the Council amending Decision No 1313/2013/EU on a Union Civil Protection Mechanism [2021] OJ L185/1.

[8] See, for instance, Art 165(4) TFEU, which is the legal basis for the Erasmus+ programme.

[9] See Francesca Ippolito, Maria Eugenia Bartoloni and Massimo Condinanzi (eds), *The EU and the Proliferation of Integration Principles under the Lisbon Treaty* (Abingdon, Routledge, 2019).

a supplementary legal basis for the act. This phenomenon can be illustrated by the changing legal bases of the European Social Fund. Whereas the ESF Regulation of 2013 had the sole legal basis of Article 164 TFEU (which mentions the Social Fund explicitly), its successor, the ESF+ Regulation of 2021, had multiple legal bases, reflecting the fact that the new fund had absorbed some smaller funds with partially different policy objectives.[10]

3. The Constraints of Public Finance Law

The possibility for the Union to spend money for the pursuit of European public goods is not only constrained by the principle of conferral and the legal basis requirement, but also by the rules of EU public finance law laid down in the Treaties. Among the latter, there is an overall constitutional constraint, expressed in Article 310(4) TFEU, namely that 'the Union shall not adopt any act which is likely to have appreciable implications for the budget without providing an assurance that the expenditure arising from such an act is capable of being financed within the limits of the Union's own resources and in compliance with the Multiannual Financial Framework'. The Multiannual Financial Framework (MFF) is indeed a major feature of EU public finance law. The annual budget of the Union is to a large extent pre-ordained by the seven-yearly MFF. In practice, the adoption of each new MFF is accompanied by the adoption or revision of all the Union's spending programmes, most prominently the agricultural and structural funds but also the myriad of other funds in policy domains such as migration, research, education, culture and external relations. For this reason, the negotiations of the MFF are not only about the amount of EU expenditure but also about the content of EU spending policies. The political and legal importance of the MFF is reflected in its decision-making rule: it must be adopted by the Council acting unanimously, and with the consent of the European Parliament.[11] As was shown at the time of adopting the MFF for 2014–20, this means in practice that a decisive role is played by the European Council, where a political compromise must be reached that is acceptable to all the member states. A number of European Council meetings took place in in 2012 and 2013, and the final compromise was a very detailed document that was then turned into a formal regulation by the Council. The consent power given to the European Parliament under Article 312 was very much blunted by the need for unanimity at the European Council.[12] Something similar happened

[10] Regulation (EU) 2021/1057 of the European Parliament and of the Council establishing the European Social Fund Plus (ESF+) and repealing Regulation (EU) No 1296/2013 [2021] OJ L231/21. The legal bases of this regulation are Art 46(d), Art 149, Art 153(2)(a), Art 164, Art 175(3) and Art 349, all of the TFEU.

[11] Art 312(3) TFEU.

[12] See the detailed account of the negotiations on the 2014–20 MFF by Richard Crowe, 'The European Council and the Multiannual Financial Framework' (2016) 18 *Cambridge Yearbook of European Legal Studies* 69.

in July 2020, when the negotiations of the 2021–27 MFF culminated in a long European Council meeting whose conclusions spelled out, in rather great detail, the amounts allocated to the various EU funds.[13] The budgetary capacity of the Union is thus limited and constrained by the overall ceiling of EU expenditure, determined every seven years in the MFF, and by the consequent setting of financial envelopes for each of the EU's spending programmes for the next seven years, with, for some of the larger programmes, a further splitting of these financial envelopes in separate allocations for each member state.

However, the EU's funding capacity can be expanded beyond the limits of the MFF in three different ways. A first, rather exceptional, way is for the MFF to be amended during its term. As the MFF is adopted by means of a regulation, it is possible to amend it by means of another regulation, as happened recently to allow for the mobilisation of a financial assistance guarantee for Ukraine.[14] A second way to expand the EU's financial capacity is through borrowing operations by the EU on the financial markets. Traditionally, such borrowing was limited in size and served for loans to the member states or to third countries, so that the EU's debt would, normally speaking, be repaid by the end-recipients of the loans at no budgetary cost for the Union. More recently, in the framework of the EU's pandemic response, the proceeds of EU borrowing have been used to fund non-repayable expenditure rather than loans – an innovative practice whose compatibility with EU public finance law is contested.[15] A third way to expand the EU's financial capacity beyond the EU budget is by setting up funds in which Union expenditure is combined with contributions by the member states, private actors or third states. An important example of such hybrid or 'blended' funding is the so-called Juncker Plan adopted in 2015,[16] now renamed as the InvestEU programme. Blended finance has become a major general tool of the EU's external relations, through the European Fund for Sustainable Development (EFSD+),[17] and was also used for

[13] After further negotiations in the second half of 2020, the MFF was adopted through Council Regulation (EU, Euratom) 2020/2093 laying down the multiannual financial framework for the years 2021 to 2027 [2020] OJ LI433/11.

[14] Council Regulation (EU, Euratom) 2022/2496 amending Regulation (EU, Euratom) 2020/2093 laying down the multiannual financial framework for the years 2021 to 2027 [2022] OJ L325/11.

[15] Päivi Leino-Sandberg and Matthias Ruffert, 'Next Generation EU and its Constitutional Ramifications: A Critical Assessment' (2022) 59 *CML Rev* 433, 450–60.

[16] Regulation (EU) 2015/1017 of the European Parliament and of the Council on the European Fund for Strategic Investments, the European Investment Advisory Hub and the European Investment Project Portal and amending Regulations (EU) No 1291/2013 and (EU) No 1316/2013 – the European Fund for Strategic Investments [2015] OJ L169/1. The European Fund for Strategic Investments is now replaced by Regulation (EU) 2021/523 of the European Parliament and of the Council establishing the InvestEU Programme and amending Regulation (EU) 2015/1017 [2021] OJ L107/30.

[17] The EFSD+ is based on Arts 31 to 40 of the Regulation (EU) 2021/947 of the European Parliament and of the Council establishing the Neighbourhood, Development and International Cooperation Instrument – Global Europe, amending and repealing Decision No 466/2014/EU of the European Parliament and of the Council and repealing Regulation (EU) 2017/1601 of the European Parliament and of the Council and Council Regulation (EC, Euratom) No 480/2009 [2021] OJ L209/1. On blended finance as a policy tool of the EU's external relations, see Andrea Prontera and Rainer Quitzow,

ad-hoc projects such as the Emergency Trust Fund for Africa, set up on the basis of an international agreement concluded between the EU, its member states, and two other countries.[18] By contrast, expenditure under the Common Foreign and Security Policy is off-budget, and EU mechanisms of foreign policy such as the European Peace Facility are entirely funded by the member states.[19]

4. The Policy Steering Role of EU Funding: A General View

For many years now, the EU has had two main spending programmes absorbing the bulk of the EU's overall budget that, because of their sheer volume, could act as policy steering tools: the agricultural funds and the structural funds.

The *common agricultural policy* (CAP) contained, right from its origins, a funding dimension which quickly became its dominant component and overshadows the EU's regulatory activity in this field. The concrete funding mechanisms and priorities have evolved over time, in order to steer agricultural activity in particular directions, by subsidising certain activities rather than others. The most prominent inflection in spending priorities is the growing emphasis on the protection of the environment. This has, in the current version of the agricultural funds, become one of the three general objectives of the CAP, despite the fact that it is not mentioned in the TFEU as one of the goals of the EU's agricultural policy.[20] This inclusion of the environment as one of the three 'pillars' (alongside agricultural sector economy and rural development) of the CAP is justified, in legal terms, by the strong environmental integration clause in Article 11 TFEU which states that environmental protection requirements '*must* be integrated into the definition and implementation of the Union's policies and activities'. However, the potential for agricultural funding to be turned to the achievement of 'new' policy goals is hindered by the fact that existing agricultural spending patterns serve important vested interests. Agricultural funding is therefore an important potential instrument of integration through funding, but it is not easily adaptable to new policy priorities.

'Catalytic Power Europe: Blended Finance in European External Action' *Journal of Common Market Studies* (early view article, 2022).

[18] Agreement establishing the European Union Emergency Trust Fund for stability and addressing root causes of irregular migration and displaced persons in Africa, done at La Valletta on 12 November 2015.

[19] Council Decision (CFSP) 2021/509 establishing a European Peace Facility, and repealing Decision (CFSP) 2015/528 [2021] OJ L102/14.

[20] Regulation (EU) 2021/2115 of the European Parliament and of the Council establishing rules on support for strategic plans to be drawn up by Member States under the common agricultural policy (CAP Strategic Plans) and financed by the European Agricultural Guarantee Fund (EAGF) and by the European Agricultural Fund for Rural Development (EAFRD) and repealing Regulations (EU) No 1305/2013 and (EU) No 1307/2013 [2021] OJ L435/1, Art 5: 'to support and strengthen environmental protection, including biodiversity, and climate action'.

The *structural funds* serve, according to the Treaty text (Article 174 TFEU), to strengthen the economic, social and territorial cohesion of the Union. Those overall objectives form a very capacious umbrella for a host of more fine-grained policy aims. The structural funds can be seen as half-empty shells that can be filled with new policy goals every seven years, when the revised fund regulations are being adopted, and occasionally even within the seven-year period, in order to address new needs. The latter happened in response to the Covid-19 pandemic, when the EU legislator created the REACT-EU programme which provided additional resources (stemming from the NextGenerationEU (NGEU) programme) to the structural funds, in particular in order to support investment in the social and health sectors.[21] Apart from their broadly defined cohesion goals, the structural funds have also been marked, over the past 10 years, by the growing importance of conditionality. Funding is made conditional on compliance by the member states with a large number of so-called enabling conditions, and EU funding can be stopped in the course of a programme for failure to comply with certain conditions. In this manner, the European Union seeks to use these funds to achieve other policy objectives apart from cohesion, including for instance gender equality and the fight against corruption.[22]

In addition to agricultural and cohesion funding, the EU has adopted an increasing number of so-called 'action programmes', especially in areas of supplementary competence such as education, culture and the integration of migrants. Supplementary competences are legally characterised by the fact that the harmonisation of national laws is prohibited,[23] and spending is thus an alternative policy tool to be used instead of rule-making. In those policy areas, EU funding is implicitly authorised by the fact that the Treaty text allows for the adoption of 'incentive measures': by providing money for specific purposes, the EU creates an incentive for the recipients (states and non-state organisations) to pursue European policy goals even in the absence of European law-making powers. Well-known examples of such action programmes are the Erasmus+ programme in the field of education and the Creative Europe programme in the field of culture. The amounts allocated to those programmes are relatively small, in terms of their share of the overall EU budget, but they nevertheless form interesting examples of integration through funding.

In other policy fields, spending has gradually developed as an ancillary policy instrument alongside rule-making and in combination with it. The most obvious

[21] Regulation (EU) 2020/2221 of the European Parliament and of the Council amending Regulation (EU) No 1303/2013 as regards additional resources and implementing arrangements to provide assistance for fostering crisis repair in the context of the COVID-19 pandemic and its social consequences and for preparing a green, digital and resilient recovery of the economy (REACT-EU) [2020] OJ L437/30.

[22] See Marco Fisicaro, 'Beyond the Rule of Law Conditionality: Exploiting the EU Spending Power to Foster the Union's Values' (2022) 7 *European Papers* 697.

[23] See Art 2(5) TFEU. The no-harmonisation rule is repeated in the specific legal bases for each of the policy areas where the EU has supplementary competences.

example is *environmental policy*, where the main emphasis of EU action, over the years, had been rule-making and standard setting, but the possibility to promote the Union's environmental goals by means of the Cohesion Fund was expressly recognised by the text of the TFEU, in both Article 177(2) and Article 192(5). Additional funding mechanisms were gradually developed, thereby contributing to a new 'policy mix' in the field of environmental and climate policy.[24] In particular, the directive of 2003 creating the Emissions Trading Scheme (EMS) contained a provision establishing an Innovation Fund,[25] whose operation was laid down in a delegated regulation of the Commission.[26] It subsidises the development of business solutions that help to achieve the decarbonisation objective of the EMS scheme, and its amount has grown over the years. Today, there is still no 'flagship' funding programme for environmental policy, but substantial funding now comes from a number of sources, including agricultural policy, the structural funds, and (for the next few years) the Recovery and Resilience Facility.

A similar, though still weaker, trend has emerged in the field of *migration and asylum* policy, where the EU originally acted exclusively through rule-making but in recent years EU expenditure in this field has grown,[27] through a substantial increase of the Asylum Migration and Integration Fund and also through unorthodox financial mechanisms such as the EU–Turkey Facility. That financial instrument has a hybrid nature, in that it combines contributions from the EU budget and from the member states.[28] The funding serves to improve the reception conditions of refugees in Turkey but its underlying policy goal, from an EU perspective, is to convince the Turkey government to try to discourage migrants and refugees from crossing the Turkey–EU border.

As a final example, the EU's *external relations* field is characterised by the use of funding programmes that seek to advance the EU's external policy objectives which, by their nature, tend to be very broad. They do so by earmarking the use

[24] For a discussion of the way the EU's climate policy has 'thickened' through a stepwise addition of new policy tools, including funding mechanisms, see Sebastian Oberthür and Ingmar von Homeyer, 'From Emissions Trading to the European Green Deal: The Evolution of the Climate Policy Mix and Climate Policy Integration in the EU' (2023) 30 *Journal of European Public Policy* 445.

[25] Directive 2003/87/EC of the European Parliament and of the Council establishing a scheme for greenhouse gas emission allowance trading within the Community and amending Council Directive 96/61/EC [2003] OJ L275/32, Art 10a(8) of the consolidated version.

[26] Commission Delegated Regulation (EU) 2019/856 supplementing Directive 2003/87/EC of the European Parliament and of the Council with regard to the operation of the Innovation Fund [2019] OJ L140/6.

[27] See Leonhard den Hertog, 'EU Budgetary Responses to the "Refugee Crisis": Reconfiguring the Funding Landscape' (*CEPS Paper in Liberty and Security in Europe* no 93, 2016); Evangelia Tsourdi and Philippe De Bruycker, 'The Evolving EU Asylum and Migration Law' in Evangelia Tsourdi and Philippe De Bruycker (eds), *Research Handbook on EU Migration and Asylum Law* (Northampton, Edward Elgar, 2022) 1–56, 30–34.

[28] Richard Crowe, 'The European Budgetary Galaxy' 13 *European Constitutional Law Review* (2017) 428, 444.

of the funds for particular purposes, such as the support of fundamental rights and good governance, and by imposing conditionality on the receipt of financial support.[29]

5. Emergency Funding and its Use During the Covid-19 Crisis

From an EU constitutional law perspective, funding mechanisms for dealing with emergency situations are not fundamentally different from ordinary funding programmes, as they too must have a legal basis in the Treaties and be implemented in accordance with EU public finance law.

Starting with the constraints imposed by public finance law, the Multiannual Financial Framework mechanism implies that unforeseen funding needs that might arise within the seven-year period covered by the MFF must somehow be integrated into the mechanism. This happens essentially in three different ways. First, the MFF provides for a general reserve that is not allocated to any of the predefined policy headings and can be used for unforeseen purposes; in the current 2021–27 MFF, this flexibility has been used especially for funding to support Ukraine and to help the member states with the reception of Ukrainian refugees. The second way has taken the form of special emergency funds, which are part of the MFF framework, even though actual expenditure is not pre-programmed (as for the other funds) but depends on the occurrence of events during the seven-year period. One example is the European Globalisation Adjustment Fund, first created in 2006, whose financial means are mobilised in response to a sudden loss of jobs in a particular company, sector or region.[30]

The third way is to address emergencies in the member states (or third countries) by means of loans to their governments that are kept off-budget. There have been, for many years now, financial assistance schemes for member states facing special economic difficulties. The distinctive element of this funding mechanism is that the disbursements are not earmarked for specific policy objectives, but are aimed at buttressing the general fiscal situation of the beneficiary state. This mechanism was put in place at the time of the first oil crisis of the early 1970s.[31] The funds did not figure as an item on the regular EU budget, but were borrowed by the EU on

[29] See, for a recent example, the macro-financial assistance for Ukraine, for an amount of €18 billion, adopted with Art 212 TFEU as its legal basis: Regulation (EU) 2022/2463 of the European Parliament and of the Council establishing an instrument for providing support to Ukraine for 2023 (macro-financial assistance +) [2022] OJ L322/1.

[30] The fund's current version is in Regulation (EU) 2021/691 of the European Parliament and of the Council on the European Globalisation Adjustment Fund for Displaced Workers (EGF) and repealing Regulation (EU) No 1309/2013 [2021] OJ L153/48.

[31] See the account of the historical development since the 1970s by Moritz Rehm, 'Shocks and Time: The Development of the European Financial Assistance Regime' (2022) 60 *Journal of Common Market Studies* 1645.

the financial markets and transferred in the form of general loans to the member state treasuries. These were relatively small loans but they became larger during the euro crisis, when the EU created the European Financial Stabilisation Mechanism (EFSM) with a total volume of €60 billion, to assist euro area states facing a sovereign debt crisis,[32] even though most of the financial assistance was not channelled through the EFSM but through funds created by the euro states acting together under international law (namely, first the European Financial Stability Facility (EFSF) and later the European Stability Mechanism (ESM)).[33]

In terms of legal bases for emergency funding, a central role is now played by Article 122 TFEU. This Treaty article contains two legal bases for EU action in economic crisis situations – a very generic one and a more specific one. Its paragraph 1 (the generic legal basis) states that the Council 'may decide, in a spirit of solidarity between Member States, upon the measures appropriate to the economic situation, in particular if severe difficulties arise in the supply of certain products, notably in the area of energy'. It was used for emergency measures in the energy sector, which is what this provision was written for in the first place,[34] but was then employed, in 2016, as the legal basis for a broader and permanent EU programme for emergency financial support when a state is hit by natural or man-made disasters.[35] This regulation of 2016 was amended in 2020, in order to allow for financial support to pandemic-related health measures taken by the member states.[36]

As for Article 122, paragraph 2 (the more specific legal basis), it allows for the Council to decide to grant financial assistance to a Member State 'where a Member State is in difficulties or is seriously threatened with severe difficulties caused by natural disasters or exceptional occurrences beyond its control'. The assistance is granted 'under certain conditions' – a clause that opens the door for the European Union to use the assistance for advancing its own policy objectives in addition to helping the beneficiary state. Prior to the Covid-19 crisis, Article 122(2) had been used in the early stages of the sovereign debt crisis as the legal basis for the EFSM, but it made an impressive comeback in the context of the pandemic crisis. It was proposed by the Commission, and accepted by the member states, as the legal basis

[32] Council Regulation (EU) 407/2010 establishing a European financial stabilisation mechanism [2010] OJ L118/1. See Vestert Borger, 'EU Financial Assistance' in Fabian Amtenbrink, Christoph Herrmann and René Repasi (eds), *The EU Law of Economic and Monetary Union* (Oxford, Oxford University Press, 2020) 963–78, 968–73.

[33] Ulrich Forsthoff and Jasper Aerts, 'Financial Assistance to Euro Area Members (EFSF and ESM)' in Amtenbrink, Herrmann and Repasi, *The EU Law of EMU* 979–1024.

[34] Council Directive 2009/119/EC imposing an obligation on Member States to maintain minimum stocks of crude oil and/or petroleum products [2009] OJ L265/9 (as this directive was adopted before the entry into force of the Lisbon Treaty, its legal basis was Art 100 EC, which is now renumbered as Art 122 TFEU).

[35] Council Regulation (EU) 2016/369 on the provision of emergency support within the Union [2016] OJ L70/1.

[36] Council Regulation (EU) 2020/521 activating the emergency support under Regulation (EU) 2016/369, and amending its provisions taking into account the COVID-19 outbreak [2020] OJ L117/3. See its Annex, 'Eligible actions'.

of the Support to mitigate Unemployment Risks in an Emergency (SURE) instrument, offering €100 billion worth of temporary financial support to the national employment support programmes.[37] Later on in 2020, Article 122 TFEU served as the legal basis for the European Union Recovery Instrument (EURI) Regulation, which is the formal basis of the whole NGEU programme.[38]

SURE was created for providing financial assistance in the form of cheap loans to all its member states, for the specific purpose of helping them to address the sudden increase of public expenditure for the preservation of employment during the pandemic. Access to the EU loans presupposes that the member states had preservation of employment schemes in place, but the SURE Regulation did not seek to impose the creation of new schemes or to harmonise existing schemes. Therefore, it did not seek to steer the content of national employment policies and it rather resembles the earlier financial assistance schemes of the EU even if the loans are earmarked for use in a specific policy domain.

NGEU could seem similar to old-style financial assistance, in that the funds are raised by the EU on the financial markets and passed on to the member states to face the economic downturn caused by the pandemic. But, unlike the earlier emergency assistance programmes, it also, and even primarily, serves as a tool for integration through funding. Indeed, the funds assembled for NGEU are spent in loans and grants allocated to the member states through a number of spending programmes that have their own policy objectives, of which the Recovery and Resilience Facility is the largest (see the next section). NGEU is thus more than a response to the economic downturn caused by the pandemic crisis. It rather appears to be a multipurpose plan, aiming to foster structural transformation of the national economies, with special emphasis on the green and digital transitions. It is a true instrument of strategic spending for the European Union.[39]

6. Expansion of the Scope of Cohesion Funding: From the European Solidarity Fund to the RRF and to REPowerEU

Article 175, third paragraph, allows for cohesion measures to be adopted by the Union 'outside the Funds'. This legal basis thus partakes in the broadly defined aims of cohesion, which were mentioned in a previous section. It allows for a broad

[37] Council Regulation (EU) 2020/672 on the establishment of a European instrument for temporary support to mitigate unemployment risks in an emergency (SURE) following the COVID-19 outbreak [2020] OJ L159/1. The crisis-related nature of the instrument is underscored by its limited duration, namely until 31 December 2022.

[38] Council Regulation (EU) 2020/2094 establishing a European Union Recovery Instrument to support the recovery in the aftermath of the COVID-19 crisis [2020] OJ LI 433/23.

[39] See Luuk van Middelaar's chapter in this volume (ch 12).

range of measures, namely any 'action' that would 'prove necessary'. Financial assistance is not specifically mentioned but is not excluded either. The broad potential of this flexible legal basis was first employed in 2002, when it served for the creation of the European Solidarity Fund (EUSF).[40] The EUSF was intended to offer rapid financial support to member states facing major natural disasters such as floods or earthquakes, but it was amended in 2020 to include major public health emergencies within its scope of application,[41] and some relatively small sums were allocated to a number of member states to deal with the health emergency caused by the coronavirus pandemic. This practice indicates that emergency funding by the EU could also be established on legal bases that do not refer to the existence of an emergency.

Article 175(3) furthermore served as the legal basis for the European Globalisation Adjustment Fund, mentioned above, and for the Fund for European Aid to the Most Deprived in 2014. The latter instrument contributed to the fight against poverty and social exclusion, objectives which are thus considered to be part of the aim to improve social cohesion. The same legal basis was mobilised for the Commission proposal for a Just Transition Fund. This instrument was initially presented in January 2020 with the aim of supporting the economic diversification of territories most affected by the climate transition measures (such as, for example, the coal-mining region in Poland). The Commission presented an amended proposal on 28 May 2020 in which it proposed that the Fund should be one of the spending programmes of the NGEU package. The Just Transition Regulation was adopted in June 2021, and it was accepted, apparently without discussion, that Article 175(3) was an appropriate legal basis. Indeed, the territorial cohesion element is particularly evident in this programme.

The Recovery and Resilience Facility (RRF), the main spending programme of NGEU, was, in turn, established on the basis of Article 175(3).[42] In this case, cohesion policy was given a much wider meaning than in the previous cases. Article 3 of the RRF Regulation mentions 'economic cohesion' and 'social and territorial cohesion' as two of the six pillars of the plan, but adds four other pillars, namely green transition, digital transformation, crisis preparedness, and policies for the next generation. The EU legislator thus adopted a very broad conception of what the cohesion objective enables the European Union to do. It signals a move away from cohesion in the traditional sense (namely, the sort of measures funded by the

[40] Council Regulation (EC) 2012/2002 establishing the European Solidarity Fund [2002] OJ L311/3, later amended by Regulation (EU) 661/2014 of the European Parliament and of the Council amending Council Regulation (EC) No 2012/2002 establishing the European Union Solidarity Fund [2014] OJ L189/143.

[41] Regulation (EU) 2020/461 of the European Parliament and of the Council amending Council Regulation (EC) No 2012/2002 in order to provide financial assistance to Member States and to countries negotiating their accession to the Union that are seriously affected by a major public health emergency [2020] OJ L99/9.

[42] Regulation (EU) 2021/241 of the European Parliament and of the Council establishing the Recovery and Resilience Facility [2021] OJ L57/17.

structural funds) towards a much broader domain of macroeconomic policy measures aiming at improving the overall balance of economic development within the territory of the European Union, by making it more sustainable.

The range of policy goals which the RRF seeks to advance is quite broad: in addition to the environmental and digital 'flagships', the recovery money is intended to achieve the social policy goals contained in the European Pillar of Social Rights, and, depending on the country, a substantive portion of the recovery money is being allocated to social investment and the improvement of healthcare systems in the member states.[43] Also, 'Pillar 6' of the RRF, called 'Policies for the next generation', encourages investment in education and training.[44] As mentioned in a previous section, education and training are policy areas for which the EU does not possess law-making competences. In fact, one could say that RRF money here serves, to some extent, for the pursuit of purely national policy objectives, meaning that the steering potential of EU funding is largely absent. Generally though, the RRF possesses strong integration-through-funding features, stronger even than in the case of the structural funds. It does so for a number of reasons: (i) the strong earmarking of the expenditure towards the pursuit of Europe-wide policy priorities, namely more than half of it for green and digital transitions; (ii) the possibility offered to the Commission to impose the implementation of certain Country-Specific Recommendations (CSRs) (ie, EU-level macroeconomic policy goals) in the national plans – thereby making those CSRs better enforceable than they used to be;[45] (iii) the governance mechanism, and especially the targets and milestones which must be met before the successive instalments of the grants or loans will be paid, which allows the EU to take a harder look at whether the beneficiary state complies with the terms of the funding; those terms may include, in some cases, demanding rule-of-law reforms.[46]

It is therefore possible to see the NGEU programme as a major development of integration through funding, but at this moment in time, its policy steering effect still needs to be demonstrated. Its potential to further the policy goals of the

[43] On the social policy dimension of the recovery plans, see Silvia Rainone and Philippe Pochet, 'The EU Recovery Strategy – A Blueprint for a More Social Europe or a House of Cards?' (2022) *ETUI Working Paper* 2022.18 www.etui.org/sites/default/files/2022-11/The%20EU%20recovery%20strategy-a%20blueprint%20for%20a%20more%20Social%20Europe%20or%20a%20house%20of%20cards-2022.pdf.

[44] A recent study for the European Parliament examines the extent to which the national RRPs of eight member states incorporate measures under the 'policies for the next generation' heading: Manuela Samek Lodovici and Flavia Pesce, 'Addressing the challenges of the policies for the next generation, children and the youth, such as education and skills in national Recovery and Resilience Plans – A preliminary assessment' (*Economic Governance Support Unit at the Directorate-General for Internal Policies of the European Parliament*, PE 733.738, December 2022) requested by the ECON Committee.

[45] Louise Fromont, 'La conditionnalité des financements octroyés par la Facilité pour la reprise et la résilience' (2021) *Revue des affaires européennes* 771.

[46] In particular, rule of law reforms are included among the milestones in the national plans of Hungary and Poland. See Niall Moran, 'The Evolution of Conditionality in EU Financial Assistance under the Recovery and Resilience Facility' (2023) *REBUILD Centre Working Paper* No 5 https://rebuildcentre.eu/publication/the-evolution-of-conditionality-in-eu-financial-assistance-under-the-recovery-and-resilience-facility.

EU (its 'integration effect') depends on whether the states will be able to absorb the vast amounts of money allocated to them in the form of grants and loans; on whether the money will actually be used for the purposes described in the national plans; and, if they are, whether the expenditure will effectively produce the policy goals (such as green and digital transition) which are set out in the programme.

Policy integration by means of the RRF acquired a new dimension in 2022. Little more than a year after the adoption of the RRF, the European Commission presented its REPowerEU Plan which involved, as it announced, 'a targeted and swift amendment of the Recovery and Facility Regulation' [*sic*].[47] The proposed reform was not linked to any deficiencies in the original RRF scheme that would have come to light during its first year of application. Rather, what prompted the reform was the need to address a new crisis, unrelated to the pandemic, namely the energy market disruption caused by the Russian invasion of Ukraine. That crisis was analysed as requiring major investments to turn around the energy sector in the member states and, in the Commission's view, needed an EU-wide financial response similar to the one enacted during the Covid-19 crisis. It so happened that the RRF had unused funding which could be made available. Indeed, it had become clear by May 2022 that the loans part of the RRF (in contrast to the grants part) would not be entirely used. Only seven member states had decided to apply for the RRF loans, whereas the others either did not need that extra funding or could borrow at better or equivalent rates directly on the financial markets (or with the European Central Bank (ECB)). The REPowerEU document of the Commission proposed that the €225 billion of loans not requested so far would be made available for the purpose of strengthening the resilience of the EU's energy system, as delineated in the REPowerEU plan.[48]

Given the origin of its funding, REPowerEU will share the time-bound nature of RRF, as all the funds stemming from the RRF must be spent by 2026. Also, the funding will mainly consist of loans, although the Commission also proposed to add a smaller component of non-reimbursable expenditure ('grants'), to be repurposed from the cohesion funds (€26.9 billion) and CAP funds (€7.5 billion) and also to be drawn from the auction of Emissions Trading System allowances (€20 billion). The REPowerEU regulation therefore required an amendment to the

[47] Commission, 'Communication from the Commission to the European Parliament, the European Council, the Council, the European Economic and Social Committee and the Committee of the Regions – REPowerEU Plan', COM (2022) 230 final, 17.

[48] Commission, 'Proposal for a Regulation of the European Parliament and of the Council amending Regulation (EU) 2021/241 as regards REPowerEU chapters in recovery and resilience plans and amending Regulation (EU) 2021/1060, Regulation (EU) 2021/2115, Directive 2003/87/EC and Decision (EU) 2015/1814', COM (2022) 231 final. The Council and the European Parliament reached political agreement on its adoption in December 2022, and the Regulation was formally enacted on 27 February 2023: Regulation (EU) 2023/435 of the European Parliament and of the Council amending Regulation (EU) 2021/241 as regards REPowerEU chapters in recovery and resilience plans and amending Regulations (EU) No 1303/2013, (EU) 2021/1060 and (EU) 2021/1755, and Directive 2003/87/EC [2023] OJ L63/1.

legal instruments of cohesion and CAP, and the relevant legal bases were added to Article 175(3) but this did not affect the decision-making procedure, since all the legal bases provide for the ordinary legislative procedure.

7. Conclusion

This chapter has sought to show that there is indeed, as EU scholars have started to notice, a 'shift towards using financing rather than rule-making to influence how European Member States work'.[49] That shift is still tentative, as the overall amount of the EU budget remains limited, and the recent expansion of its volume through massive borrowing on the financial markets for the purpose of the NGEU programme is presented as a one-off initiative that should not (necessarily) lead to a stable expansion of the EU's financial capacity. However, independently from whether the NGEU and REPowerEU schemes will be continued or inspire similar schemes in the future, the current EU funding landscape is marked by the increased eagerness of the European institutions to use EU funding in a strategic way so as to advance Europe-wide policy objectives rather than (or in addition to) redistribution among the member states.

[49] Mark Dawson and Floris de Witte, *EU Law and Governance* (Cambridge, Cambridge University Press, 2022) 89.

12

Investment Politics

A New Capacity to Project Union Action into the Future?

LUUK VAN MIDDELAAR

1. Introduction

Focusing on recent years, I will 'Follow the Money' by taking it as a revealer of other political forces at play in Europe's constitution.[1] Money, after all, is not a thing in itself but an expression of relationships, starting with the relation between an object and its value. Our use of money also reveals our relationship to time, as we *save* for later, *spend* now, or *invest* for the future. My intellectual guide will neither be an economist nor a legal scholar, but a sociologist and philosopher – the great German thinker Georg Simmel who, at one point in his reference work *Philosophie des Geldes* (1900), defines money as the action of being spent:

> The meaning of money lies in the fact that it will be given away. When money stands still, it is no longer money according to its specific value and significance. The effect that it occasionally exerts in a state of repose arises out of an anticipation of its further motion. Money is nothing but the vehicle for a movement in which everything else that is not in motion is completely extinguished. It is, as it were, an actus purus.[2]

Simmel's consideration on money as *actus purus* is useful for the purpose of this chapter, as it highlights how the action of spending confers its meaning and purpose to money. Unmistakably, this financial capacity for action in the public realm forms a central feature of modern governmental systems. In the western constitutional tradition, it translates most notably into the distinction between the capacity to spend and the capacity to control that spending, defining an essential part of the relationship between executive and Parliament.

[1] For their valuable comments, suggestions and help, I should like to warmly thank Dr Vestert Borger (Leiden), Antonia Craven (Berlin), Sébastien Lumet MA (Brussels) and Dr Ruth Weber (Berlin).

[2] Georg Simmel, *The Philosophy of Money*, 3rd edn (London, Routledge, 2004) 517.

Although many scholars, including in EU studies and EU law, focus on the control function – on the ability to rein in spending on behalf of the taxpayers – it is worth remembering that the executive capacity to spend historically came first, and deserves to be studied at greater length. After all, first a political order needs to emerge out of the chaos of time immemorial and acquire some leader or King, with a Treasury at his disposal, and only then can budgetary control or a parliamentary *Königsrecht* (to use a term from the German debate) come into play.[3] Pushing the argument, one could perhaps distinguish two European legal traditions in this respect. Whereas the German legal tradition tends to focus on the Parliament, and to identify with the taxpayers on whose behalf a parliamentary assembly speaks, the French approach tends to see executive budgetary capacity as an expression of the citizenry's collective capacity to act, that is, of sovereignty, and hence puts the government centre stage. I will show some sympathy for the latter view here and look at EU finances from the perspective of the executive and, therefore, as one expression among others of the Union's capacity to act.

This is why, in this chapter, I would like to bring the lenses of political theory and constitutional law to the Union budget. In doing so, my aim is to take the budgetary evolution out of a legal and financial assessment, into a story of the European Union's executive and strategic emancipation.

First, I will briefly present the general framework of reference, anchored in the distinction between what I refer to as rules-politics and events-politics. The focus will lie on the extent to which the Covid-19 crisis has opened a new chapter in the surprise-intercepting politics of events, accelerating the Union's overall metamorphosis into a body politic.

This framework will then be applied to the evolution of EU spending. Introducing three concepts to trace and decipher that evolution, my claim will be that the Union's budgetary capacity has evolved from (only) '*programme spending*', emphasising long-term predictability and control, to (also) '*emergency spending*', as a way to deal with unexpected financial and political danger, to (also) '*strategic spending*' which relates to critical investments and budgetary foresight.[4]

Finally, I will reflect on this latter capacity and ask whether it points to a new form of European political action. What seems to be at stake, ultimately, is whether the EU is able to break away from the perpetual state of emergency, and to acquire a projection capability and become more resilient, in a world that is ever more hostile.

[3] The classic study on the executive emancipation in the transition from medieval kings to Renaissance rulers remains: John Greville Agard Pocock, *The Machiavellian Moment: Florentine political thought and the Atlantic republican tradition* (Princeton, Princeton University Press, 1975); also see Frank Schorkopf's chapter in this volume (ch 10).

[4] The overall movement, therefore, is not: from A via B to C, but rather from A via 'A and B' to 'A and B and C'.

2. The Metamorphosis: The Union's Executive Emancipation

The chain of decision-making leading to the adoption of the Covid-19 recovery funds, or NextGenerationEU (NGEU), tells us something about the European Union in moments of crisis. It corroborates the general thesis about a shift from a community focusing on 'rules-politics' to a Union also capable of engaging in 'events-politics' – a thesis I have developed in previous work and set out for the EU's pandemic response in *Pandemonium: Saving Europe* (2021). That thesis is briefly presented in the next section.[5]

2.1. Rules-Politics to Events-Politics

Originally, the institutions of the Union were mainly designed to create and develop a market. This rules-politics is an ingenious mechanism that produces consensus and support, but it works only within the agreed system, and furthermore by dint of the fiction that history proceeds along predictable lines. In events-politics, the aim is to get a grip on unforeseen, unanticipated situations. Often this form of political action is played out not within an established framework but precisely at moments when the framework itself is put to the test, in the most extreme cases by a war or catastrophe. The response to an unforeseen situation can sometimes be to create a new regulatory framework, in which case we witness an interaction between events-politics and rules-politics. One example of this is the 2012 European Council decision to create a European banking union in order to break the dangerous cycle between weak sovereigns and weak banks.

For post-war Europe, the choice was clear: rules-politics at the service of reconstruction and stability. Since the early years of the European Economic Community, political conflicts with all their dramatic potential have been transformed into manageable 'problems' that are technically soluble. Conflicting interests and incompatible visions are dealt with through a wondrous process of consultation and consideration, exchange and compromise, out of which the system then manufactures binding rules and norms for everyone – an internal market with policy coordination that spans practically an entire continent. Yet the qualities of rules-politics can take a negative turn. A multiplicity of internal equilibriums can topple over into stagnation and indecision, and a loss of connection

[5] See Luuk van Middelaar, *Alarums and Excursions: Improvising politics on the European stage* (Newcastle upon Tyne, Agenda Publishing, 2020) 11–14 for the general framework, as applied to the euro crisis (2010–12), see 21–64, and to the refugee crisis (2015–16), 91–114. For some institutional ramifications, see 173–83, and for the changed public experience, 229–38. The next section also draws upon: Luuk van Middelaar, *Pandemonium: Saving Europe* (Newcastle upon Tyne, Agenda Publishing, 2021) 21–45.

with the public. A more striking weakness is that the rule-making factory is not set up to deal with sudden and widespread adversity. Such moments of crisis therefore prise open the chest of rules. Gradually, a new European politics has emerged as a result, which can be called events-politics. A metamorphosis, whether we like it or not.

The factor of time brings the difference between events-politics and rules-politics most sharply into view. What to do if a eurozone country is on the verge of bankruptcy and the immense sum of €750 billion has to be put on the table within 72 hours to calm the markets? Or, what if from one day to the next, because of a virus outbreak, businesses are threatened with ruin and millions of people with unemployment if the public coffers are not opened for them without delay? In such cases of emergency, the acute need for readiness trumps the bureaucratic preference for patience and caution. There is no time for attuning and ironing out, for months of consultation with white papers and green papers, for postponement until after an election, or for patiently waiting until the problem blows over of its own accord. Instead, there is a need for improvisation – for steering a course between fixed rules and historical necessity, because to wait or do nothing would be irresponsible.

The major crises since 2008 have concerned not goat cheeses, lawn mowers or grain prices, but billions of euros and solidarity, war and peace, identity and sovereignty, life and death. These are sensitive, passion-rousing matters of great importance to the public at large, and they cannot be depoliticised by means of technocratic or procedural ingenuity. The commotion arising from the crisis years represented a huge change from the quiet tedium of the heyday of rules-politics – from the compliant indifference of citizens which political scientists called 'permissive consensus'. During the euro crisis, public squares from Athens to Madrid and Rome filled with defiant demonstrators. Voters discovered the ballot box as a means of settling scores with national leaders for their European performances. Previously marginal parties of protest made serious bids for power based on dissatisfaction with currency politics or the handling of migration, just as, in the most recent turmoil following Russia's invasion of Ukraine, public pressure and divisions on how to jointly deal with the fallout has shaken and toppled governments from Bulgaria to Italy.

The demands of time and the public bring us to the third major difference between rules- and events-politics: the political cast. Rapid and controversial decisions in times of crisis call for political authority, for visible and decisive powers of persuasion. When a storm arises, the bureaucratic and technocratic authority available in Brussels falls short, including that of commissioners, parliamentarians and sectoral ministers who keep the daily rules-machinery running. In events-politics other political players step onto the stage, in the form of 27 elected presidents and premiers. In the euro crisis, it was the heads of state or government, gathered together under the leadership of the German chancellor and the French president, who from 2010 onwards defended numerous emergency decisions before the national publics and thereby – along with the central bankers in Frankfurt – saved the besieged currency. This was a radical turn away from the old rules-politics, in which national leaders were deliberately kept outside the door. With new executive organs, adjusted voting rules and permanent presidencies, the Union is establishing itself in a world that demands agility, vigour and accountability. It is in this context of 'executive emancipation' that we should situate the recent deployment of new forms of joint budgetary capacity.

2.2. The Covid Moment

Before looking at the budgetary aspects of this overall evolution, it is worth briefly zooming in at the politics of the 'Covid moment'. After all, it was the fascinating interplay between the public and decision-makers during the pandemic which resulted in the decisive push toward a substantially larger Union budget and a new orientation toward 'investment politics'.

Taking up the three above-mentioned aspects of time pressure, public interest and political cast in that order, it was clear, first, that the outbreak of Covid-19 signified a moment of acute political danger. The clock was ticking. As the unknown disease spread – from early to mid-March 2020 – the only way to stop it at a humanly bearable cost seemed to be to shut down large parts of economic and social life and movements. An existential threat to the Union loomed. Prophets of doom were already predicting the euro's demise, while authoritative voices such as Pope Francis in Rome or Jacques Delors from Paris warned European nations against disunity, or their union would no longer be.

It is worth underlining the importance of the second aspect: the public's involvement. When in the early weeks a public health disaster was unfolding, the EU was slow to react. The loudest cry came from Italy, hit by the virus early on. Appeals for help went unanswered and bitter reproaches ensued. The fact that EU institutions lack the legal competences to act decisively in the field of public health impressed no one. If that were the case – if at this hour of need the EU was useless – it had to change. That is what happened.

During the Covid-19 disaster political decision-making *followed* public demand for action. By contrast, the financial storms of 2008 onwards had been calmed in top-down ways. Governments, alarmed by central bankers and experts, had to convince reluctant parliaments of the need for drastic decisions to save the banking system and the currency. The public looked on, not having asked for anything. The pandemic was different. All citizens felt threatened in their own bodies. The disease was nobody's fault. This crisis was so overwhelming – the strange lockdowns, the mass layoffs, the geo-medical 'divide and rule' strategy by Xi's China and Trump's America – that 'Europe' had to do something in response. Pandemic despair forced the Union to assume a form it did not previously possess.

Certainly, the Covid-19 outbreak led to intensely experienced moments of national belonging. Day after day, European societies counted and blessed the sick and the dead, tuned in for televised proclamations by monarchs, presidents or prime ministers, sang from balconies, and applauded medical staff in the evenings. At the same time, neighbouring states grew closer than ever in their suffering, their lockdown rules, their intensive-care policies, and their death rates. Leaving aside pandemic empathy, observing other countries had its uses at home. The media compared their own governments with others. Why was Austria testing more aggressively than France? Why were more people dying in Britain than in Greece?

But in the EU, with its single market, currency and shared borders, this went beyond mere comparison. Decisions next door had direct repercussions on people's lives. What if Germany pumped billions into its own economy and Italy could not? What if Sweden took a lax attitude to Covid-19 and kept its borders open? What if Hungary accepted a Russian vaccine? Some national publics were quick to say to their neighbours: this decision of yours is our business too. Conversely, several national leaders reached out to a broader, European public.

This is how, during the Covid-19 crisis, it once again became clear how acute danger and intense public attention bring a different political cast – the third element – onto the stage: national leaders acting in a European capacity. Few of them were more keenly aware of the stakes than the German chancellor. By Easter 2020, Angela Merkel could observe how fault-lines were hardening, how political fights over solidarity were flaring up between Europe's north and south, and how Covid-19 was driving the heart of the eurozone and its Mediterranean periphery apart economically. Therefore, she decided on 18 May 2020, after thorough consideration, to make a remarkable move. In agreement with the French president, she assumed responsibility for a €500 billion Covid-19 recovery fund, to be disbursed in the form of grants, not loans. Something that had remained taboo during the eurozone crisis was now suddenly possible.

Merkel displayed a seismologist's sensitivity to undercurrents and aftershocks in the public sphere. This unique ordeal could produce heaves and landslips, abrupt emotional eruptions. 'Our country is dying', the leaders in Rome and Madrid told her[6] – and so pandemic aid could not be conditional; that would be humiliating. Nor was it possible to ignore the fact that the Italian public's trust in the European Union was plummeting. For a German leader well-known for her 'step-by-step' approach, in her final year in office, it was enough to take the plunge.

In the following weeks and months, the initiative by the German and French members of the European Council – which took some of Germany's smaller Northern allies by surprise – was taken up and embedded into formal EU structures. On 27 May 2020, European Commission president Ursula von der Leyen presented her institution's proposal for a €750 billion rescue fund to the European Parliament, consisting of the €500 billion in grants from the Franco-German proposal plus €250 billion in loans. The 17–21 July European Council meeting, the second longest in the Union's history, unanimously agreed to pandemic

[6] Pedro Sanchez, 'Europe's future is at stake in this war against coronavirus' *The Guardian* (London, 5 April 2020).

funds of this volume, even if with a slightly different grant to loan ratio. Following some further hurdles that autumn – not least over the related rule-of-law conditionality – Council and Parliament as co-legislators finalised the agreements in December 2020, less than 12 months after the first Covid-19 cases in Europe.

All in all, the Covid moment showed a European Union convincingly engaging in events-politics, displaying political creativity, solidarity and (ultimately) unity, at least in the financial sphere.[7] Triggered by a public outcry, a productive interplay unfolded between the two sides of the Union's political executive: the European Council as the Union's crisis manager and centre of political authority, and the Commission and its president bringing ideas and its own specific EU-wide legitimacy to the table.

3. From 'Programme Spending' to 'Strategic Spending'

The European response to the Covid-19 crisis, so the previous section argued, tells us something about how the EU works when faced with existential threats. Now, I would like to zoom in onto what this could mean through the prism of budgetary politics. I would suggest that the design of emergency budgetary instruments throughout the crisis years, starting in 2010 and culminating in 2020 with NGEU, has impacted the Union's budgetary capacity in ways that closely reflect the distinction between rules- and events-politics, while it also points to a further evolution of the latter, perhaps to a new type of leadership. To better understand this evolution, it makes sense to distinguish three logics of spending and situate them through time. I propose to call these 'programme spending', 'emergency spending' and finally, perhaps still embryonically, 'strategic spending'.

3.1. Programme Spending

Looking at the first category, I would suggest that the Multiannual Financial Framework (MFF), the EU's conventional budgetary basis, is and remains at heart 'programme spending'. As such, it is the budgetary equivalent of rules-politics, insofar as it relates to traditional EU budget programmes such as the Common Agricultural Policy and Cohesion funds, which together amount to approximately two thirds of annual budgets. Tied for seven years with limited annual margins for adjustments and focused on a specific set of areas connected with explicit

[7] This analysis has to be seen in nuances as, during the pandemic, there have also been less convincing or even quite weak examples of events-politics, such as the fiasco around PPE public procurement by the European Commission (February – March 2020), mistaking a situation of war economy for a normal economy; in part repeated, then corrected, with the vaccine mandate that the institution received (see Van Middelaar, *Pandemonium* 59–62 and 93–104).

EU competences, MFFs are fully geared towards the long-term predictability of EU policies. They are primarily aimed at supporting the deepening of the internal market, including compensating for inequalities and promoting convergence. According to primary law (Article 310 of the Treaty on the Functioning of the European Union (TFEU)), the EU budget also has to balance expenditure and revenue and shall not foresee a deficit – a rule which distinguishes it from established practices in the member states. All this fits together and suits what I have analysed elsewhere as a protected, a-historical world of EU policy-making.[8]

The inelasticity of this budgetary apparatus is justified by a series of historical, legal and practical reasons. To be sure, predictability is essential for the recipients of funds – from local governments to farmers and research institutes – and represents a major advantage in itself. Just as importantly, the nature of the agreement also contributes to 'pacifying' relations between the EU institutions and among member states. This is why, in the late 1980s, the Delors Commission proposed the first of these multiannual packages, then called 'Financial Perspectives'.[9] Although MFFs have made it possible to break the diplomatic hassle of annual budgets, this also comes with a loss, since yearly budgets structure the political life and direction of a polity. In this respect, MFFs constrain the dynamism and adaptability of EU politics.

Comparing data on MFFs is rendered difficult by multiple factors, not least the fact that figures are often presented in different real prices or that Brexit deprived the budget of a major net contributor. But even a rough analysis can demonstrate that MFFs have shown their limits through time. At €994 billion (in appropriations for commitments at 2011 prices), the 2007–13 MFF was incapable of adapting to unforeseen expenses and had to be repeatedly revised, albeit within the ceilings set previously. Most of the response to the euro crisis from 2010 onwards consequently took place outside this financial framework. At €960 billion (in appropriations for commitments at 2011 prices), the 2014–20 MFF was even less ambitious, admittedly in order not to overburden the fiscal capacity of countries recovering from financial turmoil and increased government debt.[10] Early on, the budget was stretched to its limit and flexibility instruments outside the general budget were used extensively.[11] It proved for instance insufficient during the refugee crisis in 2015–16.

Ahead of the pandemic, the EU budget was therefore notoriously too small and rigid to deal with surprises, while negotiations for the new 2021–27 MFF did

[8] See Van Middelaar, *Pandemonium* 27–33. For a more elaborate account of the 'Community years' (1958–89) as shielded from history: Luuk van Middelaar, *The Passage to Europe: How a Continent Became a Union* (Yale, Yale University Press, 2020) 158–80.

[9] See N Piers Ludlow's chapter in this volume (ch 9).

[10] Data taken from European Commission Directorate-General for Budget, *European Union Public Finance*, 5th edn (Luxembourg, Publications Office of the European Union, 2014).

[11] European Commission, 'Flexibility and special instruments' *(European Commission Website)* https://ec.europa.eu/info/strategy/eu-budget/long-term-eu-budget/2014-2020/spending/flexibility-and-special-instruments_en.

not show signs of improvement in this respect. As late as at the end of 2019, as the first cases of Covid-19 were reported in China, negotiations at political level were at a dead end, critically delaying the adoption of the MFF.[12] Some countries were floating further cuts.[13]

Suddenly, Covid-19 profoundly shattered deeply entrenched taboos and overturned part of the philosophy of EU finances. As we saw in the previous section, in a matter of just a few months, the Union's leadership improvised and delivered an unprecedented budgetary solution, with an ad hoc recovery fund added alongside the new MFF – the two together amounting to a massive €1824 billion.[14] In and of itself, the 2021–27 MFF was set at €1074 billion (in appropriations for commitments at 2018 prices), which was an increase compared to the previous framework but one which did not alter the existing philosophy nor step out of the straitjacket of traditional 'programme spending'. The renewal was on the other half of the package and it built on earlier experiences from the euro crisis.

3.2. Emergency Spending

The budgetary breakthrough lies with the NGEU package, added alongside the MFF and which almost doubles the financial capability of the EU. NGEU amounts to a total of €750 billion, almost 90 per cent of which is spent via an ad hoc Recovery and Resilience Facility (RRF) split into €360 billion of loans and €312.5 billion of grants. The remaining 10 per cent is directly integrated into MFF programmes. The NGEU recovery package is anchored in Article 122 TFEU,[15] which is a solidarity clause that provides for financial assistance or other measures in case of a severe difficulties, and the looser Article 175(3) TFEU,[16] which pertains to specific actions leading to the strengthening of the EU's economic, social and territorial cohesion. Both legal instruments had already been used during or shortly after the euro crisis, albeit in less ambitious proportions.[17]

This economic recovery plan, alongside the State aid Temporary Crisis Framework[18] adopted as of early March 2020 by the European Commission,

[12] Jorge Valero, 'Pressure mounts on EU leaders to reach MFF deal within days' (*EURACTIV*, 19 February 2020) www.euractiv.com/section/future-eu/news/pressure-mounts-on-eu-leaders-to-reach-mff-deal-within-days.

[13] Guriev Gotev, 'Von der Leyen criticises Finnish presidency's EU budget proposal' (*EURACTIV*, 4 December 2019) www.euractiv.com/section/future-eu/news/von-der-leyen-criticises-finnish-presidencys-eu-budget-proposal.

[14] European Council, 'Multiannual financial framework 2021-2027 and Next Generation EU' (*European Council Website*, 2020) www.consilium.europa.eu/en/infographics/mff2021-2027-ngeu-final.

[15] Which forms the legal basis for the Regulation establishing the European Union Recovery Instrument.

[16] Which forms the legal basis for the Regulation establishing the Recovery and Resilience Facility.

[17] Bruno De Witte, 'The European Union's Covid-19 Recovery Plan: The Legal Engineering of an Economic Policy Shift' (2021) 58 *CML Rev* 635.

[18] Communication from the Commission on the Temporary Crisis Framework for State aid measures to support the economy in the current COVID-19 outbreak [2020] OJ CI91/1.

and the Pandemic emergency purchase programme (PEPP) introduced by the European Central Bank (ECB) around the same time,[19] could be considered as the culmination of the second category of spending, which I here label 'emergency spending'. However, to better apprehend this crisis response, one must trace back the roots and characteristics of emergency spending to its first occurrence as an answer to the shocks of the euro crisis years. Even if that budgetary action was but a part of the complex and multifaceted crisis response that occurred in disorderly steps over the span of several years, it was a decisive part.

The first instance when the euro was saved thanks to emergency spending occurred in May 2010, when risks were running high that a Greek default would send shockwaves to the whole currency union and beyond. The operation came in two parts. The Commission proposed a European Financial Stabilisation Mechanism (EFSM). It was swiftly adopted as a Council Regulation, on the basis of Article 122(2) TFEU, and provided for the Commission to raise funds on the financial markets, guaranteed using the EU budget as collateral.[20] However, this capacity was limited to a maximum amount of €60 billion, to be disbursed exclusively as loans to assist member states facing a sovereign debt crisis. This limited amount was a direct result of the inflexibility of the 2007–13 MFF: the €60 billion corresponded to the Union's available budget payment ceilings.

Furthermore, it was designed in an emergency situation where €500 billion was needed. The Commission had originally proposed to use the EFSM for the remaining €440 billion, too, with the extra amount to be guaranteed by the member states.[21] This plan was considered politically unfeasible ('eurobonds!') and legally unsound – a remarkable contrast to what proved possible 10 years later. In May 2010, for the remaining funds, eurozone governments therefore decided to act outside the scope of the Treaty, even outside public law, and founded a special purpose vehicle: the European Financial Stability Facility (EFSF). Incorporated as a company under Luxembourgish law, it was initially equipped with a lending capacity of €440 billion through the issuance of bonds and other debt instruments on capital markets, guaranteed by the euro area member states. The instrument was conceived as a last resort facility and exclusively geared towards providing loans with strict conditionalities attached.

Those two temporary instruments were later superseded by the permanent European Stability Mechanism (ESM), with some of the EFSF funds being

[19] European Central Bank, 'Pandemic emergency purchase programme (PEPP)' (*European Central Bank Website*, 2022) www.ecb.europa.eu/mopo/implement/pepp/html/index.en.html.

[20] Note the more limited legal base compared to the 2020 European Union Recovery Instrument, which is based on Art 122 TFEU as such, and not just on either para 1 or (as in this case) para 2.

[21] Commission, 'Proposal for a Council Regulation establishing a European financial stabilization mechanism' COM (2010) 2010 final, 3. See in particular Art 2(2): 'Subject to Article 3, the outstanding amount of loans or credit lines to be granted to Member States under the present stabilization mechanism shall be limited to the margin available under the own resources ceiling for payment appropriations.' As well as Art 3 (1): 'Loans and credit lines above the ceiling referred to in Article 2(2) shall benefit from the joint and pro-rata guarantee of the euro-area Member States.'

transferred to the ESM.[22] This new mechanism was set up as an intergovernmental organisation under public international law. It was contracted by euro area states, but still outside the EU framework, although closely related to it, to the dismay of many Brussels observers. The intricate political and legal operation took two versions of the ESM Treaty and also required – a German demand – a 'surgical' amendment to the founding treaties, with a brief third paragraph being added to Article 136 TFEU.[23] There was clearly not enough flexibility within the system to deal with shocks.

With hindsight, one can see how the financial crisis broke the straitjacket of budgetary policy and spending capacity at European level. During the crisis, it became clear that existing rules and instruments had not been designed to deal with a crisis. Under the pressure of events, emergency funds had to be improvised, alongside stricter fiscal rules and more robust macro-economic oversight. As such, the drama of the euro crisis was in part the EU's struggle to design ad hoc funds.

The same shift took place at the level of central banks. The role played by the ECB is outside the scope of this chapter, but it is nonetheless important to note that the Frankfurt-based institution operated a historic shift from a mandate-tied, rules-politics approach to one also able to engage in events-politics. It did so by crossing, as early as May 2010, with tacit consent from the German Chancellor, one of the (three) main red lines of German monetary orthodoxy, that of no monetary financing. The fact that Mario Draghi added the element of 'bluff' to the ECB's toolkit with his 2012 'whatever it takes' statement (and in particular with the few words he personally added for the financial markets: 'and believe me, it will be enough') makes clear that this shift was deeply political. During the 2007–08 financial crisis, the ECB had already decided to make non-conventional monetary policy interventions for the first time in order to deal with high and sudden risk. This was a prelude to its action during the euro crisis, when it implicitly adapted its stability mandate to include not just price stability but also financial stability.[24] The array of monetary and banking policy decisions introduced since the outbreak of the pandemic have confirmed and amplified this course of action,[25] driven by events.

[22] The EFSM has nonetheless been used as late as 2015, long after the formal entry into force of the ESM Treaty, in the context of a bridge loan for Greece, and prior to the establishment of a new loan package.

[23] The inserted paragraph reads: 'The Member States whose currency is the euro may establish a stability mechanism to be activated if indispensable to safeguard the stability of the euro area as a whole. The granting of any required financial assistance under the mechanism will be made subject to strict conditionality.'

[24] Evolution traced in great detail in Vestert Borger, *The Currency of Solidarity. Constitutional Transformation during the Euro Crisis* (Cambridge, Cambridge University Press, 2020).

[25] Pierpaolo Benigno et al, 'The ECB's Measures in Support of the COVID-19 Crisis' (Policy Department for Economic, Scientific and Quality of Life Policies at the Directorate-General for Internal Policies of the European Parliament, Monetary Dialogue Papers PE 658.225, March 2021) requested by the ECON Committee.

The European financial inventiveness exhibited during the years of the euro crisis created some openings but also showed constraints for budgetary politics. It opened the door to a new general approach, which several proposals tried to institutionalise afterwards, from the so-called 'Five Presidents' Report on completing Europe's Economic and Monetary Union'[26] to the Franco-German Meseberg declaration from June 2018.[27] However, most of the attempts undertaken in the period from 2015 to 2019 failed or fell short of delivering significant effects. For instance, despite several reform attempts up until as late as 2020, the ESM has not yet been incorporated into EU law and remains a separate treaty. Another telling example is the French attempt to create a specific 'budget for the eurozone', a political tool that would serve to absorb financial shocks. This flagship idea, taken up notably in president Emmanuel Macron's 2017 Sorbonne speech, faced strong German and Dutch resistance. The stalemate resulted in the still-born Budgetary Instrument for Convergence and Competitiveness (BICC), agreed at Eurogroup level in October 2019.[28] Its scope was reduced so much that its benefits were highly questionable.[29] As I commented in 2019, it looked 'as if the eurozone is waiting for another crisis … to improve its resilience'.[30]

The Covid-19 pandemic was that crisis. It led to an exceptional instance of 'emergency spending', and to the EU engaging successfully and ingeniously in events-politics. What is more, I would claim that, this time around, European leaders and policy-makers even went beyond the mere improvisation displayed in earlier times. They put this crisis to good use, triggering a shift beyond strait-jacketed programme spending and ad hoc instruments towards more strategic investments, akin to executive budgetary foresight.

3.3. Strategic Spending

Admittedly, the response to Covid-19 started with improvisation. When the pandemic shattered deeply entrenched taboos, first measures naturally drew on experiences from previous crises. As mentioned above, EU fiscal rules were suspended as of early March 2020[31] to allow EU governments to increase national

[26] Jean-Claude Juncker et al, 'The Five Presidents' Report: Completing Europe's Economic and Monetary Union' (European Commission, 2015).

[27] Présidence de la République française, 'Meseberg Declaration – Renewing Europe's promises of security and prosperity' (*Élysée*, 19 June 2018) www.elysee.fr/en/emmanuel-macron/2018/06/19/meseberg-declaration-renewing-europes-promises-of-security-and-prosperity.

[28] Mario Centeno, 'Summing up letter: Eurogroup in inclusive format (09.10.2019)' (*Consilium*, 23 October 2019) www.consilium.europa.eu/media/41173/summing-up-letter-eg-9-october-2019.pdf.

[29] Lucas Guttenberg, 'New beginnings: A new approach to Eurozone reform' (2019) Jacques Delors Institute.

[30] Van Middelaar, *Alarums & Excursions* 216.

[31] At least until 2024, as per: János Allenbach-Ammann, 'EU fiscal rules to be suspended for another year' (*EURACTIV*, 23 May 2022) www.euractiv.com/section/economy-jobs/news/eu-fiscal-rules-to-be-suspended-for-another-year.

public investments, just as they had done during the banking crisis. Joint expenditure was also engineered, at first by mobilising familiar sources: European Investment Bank[32] and Commission funds to help companies. More innovatively, member states designed the €100 billion Support to mitigate Unemployment Risks in an Emergency (SURE) loan programme, to help member states finance social security expenses. It was based on Article 122 TFEU and underpinned by a system of voluntary guarantees.[33] All this was set up before it became clear that something still bigger and unprecedented was needed.

Pushed by the pressure of public opinion (as seen above) and despite strong disagreements, leaders drew on lessons learnt in the euro crisis years. After the red line of monetary financing, the two other red lines of German monetary orthodoxy were crossed: transfers and common borrowing. For chancellor Merkel, the 'exceptional situation' of a human tragedy hitting all member states in a 'symmetric shock', allowed for 'an exceptional and one-off effort'.[34] In this respect, and in terms of the North / South political dynamics displayed in spring 2020, it was a euro crisis 2.0, but with Germany, under Merkel's leadership, leaving the North for a one-off Centre. The Federal Republic forced its smaller northern allies to swallow defeat on the principle and align themselves on a new paradigm, at least on this occasion.

Besides the changed political dynamics, this new occurrence of improvisation was also different in institutional form. First, although building on previous instruments and legal bases, these new remedies were not devised fully outside EU structures. This was facilitated by the fact that decisions had to be taken at a moment when the 2021–27 MFF struggled to get approval. The lack of agreement (a February 2020 summit dedicated to the budget had failed blatantly) proved a blessing in disguise: the more open issues and problems there were, the more chance of trade-offs and buy-offs, and so of an agreement. The situation provided the opportunity to create something more anchored to the EU framework than vehicles designed during the euro crisis.

In this respect, the linkage of the pandemic funds to the Own Resources Decision (ORD) points in two directions. On the one hand, it firmly embeds the new funds in the Union's institutional structures (something which the

[32] European Investment Bank, 'EIB Board approves €25 billion Pan-European Guarantee Fund in response to COVID-19 crisis' (*EIB Website*, 26 May 2020) www.eib.org/en/press/all/2020-126-eib-board-approves-eur-25-billion-pan-european-guarantee-fund-to-respond-to-covid-19-crisis.htm.

[33] De Witte, 'The European Union's Covid-19 Recovery Plan'.

[34] eg speech from Federal Chancellor Angela Merkel to the European Parliament in Brussels, 8 July 2020 www.bundesregierung.de/breg-de/suche/rede-von-bundeskanzlerin-merkel-zur-deutschen-eu-ratspraesidentschaft-2020-vor-dem-europaeischen-parlament-am-8-juli-2020-in-bruessel-1767368 ('eine außergewöhnliche und einmalige Kraftanstrengung', which the official translation inadequately renders as 'an exceptional and unprecedented exertion'). The notion of a 'symmetric shock' affecting all EU Member States, in contrast to 'asymmetric' ones hitting those with weak economic stewardship, was expressed by Merkel as early as 6 April 2020 in a press conference: www.bundesregierung.de/breg-de/suche/pressekonferenz-von-bundeskanzlerin-merkel-zu-den-massnahmen-der-bundesregierung-im-zusammenhang-mit-dem-coronavirus-1739654.

Commission was keen to achieve). On the other hand, it constitutionally underlines, since the Decision requires a unanimous parliamentary ratification, that the funds were supposed to be a one-off operation, targeted at the exceptional economic fallout of the Covid-19 crisis (a crucial point for Germany).[35] Therefore, in one and the same movement, the possibility of a repetition has been institutionally facilitated and the political veto against such repetition put in place. Time will tell how this will play out. Officially, NGEU is supposed to be non-permanent, with the funds paid back by 2058 at the latest. However, it is safe to say that many in Brussels, Paris and beyond consider that an important precedent has been set – and a precedent which may well be built upon rather soon, for instance to face the imminent economic fallout of the Ukraine war.[36]

A second difference concerns conditionality. Early in the Covid-19 crisis, using the ESM – the dedicated euro crisis instrument – was an option put on the table, with finance ministers agreeing in notoriously ill-tempered Eurogroup meetings in the spring of 2020 to equip it with a €240 billion public health credit line. However, the stigma attached to the ESM in Southern Europe made it politically unsuitable for use during the pandemic. Accepting financing conditionalities was considered deeply humiliating in Rome and Madrid, as hundreds of people were dying daily – a sentiment widely if not unanimously shared. The recovery funds, in particular the Recovery and Resilience Facility (RRF), have therefore been set up differently. To access funding, member states must meet milestones set out in their respective National Recovery and Resilience Plans, which are designed within the framework of the European semester.[37] This set up has been criticised[38] for its multiple loopholes and the risks it poses for effective medium-term sustainable growth, as well as the difficulty of ensuring proper implementation and absorption.[39] But it nonetheless constitutes a clear departure from the severe conditionality mechanisms designed during the euro crisis, which fed public resentment in Southern Europe. It is also significant that, regarding the legal basis, a large part of economic policy-making has in the process been moved from the Treaty section on economic and monetary policy (Articles 119 ff TFEU) to the

[35] Council Regulation (EU) 2020/2094 establishing a European Union Recovery Instrument to support the recovery in the aftermath of the COVID-19 crisis [2020] OJ LI433/23.

[36] Thu Nguyen, 'EU Economic Policy Coordination After the Recovery and Resilience Facility' (DFG-Research Training Group DynamInt Conference at Humboldt-Universität zu Berlin, Berlin, 9–10 June 2022).

[37] Thu Nguyen, 'EU Economic Policy Coordination After the Recovery and Resilience Facility' (DFG-Research Training Group DynamInt Conference at Humboldt-Universität zu Berlin, Berlin, 9–10 June 2022).

[38] Thomas Wieser, 'What Role for the European Semester in the recovery plan?' (*Economic Governance Support Unit at the Directorate-General for Internal Policies of the European Parliament*, PE 651.368, October 2020) requested by the ECON Committee.

[39] Guntram B Wolff, 'Without good governance, the EU borrowing mechanism to boost the recovery could fail' (*Bruegel*, 15 September 2020) www.bruegel.org/comment/without-good-governance-eu-borrowing-mechanism-boost-recovery-could-fail.

section dealing with economic, social and territorial cohesion (and in particular Article 175 TFEU), giving the latter a whole new scope and dimension.

Finally, compared to previous crises, NGEU also initiated a change of nature and philosophy towards more strategic investments. Indeed, the fund acts as more than a means for immediate relief against the economic downturn brought about by the crisis and is also meant to foster structural change, articulated in particular around the 'twin' green and digital transitions.[40] Targets for climate and digital spending are 37 per cent and 20 per cent respectively; according to the Commission, they are both likely to be achieved.[41] Hence, the most striking difference between the euro crisis and the Covid-19 funds lies in the fact that whereas the former were designed as reactive rescue packages with strict conditions to avoid loss of market confidence in the currency union, the latter were created as a proactive strategic investment capability. This fundamental difference sets the stage for what I would like to call 'strategic spending'.

4. Strategic Spending as a New Form of European Executive Action?

4.1. Progressive Political Self-Assertion and Strategic Spending

As set out in the previous section, the resolution of the financial crisis was improvised but opened the door to a new approach that has been expanded and reinforced during the Covid-19 crisis. Now we can reflect on the outcome of this new capacity for political action, via massive financial investment, and whether it indeed represents a new form of executive action at European level. During the euro crisis, emergency funds allowed for the absorption of financial shocks – to *spend now* – and face the emergency. But such actions only came about after disaster was narrowly averted. The test is, therefore, whether the EU is able to break away from the perpetual state of emergency and acquire a projection capability, to spend now *and* to invest in the future.

The relationship to time and the future is at the very heart of any community's political life. It also determines the scope, style and public expectations of political leadership, as the European Union currently discovers. To understand how this plays out, it is worthwhile putting budgetary considerations aside for a moment

[40] European Commission, '2022 Strategic Foresight Report: twinning the green and digital transitions in the new geopolitical context' (*European Commission Website*, June 2022) https://ec.europa.eu/commission/presscorner/detail/en/IP_22_4004.

[41] European Commission, 'The Recovery and Resilience Facility' (*European Commission Website*, Summer 2020) https://ec.europa.eu/info/business-economy-euro/recovery-coronavirus/recovery-and-resilience-facility_en.

and briefly looking at Alexandre Kojève's *The Notion of Authority* (1942). In this short book, the Franco-Russian philosopher distinguishes four leadership types: Judge (*le Juge*), Father (*le Père*), Combatant (*le Maître*) and Leader (*le Chef*), all with their specific temporal mode. Of the four, the Judge, deriving his authority from a neutral position outside the fray, stands 'outside time', while the other three all represent a specific mode of being in history. The Father embodies the authority of tradition and the *past*. The Combatant, a person ready to risk his life, is strong in the *present*. The Leader, finally, gains respect by putting forward ideas for the *future*.[42] These are ideal-types, as Kojève himself readily conceded; any individual political leader will in practice rely on a combination of them. Nevertheless, an overall trend is clear. As the author observed back in his day: in contemporary societies, the centre of gravity of leaders' political authority shifts from warrior-type assets (strength, courage) and the incarnation of tradition (age, wisdom) to the ability to propose a vision for the future (intelligence, expertise).

This perspective on time and executive authority also gives an insight into the EU's specific conundrum in this respect. Created in the 1950s as a policy-making system shielded from the forces of history, so almost outside time, the Union has traditionally – and unsurprisingly – above all been endowed with the authority of the Judge, or arbiter. However, faced with historic events knocking on the door, in a series of twists and turns, it is discovering that it has to assume a position in time. And perhaps even more so than those of other political bodies, who have the past at their disposal, EU leaders must gain authority and respect by acting in the present and proposing a way forward into the future. After all, politicians representing an organisation proud of its break with Europe's war-torn past, can hardly embody some immemorial tradition as 'Father' or 'Mother'. As to action in the present, EU leaders can of course not literally put their own lives at stake, 'Combatant'-style. However, during the banking and currency crisis, their executive action for the first time explicitly took the form of a 'battle' against a formidable adversary, that is, the financial markets, in order for the euro to 'survive'. In the pandemic, while fighting an acute danger, EU leaders also took up the role of future-oriented Leader(s). By stepping out of the role of Judge, and going beyond emergency action, EU leaders took the right path. I am not suggesting that the part of far-seeing Leader has already been taken up credibly and successfully – neither in Brussels nor in the EU capitals – but strategic foresight is what Europe's geopolitical situation is asking for and what the public expects.

Hence my claim that the Union's budgetary turn to strategic spending should be seen in the much wider context of its *geopolitical awakening* of recent years. Russia's brutal invasion of Ukraine has accelerated and deepened the awareness but did not trigger it. A sentiment of existential vulnerability was already palpable, certainly in Berlin and Brussels, in the early days of the US presidency of Donald Trump (2016–20). It is clear that a series of phenomena including the assertiveness

[42] Alexandre Kojève, *The Notion of Authority* (first published 1942, London, Verso Books, 2014).

of Xi Jinping's China, the growing divergence between European and US economic and territorial interests, the actions of Putin-style strongmen across the globe, and the myriad of factors prompting the resurgence of asymmetries and geopolitical disruptions,[43] have been forcing the Union to become a more strategic entity. Although its decision-making structure remains inevitably siloed and improvised responses tend to lack a strategic synthesis, a broader paradigm shift is emerging. It is having an impact on EU views and approaches to economic and industrial policy since at least 2016. NGEU ties in with these wider developments.

Industrial policy is perhaps the most telling example. Traditionally, the EU focused its efforts on 'horizontal' measures, that is, enabling an environment in which innovation can flourish, based on the facilitation of market choices, and on strictly limiting the space for direct or 'vertical' interventions benefitting specific sectors or individual companies by national governments with a strict state-aid framework. In the last few years however, we have witnessed a turn to something akin to 'vertical' industrial policy, urging governments to more directly guide the supply side of the economy towards key sectors.[44] The objective is to avoid the errors of the 1970s (which ended up 'backing losers' rather than 'picking winners') by fostering specific, future-oriented industrial 'ecosystems'. The Union institutions do so with a view to outside threats and competitors, in a world of intensifying geoeconomics rivalry.

In this field too, the pandemic has been a catalyst in showing the vulnerabilities of a purely market-based approach – painfully visible in a global struggle for protective equipment and vaccines, with phenomena such as 'mask diplomacy' and geo-medical divide-and-rule by China and the US. At the heart of today's geostrategic rivalry, supply-chain disruptions have significantly increased since the beginning of the Covid-19 crisis[45] and with the war in Ukraine. But these disruptions have structural causes which go beyond Covid-19.

Supply chains are turning into tools of geopolitical power. Engaged in a power competition around key resources and production chains, not least for energy, rare earth, semiconductors and batteries, major powers assess their strategic situation and devise remedies. In this respect, the US has assessed its supply chains' vulnerabilities and dependencies,[46] and so has the EU with the Commission's landmark

[43] Jean Pisani-Ferry, 'Global asymmetries strike back' (*Bruegel*, 2 September 2021) www.bruegel.org/comment/global-asymmetries-strike-back.

[44] Advisory Council on International Affairs, 'Designing smart industrial policy: new departures for the Netherlands within the EU' (AIV Advisory Report no 120, 18 March 2022) www.advisorycouncil-internationalaffairs.nl/documents/publications/2022/04/01/designing-smart-industrial-policy.

[45] Federal Reserve Bank of New York, 'Global Supply Chain Pressure Index (GSCPI)' (*FRBNY Website*, 2022) www.newyorkfed.org/research/policy/gscpi#/overview.

[46] The White House, 'The Biden-Harris Plan to Revitalize American Manufacturing and Secure Critical Supply Chains in 2022' (*The White House Website*, 24 February 2022) www.whitehouse.gov/briefing-room/statements-releases/2022/02/24/the-biden-harris-plan-to-revitalize-american-manufacturing-and-secure-critical-supply-chains-in-2022.

report on Europe's strategic dependencies.[47] In turn, via massive investments, major powers try to maximise their ability to attract or build the necessary industrial capacity on domestic soil and diversify critical supply lines.[48] The approach aims at targeted investments to reduce vulnerabilities and acquire control over core networks and sectors.

In this endeavour, the Union first focused on defensive tools, via initiatives such as the modernisation of the EU's trade defence instruments (TDIs), including the updated EU anti-dumping methodology.[49] This was a revolution in itself, in light of the EU's historic preference for 'offensive' trade instruments, geared towards opening foreign markets and creating a global level playing field. The 'China shock' – very visible in a series of take-overs in the German high-tech industry from 2016 onwards – has tilted the balance. More recently, the Commission's proposal for an anti-coercion instrument[50] or the regulation on foreign subsidies distorting the internal market[51] are part of the same logic. However, the political focus is now shifting to measures beyond the realm of TDIs in order to actively strengthen industrial ecosystems.

4.2. The EU Chips Act

The clearest illustration of this embryonic investment strategy at European level, or 'strategic spending' as I should like to call it, is the EU Chips Act, which is a massive subsidy programme for semiconductors unveiled in the first half of 2022. In this field, where Europe only has roughly 10 per cent of the global market share, the plan aims to expand its share of the semiconductors market to 20 per cent by 2030. The means for the €43 billion investment plan[52] should mostly stem not from the EU budget but from member states via relaxed state-aid rules for microelectronics – a sector which has been designated an Important Project of Common European Interest (or IPCEI). All this makes the EU Chips Act a cumulative strategy combining not only a research and production boost, strengthened

[47] European Commission, 'EU strategic dependencies and capacities: second stage of in-depth reviews' (*European Commission Website*, 22 February 2022) https://ec.europa.eu/docsroom/documents/48878.

[48] Shearwater Global, 'A Smart EU Industrial Policy – Lowri Evans & Hans Kribbe in conversation' (*Shearwater Global Website*, 4 May 2022) http://shearwater.global/media/55/a-smart-eu-industrial-policy.

[49] European Commission, 'EU modernises its trade defence instruments' (*European Commission Website*, 23 January 2018) https://ec.europa.eu/commission/presscorner/detail/en/MEMO_18_396.

[50] European Commission, 'EU strengthens protection against economic coercion' (*European Commission Website*, 8 December 2021) https://ec.europa.eu/commission/presscorner/detail/en/ip_21_6642.

[51] Council of the European Union, 'Foreign subsidies distorting the internal market: provisional political agreement between the Council and the European Parliament' (*Council of the European Union Website*, 30 June 2022) www.consilium.europa.eu/en/press/press-releases/2022/06/30/foreign-subsidies-regulation-political-agreement.

[52] Andy Bounds, 'EU launches €43bn push for chip factories as shortages hit manufacturing' *The Financial Times* (London, 8 February 2022).

manufacturing capacity, and the joined monitoring of supply, but also massive investments.[53]

Setting aside legitimate concerns regarding potential trade-distorting effects and economic shortfalls associated with the Commission's approach,[54] this is a major policy shift from previous practices regarding the channelling of funds towards industrial goals, much more akin to the capacity deployed by the governments of major powers. In comparison, the US government has unveiled a $52 billion five-year investment plan for its chip industry,[55] while South Korea is looking to unlock $450 billion over 10 years[56] and Japan approved a $6.8 billion investment package last year.[57]

This sectoral example tells us that investments are increasingly used at European level as an executive capacity to act in pursuit of political objectives. Money, to allude to Georg Simmel referenced above, is 'the vehicle for a movement'[58] – it is *actus purus*.

To grasp how this evolution fits within the EU budgetary framework in practice, it is striking to observe that, based on calculations by the European Commission,[59] around 66 per cent of the RRF funds of NGEU will be directed towards climate and digital objectives, exceeding the mandatory 57 per cent set out in member states' National Recovery and Resilience Plans (NRRPs).[60] Strategic spending, understood as such, can be seen as the emergence of a European capacity to act in accordance with political aims. It is a crystallisation of a trajectory taken mostly in relation to competitors and rivals, catching up or trying to get ahead. Such new investments go beyond the mere reaction to events and insert themselves into a wider shift towards a more future-oriented, more strategic Union, which is capable of leadership.

[53] European Commission, 'Digital sovereignty: Commission proposes Chips Act to confront semiconductor shortages and strengthen Europe's technological leadership' (*European Commission Website*, 8 February 2022) https://ec.europa.eu/commission/presscorner/detail/en/ip_22_729.

[54] Niclas Poitier and Pauline Weil, 'Is the EU Chips Act the right approach?' (*Bruegel*, 2 June 2022) www.bruegel.org/blog-post/eu-chips-act-right-approach.

[55] The White House, 'Biden-Harris Administration Bringing Semiconductor Manufacturing Back to America' (*The White House Website*, 21 January 2021) www.whitehouse.gov/briefing-room/statements-releases/2022/01/21/fact-sheet-biden-harris-administration-bringing-semiconductor-manufacturing-back-to-america-2; Stephen Shankland, 'Biden to Congress: Pass Bill to Fund US Chip Manufacturing' (*CNET*, 2 March 2022) www.cnet.com/news/politics/biden-to-congress-pass-that-bill-to-fund-us-chip-manufacturing.

[56] Sohee Kim and Sam Kim, 'Korea Unveils $450 Billion Push for Global Chipmaking Crown' (*Bloomberg*, 13 May 2021) www.bloomberg.com/news/articles/2021-05-13/korea-unveils-450-billion-push-to-seize-global-chipmaking-crown.

[57] Yuri Furukawa and Takashi Mochizuki, 'Japan Approves $6.8 Billion Boost for Domestic Chip Industry' (*Bloomberg*, 26 November 2021) www.bloomberg.com/news/articles/2021-11-26/japan-approves-6-8-billion-boost-for-domestic-chip-industry#xj4y7vzkg.

[58] Simmel, *The Philosophy of Money*.

[59] European Commission, 'Recovery and Resilience Scoreboard' (*European Commission Website*, 2022) https://ec.europa.eu/economy_finance/recovery-and-resilience-scoreboard/index.html.

[60] Commission, 'A competition policy fit for new challenges (Communication to the European Parliament, the Council, the European Economic and Social Committee and the Committee of the Regions)' COM (2021) 713 final.

4.3. REPowerEU

A final telling illustration of the potential behind this embryonic capacity as a new form of political action is REPowerEU. Following Russia's aggression against Ukraine, a plan was announced in late May 2022 by the European Commission to drastically and swiftly reduce dependence on Russian fossil fuels.[61] The Commission proposes to make targeted amendments to the RRF Regulation in order to integrate dedicated REPowerEU chapters into member states' existing recovery plans. Just like the EU Chips Act, this plan comes with short- and long-term measures, ranging from the diversification of energy supplies to the creation of a 'joint purchasing mechanism' to negotiate gas contracts on behalf of member states, or the revision of renewable targets.

Interestingly for the purpose of this chapter, the plan aims to make massive strategic investments, but this time via the budgetary means developed as part of NGEU.[62] Indeed, besides a plan to sell roughly €20 billion worth of additional Emission Trading System (ETS) allowances and the transfer of up to approximately €35 billion of cohesion and CAP funds, the bulk of the funding would stem from the repurposing of the €225 billion unused loans from the RRF.[63] As pointed out by analysts,[64] it remains to be seen how precisely this money would be rechannelled, whether as loans with the pitfalls and risks associated, or as new grants. But the approach itself is a good illustration of what 'strategic spending' can look like, as an improvised response to a crisis, embedded in the European budgetary framework, and which fits into more strategic and long-term executive action.

5. Conclusion

In a famous lecture held in 2000 at Humboldt University,[65] Joschka Fischer kick-started an EU constitutional debate by asking a profoundly political and taboo question: where do we find the Government – the Executive Branch – in the

[61] European Commission, 'REPowerEU: A plan to rapidly reduce dependence on Russian fossil fuels and fast forward the green transition' (*European Commission Website*, 18 May 2022) https://ec.europa.eu/commission/presscorner/detail/en/IP_22_3131; Commission, 'Implementing the RE Power EU action plan: Investment needs, hydrogen accelerator and achieving the bio-methane targets (Staff working document)' SWD (2022) 230 final.

[62] Jorge Liboreiro, 'Five things to know about the EU's big plan to become independent from Russian fossil fuels' (*Euronews*, 24 May 2022) www.euronews.com/my-europe/2022/05/18/five-things-to-know-about-the-eu-s-big-plan-to-become-independent-from-russian-fossil-fuel.

[63] European Commission, 'Financing REPowerEU' FactSheet (*European Commission Website*, 18 May 2022) https://ec.europa.eu/commission/presscorner/detail/en/fs_22_3135.

[64] Andreas Eisl, 'An ambitious plan without adequate financing?' (*Jacques Delors Institute Website*, 15 June 2022) https://institutdelors.eu/en/publications/an-ambitious-plan-without-adequate-financing.

[65] Joschka Fischer, 'From Confederacy to Federation – Thoughts on the finality of European integration' (*European Commission Website*, May 2000) https://ec.europa.eu/dorie/fileDownload.do?docId=192161&cardId=192161.

European Union? Two decades on, following a series of crises, we see the rise of a more strategic Europe, better able to act, including via the power of the purse.

As I illustrate in *Alarums and Excursions*, the desire among the political leadership of the European Union to break free of the permanent state of emergency has been running high for a number of years. At the June 2017 European Council, Angela Merkel uttered a heartfelt cry: 'Enough of crisis management! The hour of strategic choices has come.' while Emmanuel Macron stated his intention to end the Union as the 'curator of crisis management'.[66] Five years on, crisis management has occurred in a proportion few could have expected back then, and it is too early to say if their wishes have been granted. But in light of the developments set out in this chapter, I argue that something has indeed changed.

Zooming out and taking a long-term perspective, it is possible to discern how the pandemic funds, the policy tools initiated in the context of the twin transitions of climate and digitalisation, or the renewal of industrial policy, all pertain to a new self-confidence in projecting the Union's capacity to act. In my view, this change is deeply bound to the vulnerability the EU has experienced in a series of shocks since the global banking crisis, via the Trump election and culminating now in the Ukraine war. Throughout this process, the EU has become aware of its own mortality: a sobering but also liberating experience, ushering into the deeply geopolitical and historic moment in which the EU finds itself now. With this new capacity to act, one can decipher something akin to the progressive emancipation of executive power: a new claim of strategic leadership, of which budgetary capacity is an important part.

As far as the capacity to deploy financial tools is part of this evolution, this chapter also aimed to illustrate that the European Union, as a constitutional order, experienced budgetary capacity in reverse. It acquired the capacity to control spending before the capacity to spend. In terms used at the outset: first a Parliament, then a King with his Treasury. On the one hand, it is now up to leaders and policy-makers to prove this spending capacity's use for the Union's citizenry. On the other hand, it is up to EU scholars to study this fascinating nascent executive capacity, its ramifications and further developments.

[66] Van Middelaar, *Alarums & Excursions* 214.

Epilogue

Money, Money, Money

MATTHIAS RUFFERT

1. No Supranational Surplus

Politically and economically, the European Union is a success story because it added to the member states' performance a surplus that was not only out of reach for one or some of them but that could not be attained by any state on its own – in a sense, a supra-national surplus. It is the 'area without internal frontiers' – both politically and economically. In political terms, the success is obvious. It became evident to those who did not believe in it when the borders were temporarily closed between European neighbours in the early weeks of the pandemic, and its effect is visible in the ongoing quarrel about Brexit effects in Northern Ireland. In economic terms, the wealth-creating effect of the internal market is also beyond doubt. For those who are looking for proof, the economically detrimental effects of Brexit should be sufficiently evidential. But the internal market is more than just free trade in goods. It creates a common economic area with respect to all commodities or factors of production. It builds a level playing field for competition that enhances wealth, and it is complemented by a common policy to protect competition against cartels and abuse by dominant undertakings. It creates a ground for regulation that is able to protect the common good in Europe and – via the famous 'Brussels effect' – on a global scale.[1] True, there are coincidences of the internal market's economic model with neoliberal theory which are all the more astonishing as the neoliberals were to a large extent opposed to the creation of the European Common Market in the early days of market integration.[2] But it would not be fair to say that the success story until now was all ideology.

Creating the supra-national surplus of the internal market does not need a budget. Neither does the common currency as designed by the Treaty of

[1] Anu Bradford, *The Brussels Effect: How the European Union Rules the World* (New York, NY, Oxford University Press, 2020).

[2] This is made particularly clear by Christian Joerges, 'Europa nach dem Ordoliberalismus: Eine Philippika' (2010) 43 *Kritische Justiz* 394, 399.

Maastricht, which can be seen as the monetary extension of this market. But of course, it would also not be fair to state that the internal market and the common currency had no redistributive effects. This is why we can observe high political pressure to complement the internal market and the eurozone with budgetary capacities. Such pressure has been visible since the negotiations of the Treaty of Maastricht at the latest,[3] and it has been highly pertinent since the state-debt crisis of the early 2010s. Strangely enough, the 'White Paper Process' triggered by the European Commission did not result in any outcome, except in the field of economic and monetary policy, where a bundle of reform proposals was presented in December 2017.[4] It contained a proposal for 'New Budgetary Instruments for a Stable Euro Area'.[5] The debate on this proposal – not to mention its adoption – was postponed from Council to Council. Maybe this was not the best strategy by the governments opposed to these budgetary instruments. At any rate, it was in the early months of the Covid-19 crisis when European politics, facing the televised view of the lorries carrying the coffins of the Covid-19 victims in Bergamo, took the idea up again, resulting in NextGenerationEU (NGEU). A Hamiltonian moment? A constitutional moment? The beginning of a new era? The end of an era (for instance, of neoliberalism[6])? Certainly, NGEU signifies a shift in strategy. Steering by expenditure is nothing that could not be undertaken by any member state, and nothing particularly supra-national. Public expenditure has been used for ages to attain certain goals by all states, and also, albeit in a limited manner, by the EU. It brings political normality to the EU level. NGEU is also an obvious means to finally create a transfer Union. We can only argue to what extent it does so.

2. Doubtful Power

It is crucial to see that NGEU is built on debt. There is apparently not enough political power to draw the necessary financial means from elsewhere, that is, to raise taxes or to save resources in other policy fields and to shift them into what is now considered necessary for the future of Europe. This is debatable in economic terms,

[3] A proposal made by the Commission to establish a general mechanism of support was rejected, see Jean-Victor Louis, 'Guest Editorial: The No-Bailout Clause and Rescue Packages' (2010) 47 *CML Rev* 971, 982 ff, referring to IGC, Contributions of the Commission, Communication, Bull CE, suppl. 2/91 (21 August 1990) 42, Art 104; see also the 'Projet de Traité portant revision du Traité instituant la Communauté économique européenne en vue de la mise en place d'une Union économique et monétaire' SEC(90)2500 (Brussels, 10 December 1990) Art 104.

[4] A deeper analysis can be found here: Matthias Ruffert, 'The Future of the European Economic and Monetary Union: Issues of Constitutional Law' in Francesca Bignami (ed), *EU Law in Populist Times: Crises and Prospects* (Cambridge, Cambridge University Press, 2020) 33–66, 47 ff.

[5] Commission, 'Communication from the Commission, New Budgetary Instruments for a Stable Euro Area within the Union Framework' COM (2017) 822 final.

[6] See Thomas Biebricher's chapter in this volume (ch 4).

and of course the vicious circle of budgetary deficits, the purchase programmes of the European Central Bank (ECB) that made it a major creditor of the member states,[7] and the effects of all this on the capacity to fight inflation are discussed in the field of political and economic analysis.[8]

Incurring debt is also a legal issue. We know that until 2020 the Commission was convinced that the EU could not become a debtor ('borrowing for spending') beyond 'back-to-back-lending'[9] which only meant transferring the benefit of a better rating in the financial markets to member states in need of such benefit. NGEU was challenged in the Bundesverfassungsgericht (German Federal Constitutional Court).[10] The Bundesverfassungsgericht, although it fell short of repeating its PSPP move,[11] established two limits to borrowing by the EU. First: 'The Treaties do not contain a specific competence conferred in accordance with Article 5 (1) (1) and Article 5 (2) of the TEU that enables the European Union to borrow on the capital markets.'[12] According to the German court, borrowing money is a power that must expressly be given to the EU – which it was not – and this closes the door to any plans to perpetuate NGEU into the ordinary budget, even against the will of the current Federal Chancellor of Germany. Of course, it is by no means clear whether the Court of Justice of the European Union (CJEU) would follow the same approach. In legal terms, it is convincing. Article 49 ECSC Treaty (until 2002) empowered the High Authority to contract loans, and so Article 172(4) Euratom Treaty still does so with respect to the Council as well as Article 20(1) EIB Statute with respect to the EIB. A parallel competence for the EU or the Commission is missing.[13] Second:

> It cannot be clearly ruled out that Art. 5 of the 2020 EU Own Resources Decision satisfies the requirements for the authorisation of the European Union to borrow on capital markets as 'other revenue' within the meaning of Art. 311(2) TFEU and that it does not encroach upon the rules of primary law governing the EU's financial system. In this respect, it must be established, in particular, that the financing through own resources is not undermined by revenue obtained from other sources.[14]

In other words, under certain conditions borrowed funds can be other revenue, the main condition being that the borrowing is limited in volume. This limitation

[7] In February/March 2023, the ECB held €2.585 bn under the public sector purchase programme (PSPP) and €1.683 bn under the pandemic emergency purchase programme (PEPP) (data available at www.ecb.europa.eu).

[8] See Paul Tucker's chapter in this volume (ch 1).

[9] This has been meticulously shown by Päivi Leino-Sandberg, 'Who is ultra vires now? The EU's legal U-turn in interpreting Article 310 TFEU' (*Verfassungsblog*, 18 June 2020) https://verfassungsblog.de/who-is-ultra-vires-now-the-eus-legal-u-turn-in-interpreting-article-310-tfeu.

[10] On the following see Matthias Ruffert, 'Das Eigenmittelbeschluß-Ratifizierungsgesetz und das Urteil des BVerfG vom 6. Dezember 2022', Zeitschrift für Gesetzgebung 2023, forthcoming.

[11] BVerfGE 154, 17 (English language version available at http://www.bverfg.de/e/rs20200505_2bvr085915en.html).

[12] BVerfG, Judgment of the Second Senate of 6 December 2022 – 2 BvR 547/21 – para 150 (English language version available at http://www.bverfg.de/e/rs20221206_2bvr054721en.html).

[13] This is explained in Päivi Leino-Sandberg and Matthias Ruffert, 'Next Generation EU and Its Constitutional Ramifications: A Critical Assessment' (2022) 59 *CML Rev* 433, 456 f.

[14] BVerfG, Judgment of the Second Senate of 6 December 2022 – 2 BvR 547/21 – para 162.

must take the 'multiannual financial framework of the European Union (*cf* Art. 312 TFEU) … as the relevant point of reference'. As NGEU does not exceed the EU budget over the seven years of the Multiannual Financial Framework (MFF), the Bundesverfassungsgericht could not identify a 'manifestly evident' infringement of Germany's competences.[15] In light of the Court's standard of review, this result is acceptable, although it appears to be an obvious compromise – one judge filing a well-argued dissent[16] – and is also backed by arguments that are not wholly convincing, a somewhat amusing one being:

> In fact, Art. 318 (1) TFEU – which obliges the European Commission to submit to the European Parliament and the Council an annual financial statement of the assets and liabilities of the European Union – is an indication that the possibility of debt on the part of the European Union is naturally assumed.[17]

'Liabilities' in the English text does not necessarily imply debt incurred by a process of borrowing but may for example be created by any contract (other than a loan) or tort. The word 'Schulden' (ie debt) only appears in the German text. It is also not clear whether the Court would really apply the volume of the MFF as a threshold to possible borrowing as 'other revenue'.[18] And, again, it is by no means clear that the CJEU would follow this approach.

For the time being, it is difficult to be optimistic with respect to further economic development. There is enormous political pressure to perpetuate and deepen the debt-driven programme in NGEU. With its shrinking population and lack of innovative technologies – such as the digitisation economically taking place elsewhere – and the loss of any incentives to eliminate structural deficits, the Union is not on the same path to success it had taken with its original approach. Brexit on the one hand, and all possible accessions on the other hand, do not really offer perspectives of economic strength – all good political reasons for accession that may exist in individual cases set aside. But prognoses for the future are not the legal scholar's business. Things may also develop differently if a reasonable way (compatible with the Treaties, probably after changing them) to finance the tasks of the Union other than debt is found and if the integrative effect that its proponents expect from programmes such as NGEU become clearly visible. In the end, all's well that ends well.

3. A Risk for EU Law Scholarship

The legal creativity as described has effects on EU law and its scholarship. Similarly, the uncertainty emanating from the absence of a decision of the CJEU

[15] ibid paras 196 ff.
[16] ibid dissenting opinion of Judge Peter Müller.
[17] ibid para 155.
[18] On this issue see Christoph Ohler, 'Next Generation EU: Vereinbarkeit der zweckgebundenen Kreditaufnahme durch die EU mit dem Grundgesetz' (2023) 78 *Juristen Zeitung* 204, 207.

bears an influence. We should remember that even during the high times of the state-debt crisis, it took the CJEU a few months to issue its judgment in *Pringle* and clear most of the questions surrounding Article 125 TFEU and the legality of rescue packages.[19] Now, the possibility that we will never know the Court's view on Article 122 and Article 311 TFEU can by no means be excluded, although their scope is rather stretched by constitutional practice, to say the least.

Indeed, after the 'sleeping beauty' of Article 122 TFEU[20] was kissed awake during the Covid-19 crisis – its application before having been rather limited[21] – it somehow became a super-norm for Council activities in times of despair. It served as the legal basis for Support to mitigate Unemployment Risks (SURE) and the Recovery and Resilience Instrument (EURI).[22] Later, it was taken as the basis for a programme for the acquisition of vaccines.[23] The war in Ukraine and the subsequent closure of the Nord Stream gas pipeline triggered the adoption of the Regulation on coordinated demand-reduction measures for gas[24] and in a sense also the programme REPowerEU to use the funds accumulated in the EURI to finance the burden caused by the non-availability of Russian gas[25] and therefore for a purpose which is without any reasonable doubt outside fighting the consequences of the pandemic. The *dernier cri* is a regulation for the accelerated deployment of renewable energy.[26]

Of course, none of these activities are pernicious as such nor should they be generally rejected. But using Article 122 TFEU as a legal basis leads to a power shift. The Parliament is out of the game, and all the safeguards of Article 352 TFEU

[19] Case C-370/12 *Thomas Pringle v Government of Ireland and Others* ECLI:EU:C:2012:756.

[20] Metaphorical expression used by Alberto de Gregorio Merino, see his chapter in this volume (ch 5).

[21] Minimum stocks of fuel: Council Directive 2009/119/EC imposing an obligation on Member States to maintain minimum stocks of crude oil and/or petroleum products [2009] OJ L265/9, which follows Council Directive 2006/67/EC imposing an obligation on Member States to maintain minimum stocks of crude oil and/or petroleum product [2006] OJ L217/8. European Financial Stabilisation Mechanism: Council Regulation (EU) No 407/2010 establishing a European financial stabilisation mechanism [2010] OJ L118/1. Emergency Support: Council Regulation (EU) 2016/369 on the provision of emergency support within the Union [2016] OJ L70/1, as amended by Council Regulation (EU) 2020/521 activating the emergency support under Regulation (EU) 2016/369, and amending its provisions taking into account the COVID-19 outbreak [2020] OJ L117/3.

[22] Council Regulation (EU) 2020/672 on the establishment of a European instrument for temporary support to mitigate unemployment risks in an emergency (SURE) following the COVID-19 outbreak [2020] OJ L159/1; Council Regulation (EU) 2020/2094 establishing a European Union Recovery Instrument to support the recovery in the aftermath of the COVID-19 crisis [2020] OJ LI433/23.

[23] Council Regulation (EU) 2022/2372 on a framework of measures for ensuring the supply of crisis-relevant medical countermeasures in the event of a public health emergency at Union level [2022] OJ L314/64.

[24] Council Regulation (EU) 2022/1369 on coordinated demand-reduction measures for gas [2022] OJ L206/1.

[25] Regulation (EU) 2023/435 of the European Parliament and of the Council amending Regulation (EU) 2021/241 as regards REPowerEU chapters in recovery and resilience plans and amending Regulations (EU) No 1303/2013, (EU) 2021/1060 and (EU) 2021/1755, and Directive 2003/87/EC [2023] OJ L63/1.

[26] Council Regulation (EU) 2022/2577 laying down a framework to accelerate the deployment of renewable energy [2022] OJ L335/36.

are circumvented. At least, there is some chance that in one of the cases described the Court will have another say on Article 122 TFEU. It already did so in *Pringle* and rejected the idea of a permanent mechanism of financial assistance under section 2 and of any financial assistance at all under section 1.[27] The Court will also have to consider whether both sections of the article can really be read together. It is developed elsewhere that this is wrong,[28] and it should be added, that both sections have a completely different history which, by the way, never hinted at anything comparable to a general transfer mechanism.[29]

It is obvious that the re-reading of the provisions of the Treaties will change the face of the EU. It should also not be underestimated that such re-reading changes the role of EU law[30] – and of its scholarship. If we as EU law scholars leave the development of the law to a conglomerate of high-level consensus, creative legal design by the legal services of the institutions and a Court that is not ready to provide necessary checks and balances, we run the high risk of seeing the purpose of our profession significantly reduced. The very nature of EU law and its application should leave sufficient space for meaningful scholarly debate between the unhappy choices of blatant opposition or subservient apology.

[27] Case C-370/12 *Thomas Pringle v Government of Ireland and Others* ECLI:EU:C:2012:756, para 65 on section 1. It is revealing to consider the passage on section 1 in para 116 of the judgment: 'Since Article 122(1) TFEU does not constitute an appropriate legal basis for any financial assistance from the Union to Member States who are experiencing, or are threatened by, severe financing problems …'.

[28] Leino-Sandberg and Ruffert, 'Next Generation EU' 445.

[29] Matthias Ruffert, 'Not kennt kein Gebot – Art. 122 AEUV als neue Generalermächtigung?' in Festschrift für Rudolf Streinz, forthcoming.

[30] See Päivi Leino-Sandberg's chapter in this volume (ch 8).

INDEX

www.ingramcontent.com/pod-product-compliance
Ingram Content Group UK Ltd.
Pitfield, Milton Keynes, MK11 3LW, UK
UKHW020246290926
15470UKWH00002B/774